to make friends rather than to divide the population. The offence given was always indirect.

Above all, the problem with the search for a fixed divide-and-rule policy is that it easily runs away with itself to no good purpose. It lacks boundaries; almost anything can be brought into the accusation. For example, some insist that the Nagri decision of 1900 was designed to raise religious tensions. But MacDonnell could stand accused in the light of any decision he made, because all possible outcomes were bound to benefit or disadvantage some interested party or other.

The whole idea has now turned into a conspiracy theory, simple to apprehend and apparently based on real events, but in which balance and context vanish, leaving a prosecution argument unchallenged. Commentators praise the Maharaja of Baroda as an enlightened ruler for making reservations for Scheduled Castes in 1906, but accuse the British of cynicism and insincerity for doing the same thing. Divide and rule remains very much in the eye of the beholder.

One internet favourite is the letter from Lord Cross, a hardline Conservative writing from London to Viceroy Dufferin, in 1887: 'This division of religious feeling is greatly to our advantage and I look for some good as a result of your Committee of Inquiry on Indian Education and on teaching material.' Damning, perhaps, till we learn that no such committee of inquiry took place. There had been one five years before—the Hunter Commission of 1882, which had recommended, as a matter of official policy, 'That care be taken to avoid, as far as possible, the introduction of textbooks which are of an aggressive character, or are likely to give unnecessary offence to any section of the community'.[19] Lord Cross was off-message.

The point so frequently missed is that the British were keen to cultivate loyalty where it could be found, which was a much easier and more helpful thing to do than trying to stir up social tensions. The Raj was always attempting to deflect its most dangerous enemies while encouraging its closest friends. For instance, it was always more anti-nationalist than pro-Muslim.

The Congress was a small and relatively insignificant force before 1920, and the British were happy to engineer potential alliances against it. But they did so using two social axes—rich and poor, loyal and disloyal. Religious considerations were subordinate to these more telling polarities. Men of rank and ability, Muslim or Hindu, were brought into high-level imperial councils from 1907. It was pliability that counted; Congressmen had to wait till 1946.

Within the official strategy there were therefore two interlinked strands. There was a principled drive for the protection of minorities, which was a main justification of empire, and included trying to protect groups such as Muslims or Scheduled Castes and Tribes. There was also a search for political support that was less principled, and involved the grant of privileges and honours to princes and eminent persons of all faiths. This was the very essence of 'oblige and rule'.

The aim in both cases was to promote loyalty, not to stir up animosity. Religious issues connected with sacred buildings or the use of roads were inevitable outcomes of complicated social conditions, and were not dreamed up by officials, who had to pick up the pieces whenever riots brought loss of life and damage to property. Raj officials persistently believed they were protecting Indians from each other, not setting them at each other's throats.

Across the years 1905–26, we can find multiple test cases. If the Partition of Bengal was dividing and ruling, then what was the reunification of Bengal in 1912? Was this a further attempt to divide opposition, or just a recognition that the decision of 1905 had been a mistake? And why move the capital from Calcutta to Delhi at the same time, thus offending as many people as might have been pleased with the reunification of Bengal?

Or take the creation of religious electorates in the reforms of 1909. Divide and rule, or an attempt to make sure that the 'representative principle' could be introduced with due regard for sectional interests? From the point of view of British political theory, special electorates guaranteed a voice to dispersed minorities, by rejecting the 'territorial principle'. The idea that Muslims who were both loyal and economically significant would be outvoted wherever they lived was an intolerable thought, and a highly undemocratic outcome. Ask: if a system of open competition had been introduced, with hardly a Muslim elected anywhere, what kind of legitimacy could such a system have claimed?

Nor were separate electorates entirely separate; the term is misleading. Muslims could stand as candidates and vote in the open constituencies or in the reserved seats. A less emotionally loaded term is 'reserved electorates'. Nor was this a Hindu–Muslim issue, as almost any Indian commentary on the Act will assert somewhere. Reserved seats were granted not only to Muslims; they were also used to give an elected voice to European commercial interests, universities and chambers of commerce.

Finally, why did the British force through the Rowlatt Act in 1919, or appoint the 'all-white' Simon Commission in 1927, both of which unified the entire Indian political establishment at inconvenient times?

All of this looks more like improvisation or incompetence than brilliant strategy, as does the way the British smiled upon the birth of the Indian National Congress in 1885, before realizing that it might become a forum for disloyalty, not just a means of finding out what educated Indians were thinking. And what of the extraordinary effort the British took to spread English-language education—the common ground that allowed so many Indians to come together? This policy alone did more for India's national unity than centuries of Sanskrit or Persian education had done. How does this spectacular own goal fit into the secret master plan?

The last clinching proof of a divide-and-rule policy is usually considered to be the Partition of 1947. But again, this is mistaken. The British did not want to partition India. There is a mountain of documentary evidence to support this, plus sound political and strategic reasons why they would not want to. It was actually Indian leaders who wanted partition. Jinnah asked for it repeatedly and, in the end, senior Congressmen accepted its necessity. Partition was an Anglo-Indian compromise.

It is vitally important here to appreciate that the end of empire entailed the advent of democracy, and with it a major shift in political realities.

India's composite culture had managed to cohere as well as it did partly because the political and religious maps of the country had never been superimposed; feudal monarchy never emphasized religion as a political issue in the same way that majority voting does. With the advent of democracy, the disorderly localism of India's religions suddenly became an acute problem of political geography that no boundary lines could satisfactorily unpick.

Loyalty to a regime was abruptly replaced by loyalty to a community. In an empire or a monarchy, subjects only have to swear allegiance to be protected, but in a democracy, members of majority communities are given real potential power over all their neighbours. The imminent prospect of this transition is what drove partition and its attendant bloodshed, not some long-term government policy.

Uncritical reliance on the idea of 'divide and rule' leads to the unsatisfactory and absurd conclusion that major figures including Gandhi, Jinnah, Sayyid Ahmad Khan, Nehru and Ambedkar were all unwitting British stooges, incapable of independent thought or action. It also assumes that the British magically knew how not to cross the precise point at which the political benefits of dividing Indians tipped over into unproductive chaos.

The truth, attested throughout history, is not that conquerors divide to rule, it is that people who will not cooperate risk being conquered by groups that can. If there was one resource that the British had in abundance and that the Indians lacked, it was not guns or courage, but the quality of collective purpose—what Ibn Khaldun in the fourteenth century CE called *assabiyya*. British *assabiyya* was a product of political stability, which in turn rested on institutional developments that by 1757 had put Britain ahead of all her European rivals.

Germany, prior to unification in the nineteenth century, was as divided as India, and as frequently conquered and plundered. Italy, when united under Roman leadership, held the whole Mediterranean basin in her grip. Not so in the centuries that saw the division of the country into competing states and regions, which were variously picked off and seized by invaders as opportunity allowed. Unite and rule, divide and be ruled, is the lesson.

Of course, some sections of Indian society were able to cohere very well. Bohras, Khojas, Marwaris, Parsis and others formed tight groups, which usually prospered as a result. But they did not habitually cohere with each other or with the wider society. Even the Marathas, a strongly self-identifying group with high military expertise, failed to cooperate to defend the putative Indian nation. The divisions that the British exploited were ready and waiting.

Some kind of national consciousness may have been real, and much effort has gone into trying to find it. But even if such a consciousness did exist, which can never be definitively proved, it was a weak force, with no institutional arrangements in place to represent it. At the most granular level, of individuals and families, it was easy for local people to make their peace with the British. The British set out to do this, and succeeded.

Properly understood, the 'policy' of divide and rule was a continuous search for support wherever it could be found. But it was a form of politics that, for the sake of the empire, could not be acknowledged as political.

Imperialism and divide and rule have limited value as explanatory concepts, but they did not spring up at random. They are linked, and it is important to appreciate the genuine utility they had in their historical context, as part of the British search for legitimacy and the Indian quest for unity.

The British made self-certified claims about their superiority in order to provide a justification for imperial rule that lay beyond the power of Indians to deny. Indian accusations about divide and rule helped to counteract the friability of the national movement.

What the two sides said about themselves and their opponents gives a strong pointer to the areas in which they were most vulnerable. If you want to know where a castle's weakest point is, look for its most elaborate defences.

Elites and Masses: Five Groups

Anglo-Indian history was shaped by the interaction of five main social groupings, and especially by the dynamic relationship between three elite groups—two small and one large.

The two small groups were the British invaders and the progressive Indians who favoured degrees of reform or modernization. Both were centred in the presidency towns—Calcutta, Madras and Bombay. The British ruling cadre never rose above about 1,500, while the modernizing Indian intelligentsia still only numbered less than one per cent of the population by the beginning of the twentieth century. Thus Viceroy Dufferin's dismissal of the Indian National Congress in 1888 as representing 'a microscopic minority' had a certain truth to it, but his jibe also reveals a remarkable blindness to the irony of his own position. As he spoke, the European population of Calcutta was well under 20,000, not even a tenth of the size of the town's bhadralok, or middle classes. When it came to comparative scales of unrepresentative microscopy, Dufferin was hardly in a position to boast.

Through the early decades of British rule, these two small groups appeared to share an interest in social and economic modernization. Yet despite this early rapport, the British ruling clique ultimately thwarted the ambitions of the Indian progressives. The modernizing urban elite did not take up arms in 1857, but the British declined to reward them for their loyalty. After the traumatic events of that year, the British transferred their support and patronage from the small progressive, urban grouping to a third, much larger and economically more powerful group, India's conservative landholders. This new alliance was to have far-reaching political and economic consequences.

There were two other mass groupings: the domestic British electorate and the Indian peasantry. Neither had any way of exerting direct political influence, and neither, through the years 1757–1919, made the political weather, though as franchise extensions proceeded in Britain, the British electorate became marginally more influential. Its most direct intervention in Indian affairs came in 1880, when it unseated a Conservative government and installed Gladstone's Liberals. This had an immediate impact on Indian policy, bringing an end to military involvement in Afghanistan, and the reversal of a number of the social and political policies of Viceroy Lytton. But this event is noteworthy only for its rarity. When Viceroy Irwin (1926–31), a Conservative, was obliged to serve new masters in the wake of Labour's 1929 election victory, the government's stance barely altered. British policy in India always took account of underlying economic and strategic imperatives that remained broadly consistent.

Even in the twentieth century, with an expanded franchise, the masses in Britain were largely uninterested in imperial affairs. They were content to enjoy cheap food from the empire while earning good returns—wages or dividends—from export industries and overseas investments. And because India rarely became a serious party issue, usually senior postings there were not strongly political.

Imperial proconsuls represented an elite within an elite. Only thirty-two men achieved the rank of Governor-General between 1773 and 1947, and between 1798 and 1921, with the exception of John Lawrence (1863–9), they all came from noble families. Not all of the other twenty-three were great hereditary landowners—Ellenborough's father was a judge and Lytton's a successful novelist—but all owed the job to their status, not their status to the job.

Of all thirty-two, three were the sons of prime ministers, and only the first, Warren Hastings, died without noble rank. They often had very similar patterns to their education. Between 1858 and 1910, seven out of eleven went to Eton, and three successive viceroys, from 1888 to 1905, were educated at Balliol College, Oxford. Many were closely related; brothers-in-law succeeded each other in 1844, the two Elgins were father and son, the two Hardinges grandfather and grandson, and the two Mintos great-grandfather and great-grandson.

The British electorate and the Indian peasantry both lurked offstage through most of the drama. Neither was particularly radical, though heroic attempts have been made in recent years to trace a lineage of popular democracy within India's history of tribal revolts, and by using broad concepts like 'peasant radicalism'. But evidence is still lacking of recognizably modern political consciousness among these 'subaltern' groups. Illiterate people tend not to leave much of a documentary record, yet the onus must always be on researchers to show us that such consciousness truly existed. Attempts to tell history 'from below' necessarily involve attempts to recover 'lost voices', but how often this shades into ventriloquism is an open question.

Peasant radicalism may even count as an oxymoron. Peasants are notoriously resistant to change, and are often deeply conservative, socially and religiously. They usually want to stay on the land, but with better conditions. Given their greatest opportunities for radical action, in 1857 and 1947, there was little coordinated activity that ventured beyond destruction.

Rather than political revolution, peasants usually wanted to remove particular oppressors, or to achieve fairer running of the system under which they lived. They generally lacked appropriate experience, education or political vocabulary to help them beyond these practical objectives until quite late in the story. Instead, popular leaders often cloaked themselves with maverick religious authority, in a procession of messianic figures such as Dhoondiah Waugh, self-styled 'King of Two Worlds' in 1800, down to Birsa Munda in 1899.

Political militancy was in short supply within all five groups. The British electorate, for reasons of self-interest, remained generally pro-imperial, while the Indian peasantry, for lack of articulacy or organization, was unwilling or unable to press for constructive reform, except perhaps when under Communist leadership, as in the Telangana rebellion of 1946–51.

Importantly, the political ambitions of the educated Indian modernizers were also circumscribed. They had no wish to destroy the colonial system of government, because they wanted to take it over and use its power to implement reform. As a result there was always a grain of conservatism hidden within the mainstream of the Indian nationalist movement. Furthermore, many of the movement's leaders had social positions and economic interests to defend. Demands for radical change were the preserve of fringe actors.

Within the five groups, the most conservative became the British official class; by 1920, the Raj itself was the anti-reform party, propping up the landed bloc. And victory eventually went to a vanguard splinter within the Indian modernizers, led by Jawaharlal Nehru. The tradition of meeting the West on equal terms and guiding India forward using the best of Western models finally flowered in his person. Heir to two cultures, the mature Nehru was a man who divided himself to rule.

Modernity: Britain and India

The Anglo-Indian connection was instrumental in nurturing liberal democracy in both Britain and India; there was a degree of interactive influence that has not been fully appreciated.

Albeit reluctantly, India became the theatre for the longest and by far the most constructive connection between the 'ancient' East and the 'modern' West, though these terms are misleading. The only reason to use them is that they were so influential within official British thinking, and can thus help us to understand what emerged and why.

Modernity has been an immensely powerful agent for political and social change all over the world, and India was not going to be spared—she was too centrally placed in the world's trade routes, too hard to defend, and too blessed with valuable resources. Modernity was coming; the only questions were when and how. And there was a demand for it too; many Indians willingly adapted their lives and attitudes. However, as in Europe, both winners and losers emerged from the process.

Before exploring the interrelated impact of modernity in Britain and India, it is necessary to set out a working definition of what modernity is. Modernity as a historical phenomenon is a social, cultural and economic package, whose chief characteristics have been scientific rationalism, bureaucratic government and capitalist money relations. Over time it has produced liberal politics, impersonal state institutions, secular public culture and economic individualism. Its upsides include representative government, religious tolerance, personal liberty and enormously improved standards of living for those further up the social scale. Its downsides are disconnection from tradition, social dislocation, and an enormously increased capacity for destructive power, both military and environmental.

Modernity was not a package defined by one generation or one national grouping, but it reached a critical combination of vigour and acquisitiveness in Europe by around 1750. The processes that created it lacked consistent direction and were occasionally violent; mostly they were fairly slow. But to the great civilizations of the Orient, modernity came at shocking speed. When caught in its path, Indians had very little choice about how it would be absorbed, because the military side of the package overwhelmed them before the rest had fully arrived.

It was only in the mid-eighteenth century that direct pressure to modernize arrived in India, through the extension of European wars. After around 1750, the Maratha states and the rulers of Mysore adopted new attitudes to governance and warfare, while Raja Serfoji II of Tanjore later displayed a purer kind of curiosity. Many Indian princes took on European military advisers, and both Muhammad Ali Khan Wallajah (Nawab of Arcot, 1751–95) and Nasir al-Din Haidar (King of Awadh, 1827–37) had British medical staff.

But India's relationship with modernity was problematic from the start. Political, technological and cultural change, so closely interwoven in

Europe, never combined in quite the same way in India. Ideas of progress and prosperity never became as directly connected as they were in the West, where mechanization and changes in patterns of employment brought tangible improvements across the whole social spectrum. In India, access to world markets very often meant doing the same things as before, but not always with greater reward. Indians were denied choices right from the start.

India became increasingly static under colonial rule, and remained so despite all British efforts at stimulation. Neither reformist social legislation before the Uprising of 1857 nor public works projects after it managed to start the virtuous circle of growth and change. In Britain, state, society and economy expanded together. In India, it was only the population that grew.

Colonial modernity failed to produce the economic fluidity witnessed in Europe. Economic power stayed broadly in two places—with the European holders of capital, and with the larger Indian landlords. This situation hardly changed at all during the whole British period, which meant that India was very slow to grow a domestic industrial sector, and that there was a general shortage of liquid capital in the country at independence.

Above all, the strongest natural alliance in Indian politics turned out to be between the modern, political, military power of the colonialists and the traditional, social, economic power of the indigenous landholding classes.

India's small Western-influenced intelligentsia was culturally distinct, but only marginally important politically, and had little economic power. It was not a 'class' in that sense. So, with only limited political and economic heft, and at odds with traditional Indian society, its role was destined to be peripheral. It was Gandhi's outreach that brought real political power to the Indian National Congress by giving it a mass following, albeit one with which some of its leaders were not always in full sympathy. Over the period 1885–1947, not all Congress leaders welcomed the entire modern package, but they all wanted liberal institutions and free speech, even if they did not advocate social and economic agendas of full equality.

Broadly, the Congress represented the pro-modernity faction within Indian society, visibly distanced from religious conservatives within the major faith traditions, and separate from and opposed to the feudal autocrats in the 'princely states', whose rulers generally remained resistant to political and cultural change, except in its most gimcrack and superficial forms, such as French jewellery or Rolls Royce cars. Crucially, such rulers did not need to embrace nationalism to give themselves status or to enhance their incomes or prospects of employment. It was the progressive middle classes who were seeking new opportunities and new definitions of their identity.

But, driven by self-interest, the British betrayed the hopes of the modernizing few and opted for crude domination, above which they proved repeatedly unable to rise. Whenever modernization was set against control, the British chose authority and stasis over modernity and change. Questions always needed to be answered in primarily imperial terms: modernize India—at whose expense, and for whose benefit? As the most exploitative relations of primitive industrialization were being abandoned in Britain, in India they lived on. Social exclusion and rigid hierarchy continued as features of British Indian society.

What India ended up with was a stunted and incomplete version of modernity, tailored to suit British interests. Equality before the law and impersonal government were the most distinctly modern features of British India, but legal equality was primarily confined to relations between Indians, not between Indians and 'European British subjects'. And the impersonal government was rarely as disinterested as it pretended.

Modernity and India: Religion and Politics

Once alien forces had propelled modernity into the heart of traditional Indian society, a sense of crisis and defeat was widely felt. But the cultural relationship that followed should not be represented purely in terms of domination. Contact with the West produced a range of reactions including acceptance, rejection, and degrees of assimilation across personal and political arenas. Differing attitudes to modernity appeared within Hindu, Muslim and Sikh traditions, and all three produced conservatives, moderate reformers and militant radicals.

This subject has been greatly complicated over recent decades by the academic fashion for alleging that the British 'invented' the faith communities of India. This claim is founded in retro-anti-colonialism, and is only true in very restricted senses. Muslims, Sikhs, Jains and Parsis were genuine historical, self-identifying, locally cohesive social groupings, based on scriptural, liturgical and cultural distinctiveness. What the British presence did was to give faith communities shape, power and a degree of rivalry as *political* entities. This was a complex process, which fully reflected the pluralism of India's established social structures, and ultimately hinged on the introduction of representative institutions.

The outcome of this process was the elevation of the two largest religious communities into national blocs, and the centralized colonial state undoubtedly played a part in this development. But again, this was not a straightforward process, and involved a considerable degree of interaction. The British created political and administrative structures, which select groups of Indians then used for their own purposes. The most significant feature of this interaction was the creation of self-awareness among the Hindu 'community', which was more numerous and diverse than other groupings, and whose distinctive essence was not based on one central, historical point of reference.

However, the term 'Hindu' is problematic. The people now referred to as Hindus did not refer to themselves as such before the British era, and in the eighteenth century the British usually called the non-Muslim inhabitants of India 'Gentoos', adapting Portuguese usage. The invention of the term 'Hinduism' is credited to Ram Mohan Roy (1772–1833) in 1818. With these caveats noted, the term Hindu is nonetheless convenient shorthand for the majority of inhabitants of India who followed the traditional indigenous way of life, and worshipped the pantheon of local deities described in ancient Sanskrit texts.

Among Hindus, attitudes to modernity played out across a range of issues, including ritual observance, scriptural authority, family relations and caste. These matters were closely interlinked within a tradition that was never willing to isolate its concepts of society, law, duty and purity. Consequently, social reform meant reform of religion and vice versa. The joint family remained at the heart of social reform, and the best-known colonial intrusions into Hindu affairs—the abolition of sati (the voluntary immolation of a widow on her husband's funeral pyre) in 1829, the Widow Remarriage Act of 1856 and the Age of Consent Act of 1891—centred on the intimate family. And all were called for by sections of the community as vociferously as they were opposed by others.

For Hindus, where to find correct religious guidance was a crucial question, complicated by three factors: the multiplicity of scriptures, the lack of a centralized clerical hierarchy, and the canonical belief that revelation is continuously available to pious seekers. This set up a confusing situation in which Hindu modernizers could claim high authority as convincingly as traditionalists, and religious and political figures could be both conservative and radical at the same time. It is hard to define the views of B.G. Tilak (1856–1920) or the proto-revolutionary spirituality of Sri Aurobindo (1872–1950) as either definitively modern or traditional, and the great achievement of M.K. Gandhi (1869–1948) was to unite the religious-traditionalist masses with some of the most committed modernizers.

Religious leaders were forced to negotiate a path between preserving and reforming traditional observances. Ram Mohan Roy tried to select the best of Western ideas while retaining his own heritage. The Brahmo Samaj, which he founded in 1828, promoted a strict, rational monotheism purged of popular ritual practices. Roy should thus be seen as a modernizer rather than as a Westernizer.

The debates of his time were also more nuanced than they are often presented. Roy called for the abolition of sati on the modernist (yet also indigenist) grounds that it had no authorization in scripture, while his main opponent, Radhakanta Deb (1784–1867), was hardly a textbook traditionalist. Deb advocated education for girls, and ran Calcutta's Hindu College, which taught Western science. His stance was not specifically in favour of sati; he simply believed that the British had no right to legislate about it.

The connection between Hinduism and conservatism was always flexible. Dadoba Pandurang (1814–82) attacked idol worship in the 1840s, as did Dayananda Saraswati (1824–83) in the 1870s, while others, including Swami Vivekananda (1863–1902), considered it harmless or even beneficial. The institution of caste also polarized opinion, with the Arya Samaj strongly against, as were Ishwar Chandra Vidyasagar (1820–91), Narayana Guru (1856–1928) and Jyotirao Phule (1827–90), who met opposition from orthodox Brahmins in Bengal, Kerala and Maharashtra respectively. Caste, however, continued to be a bedrock belief for other devout Hindu figures, including Vivekananda and Gandhi, who insisted that its true meaning had been corrupted.

The close connection between community, society, law and religion meant that major public figures were always straddling a line between religion and politics. This line could become very blurred, especially when it came to the twin problems of loyalty to the colonial regime and the growth of national identity.

The writer Nabagopal Mitra (1840–94) considered that there was a fundamental, necessary connection between Hinduism and nationalism, a link that became increasingly close after Swami Vivekananda had put together his influential package of Practical Vedanta—strength, activity, self-worth, and service to the masses. This message, which first appeared around 1890, was the germ of an effective anti-colonial national ideology, and it shaped the thinking of a whole generation of nationalists with undoubtedly Hindu outlooks—Tilak, Gokhale and Gandhi chief among them.

But not all Hindus could be described simply as nationalists. The 'father of Hindi literature', Bharatendu Harishchandra (1850–85), while certainly a patriot, was generally pro-British, and nearly all major political and literary figures established positions of nominal loyalty, tempered with various degrees of criticism. Not all these positions were entirely prudential. Some genuinely felt that British rule brought a degree of benefit, such as the blessings of peace, modern government and technology. More ominously, some were simply thankful that Hindus had been delivered from Muslim rule.

Attitudes to modernity among Hindus were also closely linked with attitudes to the remote past. Many writers, R.C. Dutt and Dayananda Saraswati among them, were keen to emphasize the glory of early Vedic civilization. Such pride could either serve as a broad support for faith in India's future or express a narrow chauvinism about the present, including the claim that large parts of modern science and technology were actually ancient Hindu discoveries or inventions. In Dutt's hands, the past offered a model of tolerance and virtue; in Dayananda's, scripture was promoted above history, and Hinduism above all other faiths. This latter tendency was in full cry by the mid-1890s, and reached a peak in 1906 with *Hindu Superiority* by Har Bilas Sarda.[20] Devout Hindus, he implied, should not be fearful of modernity when their illustrious forefathers had long ago surpassed the modern West with advanced weaponry and flying machines.

Such confusions about modernity were not the result of any absence of rationality or flexibility within Indian society. They are more easily understood if we remember that modernity developed organically in Europe through internal stresses, while in South Asia it came as an external shock. The impact of alien intrusion did initially produce degrees of social and political fragmentation, but as confident relationships to modernity emerged, Indians gained access to a new form of unity: national identity.

However, the possibility of developing unitary representation of a diverse population through the use of religion remained challenging, and nationalists could only hope to build a truly national movement by addressing secular issues in secular language. The early leadership of the Congress, which included Muslims, Parsis and Christians, clung to this formula, while the sensitive issue of social reform was delegated to the National Social Conference, which met annually after the Congress sessions were over.

But even in purely secular matters, the restricted scope for public discussion in colonial India meant that political activity was often represented as a matter of religion, because most of the existing forms of personal identity—and many forms of traditional grievance—carried a religious character. This could be most clearly seen in parts of India where class and economic divisions, such as between peasants and landholders, coincided with religious differences, which was the case, for example, in Malabar and large parts of Bengal and Punjab. The Congress avoided these alignments very consciously and sought to promote modern issues.

More overtly religious movements, such as the Faraizi, the Arya Samaj, the Mahimas, the Deobandis, and the various jihadi groups, were usually archaists and could not find or did not want a place in conventional politics, and tended to organize outside Raj institutions.

Religion, therefore, did not make India intrinsically or permanently ancient; some strands of Hindu thought were as progressive and modernist as Evangelical Christianity was in Britain. Nor was Indian society entirely dominated by religious distinctions. To talk glibly of religious blocs is to adopt the imperial British idea that Indian society was primarily defined by faith communities. It could look a little like that from the outside—especially viewed in terms of indigenous traditions of law—and the stubbornness with which senior British figures held to this view was partly due to its political and administrative convenience.

This official tenaciousness is important, because it made the British unwilling to challenge religion, which meant that they ended up preserving its presence in politics. Eventually this led them to affect, and even exaggerate, the processes they thought they were objectively observing.

The British perceived 'communal' tension between Hindus and Muslims as an ancient phenomenon, predetermined by the essential 'nature' of the faiths and the 'races' involved. Congress writers contested this view, and claimed that interfaith harmony had been destroyed by the arrival of the British, and would be restored by their removal. Neither view was entirely correct or disinterested.

Though inter-communal tensions can be seen to have increased through the later Raj period, it long remained difficult to mobilize anything that could be called 'the Hindu community', because of the wide range of outlooks and interests among Hindus. Attempts to do this through the Hindu Mahasabha completely failed in electoral terms. Truly unifying 'Hindu' issues were rare, with cow protection chief among them from the late 1880s. The symbols, slogans and personalities required to create a national constituency only emerged in the twentieth century, and became part of the Gandhian platform.

By comparison, collective mobilization of India's Muslims should have been an easier task because, despite the various subdivisions of sect, class and region, the idea of the umma (Muslim community) was long cherished—grander than jati, more relevant than varna. But crucially, the umma was not a political idea until the arrival of electoral politics.

Here another irony intrudes, which is that although a national Muslim community existed in theory, in practice it proved much harder to mobilize than the secular nationalism represented by the Congress. Regional Muslim leaders had little use for a national platform, and the institutions created by British reform packages effectively undermined the need for central representation of any grouping that might be called Muslim. It was only a series of circumstances in the late 1930s, and the powerful determination of M.A. Jinnah, that finally brought this about. Separate electorates were of little value to the 'second nation' project until then.

In reality, the most relevant factor in the rise of communal identities was not colonial government per se, but the advent of electoral politics. The introduction of democratic processes must, by definition, run ahead of the existence of stable political parties, leading to two possible outcomes: community mobilization along familiar lines or demagogic populism. India got both.

The main problem was building structures to link the local and the national. Indian nationalists have always found this hard to admit, because the national movement did not manage to do it very successfully. The diversity of Indian society was an obstruction which could be addressed administratively, by party organization, but it proved very resistant ideologically. No matter how often the Congress asserted that it was representative of everyone, political realities meant that it never could be. Leadership ultimately can only be shared so far, and the more socialist and secular its message became, while its membership became increasingly Hindu, the less likely Muslims and other minority political and ideological elements were to support it.

Pre-colonial India was a land of monarchs, whose power had little to do with religious identity. But electoral politics necessarily had to be connected with majorities and minorities at every level, from local to provincial to national. Here was a new and troubling factor, which the British took more seriously than most Hindus, but not all Muslims.

The introduction of elections meant that a historically plural society suddenly had a single form of political contestation thrust upon it, a form that valued public processes—what would now be called transparency. Such a system needs clear definitions, not the obfuscation of court politics, personal dealings or patronage behind closed doors. It happened that the clearest definitions, or at least the ones with most direct appeal, were religious.

Religion in its social context, as distinct from personal spiritual practice, carries an inescapably collective component, and political activism can always be facilitated by religious connections, if available. It should therefore not be a surprise that a form of politics developed in India that recognized and incorporated religious definitions. A more serious point is that this transition was not well handled by any of the parties, colonial or indigenous, some of whom had an interest in denying its reality, while others drew real advantage from its existence.

In colonial India, religion was only one potential basis of division within society, and it could combine with all sorts of other issues. So, some nominally religious conflicts were about local government, economic competition, bureaucratic rulings or public spaces. Other forms revolved around caste privileges or government employment. The terrain of contestation was further complicated by internal migration, urbanization and the development of new industries. All this went on under the supervision of a government that was almost always prepared to appease the loudest voices that addressed it. The result was a fragmented picture that defies easy classification now, just as it was confusing then.

Colonial rule was not an essential precondition for the appearance of rivalry between religious groups. Such rivalry only required a government that entered into forms of representative dialogue with its subjects, and included a competitive element within its political structure. The British Raj did both.

Opposition, Collaboration and Division

Indians as a body did not 'nationally' resist the arrival of the British, nor did all Indians try to expel them in 1857. Nor was there a totally unified drive for national liberation in the later Raj, when substantial parts of the Indian population, including the princes and many Muslims, were highly ambivalent about the kind of self-government envisaged by the Congress.

A long list of major Indian figures formed types of partnership, political or commercial, with the British, including Ram Mohan Roy, Sayyid Ahmad Khan, several generations of the Tagore family, dozens of major bankers and merchants, hundreds of native rulers, thousands of lawyers, tens of thousands of petty officials, and hundreds of thousands of soldiers (sepoys). The most important point about these people is that they had little choice but to become enmeshed in the British colonial system. Many of the more prominent among them were frequently criticizing British rule, while still trying to move towards a partnership in modernity.

This was a real and continuing dilemma, and standard histories are not very sympathetic to it. They tend, instead, to deny its existence outright, or seek to dissolve it by turning colonialism into a much more powerful force than it could ever possibly have been—particularly not without local cooperation. Indians have frequently been reduced to the role of passive victims in the story, which is both dismissive and inaccurate.

Virtually all the great names of Indian nationalism had close relationships with British institutions. M.G. Ranade was a High Court judge, G.K. Gokhale sat on official councils for years. R.C. Dutt spent a long, under-rewarded career as a civil servant before turning in frustration to economic criticism of the Raj. There was a long list of nationalist politicians who were educated at the Bar in London, including Pherozeshah Mehta, W.C. Bonnerjee. M.K. Gandhi, M.A. Jinnah, Badruddin Tyabji and Jawaharlal Nehru. In this, as in much else, B.G. Tilak stands as something of an exception, having managed to make a living without the good offices of the Raj. Tilak apart, prominent thinkers who managed to avoid colonial influence were mainly religious figures, such as Dayananda Saraswati, or were confined to the fringes of mainstream politics, such as Sri Aurobindo or V.D. Savarkar.

There were always critics of colonial rule among the British too, across the political spectrum, and on both sides of the traditionalist–modernist divide. James Silk Buckingham, editor of the radical *Calcutta Journal*, was deported for opposition to the government in 1824, at a time when loyalist opinion in Calcutta was being voiced by a rival newspaper, *John Bull*. Within Parliament, liberal and radical voices were always raised against colonial government. Henry Fawcett was an outspoken critic of Raj economic policies in the 1870s, and from the mid-1840s to the early 1880s John Bright—businessman, reformer and free trader—kept up a stream of anti-imperial rhetoric inside the Commons chamber, at public meetings, and in letters to the press.

There was even dissent among the top ranks in India. General Charles Napier was a savage critic of British rule through the 1840s, even as he did its most rascally work in annexing Sind. Lord Hobart's term as Governor of Madras from 1872 to 1875 was marked by controversy over his liberal views, at the same time as imperial conservatism was about to reach its peak in the Durbar of 1877. Lord Lytton (1876–80), possibly the most traditionalist of all viceroys, was followed by Lord Ripon (1880–4), certainly the most progressive.

Political dissent was matched by religious confusion. In the early nineteenth century Charles 'Hindoo' Stuart (c.1758–1828) whole-heartedly embraced local religious practices at the same time as British missionaries based in Serampore were trying to stamp them out. Sir Francis Younghusband (1863–1942), 'conqueror of Tibet', moved from a straightforward imperialist outlook to a complicated mystical worldview, which by the late 1920s included support for Indian self-government and an ambitious project for the empowerment of Indians that he called 'remasculation'. Annie Besant (1847–1933) even managed to be both a religious traditionalist and a political modernizer at the same time.

Raj loyalism and modernism did not necessarily go together, and the longer the Raj lasted, the less they were in harmony.

The Domestic Debate

During the British rise to supremacy in India, military conquest rarely presented a moral problem for the public at home. British rule was universally viewed as better for India than Indian rule, and there was broad agreement that it was in Britain's interests to hold onto the new territories. Nevertheless, there were always repelling poles discernible in British political discussions about India, and after about 1815 these can be characterized on a left–right spectrum. Those on the left of British politics—liberals and radicals—sided with peasants against landlords, favoured the inclusion of Indians in government, and thought that British standards should be exported, whereas those on the right—Tories, later Conservatives—wanted to support traditional Indian social systems, to avoid cultural exports and to rule by shows of strength.

In sum, these disagreements were about whether it was better to hold onto India by good governance or by force. The common middle ground was always to try to keep the peace—if necessary by aggressive preemption—and to preserve India's people in the most advantageous condition as taxpayers and consumers.

Across the nineteenth century, these two viewpoints determined the detailed contents of controversies over land rights, education, tariff levels, taxation policy, social leadership, border security, political consultation, and the employment of Indians in government. For instance, in the 1880s Lord Kimberley, a Liberal, was prepared to concede that India's new university graduates were representative of the Indian population at large. His Conservative successor as Secretary for India, Lord Cross, absolutely denied this.

A variety of views sympathetic to Indian interests and aspirations appeared among free traders, liberals, radicals, socialists and communists. On the other side of the argument, matters were much simpler. For Tories, it was not political inclusion that mattered in India. The creation of prosperity—later called 'uplift'—was always an absolute priority. It literally had to come first, because it would produce contentment much more surely than schemes designed to promote abstract notions of fairness. Prosperity, crucially, could be shared, whereas governmental responsibility—i.e. power—could not. This was perfectly in line with the basic Tory view that people need, and like, leadership.

There was another important distinction. Liberals were always less satisfied with India, and assumed that social conditions should be ameliorated in the interests of the local population. Conservatives were quite happy with existing Indian arrangements, so long as the 'natural leaders' of society were still in charge, and were kept friendly. This attitude underwent a later development, when many conservatives began to adopt the protection of the Indian peasant as a bulwark of imperial policy. This was partly to avert revolt among the largest sector of Indian society, but it was also part of a strategy to undermine middle-class demands for political inclusion. Late imperialists, such as Harcourt Butler and Winston Churchill, insisted that ordinary Indians did not want votes or participation in government; they wanted security of tenure, protection from moneylenders, and swift, impartial justice.

It was also those towards the right who were more willing to believe that lessons could be learned from Indian practice. J.F. Stephen, though once a liberal, wrote to Viceroy Lytton in 1878, saying that India was 'the best corrective in existence to the fundamental fallacies of Liberalism'.[21] Monarchy, aristocracy and paternalism all had a great appeal to traditionalists and authoritarians in Britain. How well all these things were seen to be working in India probably helped to preserve many of the traditional elements still visible in the British state today.

Running alongside these differences was the issue of centralization or, seen in another light, state power. During the years of active conquest there was a strong drive towards increased central control, which peaked in the 1833 Charter Act. After 1857 the opposite became true, as the need for more detailed and responsive administration became paramount. Taking more power at the centre was the best way to propel modernization, but it also ran directly against classical laissez-faire principles.

There were no clear answers about big or small government, national or local responsibility, or degrees of inclusion. The result was a constant readjustment of military, administrative and revenue systems. 'Single' officers and committees swapped functions between 1793 and 1835. Fiscal devolution ran strongly through the late nineteenth century at the same time as amalgamation and centralization were in full swing in military and railway policy. Increased decentralization was recommended by a royal commission in 1907, but in practice viceroys continued to take more powers at the centre, as local and provincial government became increasingly Indianized.

Over the whole British period, a distinction emerged between active reformers who needed a strong state as a tool, and cautious conservatives who didn't. Early state builders include Cornwallis, Bentinck and Dalhousie; early non-interferers include Warren Hastings, Elphinstone and Ellenborough. Eventually this was a battle that the conservatives won by default, because lack of funds ensured that the British Indian state stayed small. But significantly, the reforming ambitions of the high Raj were inherited by the leadership of the Indian National Congress, and arguments about the role of central government in social reform persist in India to this day.

One last influential shift during this period should also be mentioned—the progression in British minds from thinking of India as rich to thinking of her as poor. This happened quickly among individuals—well before 1800—but much more gradually at a domestic political level. This reassessment provided a convenient political justification for authoritarian government, because a country too poor to educate and organize itself was obviously more in need of firm leadership than one with a strong internal economic and political dynamic.

Though dissenting voices were heard,[22] there was much more agreement about the empire in Britain than might be expected on any political issue of such magnitude over such a long period. It is also surprising at first sight to find so many professed liberals so willing to collaborate in its maintenance. This was partly because of the powerful force of self-interest, on both personal and national levels, but it was also the result of a concordance between the two major schools of domestic political philosophy, Whiggism and Toryism.

Overseas empire worked as an accommodating space both for the Whig belief that power corrupts and the Tory belief that dominance is natural. These two ideas often found it difficult to cohabit in Britain, but they could combine forcefully and purposefully abroad. The result was a project whose aim became to make sure that government ennobled those who bore its burdens. Here, beyond economics, lay the empire's most lasting domestic appeal.

India and the Modernizing of Britain

Taking on government in India had a much deeper effect on Britain than is usually acknowledged, and it should be ranked as one of the four most important socio-political milestones in British history, alongside the Norman Conquest, the Black Death and the Civil War. This is because the experience of ruling India profoundly changed British political culture and practice.

The Indian connection thrust genuinely new elements into national life. It raised fundamental questions about the purposes and mechanics of government, and changed perceptions of the basis of legitimate rule in Britain. This brought an end to inward-looking parochial Whiggism, propelled a transition to outward-looking universal liberalism, and ultimately stimulated the introduction of modern political accountability.

Governing in India provided a deep and continuing political education for the British ruling classes. Between 1793 and 1813, 9,000 volumes of official correspondence were received from India, 4,000 were sent in return, and 3,000 were exchanged between senior officials of the East India Company. This represented a very protracted seminar on governmental science, and was unlike anything ever thrown up by domestic British administration. Before responsibility for India arrived in London, the prime sources of political instruction for the British elite had been constructing their own self-governing institutions and, latterly, the fraught relationships with Ireland and the American colonies.

This widening of perspective gradually showed up how inadequate British political theory—based principally on the philosophy of John Locke—was to the task of managing complex systems. Locke's ideas on government were too specific and theoretical for the maintenance of a single political system strung across two very different and widely separated social systems.

A long list of major figures whose ideas fed into the broad stream of modern liberal thinking were concerned with and influenced by Indian affairs. The thoughts and attitudes of Edmund Burke, Adam Smith, Thomas Macaulay, Charles Trevelyan, John Stuart Mill, James Fitzjames Stephen, and Henry Maine were all heavily shaped by Indian issues.

Whiggism, the dominant political theory in Britain after the Revolution of 1688, originally developed in response to a particular political problem—how to create stable government while retaining both monarchy and aristocracy. Whiggism idealized a limited executive power supported by an elite social base that policed itself for undue ambition. Its cornerstone was 'property', and its bugbear was arbitrary power. A conservative but flexible affair, Whig government was effective among small numbers and over short distances—that is, it worked well enough in England. And though it proved too self-interested and unresponsive to satisfy the American colonists, who overthrew it between 1775 and 1783, it enjoyed a long afterlife in India. It is important to realize how much old-fashioned Whig thinking was carried across into what has been dubbed 'imperialism'.

Whiggism was a systematic compromise between those in society who were most significant, socially and economically, and this made it potentially compatible with government in India. As Viceroy Lansdowne recommended in 1893, the representation within any proposed new British Indian institutions should be of 'types and classes rather than areas or numbers'.[23]

The post-1857 compact between the Indian princes and the Raj was essentially an old-style, decentralized Whig arrangement. This may seem a strange idea at first sight, but it must be emphasized that Whiggism revolved around political accommodation with important 'interests'. It was about elite inclusion, not democracy. In Britain, it encompassed aristocrats and leaders of commerce; in India, it was landowners and the leaders of significant religious minorities.

Winston Churchill was perfectly aware of this. In 1920 he said: 'Our reign in India or anywhere else has never stood on the basis of physical force alone ... The British way of doing things ... has always meant close and effectual cooperation with the people of that country.'[24] He didn't, of course, mean all the people—just the important ones. In his words we can also distinguish the tail end of the classic legitimization rhetoric of the previous century. The kinship between high imperialism and old-style Whiggism could hardly be clearer. This can help us understand how the Morley–Minto reforms of 1909 were designed to represent competing 'interests' not straight majorities, using a franchise that stayed small and elitist through the next two reform packages, of 1919 and 1935. By then, true liberalism had long gone missing. The British could be Whigs in India, even liberals up to a point, but they could never be democrats.

Through their early experiences as rulers in India, the British ran up against the limits of Whiggish practice, because the devices that restrained aristocrats in government at home, such as personal honour, peer scrutiny and social sanction, turned out to be ineffective in the East, where power had necessarily to be condensed into highly concentrated points, and temptation, opportunity and isolation tended to dissolve the familiar domestic restraints. Government intervention in the East India Company's affairs was designed to address this problem, by buttressing Whig practices. The later Raj coped with the same issue by sharing some of the burden with India's 'natural' leaders, decompressing concentrations of power, and adding small amounts of representative opinion to delegated bodies.

The British conquered India in a wholly traditional style, but then began to run India in a way that Indians had not. The British then began to run Britain in a new way too, and 'responsibility'—what we now call accountability—became the gold standard of legitimacy in both countries. Hard on its heels came probity and efficiency, hallmarks of modern governance. But over time India was left behind under the old system, as the British became increasingly unwilling to export modern ideas and institutions to India. There was no safe place to fit self-government for subject peoples into the empire, and the reluctance of British politicians to accommodate new demands, or remake the imperial relationship sufficiently quickly or imaginatively, dictated the glacial pace of moves towards Indian independence.

This constituted a sustained betrayal of the vanguard elements within Indian society, which had looked for leadership, help and protection from the British. These modernizers, who had been a main support in the early nineteenth century, became the inveterate enemies of the twentieth-century Raj.

The later parts of this story have tended to overshadow the whole relationship, but the connection also saw India leading British political developments in a wide variety of areas: acceptance of government obligations to the governed (1788–95), a full time paid police force (1793), enactment of a citizen's right to sue the government (1793), the end of religious discrimination in access to public service employment (1833), education as a state obligation (1813–54), the first engineering college (1846), the use of competitive entry exams for public service (1854), the grants-in-aid (subsidy) system for schools (1854), codified criminal law (1861), government protection of archaeological sites (1863), state investment in roads and canals

(1830s and after), and nationalized railways (1920). Lastly, the culture of public service nurtured in India helped to normalize the idea that gentlemen should expect to do their public duty without undue financial reward.

As governmental powers and responsibilities increased, the nature and functions of the state—one of the key battlegrounds of modernity, and the basis for much of the left–right divide in politics—were first addressed not in Britain, but in India. Pivotal decisions were made on the subcontinent: that the state must not be corrupt, that it must be meritocratic in employment practices, neutral in religion, and interventionist wherever necessary. All of these things were true of the government of British India—i.e. the East India Company—before they were established and accepted in Britain; and taken together they made the Company state a liberal state in embryo.

Over the years there was also a constant stream of words, objects and ideas that India gave to Britain, which became part of the modern post-imperial nation. These included karma and korma, gymkhanas and polo, tonic water and India Pale Ale, municipal cemeteries, monitorial teaching methods, the study of comparative religion, yoga, military rockets, the Brighton Pavilion, paisley-patterned fabric, cashmere, chintz, fingerprinting, snooker, a modern syllabus in higher education, useful words like mogul, guru, cushy, jungle, bungalow, loot, doolally and thug, and a body of extraordinary literature, including the brilliant work of G.V. Desani. None of these things might, in themselves, be seen to justify the relationship as it developed, but what they show is that the long Anglo-Indian relationship was more stimulating than stultifying, and that it was not all about exploitation.

Finally, it was Indian influence that knocked the word 'British' from the title of the Commonwealth.

In 1813 Sir Thomas Munro told a House of Commons Select Committee: 'If civilization is to become an article of trade between the two countries [Britain and India], I am convinced that this country will gain by the import cargo.'[25] At the time, the idea would have seemed extraordinary to his audience, but he was proved right.

India and Liberalism

Although the French Revolution's most famous slogan—'Liberty, Equality, Fraternity'—distilled the essence of liberalism, France was not actually a stable liberal country until the 1870s. Meanwhile, what liberalism might mean in practice was being worked out in Britain, and India was a vital part of this process.

The British first adopted liberal principles not at home, like the French, but overseas, to justify colonial rule in India. This may seem paradoxical, but the shift only happened once the EIC had lost its trading monopoly in 1813, and James Mill's *History of India* (1817) had made the case that India was urgently in need of enlightened government. British administrators then realized that it was possible to use liberal principles as a mandate, without adopting liberal consultative mechanisms, as long as the intentions of the government were good. This aspiration remained the principal internal support for British rule until 1947. The reality of popular sovereign government could be withheld or delayed, as long as good men were trying to do good things.

Deluded, deceitful or intermittently justified, this is what the British told themselves until the very end of the Indian empire. It was the perfect solution to the increasingly awkward situation in which British politicians found themselves after 1757—namely, that they could not escape all responsibility for the internal affairs of another country that had fallen under British control.

This first hit home in Britain when through the 1760s the American colonists were railing against 'taxation without representation', while in India the British were trying to run a system based entirely on that principle. This was a sign that India was going to present new problems that required new responses. Here was the germ that grew into mature liberal thought, but the start was halting.

Robert Clive had few structured thoughts about what he was doing, and he hid British rule in Bengal behind a puppet nawab and the concept of dual government. Warren Hastings, though more cerebral, faced much greater difficulties and was unable to lay down any systematic approach. As a reaction to Hastings's regime, Edmund Burke then developed a moral theory of colonial rule, which stressed the importance of ethical governance in foreign lands. This proved the way forward.

Burke tried to hold Hastings to a set of standards that had never been explicitly stated in England before, and these provided the grounding for the later British arguments for imperial government, through a set of eternal moral principles. To distinguish this from the French roots of modern liberalism, it should be noted that Burke formed his ideas before the Declaration of the Rights of Man was drawn up in Paris in 1789. Indeed he fiercely attacked the new French ideas, and in his *Reflections on the Revolution in France* (1790) he explained at length why such novel, artificial principles were to be resisted.

And so they were in official circles in Britain, until around 1830, when a long, reactionary period came to an end with the fall of the Duke of Wellington's first ministry. But Burke had opened a constructive pathway for British thinkers and governors. Superficially, he seemed to share some of the anti-authoritarian attitudes of his more radical contemporary Thomas Paine, but he started from a different place. Burke's critique of government was looking down from above, Paine's up from below; Burke was concerned with the obligations of governors, Paine with the rights of citizens. In a British context, the crucial difference was that Paine's ideas found no official favour in India, whereas Burke's did. Burke's ideas constituted a philosophy of ruling, and could support the idea of empire, whereas Paine's concept of rights could not.

The trial of Warren Hastings marked the first intellectual flowering of this quest for legitimization—the desire to base colonial rule on something other than pure force. And as British political life became increasingly liberal, Burke's insistence that rulers must govern in line with universal moral principles gained support. Flouted though it often was, this ideal acted as a lodestar within imperial thinking that could not be ignored. From a British perspective, the rights of Indian widows to be safe from sati, or of Indian men to be free from torture during tax collection, were founded on Burke, not Paine. And once these rights were established in India, there was no way that they could be denied to British subjects in Britain, whose prime protection till then lay in specific laws or in the kindly paternalism of the ruling classes.

The first political philosophy that the British developed in India was thus not nationalism, or imperialism; it was liberalism. And this process started at least as early as Burke's denunciation of Hastings.

Liberalism as theorized in France was a revolutionary creed of novel possibilities, which found its way into the minds of young British idealists, like the poet Shelley and his circle, via the world of letters. But it found its way into government in Britain via India, where it lent guidance to a regime that was entirely unrepresentative. The British gradually came to think of Indians as having rights, and even if these did not include the right to make decisions of state, they certainly included rights to good government and impartial justice. Britons at home enjoyed these entitlements, but the idea that Indians should have them too was a liberal idea.

The East India Company went on to develop an unusually advanced role as a government in India—shouldering responsibility for a range of functions including education, public health, investment in infrastructure, and roles in economic regulation that went well beyond anything considered appropriate domestically. While in Britain the reforming prime ministers of the 1830s described themselves as Whigs, and there was no official Liberal Party till 1859, in Indian affairs liberal sympathizers were in positions of responsibility from around 1820, as a small coterie of educated men took positions of influence within the EIC's administration, home and abroad, and on the staff of its college at Haileybury.

But the liberalism of the rulers did not devolve on the ruled to any great degree, and Indians did not enjoy full liberty under British rule. Instead they had to make do with another part of the liberal package—equality. Some were not comfortable with this initially, because it cut across so many of India's social and legal traditions, but it did eventually go on to become a central principle of the nationalist movement—an autonomous Indian reaction that intensified the drive towards democracy. But the British were very uneven in their commitment to equality, even in the bare sense of equality before the law, and later it was official ambitions in precisely this area that set the expatriate community against its 'own' government most seriously. The thought of being set at a level with an Indian in a courtroom was at least as offensive to an indigo planter as being levelled with a ryot (peasant) was to a raja. British politicians and officials never had any objections to equality—at least not among Indians. It was liberty that remained absent, and the classic liberal package never took its full shape in British India.

In Britain, though, liberalism flourished in the backwash of government responsibilities in India. Better administrative practice, punctilious public accounting, competitive entry to public office, an advanced role for government in social legislation—all can be traced to the experience of holding and ruling India, rather than to popular pressure for critical inquiry into the governance of Britain.

Liberalism is imaginative and projective; Toryism is pragmatic and accepting. Liberalism thus found a congenial playground in India, where visions of modernization and social reform were allowed free rein. Here lies the root of the split between the liberal approach, to intervene, and the Tory approach, to leave alone.

Political power and administrative practice were dissected and examined in India in ways they had never needed to be in Britain, where traditional forms of social power reliably supported central authority. British India was different; government and society remained artificially separated. Experience also taught that the division of government into three branches—executive, legislative and judiciary—was not applicable in India and could not be directly imported. It fitted very awkwardly with the traditional distinction within Mughal government between departments of revenue (diwani) and of public order (nizamat), which both carried judicial powers, and had no close parallel in European practice.

A new analysis of government was slowly developed in India, based on problems of magistracy and taxation in Bengal, leading to a much clearer appreciation of necessary distinctions, such as between assessment and collection of revenue, or across subcategories of government such as administrative, fiscal, judicial, civil, police and military powers.

India expanded the political imagination of some British Whigs, such as Lord William Bentinck, and the limited liberalism deployed in India also had a transformative effect on some less aristocratic Indians. Many nationalist leaders, including S. Banerjea and G.K. Gokhale, were devotees of Burke,[26] and even in the 1820s the Bishop of Calcutta, Reginald Heber, claimed to have found 'advanced' Indian Whigs in the town.[27] The advent of modernity in India was genuinely multiform.

But there was one dominant, non-indigenous strand to it, with a powerful rationale of its own.

'Our Work': Legitimacy in Action

In 1905, after seven arduous years as viceroy, Lord Curzon told an audience at the Byculla Club in Bombay that there were two things about British rule of which he was certain: 'our work is righteous and…it shall endure'.[28] Even with more than a century's distance, the phrase 'our work' is still striking, and it raises important questions. What 'work' was this, who was doing it, and why?

The bulk of the work was ruling, which Indians were not supposed to be able to manage for themselves. Another element was the importation of 'progress', which Indians were assumed to lack the means to generate. This meant that the work was to be done exclusively by Britons. Most importantly, the work was necessary, and it therefore served as a reason to stay on, as rulers with real claims to legitimacy.

Talk of 'our work' came into vogue in the middle of the nineteenth century as Lord Dalhousie was forging ahead with his reforms. A letter to *The Times* of 6 November 1849 asked: 'Is our work in India ever to have an end?' Curzon, therefore, was not the first, nor by any means the last, to use the expression. In 1929 Stanley Baldwin, Conservative leader of the

Opposition, used it five times in a debate on the status of India within the empire. Lord Jowitt, the Labour Lord Chancellor, told the House of Lords in February 1947 of how, as a schoolboy, he had read 'the stirring story of our work in India'.[29]

Originally, perhaps, a borrowing from evangelical literature, the phrase was enjoying the peak of its currency as the twentieth century opened. In 1900 Sir William Lee-Warner, a former senior Raj official, delivered a lecture at the Imperial Institute in London under the title 'Our Work in India in the Nineteenth Century'. Sir William's address was all about the building of bridges and canals, the bringing of justice, order and good government. Nor was this self-satisfaction confined to conservative empire-lovers like Curzon and Lee-Warner. Even a liberal sceptic such as J.A. Hobson, author of the seminal *Imperialism: A Study* (1902), could write, 'Our work there [India] is the best record British Imperialism can show.'[30]

We can easily dismiss all this as self-congratulation, which it was, but Curzon and the others certainly believed what they were saying. Even Hobson was prepared to admit: 'Nowhere else in our Empire has so much really disinterested and thoughtful energy been applied in the work of government.'[31] Here, apparently, was a noble project, missionary in tone and suffused with moral sensibility.

But there were covert meanings and purposes in play. At a surface level 'our work' was to modernize and improve India and her people, while at a deeper level it was intended to sanctify the superior status of those doing the work. In other words, the whole idea of necessary 'work' lay at the heart of the legitimization project. Many contemporaries were well aware of this. In 1885 Arthur Cotton, the great hydraulic engineer, remarked that public works were 'a legitimate way of consolidating our power'.[32]

The language used by the first Britons to take up government in India stands in stark contrast. Their dispatches confined themselves to talk of interests, advantage and honour. In those days it was not 'work', nor was it 'ours'. But over the intervening decades, the narrow responsibility of ruling evolved into a much wider project of development, while responsibility for it broadened out from a small merchant company to an entire nation.

For the British, by around 1900, the 'work' had become not a matter of pleasing themselves, but a political requirement disguised as a moral burden taken up on behalf of others. In his Byculla speech Curzon also explained that all his efforts were actually for the benefit of India's poor peasants. The nobility of this undertaking moved him deeply, and his highest flights of rhetoric were always on this theme. The obligation to protect, enlighten and uplift mankind intoxicated him. He was reluctant to call this project 'imperialism', as were most other India veterans, but he was happy to attribute imperialism to others—notably Lord Rosebery, a former prime minister and leading Liberal figure of the 1890s. Addressing Rosebery in friendly fashion at a public dinner in 1898, Curzon remarked that imperialism was becoming 'less and less the creed of a party and more and more the faith of a nation'.[33]

This was not mere whimsy. In 1892 Curzon had faced the great Liberal leader Gladstone across the floor of the House of Commons in a debate over proposals for Indian council reform, and on that occasion had heard him utter words that are unmistakeably imperialist in tone. Gladstone, usually reckoned as a great critic of empire, was happy to agree with Curzon about the 'work', though he called it a 'task', which he described as both 'noble' and 'peculiar'—meaning special. He said: 'this nation to which we belong has undoubtedly had committed to it a most peculiar task in the foundation and the government of extraneous territories'.[34]

In opposition at the time, Gladstone went on to appeal to one of his own party not to force a vote on an amendment to the government's rather vague proposals to extend the 'elective principle' to Legislative Councils in India, on two grounds. Firstly, the governance of India was fraught with 'difficulties' and it was prudent to leave some latitude to the men charged with its execution. Secondly, it was not a good idea to divide the House on a matter of Indian governance, because it might 'convey a false impression'. Better, while under Indian eyes, to convey the 'truth' that 'united views substantially prevail in this House'.[35] These positions went on to enjoy cross-party support in imperial debates till the end of empire.

The imperial consensus appealed for by Gladstone, and assumed by Curzon, was as much pragmatic as it was ideological. It worked well as a system of present-day justification. But unlike many of his Liberal opponents, Curzon could see no end to imperial selflessness. On that Bombay evening in 1905 he put down a bold claim on the future: 'I do not think that our work is over or that it is drawing to an end.'[36]

Curzon had little time for Indians who thought that they should also be included in the work, and he thus ignored the one political issue—self-government—that was the logical outcome of the labours in which he took such pride. His mentality could not address any demand for swaraj, reflecting the fact that one simple question remained unanswered at the centre of all the imperial harangue. That question, asked by millions of Indians, was: why? Why are you shouldering the burden of government unaided, when we don't want you to? Mainstream British political opinion had no ready answer.

Before the First World War, self-government for India was not on the agenda. Even the future Labour prime minister Ramsay MacDonald, undoubtedly a man of the left, felt able to write in 1910 that 'for many a long year British sovereignty will be necessary for India'. Unlike Curzon, however, he could see a way forward—consultation. If India were 'consulted by her guardian, and given wide liberty to govern herself in all her internal affairs, she may present many difficulties and create many fears, but that is the only way to abiding peace and to the fulfilment of our work in India'.[37]

But in reality that work, of promoting economic, political and social progress, was never just a British affair. Curzon may have been unwilling to see it, but influential Indians had long been working to promote development and reform in their country.

A small but influential segment of Indian society had always broadly supported moves towards modernity, in the conscious knowledge that it risked enhancing the capabilities of the alien power. M.G. Ranade was all in favour of progress, or 'change for the better' as he defined it. Indians critical of their own society throughout the period 1750–1950 are now classified as 'social reformers', a description that scarcely does justice to the range of their interests. Not all wanted to follow Western models, but in differing degrees many did, in a long line from Dwarkanath Tagore to Jawaharlal Nehru.

Ranade hoped to see social and economic changes that would 'ensure the permanent triumph of the modern spirit in this Ancient Land'.[38] For nearly all of the social reformers, the question was not whether the modern spirit should be admitted, but exactly how it should be expressed and managed. Prominent figures from Ram Mohan Roy to Swami Vivekananda were keen to pick out the technological plums of the modern West while leaving its amorality and godlessness alone.

Under the colonial regime, however, the Indian contribution had to remain unacknowledged, for if Indians could do this kind of work for themselves, what exactly was the value of British rule?

Two Systems

It was, as Gladstone pointed out, a 'peculiar' national destiny that obliged the British to create two very different governmental systems. After 1688 they built an oligarchic quasi-representative structure in Britain to check monarchical ambitions; after 1784, they designed an autocratic military regime in India to resist insurrection. Between rulers and ruled, the two systems faced in diametrically opposite directions, and enjoyed very different futures. The first was able to grow and adapt, while the other managed to exercise control but became increasingly sclerotic. The two systems diverged slowly, and because both were theoretically grounded in parliamentary sovereignty, and were thus both legitimate in British eyes, the British were able to think of themselves as guardians of liberty at home while being more or less the opposite in India.

The British were obliged to design a state structure in India virtually from scratch, because the one Warren Hastings lashed together between 1772 and 1784 was considered to have failed. He had tried to adapt traditional Indian practice while adding a British top layer to it, but this compromise never worked well. Absence of supervision, abundant temptation, scarcity of reliable information and poor communication between Calcutta and the mofussil (rural areas) created multiple problems. When placed in Indian shoes, Europeans often behaved worse than their native predecessors. Hastings's system lacked discipline, so British politicians resolved in the early 1780s to supply standards and enforce them. Pitt's India Act of 1784 and the Cornwallis Code of 1793 were the results.

Traditional ruling practices in India were replaced by specific rules, designed to reduce personal discretion. What the British most feared in their own rulers—arbitrary power—they were determined, at least initially, to deny to those placed in authority in India.

Just as the US Constitution was designed to thwart the central executive, so the objective of the Cornwallis system of 1793, its near contemporary, was to restrain the EIC's servants in India. The collective self-regulation that it set up, by means of boards and committees, worked fairly well in enforcing honesty within government in India after 1784, but not in achieving efficiency. Day-to-day government was not facilitated, and judicial decisions slowed to a crawl. Meanwhile tax revenues, instead of sticking to British fingers, stayed somewhere out in the rural areas, hidden behind an opaque wall of legal and customary technicalities.

As the British domain expanded, a less elaborate style of administration, the Munro system, was pioneered in the Madras Presidency through the late 1790s. This relied on single officers, and was simpler and cheaper, being designed to reduce overheads and stimulate agricultural output, not to defend the administrative machine against abuse from within.

When faced with the need for greater executive responsiveness, Whiggish pessimism about power gradually lost ground within administrative thinking in India, and Munro's approach gained the upper hand around 1812–14. With the governmental brakes now off, the favourite Whig devices—boards and committees—were replaced by a new authority figure and emerging imperial hero, the enlightened 'man on the spot', in whom trust could be safely reposed.

The most energetic reformers, Bentinck and Dalhousie, were both supporters of this kind of decisive administration, known as 'single-seatedness', and as a device it stuck. The only important change to the system occurred after the Uprising of 1857, when the creation of a national system of superior courts meant that single officers gradually lost elements of their judicial functions.

The British installed local absolutism beneath an upper layer of accountability, leaving a mongrel system that joined an idealized Tory base to a superficially Whig superstructure. Efficiency and accountability were both assured by the employment of familiar domestic methods.

Early British experiences in India had been about abuses of government—by the EIC's own men—but through the early nineteenth century, personal honour came back into favour, repackaged as a scaled-down version of national honour, once the bad men in India were no longer seen to be the Company's unsupervised servants, and began to be various Indian stereotypes, including bandits, moneylenders and religious fanatics. Here was the imperial mission, carried forward by imperious men.

The British as governors sought efficiency and good practice, not the active repression of Indians, who were simply excluded from politics. India, therefore, was most often a laboratory for good governance, not bad. Much of what was good was then selectively re-imported. This will surely not be a popular suggestion with visceral anti-colonialists, but the evidence is overwhelming. The British learned nothing about repression which they re-imported; the import cargo was all good.

The British displayed public arrogance and titanic condescension in India, but they were prepared to be self-critical, at least in private. Colonial rule was subjected throughout to scrutiny which, though sporadic, was nonetheless intense. There were major parliamentary inquiries in 1767, 1772–3, 1781–2 and then every twenty years from 1793 to 1853. Henry Fawcett's parliamentary Finance Committee, which was consistently critical of the Raj, sat from 1871 to 1874, and numerous special commissions were set up in India from the 1880s through to the

1930s, to examine everything from famine, education and currency, to railways, civil service recruitment and relations with princely states. A pioneering development in this strand was the Madras Torture Commission of 1854–5, set up to examine the alleged use of coercion by the Presidency's native policemen to extract revenue payments and, much less frequently, confessions to crimes. In light of the Commission's findings—that torture was indeed commonplace—the whole structure of policing in British India was revised in the early 1860s.

The British were not complacent about India, and did try to keep abreast of how the whole system was working. They were, in fact, a lot more curious about the effectiveness of government institutions and policies in India than they were in Britain. Here again the driving force was the need for legitimacy.

But what really went missing was imagination. The great apologists for the mature Raj, Kipling and Curzon among them, were always selling a rosy vision of the present. The imperialism they promoted was based on a selective reading of history, but it had little to say about the future.

There was no officially sanctioned view of India's future anywhere in British thinking until the Montagu Declaration of 1917, 160 years after the original seizure of Bengal. Conservatives and liberals alike recognized that the Raj could not last forever, and that one day it must either fall or melt away into Indian self-government, but there was no agreement over the timetable that this might involve—centuries were mentioned—nor was there any true consensus as to how, in practical terms, any gradual liberalization should be conducted.

This was not just bloody-mindedness. As the Anglo-Indian relationship developed, it became increasingly difficult to tinker with it. A thicket of vested interests grew up, ensuring that to contemplate change was to risk mobilizing entrenched opposition on an unforeseeable scale. Instead, India became the one area in which all parties veered to the right, i.e. towards caution, social conservatism, and the acceptance of cultural and ethnic differences as 'natural' and probably unbridgeable. With the possible exception of Lord Dalhousie, a 'blue shift' affected liberal British minds from Sir William Jones and Thomas Macaulay, through John Morley, to Ramsay MacDonald and beyond.

India simply was not Britain, and even the most idealistic politicians eventually came to recognize this. In another subtle turnabout, British politicians stopped thinking of India as an archaic version of Europe, and began thinking of her as a chaotic version of Ireland. Finally, they accepted

India as India, but with the vital proviso that she was not yet ready to be handed back to her inhabitants.

Colonial rule became colonial fossilization, and India thus missed out on the intermediate stages of her own modernization.

New Outlines: Legitimacy and Unity

We can now construct a new outline of Anglo-Indian history, by tracing the progress of the legitimacy and unity projects, taking note of the factors that influenced them, and their interactions, especially in the later nineteenth century.

Legitimacy

British rule had several interactive components. In India, there were local and central levels of government. In London there was the EIC directorate, and constant political contestation beneath an upper level of governmental control. As British understanding of legitimate government continued to develop, and as circumstances altered in India, the relationship between these moving parts was constantly changing, but can be divided into three main historical phases.

The first phase (1765–84) was characterized by weak control of Indian affairs from Britain, leading to indiscipline, administrative improvisation and straightforward extortion disguised as government. The EIC's position was both anomalous and precarious, so its leading figures in both London and India were keen to establish credentials to support the legitimacy of its rule. Thus Robert Clive negotiated the Treaty of Allahabad in 1765 with Emperor Shah Alam, in an attempt to merge the Company-as-ruler into the Mughal imperium. Similarly, the directors later ordered Warren Hastings to abandon Clive's Dual System and to step out from behind the puppet nawab in 1772, to try to ensure better government in Bengal, along with enhanced accountability to the Company in Leadenhall Street.

Initially, politicians in London were not unduly troubled by misrule in India, but through the 1760s they gradually became aware of its negative domestic impact, including near bankruptcy for the Company and the arrival of rich, 'unattached' men in Parliament. The Regulating Act of 1773 was a first attempt to grapple with the expectations of the domestic political audience, but it failed to depoliticize the Company or discipline its government in India.

Concerns peaked in the early 1780s, and led to a second phase of legitimization, which began with decisive intervention in 1784, and lasted till around 1870.

Pitt's India Act of 1784 created a Board of Control, composed of members of Parliament, to supervise the Company's military, governmental and diplomatic affairs; commerce was left to the Court of Directors. This effectively converted the Company-as-ruler into an arm of the British state. The prime benefit to the Company was that it was henceforth securely founded in terms of familiar domestic legality, while politicians reserved the right to criticize it. The 1784 Act had a subsidiary legal objective—to provide legal 'redress' against the Company in India—but its main political intention was to protect Britain from India, not India from Britain.

Pitt's Act was followed by the Cornwallis Code of 1793, which was designed to reduce 'discretion' (i.e. personal power) in India by means of extensive written regulations. It also further separated the Company's various activities—trading, governing, diplomacy—as if they were constitutional functions.

But as the enormous conquests of 1792–1818 were absorbed, Cornwallis's cumbersome structure of separated powers remained confined to Bengal, while several parallel, 'Non-Regulation' systems, founded on less formal administrative arrangements, were adopted. These usually relied on single local officers, supervised at a distance by senior men, acting in boards, councils and courts.

For compelling reasons of cost and efficiency, Whig principles were gradually abandoned at the local level; superior character under high-minded supervision was deemed to suffice. In India the employment of fewer, better men was the answer to the problems of expansion. This represented a return to the kind of Tory paternalism that was becoming untenable in Britain as demands for political reform grew in the early nineteenth century.

A clear fracture between the base and the superstructure of British rule thus developed at around the time when it became accepted that the Cornwallis Code had failed in practice. This realization was followed by a relapse into indigenous idiom, marked by the rise of the Munro school of government after 1812, and its variants in the Delhi region and later the Punjab. This was another, subtler form of legitimization, as Indian norms became acceptable within local government.

Pitt and Cornwallis had done their best to take 'discretion' out of Indian affairs, but it was then reintroduced gradually, as the Company's trading activities withered, then completely disappeared after 1833. Paternalist ideals then had space to develop, a process intensified with the injection of muscular Christian righteousness from the 1830s. At ground level this is what imperialism came to be—a code of high principles to give guidance where no direct accountability could be acknowledged.

After about 1820, a generation of technocrats also began to experiment with scientific revenue assessment, social improvements, and English-medium education. This proto-liberalism grew up autonomously within the Company's structures and was not a by-product of mainstream British politics. As the EIC lost its trading role, it developed a kind of conscience about its activities, which made it susceptible to the liberal agenda. The new outlook was undemocratic but high-minded. It was also heavily stamped with the Utilitarian habit of reducing everything to matters of rational economics.

In London, most politicians lost interest in India during this period, except at times of charter revision or major warfare, though the more proactive presidents of the Board of Control, such as Lord Ellenborough, involved themselves with wider strategy. The directors also had little to do in London, apart from supervising the tea trade with China and dealing with patronage issues. All the significant activity was in Calcutta, where policy issues were now being settled.

Over the period 1820–57, liberal British, not traditional Indian, norms rose to dominate the development of central policy in India, culminating in Lord Dalhousie's reforms after 1848. The maintenance of law and order, social improvement and economic development became the professed objectives of British rule. Political inclusion of local notables was even countenanced by Dalhousie, and in his time the domestic and Indian theatres moved closer than they ever were again. But this was a sign that the balance within EIC governance between respectful conservatism and liberal reformism was becoming unstable.

In hindsight, Dalhousie's policies, especially in education, were always likely to lead to an impossible dilemma—how to elevate and educate a population that was also required to remain politically passive. This dilemma was removed by the revolt of 1857, which shifted the British into a more conservative political stance, while liberal aspirations remained as a continuing claim to legitimacy.

Although the Company's rule was replaced by closer control from London after 1858, the domestic and Indian systems soon became permanently distanced, by expanded democratic inclusion in Britain; the Reform

Acts of 1867 and 1884 had resonances in India too. Before 1857 the British, as a matter of convenience, were trying to make India more like Britain. After 1867 they were trying, as a matter of caution, to ensure that India remained as unlike Britain as possible.

The year 1857 represented a serious crisis of legitimacy, as powerful sections of Indian society showed how discontented they were, and how much damage they could do if roused. Most of the reforms after 1857 were aimed at two principal blocs: the landed elite and the peasantry. This contrasted with most of the reforms that had preceded the revolt, which were focused on the modernizing middle classes.

This second governmental phase always prioritized collecting revenue while using law and order as its justification, and strong traces of this policy continued beyond 1857. Though the Uprising abruptly changed the surface of politics, no new basis of legitimacy emerged immediately.

It was parliamentary reform that removed the possibility that Britain and India could develop modern institutions in parallel, and it was this schism that introduced the third phase of legitimization (c.1870–1947). Once a mass franchise had been conceded at home, it became impossible to sustain a single philosophy of government to justify the position of the British ruling class in both continents.

Modern machines in India could help British businesses, but modern political institutions were unlikely to yield any kind of useful return. Representative democracy would inevitably make India less amenable to British control. The third phase then simply prioritized the assembling of support that could be publicly displayed, using promises of increasing association in government.

These last seventy-odd years of the Raj represented a protracted though quiet crisis of governance as the British finally faced serious ideological discomfort, while the economics of the empire became ever more complex and Indian political aspirations proved increasingly difficult to control.

The attitude adopted by the British after 1870 was therefore different, and has been described as 'liberal authoritarianism'. This term reflects the distance that had developed between elements of British rule in London, Calcutta and the mofussil, but it is an ungainly and slightly misleading expression. Liberal authoritarianism equally well describes the main thrust of British policy during the Bentinck era, when there was no upper-level inclusion of Indians, whereas there was after 1861. But the third-phase system was undeniably more Whiggish, because of the presence of unelected Indian notables within imperial councils. The main point here is that the Raj was politically more inclusive post-1857, but culturally more supremacist. The political necessity to appease significant interests could be conceded in private, but the principle of representative inclusion could not be acknowledged publicly.

The later Raj had liberal aspirations to be modern, but it could only rely on a rationale of power that was ancient. As India failed to flourish, the British simply announced that imperial control was needed to remedy the situation. Indians, it was said, could neither defend nor govern themselves, and therefore as defenders, governors and educators the British must remain. Power continued to justify itself.

A paradoxical mixture of attitudes grew up as the government increasingly felt itself charged with the maintenance of order against forces of anarchy (the peasantry) and self-interest (the middle classes). The only safe way forward was to rely on the socio-economic power of the landowners, and in return they endured the least interference from alien control. In terms of representation, the system became wider at its top, while the base remained as narrow as possible. The Whig enthusiasm for improvement was reconciled with the Tory love of authority.

This last phase was the most rigid, and required a heightened degree of cultural arrogance to support it. The only other remaining option was to hand government back to the Indians. Schemes to do this were laid out, but they were tentative and slow, hedged about with 'safeguards' and special powers.

For the sake of legitimacy, imperialism was required to grow from a notional handbook to a constitutional document. From the 1860s onwards this need was directly faced within the white 'dominions of settlement' which, starting with Canada in 1867, were granted degrees of self-government. Imperial ideas of stewardship in the East became increasingly necessary after democratization in the West, but India was always a case too far. Victoria's elevation, in 1877, to the rank of Empress of India while she remained merely a constitutional monarch at home typified the fractures in the foundations of legitimate government.

The third phase of British rule began exactly at the moment when the Raj's money started to run out and modernization was no longer helping to make the country more governable. Through the 1880s there was a gradual collapse of political willingness to invest expansively in public works, at the same time as straitened finances made it more difficult to fund them. This change of emphasis was accompanied by a clear parallel shift in the liberal mindset. Earlier in the century, liberal criticism had been directed at society in both Britain and India. After the advent of high imperialism, the critique was directed solely at India.

So what followed the Uprising of 1857 was not the arrival of democratization but the importation of a revised, authoritarian ideal, which was, in effect, a reconfirmation of the previous century's belief that only certain people were fit to rule. This Whiggism 2.0 never acknowledged restraint by local representative bodies. It therefore needed superior men to run it, so the last phase of colonial rule witnessed the most strenuous attempts to paint the British in India as heroes.

Reform, meanwhile, was slow, with the introduction of consultation (1909), local responsibility (1919) and provincial autonomy (1935). Indian high-ups were inducted, significant interest groups were appeased, but representative bodies were still denied sovereign rights.

This reworking of the imperial machine was accompanied by cautious changes in political language. Words like nomination, appointment, selection or invitation were used when referring to consultative bodies, which were only slowly acknowledged as representative, even when degrees of election were involved. The object was to avoid admitting the existence of political, as opposed to purely legal, rights.

This tendency also found expression in the unwillingness to write the detailed provisions of reforms into parliamentary statutes; these were left at the level of regulations, drafted by officials in India. Parliament, we can remind ourselves, always felt itself entitled to exercise sovereign power over India. All the major pieces of legislation concerning the governance of India, from 1773 to 1947, were voted through the lobbies in Westminster. This, of course, looks like pure imperial arrogance, but to the British ruling classes it was the most fundamental safeguard and a vital guarantee of the legitimacy of British power in India.

After about 1890, British officials gradually drifted into a state of bemused inactivity, which they justified by ideas about India's ancient nature and stubborn backwardness. A general commitment to 'uplift' remained, but without sufficient money or political will to deliver it. Not entirely coincidentally, this loss of coherent direction within the Raj occurred at the same time as the progressive Indian vanguard began to abandon hopes that the British would deliver on their promises. This allowed the elite liberal nationalism of the early Congress to be overtaken by a popular cultural awakening, with distinct religious overtones, which began with Vivekananda and led through Tilak to Gandhi.

The nature and course of India's independence movement was largely determined by this shift of energy, which heralded the permanent decline of the British legitimization project, and opened a critical phase in Indian efforts to unite. Popular mobilization in India moved downwards and outwards from the elite, reaching a new extent in the crisis of 1919–22. This was met by cautious rearguard actions by British politicians, even those nominally of the left. The two weak Labour governments of the 1920s could not envisage any Indian policy other than to take painfully cautious steps towards granting self-government. In practice, this was barely distinguishable from Tory policy.

This outline shows how the British ruling class searched for legitimacy, both at home and abroad, and how these searches were linked. It is clear that as Britain became an increasingly liberal country, the need for legitimacy became correspondingly greater in India.

Equally important for our understanding of the later Raj is the story of the quest by India's people for unity.

Unity

Large-scale political structures were a rarity in ancient and medieval India. There was little need for them, as India's social systems were well organized at local level. Such large structures as did emerge tended to fall away into their constituent provinces whenever strong rulers were followed by weak, or regions grew too powerful for the centre to hold them.

After 1757, the need for unity became urgent in the face of determined foreign intrusion, but British success across the period 1757–1805 saw little change in the prevailing attitudes among Indian rulers; they remained addicted to military rivalry. Once the Marathas had failed to consolidate their superiority over the years 1761–84, and with the defeat of Tipu Sultan, who stood alone against a British-led coalition in 1799, prospects for a coordinated Indian resistance were lost, only to be briefly revived in 1857–9.

The first serious attempt to act in a spirit of national unity came in 1857 from the lower ranks of the army, not the nobility. Then, after the defeat of the Uprising, the quest for unity underwent a permanent change. Internal disarmament allowed for the emergence of a non-violent unification project, and the Congress took centre stage. Its early liberal nationalism was unproblematic. It followed European models, and it was an unapologetically elite affair, with no ambition towards democratic inclusion. But because of these very qualities, the early Congress was also ineffective in pressuring the British. Politically it could not mobilize mass support, and remained becalmed within the Raj's own institutions. Intellectually, the Congress quailed at defining the Indian 'nation' as much beyond the limits of its own membership, which was small, educated, Anglophile, and part-time. The main problem was then how to democratize nationalism while still controlling it.

The Western-style liberal nationalism of the early Congress remained at some distance from the kind of social and cultural centre ground that could energize a new nation, and it was not until the movement developed a heightened cultural relevance that its power was fully realized. The Congress only became truly popular once it had adopted a paradoxical, mixed character, as nationalist, secular and 'Hindu'. Perfecting this combination was Gandhi's distinct contribution to the movement, but he never found a way to escape the contradictions it contained.

The concept of secular nationhood that he used avoided potentially divisive religious traditions, but the symbolism capable of expressing it automatically pulled the movement into the Hindu cultural sphere, as did the allegiances and sympathies of the majority of its expanded membership. Gandhi adopted Vivekananda's attitude to Hinduism, as the religion he preferred but not the only one of value, and this approach was enormously helpful in allowing for maximum outreach. But its subtlety was easily lost in a mass movement. Ramrajya being preached by a man who looked like a sadhu sent a message that was unmistakeably Hindu in tone.

Gandhi's greatest success was that his very personal style of leadership made the Congress appear more united than it actually was, but there were limits to his unifying powers. Though he tried, he could not maintain the movement's religious diversity. From 1922 onwards, after the dissolution of the grand Congress–Khilafat alliance, Muslim support gradually dwindled, especially in areas where Muslims preferred local self-government to being ruled at a distance by leaders they did not consider to be like them. Congress leaders underestimated this disjuncture, while Jinnah overemphasized it. These twin political strategies were to have national consequences.

Gandhi also avoided laying down a clear attitude towards tradition. Though the Congress always espoused a modernizing agenda, many of its leaders, and most of its mass following, were quite traditional in their sympathies. Gandhi made no explicit attempt to resolve this contradiction and successfully relied on his political persona to bridge the gap. His outlook was partly archaic in its idealization of village simplicity, but he was also quite accepting of contemporary circumstances. The Congress constitution he drew up in 1921, as a blueprint for swaraj, was modern and democratic.

His opposition to machinery and cities has also been exaggerated; his dislike of them was based on their tendency to promote dehumanization and immorality. *The Gandhian Plan of Economic Development*, drawn up by S.N. Agarwal in 1944, made space for industry and capitalist relations.

All these pragmatic balances meant that the national movement was never entirely clear in its attitudes to modernization. Socialists in the Congress had little liking for village India, while others leaders harboured traditional and distinctly more 'Hindu' sympathies. Sardar Patel and Rajendra Prasad had conservative views on social issues, while Madan Mohan Malaviya was also a member of the Hindu Mahasabha, where he shared a platform with much less liberal figures. The Congress's main policy statement, the Karachi Resolution of 1931, had a whiff of compromise about it, and it was as much about rights to equality, freedom and economic justice as it was about socialism—not mentioned but only hinted at—with state control of 'key industries'. The decade that followed was not marked by the recruitment of keen leftists to the party, but by an influx of the rural gentry.[39]

Many intellectuals have since assumed that mass movements must be socialist, but the history of the Congress offers evidence to the contrary. The Congress was always a coalition as much as a party—Gandhi thought of it as a parliament—and its internal cohesion relied to some degree on a series of truces. The fact that the designing of modern India in the Constituent Assembly after 1947 was driven by some of the keenest modernizers was a specific circumstance, not the expression of a popular choice. It was mainly Gandhi's patronage of Nehru that facilitated it.

Gandhi assured Nehru's accession to the leadership in 1946 because he believed him to be the best man to negotiate demission with the British. Though many Indians today would not accept that the Mahatma was right, under Nehru's leadership India stayed democratic, but with an indistinct relationship to modernity.

Nehru may have thought he was ushering in an era of modernist reform, yet the process was skin-deep. India's rural elite, long nurtured by the British, thwarted him at every turn as they queued up to join the party, once it became the sole vehicle for patronage in the land. Law-making and social change are very different things, and the results of the fine words in the constitution were scanty. It was to take decades before modern ideas can be said to have penetrated very far into the mofussil.

This reflected the fact that the bulk of traditionalist, powerful Indians had swung behind the Raj for its last ninety years. The princes and large landowners were left unmolested after 1858, and this is the premier fact of later Raj history, one which rather complicates attempts to make clear distinctions between 'internal' and 'external' exploiters.

The stay-at-home urban modernizers of 1857 never had a chance to develop their ideas fully, so we can only guess at what might have happened had they been given more opportunity to mould India's future. But from the 1890s, mass popular movements in India were much less British-influenced in outlook and vocabulary than the Anglophile modernism that had preceded them. Modernism in India then became a pragmatic blend of indigenous cultural elements, which eventually matured into a viable national platform, while imported ideas—liberalism, socialism, revolutionary communism—all failed to appeal as broadly.

The most potent recipe for national unity was the hybrid package assembled by and incarnated in Gandhi, which had no exact parallel elsewhere. Its authentic uniqueness can be measured by the fact that it cannot be described except by neologisms, like Gandhism or Gandhigiri.

Vivekananda and Gandhi addressed and motivated people as individuals, and this was their great strength. Tilak, Jinnah and Ambedkar did not, and relied on sectional appeals based on fixed identities. This is what made the Vivekananda–Gandhi approach both modern and distinctly Indian, and also made it comprehensible and compelling to a largely uneducated population. It refused to promote Western ideas over local, but it embraced the concept of individual choice, and placed it within the context of Indian society in a way that was modern. It treated Indians as individuals with choices, and choice and modernity go together. Swaraj was a national issue, but it was also personal—political autonomy writ small. Gandhi made this link repeatedly. It was always choice that made the 'freedom movement' truly a movement for liberation.

1857 reconsidered

In 1857 there was a massive rebellion against British rule across large parts of north and central India. Its concentration in time has frequently led historians to treat the insurgency as if it were one single, identifiable thing—a popular, national liberation struggle, but it is not clear that the complex events of 1857–9 really merit one unitary classification. There is certainly no compelling reason to label the rebels of 1857 as either visionary nationalists or proto-Marxists. Recent research has shown that the rebellion was more widespread than the British liked to admit, but also that it was very disparate.

Nor are its principal causes a mystery; they were well known and well understood at the time. Subsequent investigations have not revealed new causes; they have only given us more and more case studies of individuals who acted for various reasons—combinations of dispossession, attachment to tradition, fear, self-interest, coercion and guesswork about who was most likely to win. Simply put, the principal cause was resentment of foreign intrusion. British rule had created disadvantages for a great many Indians. The objective therefore was simple: to drive out the foreigners on account of the social, cultural and economic damage they were perceived to be doing to individuals, occupations, lifestyles and institutions.

Different sets of people were hoping for different things from joining the rebellion. It would be quite unrealistic to assume that dynastic players, large landowners, peasants and tribal groups all agreed on any desired outcome beyond the expulsion of the British. To generalize this as 'resisting colonialism' is anachronistic. The rebels of 1857 were resisting oppressive and unresponsive government in the way they had traditionally resisted it, from whichever socio-economic group was handing it out. Considering their support for the Mughal dynasty and other hereditary rulers, it would surely be at least as accurate to describe the rebels as 'promoting feudalism'.

We know what the revolt was against. What is not clear is what it was for. Like most mass movements, it was much clearer on what was wrong than on how to put it right. The rebels had no clear organizational structure, only a clutch of individual leaders, which multiplies the problems of interpretation, because each leader had a separate agenda. In a situation where there were multiple triggers and multiple participants, we can only get ourselves into conceptual trouble if we amalgamate all the discontent from distinct sections of the population and try to turn it into a coherent 'national' grievance, especially at a time when the political nation was yet unborn.

Some of the mutineers faced this problem by seeking to revive the Mughal dynasty, but this was not an attractive prospect to many of the people they needed to recruit for the movement to succeed. Would a Maratha prince like Nana Sahib really have been willing to accept the Mughal suzerainty that his predecessors had fought so hard to throw off?

Who didn't join the rebels, though, is a more interesting matter than who did. The most significant group that declined to rebel was the urban bourgeoisie. They represented the small but significant hopes for modernization that existed in Indian society—at least within the presidency towns.

Above all, the most important questions about 1857 are not about its causes, but about its effects. Why was it followed by such a long period of peace, among both the Indian princes and the Indian progressive classes? Why, in other words, did 1857 mark an end to mass violent resistance, not a beginning? Why was it not until around 1920 that similarly widespread discontent against the Raj reappeared?

Violence certainly resurfaced in numerous parts of the country after 1857, but it was local and sporadic, and was often related to the specific grievances of tribal groups, such as the rebellions by the Koyas in 1879–80 or the Bhils in 1881. Armed resistance that tried to rally the spirit of 1857 more directly, such as Phadke's rebellion of 1879 in the Poona region, struggled to attract widespread support.

These insurrections were nowhere near as organized and coordinated as the political movements that followed. The first national political groups began to appear through the 1870s, and culminated in the birth of the Indian National Congress in 1885. The construction of these organizations was related to an important switch of mentality among educated, anglicized Indians. Before 1857, they had mostly thought of themselves as British subjects with grievances. After 1857 men like Dadabhai Naoroji and Surendranath Banerjea began to think of themselves as Indians with rights.

Such men were never uncritical of British rule, but they idealized it, and a period of conceptual evolution was required to think through the implications of the change in their identity from British subjects to autonomous Indians. This was a difficult and uncertain process that eventually split Moderates from Extremists within the Congress. Moderates, like Naoroji, stayed within the boundaries of British constitutional practice, whereas Extremists, like Tilak, referred to their own roots for inspiration and justification. Moderates stayed away from violence, which had not succeeded in 1857, while Extremists felt that British intransigence could only be countered by more direct and forceful action.

Much of the political and religious debate in India after 1857 was about the rediscovery of India's past and a search for ideas and institutions that connected appropriately with tradition. Congress Moderates found this difficult, while Extremists felt it unnecessary. But the debate was not confined to Congress circles, and a range of responses followed, some of which were entirely modern in tone. These included the appearance of political parties, revivalist religious movements, caste and professional associations, and even terrorist cells. All of this represented a search for a positive agenda that went beyond British liberalism, which was increasingly regarded as a failing vehicle for Indian aspirations. Attempting to shame the British by their own standards remained the persistently unsuccessful response of Indian liberals till 1947.

In the end, violence was not the answer, and ninety years after the Uprising the British did not leave under hostile gunfire. But the timing and the manner of that departure both attest that it was not British aspirations that were most damaged by the events of 1857, but Indian.

The lasting tragedy of 1857 remained that Indians collectively lost the chance to make a modern India of their own design. The British then took the opportunity to create a version of India that suited themselves.

PART TWO

RETELLING THE STORY

THE RETURN CARGO

2

1600–1740

SPICES, RIVALS, CHAOS, PEACE

1600–20: Spices and Rivals

Towards the end of the sixteenth century, the legendary spices and fine fabrics of India moved enticingly within reach of the English for the first time. The breakthrough was Sir Francis Drake's epic circumnavigation of the world (1577–80), which proved that Englishmen as well as 'Portugals' could reach the far corners of the earth. New possibilities began to open up.

Stories had been coming back for years from Italian and Portuguese explorers and missionaries, but from the 1580s the tales became first-hand. A Catholic Englishman named Thomas Stevens went to Goa in 1579 as a Jesuit priest, and his letters home attracted great interest. Queen Elizabeth sent a four-man mission to the Mughal court in 1583, and in 1591 one of its members finally returned after a string of adventures, including contact with Stevens. A London merchant named Ralph Fitch went to spy out Cochin in 1588, and by the time Shakespeare wrote *A Midsummer Night's Dream* in 1595, which mentions India four times, Englishmen knew that India was a rich place ruled over by a powerful despot, who lived in luxury and was a Muslim.

More hard-headedly, by 1600 London's merchants were keen to copy the Dutch and force their way into the highly lucrative seaborne spice trade, once monopolized by the Portuguese. The result was the formation of the East India Company, to which Queen Elizabeth granted a royal charter in December 1600. The Company was permitted to trade in 'the East Indies', an unspecific term meaning anywhere between the southern tip of Africa and the far end of modern Indonesia. The main objective was to trade in pepper, cinnamon, cloves and especially nutmeg.

Armed with a fifteen-year monopoly on all trade from the East Indies, the Company set about trying to fit into the complex commercial systems that criss-crossed the Orient. Nutmeg, the most profitable commodity, was known to be easily obtainable from the inhabitants of the islands where it grew, and this is why the Company's first two voyages did not land in India at all. India only became part of the trading pattern when it emerged that the spice islanders were happier to trade in Indian textiles than in bullion or European woollens, neither of which they valued. A system then grew up by which the English used silver to buy fabric in Indian ports, then sailed east to barter for spices.

In 1608 a delegation led by an experienced seafarer named William Hawkins was sent to negotiate with the Mughal emperor, whose protection and favour were now considered to be worth acquiring. Hawkins was the first Englishman to land in India on behalf of the East India Company, at Surat in August 1608. But there was no warm welcome. He faced obstruction from officials, opposition from commercial interests in Surat, and outright hostility from the Portuguese, who had no intention of sharing the spice trade with the intruders. Hawkins had his possessions pilfered, and lived in daily fear of his life for several months.

In early 1609 he set out for Agra to present himself to the Emperor Jahangir, taking letters of introduction made out to Jahangir's recently deceased father, Akbar. Despite this discourtesy and a lack of ostentatious gifts, Jahangir seems to have taken a liking to the uncouth Hawkins, and rapidly promoted him to a position of honour, where his duties, roughly speaking, consisted of keeping pace with the emperor in his drinking bouts. Hawkins could speak Turkish and this apparently stood him in good stead. He was given a senior Mughal military rank, supported by a grant of land, but he seems not to have understood that he had to go and personally collect the rents that made up his salary. The gulf in sophistication that separated early Jacobean England from Mughal India, both in manufactures and manners, was still considerable.

Hawkins's stay in Agra did not produce permission for a factory at Surat, and he was eventually forced to leave, having found no way past the hostility of certain members of the court and the Portuguese. He took ship back to England in 1613, but died on the way.

By then a new charter, granted by King James I in 1609, had extended the Company's monopoly indefinitely, and this encouraged the EIC to establish itself in Siam, Burma, Yemen, Japan and Persia. But its main prize was the tiny rock of Pulo Run, reached by the Company's First Voyage in

1603, which was the only one of the Banda Islands outside Dutch control. Trade started well, and the years 1600–23 were encouragingly profitable.

Where diplomacy had failed, in the end it was a naval victory in 1613 over the Portuguese off Swalley, north of Surat, that persuaded Jahangir to grant the English permission for a factory, after which the India trade began to open up. But the Portuguese and Dutch resented the competition, and as the Company moved into violent conflict with its European rivals, it was forced into closer contact with Eastern rulers.

Agreements and alliances now had to be made with local powers all over the East, but the Mughals repeatedly declined to receive an embassy from mere merchants. To this end, a senior courtier-diplomat, Sir Thomas Roe, went out to the Mughal court in 1615 as the first formal ambassador from the Court of St James to the Mughal Durbar at Agra.

He arrived at Surat in September 1615, and remained in India for three and a half years, following Jahangir's itinerant court wherever it led him. During this time he plied the emperor with gifts, including dogs, jewels, alcoholic spirits and an English-style coach. The coach especially pleased Jahangir, who had two replicas made of it. But politically the mission did not go well; the Portuguese were still as hostile as Hawkins had found them five years earlier. Roe got on well with Jahangir, despite the language barrier, and managed to build a civil relationship with at least one Portuguese priest, with whom he communicated in Latin.

Jahangir's son Khurram, later Shah Jahan, was also impressed with Roe, but there was no diplomatic leverage available to the Englishman to pass much beyond courtesies. The best he could do for the Company was to acquire a general permission to trade, with restrictions on the amount of armed men it could retain, but with rights for its servants to observe their own religion and to be governed by their own laws. Roe then left in February 1619, with nothing more than letters of commendation to take back to his royal master.

The directors in London were pleased with Roe's work, and particularly the economical way in which he had conducted it. His mission might have ushered in a regular diplomatic connection between the English and Mughal courts, but no successor was appointed, and as England descended into political strife, the Indian connection was neglected.

Roe has often been depicted as stiff and overly jealous of his status, but his mission to Agra was specifically intended to raise the social standing of the Company's servants, who lacked refinement in Indian eyes. He was a witty and cultured man with pretensions to penmanship, and counted among his friends several literary luminaries, including John Donne the poet and Ben Jonson the playwright. This polish is clearly apparent in both his letters and his conduct in India, where he laboured under multiple disadvantages. His punctilious formality at the Mughal court should therefore be regarded more as a reflection of his general objectives than a personal failing. As a representative of a small, distant kingdom, his single-mindedness and imperturbability can only be seen as estimable.

Roe was the first Englishman to record serious thoughts about the wider implications of the EIC's involvement in Indian trade, and the conclusions he drew were of considerable importance. He was in favour of aggressive action at sea against European rivals, but he is more frequently quoted for his strongly stated opinion that the Company should avoid fortifications or garrisons, and should confine itself to the pursuance of 'quiette trade'. This general strategy remained the Company's policy for half a century, and it was only in the light of bitter experience that the directors abandoned his principles and moved to large-scale fortifications and the maintenance of armed retainers.

1620–60: Collapse

By 1620 the EIC had factories on the Indian mainland at Cranganore on the west coast and Masulipatnam on the east, though its main base of operations at this time was in Bantam on the west side of Java. Gradually indigo from Surat, spices from Malabar, and gemstones and cotton goods from the Coromandel coast were integrated into wider trade patterns.

But conflict between Europeans continued to escalate in the East. The most lucrative areas of economic activity tended to attract rival factories, which jostled in close proximity. Far from home, with large sums at stake, violence was often the only way to settle disputes.

The Dutch gradually drove the Portuguese out of Malabar (1604–63) and Sri Lanka (1638–60), and they harried the English out of most of Indonesia, including the infamous massacre at Amboyna in 1622. Meanwhile the English defeated the Portuguese in Indian coastal waters and in the Persian Gulf where, allied with the Shah of Persia, they took the island fortress of Hormuz in 1622. The Portuguese subsequently concentrated on easier pickings in Brazil, and the Dutch dominated Indonesia for three centuries. The English, who withdrew from Japan and Siam in 1622, were left to concentrate on India. The basic division of later colonial 'spheres of influence' was thus prefigured in these early years.

Following its various Eastern setbacks, several factors combined from the mid-1620s to ensure that the EIC's early commercial promise was not fulfilled. There was a glut of pepper; the price crashed and never recovered. Then the Thirty Years War in Germany (1618–48) and civil war in England (1642–9) combined to disrupt trade. In 1630 there was devastating famine in Gujarat, and five years later King Charles I, for a fee, blessed the creation of a rival trading venture, known as Courteen's Association. Profits declined and investment dried up.

The Gujarat famine swung European interests around to the east coast, and in 1634 the English obtained permission to trade in Bengal. They then set up factories at Balasore (1642) and Hughli (1650). With the increased focus on India, Surat was released from the control of Bantam in 1636, and an important factory was founded at Madraspatnam in 1639. Fort St George was erected next to it in 1640.

English hostilities with the Portuguese were permanently ended by the Convention of Goa in 1635, confirmed in 1642, when Portugal regained its autonomy after sixty years under Spanish rule. Conflict with the Dutch, however, continued on and off until the end of the Napoleonic Wars.

1660–1700: Vigour, Hubris, Confusion

Prospects began to improve for the EIC from the late 1650s. Oliver Cromwell granted a new charter to the Company in 1657, later confirmed by the newly restored King Charles II in 1661. This charter had a much greater significance for the Indian connection than the 1600 or 1609 versions.

By 1657 two things had become apparent: that trading with India was the future, and that agreements with local potentates were absolutely necessary. The Company's outposts therefore had to be able to act as mini-kingdoms, with a range of autonomous powers. These included the authority to make treaties, and the right to exercise effective sovereignty over whoever came into the settlements, such as servants and mercenaries. Cromwell's charter thus took a more realistic view of security and a more state-like attitude to the powers of the Company. These provisions facilitated a movement to a more forward stance against both European rivals and local rulers.

The other important point was that the 1657 charter converted the Company into a more truly capitalist body, by requiring that it became a permanent joint stock company, not a society of individual merchants pooling their resources and gambling on the outcome of one-off voyages.

After 1661, therefore, the Company had a sense of permanence and a quasi-sovereign authority overseas. The simultaneous return to stability in British domestic politics encouraged new investment, and over the next twenty years there was a prolonged resurgence in business confidence. Profits reappeared and the Company's stock rose. A boom followed from 1660 to 1683, which drew powerful men into the Company's affairs, and brought it increasingly into high politics.

Expansion in India resumed with the acquisition of Bombay, which came to King Charles II in 1661 as part of the dowry of his Portuguese bride, Catherine of Bragança. The king, however, had no clear idea what to do with the place, and after seven years of losses to his purse he passed it over to a grateful Company, who were looking for a safer anchorage than Surat. Bombay also offered greater insulation from Mughal interference, and better protection from Maratha raids; Shivaji had attacked Surat in 1664. The directors were therefore more than eager to take Bombay on, especially at a nominal rent of £10 per annum. The new port flourished and soon became almost as large as the Company's other major settlement at Madras.

However, this expansion was choked off by a series of unhappy events that brought about the Company's second decline, beginning in the early 1680s. The Dutch finally drove the English out of Bantam in 1682, and in 1691 the EIC pulled out of the Siam trade, again. In Bombay a small mutiny in 1674 was followed by a much more serious affair in 1683, when troops under Captain Richard Keigwin took over the running of the port for more than a year. Discipline was not much better in Bengal. After bitter disputes between William Hedges and Job Charnock, 'the Bay' lost its own Presidency, awarded in 1681, and was placed once again under the authority of Madras. All over the East the Company's trade was disrupted by pirates, and consistently undermined by the activities of well-armed and well-financed 'interlopers', determined to flout the Company's monopoly.

Back in London, things were hardly less chaotic. The death of Charles II in 1685 was followed by the turbulent three-year reign of his brother, James II, and his replacement in 1688 by William III and Mary as joint sovereigns.

Throughout this period, the Company was under the control of Sir Josiah Child (c.1631–99), who was probably the first figure of national importance to hold sway within the Company's 'direction'. Child was the largest stockholder in the Company by the late 1670s, and he served as either Deputy Governor or Governor from 1684 to 1690. He manoeuvred his way through the uncertainties of the times, obtaining new charters by extensive bribery from Charles II (1682), James II (1686), and William and Mary (1693). But the Company's close association with royal patronage did little to endear it to the City of London's financiers, and a long series of disputes, scandals and lawsuits progressed through the 1680s and 1690s. The unwelcome result was the creation of a rival company by Act of Parliament in 1698. Chaos ensued, as the New Company's men went east and strove to discredit representatives of the Old, even as competition drove down prices in London.

Sir Josiah Child was also responsible for a frequently quoted letter of 1687, which called for 'the foundation of a large, well grounded, secure English dominion in India for all time to come'.[1] These words have sometimes been taken to prove a long-nurtured plot by the English to take over all of India, but this was hardly Child's intention. The letter talked of a dominion 'in' India, not 'over' India, and was concerned with security. He was thinking of forts and enclaves, not empire.

Child was an aggressive character, incurably bullish about the Company's prospects. The previous year he had declared that 'the subjects of the Mogull' would not be able to sustain a war against the English for a year 'without starving and dying by thousands for want of our trade'.[2] It was this kind of overconfidence that enabled him to dream of 'dominion' in India—for a haven (or havens) that would be safe from Maratha raids, Mughal extortions and armed interlopers.

A combination of these fantasies, and some perfectly real Mughal bullying, led the Company into the tangled events of 1686–90, known as Child's War. This 'war' was an attempt by Sir Josiah in London and Sir John Child in India (they were distantly related) to bring military force to bear on the emperor Aurangzeb, in order to resolve disputes in Bengal and Gujarat about payment of customs duties and the emperor's tolerance towards interlopers. The preposterousness of trying strong-arm tactics against the largest military establishment in Asia, combined with the puny size of the forces deployed to do the job, has bemused historians ever since, and is generally put down to a mixture of ignorance and vainglory on Sir Josiah's part.

But to excuse him a little, the Company's affairs in Bengal were being constantly disrupted by predatory Mughal officials. One stand-off in 1685 kept Job Charnock trapped in Cosimbazar for eight months. He finally escaped to Hughli, only to be besieged there too. Hijli then suffered a four-month blockade in 1687. Constant losses, and the indifference of the

Mughal authorities to the Company's monopoly rights, seemed to Child to call for escalated action.

In 1688, therefore, Captain William Heath was sent from England with an army of 300 men, charged with taking and fortifying Chittagong. But the plan went disastrously wrong, with the English forced to flee to Madras in March 1689. Meanwhile Bombay was besieged and its defenders driven out. After abject apologies to the emperor, the Company was allowed to return, under supervision, to Surat.

It then took patient persuasion from Job Charnock to get the Company readmitted to Bengal, and finally, in August 1690, it resumed trading at Sutanuti. The new Nawab of Bengal, Ibrahim Khan, looked more kindly on the English, and in 1691 he allowed them to settle at the small village of Kalikata. Official permission from the central Mughal authorities for these arrangements was granted in 1698. Calcutta was then re-established as a Presidency in 1700, and Fort William was built there (1698–1702).

In the short term, Child's strategy was a complete failure, but enough was saved from the wreckage to allow a long-term recovery. Aurangzeb appears to have taken a fairly mild stance by his standards, possibly because the Company's bullion was of some value to him. But he still held the English responsible for acts of piracy in the Arabian Sea, and repeatedly demanded compensation and the suppression of the pirates.

Madras remained the Company's chief trading hub. It escaped involvement in Child's War, and prospered throughout the 1680s under the governorship of Elihu Yale (1649–1721), the future benefactor of the American college that bears his name. The town then fell under the spell of the extraordinary Thomas Pitt.

Along with Elihu Yale, Thomas 'Diamond' Pitt (1653–1726) was one of the first Englishmen to work out how to make a large personal fortune in India, survive, and bring his wealth home. Indeed, he involved himself so successfully in Indian commerce that he was able to enter domestic politics. Though never a holder of high office himself, he used his money to establish a dynasty that supported the ambitions of his grandson and great-grandson, both called William Pitt, both of whom became prime minister.

Thomas Pitt's Indian career spans the years 1673–1709, during which the enormous profitability of the Oriental trade in luxury items first became properly organized. During this period, the European powers generally refrained from fighting each other in India, and conflicts were more usually with local officials, 'interlopers' or pirates.

A country clergyman's son, Pitt sailed to India in 1673, but soon left the Company's service and set up on his own account, remaining an interloper until 1688, when he made his peace with the Company and bought heavily into its stock. In the intervening years he made himself a fortune in trade and used it to buy land, including the 'rotten' parliamentary borough of Old Sarum, which opened a family association with the seat that was to last for several generations. He entered Parliament in 1689 as member for the borough, which had no resident voters. He thus completed the three-fold requirement for respectable status within English society: land, wealth and political influence. All this he had done by dint of his own talents as an adventurer and trader, and as such he qualifies as the first of the 'nabobs'.

He returned to India in 1693, intending to resume trading on his own account, but he rejoined the Company in 1695 and was appointed Governor of Madras in 1698. Madras was at the centre of the Company's highly profitable trade with China, Indonesia and Indochina, and it was also the main marketplace for diamonds from the Indian state of Golkonda. All of these opportunities put it well ahead of the Company's other centres of business, in Bengal and Bombay, and Pitt knew how to avail himself of such opportunities. He remained in Madras as Governor for eleven years, during which time the town expanded and its trade grew, in no small part thanks to a truce with the French that kept the War of the Spanish Succession (1701–13) out of India.

It was during Pitt's time in Madras that the New Company was formed in 1698, and among the fresh faces that appeared in the East was his cousin John Pitt, who tried to establish a factory up the coast at Masulipatnam. Thomas was able to see off this challenge without undue trouble, but a greater threat then appeared, when the New Company sent Sir William Norris to woo Aurangzeb in 1701. However, the mission to Agra resulted only in the aged and cantankerous emperor trying to extract an undertaking from Norris that his masters would rid the Arabian Sea of pirates. The embarrassed Englishman could not promise this, and Aurangzeb had no further words for him.

Shortly afterwards, in early 1702, the Nawab of the Carnatic, Daud Khan, marched on Madras, looking to pressure the Company into payment of tribute and further promises on the suppression of piracy. Daud Khan besieged the town by land, but he lacked ships or heavy cannon, and Pitt was able to hold out. A long stalemate ensued, during which Pitt regularly presented the nawab with boxes of fresh oranges in order to demonstrate to him the ineffectiveness of the siege. Pitt then put his legendary bargaining skills to work in order to reduce the nawab's demands. Honour was eventually satisfied by payment of the comparatively small sum of Rs 25,000.

During this hiatus in trade, Governor Pitt managed to purchase a large uncut diamond. The asking price is said to have been £100,000 but he eventually obtained it for £24,000, drawn from his personal fortune. The raw stone, of around 400 carats, was then shipped back to England to be cut. A prolonged search for a purchaser dragged on until the Regent of France, Philippe d'Orleans, bought it for £135,000 in 1717. The family fortune was secured.

Pitt's final demise in India was also peculiarly typical of the EIC. He ran foul of a member of his Council, one William Fraser, and the dispute was eventually referred to London, where the directors ruled in favour of Fraser. Pitt then departed for home in 1709. Even a man of his standing proved vulnerable to personal jealousies and petty accusations. Like others after him, Pitt discovered that exercising power in India was no way to make or keep friends.

The lessons of his life were plentiful and obvious: that the East was profitable, boldness paid off in India more often than not, diamonds were the best way to repatriate wealth, and politics were open to those with 'unattached' money.

1700–44: Peace and Prosperity

Neither the piracy, the interlopers, the emperor's exactions—he was paid a large sum in 1702—nor the rivalry between the Old and New Companies helped the Indian trade. But in 1709 a new United Company was formed, and its directors felt confident enough to obtain a charter extension in 1711. Finally, the Treaty of Utrecht (1713) wound up the War of the Spanish Succession in Europe, signalling the end of British entanglements in continental conflicts for the next thirty years. With peace in Europe and a new Hanoverian monarch—George I—securely installed at home in 1714, things looked rather more promising for the Company.

The peace in Europe was not exactly matched in India, but the so-called 'anarchy' of the late Mughal period was generally exaggerated by the imperial school of Indian historiography. It is true that Mughal authority was permanently weakened by bloody succession disputes in 1707, 1712, 1713 and 1719, and by the breakaway of three important regions of the old Mughal domain—Bengal, Awadh and Hyderabad—which became semi-independent states; large parts of western India also came under the control of Maratha clans. But trading conditions in the major coastal enclaves remained largely unaffected, and with the strong growth in demand for Indian textiles, all the European companies had their best-ever years in the period 1714–44. The French had successful factories at Pondicherry, south of Madras, and Chandernagore, upstream from Calcutta, while the Dutch at Chinsurah and the Danish at Tranquebar and Serampore also flourished. Companies based in Sweden and Ostend eagerly joined the trade.

The EIC pulled off a major stroke in 1717 when the emperor Farrukhsiyar was persuaded to grant three farmans (decrees) enhancing the Company's privileges in Bombay, Madras and Calcutta. The emperor was not really in a position to enforce what he was granting, but the general reduction of customs and tariffs made the trade more profitable, and gave the British an advantage over European rivals. Along with prosperity came increased grandeur; the Company's London headquarters—India House in Leadenhall Street—was completely refurbished in the late 1720s.

The Company also made another step towards governmental status when it was granted the right of legislative authority in India, under a new charter of 1726. Though still only a self-regulating body, much of the infrastructure of a ruling power—income, armaments, judicial and legal authority—was now in place. The Company posed no threat to the political worlds at either end of its activities; it was well set in Britain, and harboured no territorial ambitions in India. Its most pressing problems came from pirates around Bombay, and from the raids of the Marathas into Bengal, which prompted the building of the 'Maratha Ditch' around Calcutta in 1742. Nevertheless, through this period the Company employed only small numbers of armed men and spent little on maintaining fortifications. The problems it was shortly to experience in Madras and Calcutta both stemmed from the dilapidation and weakness of those forts.

Favourable trading conditions allowed the settlement in Bengal to grow rapidly, and by the 1730s the Calcutta trade was the largest item in the EIC's account. The Company extended its activities up the Ganges to the interior, in search of a variety of commodities, including raw silk, opium and saltpetre, to add to the main trade in textiles. Trade with China also expanded to include porcelain and lacquered furniture.

Tea, still at this date exclusively from China, was also becoming increasingly popular in Europe, which offered scope for expansion.

However, the EIC constantly ran up against difficulties in trying to expand its trading activities. Tea was heavily taxed in Britain and rival supplies were easily smuggled into the country, limiting the Company's sales. There was also resistance to the import of Indian textiles, and legislation in 1700 and 1720 had restricted the Company to the import of plain, undyed fabric, called 'piece goods', as opposed to finished garments. It was also a constant struggle to find any British goods to exchange in either India or China, and the Company was forced to buy its most profitable lines with silver bullion. This drain of precious metals was regarded with alarm by many at home, but before the Bengal 'revolution' of 1757 it remained unavoidable.

3

1744–1784

WAR, GOVERNMENT, PLUNDER, REGULATION

1744–65: Disaster, Recovery, Loot

Before 1744, European trading outfits generally avoided fighting each other in India, for three good reasons. It was physically impossible to exclude rival enterprises by force, there was sufficient profit in trade for all parties to prosper, and making private war brought disapproval from Indian rulers, who viewed it as disorderly and disrespectful. Priorities for the Europeans companies were therefore to stay on the right side of local powers, and to keep streams of cash moving within a trade that was easily disrupted by weather, piracy or accidents at sea.

But through the 1740s, despite all sound commercial sense, Western rivalries slowly became interwoven with Indian political struggles, primarily because important decisions concerning the European companies began to be made on the ground in India, by men concerned with immediate military, financial and personal advantages, rather than with long-term commercial interests. A major factor in this change was that the leadership of the French Compagnie des Indes fell to the capable Joseph Dupleix, who became Governor of Pondicherry in 1742. At that time the French had already been drawn into a succession dispute in the state of Tanjore (Thanjavur), but it was Dupleix who realized the potential for raising revenue locally in India through holding land, instead of relying on the intermittent flow of investment from France. It was the discovery and development of this source of income that transformed the small garrisons maintained by European companies into large armies.

The brief golden age of Indian trade ended in 1744, when Britain and France officially entered the War of the Austrian Succession (1740–8), already under way in Europe between their respective allies, Austria and Prussia. A tense period in India lasted until 1746, when Dupleix tried to pre-empt a British attack on Pondicherry by offering a truce to the Governor of Madras. Upon receiving an evasive reply, he sent a force to assault the town, which he knew to be in a barely defensible condition. Madras was successfully stormed with minimal loss, but this victory only brought the French into conflict with the local suzerain, Anwaruddin, Nawab of Arcot, who maintained that Dupleix had promised to hand the town over to him. The nawab then sent a large force to repossess it. But to everyone's surprise, the French beat off the nawab's much larger army with only a small force of well-drilled infantry supported by manoeuvrable artillery. It was a victory that unmistakeably demonstrated the potential of European arms in India, and the lesson was well learned by all parties.

The Treaty of Aix-la-Chapelle (1748) returned Madras to the EIC, but formal peace made little difference in India, where for the next six years the French and the British proceeded to embroil themselves in the dynastic affairs of Tanjore, Arcot and Hyderabad, while receiving grants of land in return for their support. The Marquis de Bussy-Castelnau distinguished himself by taking the supposedly impregnable fortress of Gingee for the French in 1750, and Robert Clive achieved similar fame for his capture and defence of Arcot the following year.

Back in Europe, the directors of the two companies became increasingly disturbed by the situation. They decided that this kind of peace was not affordable, and brought an end to the struggle by agreement in 1754. The French recalled the spendthrift Dupleix, whose ambitious attempts to manipulate the proto-state of Hyderabad had produced nothing but massive deficits, and whose only economy had been with the truth in his correspondence with Paris. When a fuller picture of Indian realities was provided by direct dialogue with the EIC, his fate was sealed. As he departed, peace returned to the Carnatic, with a pro-French nizam in Hyderabad, and British-backed rulers in Arcot and Tanjore.

Two years later the focus moved north when the young, recently installed Nawab of Bengal, Mirza Muhammad Siraj-ud-Daula, decided to attack the EIC's factory-fort at Calcutta. He was in dispute with the Company over its trading privileges, and he objected to repairs carried out to Calcutta's fortifications, undertaken because of the likely resumption of war with France. These irritations came on top of a challenge to his succession from a cousin based at Purnea, in the north of the province. Having no desire to leave a well-set enemy to his rear while he dealt with his rival, the nawab marched down to Calcutta in mid-June 1756, and took it after a short siege.

He then defeated his cousin that October, having left only a token garrison to defend Calcutta. So when the EIC sent Robert Clive to recapture its prime asset in India, the town was easily retaken, on 2 January 1757. The nawab made a botched attempt to retake it, but was forced to come to terms on 9 February 1757, giving the Company guarantees of security and a large sum in compensation for goods and property destroyed.

The British now had a powerful force in Bengal, which included royal troops, and when news came that war with France had been officially declared, the opportunity to capture Chandernagore seemed too good to miss. The chance and the town were duly seized, leaving Colonel Clive and Admiral Watson in undisputed military control of the region. Senior members of the Bengali business elite now took their chance to conspire with the British, to remove the inexperienced and unpredictable nawab. An agreement was drawn up laying out the division of the expected spoils of the coup, but one man, Omichand (Amir Chand), wanted more favourable personal terms. Clive reluctantly drew up an agreement complying with Omichand's demands, but told Watson privately that he did not intend to honour it. Watson refused to be a party to deception, so Clive forged the admiral's signature.

Regime change was then played out over the summer months of 1757, culminating in the defeat of Siraj-ud-Daula's army at Plassey on 23 June. Siraj-ud-Daula's father-in-law, Mir Jafar, was put on the gaddi (throne) in his place, and the friendless young nawab was murdered.

Mir Jafar rewarded his new patrons handsomely, and in return they repelled an invasion from the powerful state of Awadh, which lay to the west of Bengal. Clive received a large jagir (land revenue assignment) as reward, and returned to England in early 1760 as a very wealthy man. But with Clive gone, Mir Jafar became increasingly uncooperative, and was soon deposed in favour of his son-in-law, Mir Kasim. After three years Mir Kasim also proved less than fully compliant, and was deposed in his turn, to be replaced by a rehabilitated Mir Jafar. The exiled Mir Kasim then allied himself with the Nawab of Awadh and the Mughal emperor, Shah Alam, who had been chased out of Delhi a few years previously. Together they marched on Bengal in 1764, only to be decisively defeated at Baksar in October, by Colonel Hector Munro.

Mir Jafar died a few months later, and was succeeded by his young son, Najm-ud-Daula, who was hardly in a position to follow the family tradition of non-cooperation. In charge of a minor nawab, and having defeated or disposed of all rivals, the British position in Bengal was unassailable.

This 'Bengal Revolution' was just part of a wider picture of growing British strength. Units of the regular (royal) British Army arrived in India for the first time in 1754, Maratha naval capability was destroyed with the taking of Gheria (Vijaydurg) in 1756, and in 1758 the Nizam of Hyderabad revoked the grant to the French of a large stretch of coastal territory, known as the Northern Sarkars, and gave it to the EIC. This act marked a major change in the balance of power in central India. There were also decisive defeats for the Dutch at Badera (1759), and the French at Wandiwash (1760).

1765–74: Government and Regulation

In 1764 Clive was sent back from London to Bengal by the EIC to sort out the administrative confusion and rampant pillage that had been going on since Plassey, which had only intensified after his departure in 1760. He arrived in May 1765 to find commercial chaos and an empty treasury. British merchants were not only trading toll-free on their own account, but were also selling free trade licences (dastaks) to others without regard for the government's interests.

Clive set about stabilizing the situation. Firstly, and most significantly, in August 1765 he signed the Treaty of Allahabad with the Mughal emperor, Shah Alam, by which the emperor appointed the Company as his diwan (chief financial officer) for three provinces of his empire, Bengal, Bihar and Orissa. Orissa was almost all under the control of the Marathas at the time, but it suited both parties to ignore this fact. By taking on the diwani (revenue administration), Clive instituted the so-called 'Dual System' whereby the EIC took on official responsibility for one half of the Mughal administration—finance—while leaving the other half—the nizamat (military matters and criminal jurisdiction) nominally in the hands of the nawab. The Company became the emperor's vassal, and undertook to pay him an annual tribute of Rs 26 lakhs.

Next, Clive tried to wean Company servants off 'presents' (bribes) by diverting the proceeds of the government's salt monopoly to a joint fund, called the Society of Trade, in which shares could be bought. This, however, soon degenerated into yet another racket, and the directors wound it up.

Finally, he tackled abuses in the Company's army and curtailed batta (field allowances). This made him very unpopular with senior officers, and led to a small 'white' mutiny. But when he left again in 1767, due to ill health, the country was a little more orderly, though the main underlying problems of alien rule had been disguised rather than properly addressed.

Nevertheless, by 1767 the Company was a military and diplomatic power, with access to revenues estimated at £4 million per annum, a sum worth twice its annual turnover in trade. This seemed like a marvellous opportunity for the Company to raise silver locally in Bengal to pay for its annual 'investment' in goods for export to Europe. But many of the Company's servants took a different view, and simply scooped up whatever cash they could for themselves.

Despite the apparent abundance of revenue, the Company found that good government and profitability were not easily reconciled. Who was to make money, where and how became major political issues, generating a three-way tension between the British government, the Company's leadership, and its employees. The plunder of Bengal, ably documented by P.J. Marshall, was never Company policy; it was the work of unsupervised individuals let loose in a foreign land without fear of retribution.

In London, the abrupt transition from trade to government had immediate results, bringing wealth to individuals which was entirely unrelated to the Company's real trading position. EIC stock became highly sought after, not simply because of new potential profits in trade, but because owning stock conferred rights to nominate directors, and directors made appointments within the Company. Jobs in the EIC had always been prized, but with new opportunities for unofficial enrichment in Bengal, they became especially valuable. The expectation of plenty went on to disfigure the domestic politics of Britain for a generation.

Personal rivalries became political, not least between Robert Clive and Laurence Sulivan (1713–86). Their famous enmity played out in competition within the Company for internal preferment, which had a strongly individual quality about it, but there was an issue of principle too. Sulivan felt he was protecting the Company's interests against the personal aggrandisement of Clive, whom he regarded, not without reason, as something of a cuckoo in the Company's nest.

Apart from the scramble within the Company, the grant of the diwani also led senior politicians to consider ways to share in the bounty, as part of their search for extra revenue after the victorious but extremely expensive Seven Years War with France (1756–63); the shortfall in the government's accounts was estimated at about £1 million per year. With this in mind, the revenues of Bengal seemed to William Pitt the Elder to be the 'redemption' of the nation.

At the same time, the movement from trade to receipt of land revenue made the Company a governing rather than a merchant body, a development that ministers might use as grounds for appropriating some of its increased income, especially since royal troops had helped to win its victories. Concerns were raised as to how appropriate it was for merchants to become sovereigns.

Above all, it became clear that the Company's employees were not properly accountable to the directors, nor were the directors properly responsible to anyone in Britain apart from the stockholders.

All this was perceived to threaten the stability of the British constitution. By 1767, Clive and his ilk, and behind them the wealth of India, represented the greatest challenge to the British political system between the Glorious Revolution of 1688 and the Great Reform Act of 1832. 'Unattached' wealth was coming into the country in larger amounts and at greater speed than in any previous era. What was to become of these foreign riches? New money is never popular among established elites, but there were fears that, if left in private hands, this new exotic wealth might distort the traditional links between land and political influence. Alarmingly, the new nabobs looked as if they could outbid established aristocrats whenever a 'rotten' borough came up for sale. And just as dauntingly, if Indian wealth and patronage were somehow to fall into the hands of the government, it would certainly unsettle constitutional arrangements that were universally agreed to be in appropriate balance.

The acquisition of Bengal was the largest fait accompli ever to arrive in British politics, and it could not be ignored. So, as the Company took a grip on India, Parliament was forced to take a grip on the Company.

The government's first move, in 1767, was to demand £400,000 per annum from the Company, as a kickback to dissuade it from taking control of the entire Indian operation. But then war with Mysore (1767–9) and devastating famine in Bengal (1769–70) reduced the Company to the verge of bankruptcy by 1772, prompting it to request an emergency loan of £1 million from the state. All the while the Company was still paying a dividend of 12.5 per cent, which was patently absurd.

Suspicions also lurked that Company misrule was to blame for the massive loss of life in the famine, which was true. With constitutional, moral and financial concerns in play, inaction was no longer an option, and in a pattern that was to be repeated, embarrassment for the Company produced political intervention. A parliamentary inquiry was launched in 1772, which resulted in the passing of the Regulating Act of 1773.

Despite reservations about infringing chartered rights, the prime minister, Lord North, used the Act to assert the principle of Crown authority over the EIC. This was the first formal attempt by the home government to involve itself in Indian affairs, and its approach was more political than constitutional.

The Regulating Act reshaped the structure of the Company in India, with the creation of a Governor-General of Fort William (Bengal), who was given new powers over the Presidencies of Madras and Bombay. The new Governor-General, named in the Act as Warren Hastings, was to govern with a council of four; as a restraining measure the council was given the power to overrule him. In addition, the Act also made the acceptance of 'presents' illegal under British law, and set up a Supreme Court of Judicature in Calcutta to dispense British common law, primarily with the intention of regulating the affairs of the Company's employees. It also limited the Company's dividend, and contained a number of technical provisions to stabilize the Company's London affairs, particularly in the election of directors.

The rescue package contained two further measures. The government loaned the Company £1.4 million, and passed the Tea Act (1773), which allowed the direct export of tea to the American colonies, while reducing the duties on it. The idea was to expand the volume of the tea trade, but the actual effect was to shrink the size of the First British Empire. Enraged Americans rejected the cold charity of the home government, and threw the first consignment of cheap tea into Boston Harbour in December 1773. War with the colonists followed soon after. As did the death of Clive.

Robert Clive (1726–74) is usually hailed as the founder of the British Empire in India, and in a headline sense this is correct. But he always lacked the courage and imagination of a true empire builder, and he left no permanent structures behind him.

On the morning of the battle of Plassey he was not sure he should engage, and after the victory he refused to march on Delhi. On his return in 1765, he was no keener on expansion. As he was about to take command in Calcutta he wrote to the Company's chairman: 'I mean absolutely to bound our Possessions, Assistance and Conquests to Bengal',[1] and he explicitly ruled out an advance on Delhi again,[2] even with the opportunities that the victory at Baksar had opened up. When he left two years later he recommended in a minute to the directors that 'we should studiously maintain peace; it is the groundwork of our prosperity'.[3]

He is, perhaps, best understood as more a freebooter than an imperialist, who used military means as and when it suited his purposes.

He was therefore rather less like Alexander or Napoleon and rather more like two of his contemporaries in India, Charles Joseph Patissier, Marquis de Bussy-Castelnau (1718–85), and Haidar Ali of Mysore (c.1721–82), both successful commanders driven by personal ambition. But whatever he was, there has never been anyone quite like him in British history. Without mercantile training he managed to make money in everything he did. Though a self-taught soldier he became more effective in war than the professionals.

In England, Clive was that epitome of the unwelcome outsider, a 'nabob'. Though not the first of the nabobs, he was by far the richest. He was also the most visible, lifted to prominence by military victory and an expensively purchased parliamentary following.

By any measure he was a success, yet his contemporaries were loath to sing his praises. They found it hard to decide whether he was a courageous military hero or a plutocratic political villain. Both descriptions were as true as they were false, and such complexity made it unusually difficult for others to deal with him. Even an enthusiastic empire builder like William Pitt the Elder couldn't manage a consistent line. In 1757, on hearing news of the victory at Plassey, he declared that Clive was a 'heaven born general'. But proximity did not lend enchantment, and by 1770 Pitt was complaining that 'importers of foreign gold have forced their way into Parliament'.[4] It was to become a recurring motif of Anglo-Indian history that successful men were rewarded with the mistrust of the establishment they did so much to serve.

Clive sailed out to India in 1743 and returned in 1753 as the hero of the defence of Arcot, with a personal fortune of something like £40,000, largely garnered from an appointment in the military supply department. This sum was comparable to the annual income of the largest landowners in the country, so he found himself on an entirely different social plane from the humble clerk of eighteen who had gone out on a salary of £5 a year. He returned to India in 1755, and over the next five years he and the Company moved openly into power politics.

On his second return to England in 1760 his personal glory was greater as the celestial victor of Plassey but, more importantly, he was now worth something in the region of £300,000, mostly acquired from the public treasury of Bengal. He also enjoyed a substantial income of around £27,000 per annum from a jagir gifted to him by Mir Jafar.

His third term in India, from 1765 to 1767, was less personally remunerative but saw him display his finest qualities as he addressed the military and financial chaos in Bengal, and acquired for the Company a sheen of legal respectability from the Mughal emperor. He returned to London for the final time in 1767, rich, celebrated and still highly ambitious.

Clive's ultimate career aims were always cast in terms of British national politics. It is quite clear from the large correspondence he kept up through the 1750s with a whole series of prominent people that he wished to advance himself in the accepted contemporary manner. He sought patronage from within the existing Whig landed oligarchy, and latched onto Henry Fox, the Secretary of War. He aligned himself with Lord Sandwich and stood, unsuccessfully, in his 'interest' for a rotten borough in Cornwall in 1754. He also wrote regularly to the king's son, the Duke of Cumberland, who was Captain-General of the army, in a bid to curry favour in high military circles. He even paid court to the Archbishop of Canterbury.

But his political instincts were poor. Despite his status as a rising military star, the patrons he cultivated in the 1750s failed to do him any favours. Even in the early 1760s when he was a fabulously wealthy MP, he still found it difficult to attach himself to the right people. In a time of great political instability he floated between government and opposition, as he looked for support while his right to his jagir was being challenged. Eventually he threw in his lot with the prime minister of the day, George Grenville.

Thus, when he sailed east in June 1764 for his third tour in India, it was under the aegis of the highest patron in the land. But Grenville was forced back into opposition in 1765, and remained there till his death in 1770. All the while Clive's substantial parliamentary following, of up to eight members, never quite brought him the influence he might have expected. He received an Irish peerage in 1762, but the summit of his public service in England was the largely ceremonial post of Lord Lieutenant of Shropshire—scant reward for a winner of empire.

How did he fail to turn such wealth and success into real political power in Britain? His family were Shropshire gentry, and his father had been an MP for many years, so his background would hardly have been a hindrance to high status in public life. The problem was, in part, his temperament; the delicate compromises of politics exasperated him. His youthful years of energy and courage gave way to a later career of much frustration that revealed a haughty self-righteousness in him.

Yet there was something still more unsuitable about him that was obvious to his contemporaries—his financial independence. The politics of the age needed men who could be tempted or, in contemporary parlance, 'attached' through office, perquisites or honours. But Clive had already collected several lifetimes' worth. In a letter of 18 September 1772, the prime minister, Lord North, who was courting Clive politically at the time, wrote to one of Clive's allies that there was nothing in the gift of the Crown that was 'worth his [Clive's] pursuit' as he was already 'so great and so prosperous'.[5] North feared that the range of tools at his disposal, which would have secured the loyalties of other men, would have only a partial hold on Baron Plassey.

Clive never discovered the secrets of popularity. He found nothing so easy as making personal enemies, although that does not entirely explain the extreme public vilification he endured. His contemporaries were largely hostile, either from jealousy of his fame or wealth, or from disgust at his apparent rapaciousness and the hypocrisy he displayed in defending it. Even the historian Robert Orme, having lavished praise on his friend's earlier exploits in the Carnatic, felt forced to back away from chronicling Clive's later career in Bengal.

His behaviour in Bengal was certainly self-serving, and his loyalty to the EIC was highly contingent in ways that did him little credit. Having taken Bengal by conquest in 1757, nominally on the Company's behalf, Clive immediately offered to hand it to the London government, in a famous letter to William Pitt in January 1759.[6] In general, Clive showed little inclination to hold to any official Company line, a waywardness that contrasts vividly with later characters like Warren Hastings and Lord William Bentinck.

The one clear political victory he managed was to win the right to his jagir, which had made him the Company's landlord, an incongruous position that led Laurence Sulivan to question the legitimacy of the grant. Mir Jafar, as nawab, had originally given the district of the Twenty-Four Parganas to the Company, and only later re-granted a large part of it to Clive personally, along with the Persian title of Sabut Jang (determined in war), for seeing off the incursion from Awadh in 1759. Laurence Sulivan claimed that Clive's jagir was rightfully the Company's because Clive was a Company servant, and therefore not entitled to private rewards. Clive maintained that the grant was a personal favour from Mir Jafar.

The argument was pursued vigorously through 1763–4, leading to a great deal of stock splitting, as both sides tried to multiply their votes in order to manipulate the Court of Proprietors (shareholders), who elected the directors. Clive bought heavily and won his case in May 1764. His good fortune continued the next year when, with the rise in the Company's stock price after the acquisition of the diwani, he was able to sell at a large profit. He retained the jagir until his death, whereupon it reverted to the Company. Sulivan, who clung on to his holdings, was ruined in the stock crash of the late 1760s.

Aside from the dispute over the jagir, Clive had to endure one more political Calvary. When the whole subject of the Company's status and responsibilities came under parliamentary scrutiny in 1772–3, he was brought before the House of Commons to answer for his conduct. His testimony is the nearest we have to an autobiography, and it is full of telling details about Company life in India. He took a modest and contrite line, asking that if the House saw fit to take away his wealth, it might yet leave him his honour. Restraint won the day. He was tacitly reprimanded for taking money for himself, but also thanked for meritorious service—a nicely balanced, proto-imperial mixed message.

Clive died aged forty-eight, on 22 November 1774, at 45 Berkeley Square, London, in circumstances that still pose unanswered questions. The newspapers of the day were not agreed as to the cause of death. Some blamed apoplexy, while others reported some kind of fit brought on by opiates, taken against his doctor's advice. The only vaguely official version of the story is from Lord Hertford, the Lord Chancellor, who told the diarist Horace Walpole that it was down to over-medication.

But anomalies concerning Clive's funeral and burial seemed to indicate the withholding of a secret. The coffin was immediately sealed; the body was moved at night; it was interred with indecent haste, in an unmarked grave, at dusk. What kind of treatment was that for one of the richest men in the kingdom and a Knight of the Bath? Rumours of suicide began to circulate.

Clive had always been prone to depression. As a young 'griffin' in Madras he had tried to shoot himself, and he experienced debilitating bouts of mental illness regularly throughout the rest of his life. But he also suffered a great deal of physical discomfort from gout, 'derangement of the liver', and intensely painful gallstones, from which the only refuge was opium. So although suicide brought on by depression is a credible explanation, an overdose of laudanum fits very neatly with misplaced efforts to relieve his agonies.

There are, however, other completely different and highly detailed accounts that support a suicide by knife. G.R. Gleig, in his 1848 biography of Clive, records a version of events in which Clive is found covered in blood, having cut his own throat with a penknife. Dr Samuel Johnson was heard to remark that Clive's 'irredeemable wickedness' had driven him to cut his own throat, and letters show that this much more lurid explanation was circulating among society ladies in 1774. Gleig claims to have got the story directly from the descendants of Jane Strachey, who was present in the house at the time, thus making it the only eyewitness account we have. It would certainly explain why no one was ever permitted to see the body.

Intriguingly, in Robert Harvey's 1998 biography of Clive, *Life and Death of a British Emperor*, there is another penknife theory. Harvey suggests that someone else—servant, guest or kin—snatched up this puny weapon in a moment of panic to use in self-defence when confronted by Clive in one of his towering rages.

This idea gives us extra scope to choose the death we want for him, based on the Clive we wish to see. So, he was either a tormented genius in despair, who killed himself after Parliament humiliated him. Or he was the cool-headed man of affairs, his troubles behind him, looking forward to a life in national politics, who accidentally ended his unceasing pain with an excess of laudanum. Or he was the overpowering imperial brute, finally laid low as he attacked a weaker adversary once too often.

Many contemporaries thought that the principal casualty of Clive's success would be the British political system; in the end it was the man himself.

1774–85: Survival

Although Clive is chiefly remembered as the victor of Plassey, his greater significance was in bringing the problem of Indian governance very directly to the attention of the British ruling class. The chaos he set in train was the principal reason for the 1773 Regulating Act.

The Act had some success in calming down the London end of EIC politics, but it was much less successful in India, primarily because it did nothing to distance the Company's servants from the temptations that surrounded them. It also failed to bring stability because its provisions virtually guaranteed that personal rivalries would break out.

Warren Hastings found himself severely hampered by his new council, which had been carefully set up to balance political interests: two members for the Company—himself and Richard Barwell—and three for the government—General John Clavering, Colonel George Monson and Philip Francis. With the arrival in Calcutta of the three government appointees in late 1774, the council split into its two, preordained factions, with Hastings repeatedly outvoted. He had been conducting a thorough overhaul of government in Bengal, especially the revenue system, but the Company's affairs now descended into a period of disorderly acrimony.

The three-man 'Majority' had the upper hand until 1776, when the death of Monson allowed Hastings to regain control with his casting vote. The death of Clavering in 1777 further eased the situation, but the personal hostility between Hastings and Philip Francis continued, culminating in a duel between the two, fought in August 1780. Francis was wounded and chose to return home that December. This offered some respite to Hastings, but it also granted Francis ample time to prepare for a rematch.

Apart from obstruction in his own council, Hastings also suffered the consequences of decisions made by the subordinate Presidencies of Bombay and Madras, which drew the Company into simultaneous wars—with the Marathas, whose lands surrounded Bombay, and with Hyderabad and Mysore, which both adjoined Madras.

The Company's Bombay Council rashly become involved in a succession dispute, committing itself by the Treaty of Surat (March 1775) to back Raghunath Rao's claims to the office of Peshwa (titular head of the Maratha Confederacy) in return for promises of new ports on the west coast. Hastings refused to ratify this alliance but was overruled by the directors in London. The result was the First Anglo-Maratha War (1775–82). Initial success was followed by disaster, when a British army was forced to surrender at Wadgaon in early 1779.

At this point, war with France broke out again, and the Council in Madras, under the spectacularly corrupt Sir Thomas Rumbold, provoked Haidar Ali of Mysore by seizing the French port of Mahé, which was under his protection. The general weakness of the British position at this time persuaded Haidar Ali to start the Second Anglo-Mysore War (1780–4). His son Tipu then annihilated a British force at Polilur in September 1780, leaving Madras defenceless.

This was Hastings's 'Churchill moment' and he refused to buckle. He had already sent troops on a spectacular year-long march across India to relieve Bombay—too late to prevent Wadgaon—but he now sent armies by land and sea to relieve Madras. Meanwhile a second force under Captain Popham pulled off a spectacular coup by storming the supposedly impregnable fortress of Gwalior, the home base of the strongest Maratha leader, Mahadji Sindhia. Lt Col. Jacob Camac then checked Sindhia's forces at Shivpuri (Sipri), after which Sir Eyre Coote went on to defeat the Mysoreans at Porto Novo in 1781, and again at Arni in 1782. In this strengthened position, the British abandoned Raghunath Rao, bought off the Maratha ruler of Berar, who was threatening Bengal, and placated Mahadji Sindhia.

Hastings stood firm, but the final defeat of the French was also the work of Sir Eyre Coote, who was rarely credited then, or since, with the achievement.

Born in the same year as Clive, Sir Eyre Coote (1726–83) was characteristic of the early British drive for power in India in several ways. He was of Celtic stock, as were many in the armed forces, and like several other successful soldiers of the period he amassed a fortune. Finally, like nearly all of his contemporaries in India from Clive to Philip Francis, he also quarrelled with colleagues wherever he went.

He is credited with introducing to India the two-deep formation known as 'the thin red line', and he was acclaimed for his great personal bravery, which brought the best out of his sepoys, who admired him and were keen to match his courage. He returned their devotion, and developed a deep concern for their welfare. It was this relationship, as much as any great tactical skill, that lay behind his successes, and it prompted an officer who served under him to describe him as 'the soldier's friend'. 'Other generals', continued Captain Innes Munro, 'have been approved, but Sir Eyre Coote was beloved of the British Army in India.'[7]

Coote undertook four tours of duty in India between 1755 and 1783, all of which illuminate the condition of British power there.

After a shaky start to his military career against Jacobite rebels, he joined the 39th Regiment of Foot just in time to be sent to India in 1755. The 39th always carried the motto 'Primus in India' to advertise the fact that it was the first royal unit to arrive in the subcontinent—all others fighting under British colours till then were either employed by the Company or were in the pay of princely allies.

Coote was part of Clive's expedition from Madras in October 1756 to recover Calcutta, and he fought throughout the campaign that swept the British up from the mouth of the Hughli, through Calcutta, on to Chandernagore, and finally to victory at Plassey. Unlike Clive, Coote was one of the few who wanted to fight that day, and he distinguished himself after the battle by his pursuit of a French contingent into the interior. Despite the fact that Clive disliked him, Coote came out of the whole Bengal Revolution very well, in both reputation and wealth.

He returned to London in 1758 in a cloud of glory, and was soon sent back to take command of the Madras army. He arrived in late 1759 and decisively beat the French at Wandiwash in January 1760, after which he proceeded to reduce all the French outposts in the region; Pondicherry was the last, taken in January 1761. He then returned to England where, in a textbook piece of nabobbery, he purchased a country estate and entered Parliament.

Coote's third spell in India was nowhere near as successful. The directors sent him out in 1770 as a member of a commission of inquiry into the Company's affairs, which were in disarray; a severe cash-flow crisis had arisen after a disastrous war against Haidar Ali of Mysore (1767–9) and the Bengal famine of 1769–70. Coote made it safely to India, but the three commissioners who were to work with him did not; their ship, the *Aurora*, was lost somewhere beyond Cape Town in January 1770.

He held the nominal position of Commander-in-Chief, but this was not a simple matter in India, where there were three separate presidency armies. As a royal officer, he was senior to any Company soldier of equivalent rank, but he seemed unable to navigate the jealousies that were rife within the services. He proceeded to make himself unpopular with just about everyone, and returned to Europe overland in 1771. Warren Hastings, then still a junior in the Madras Council, was pleased to see him go, remarking: 'God forbid that he should ever return to any part of India.'[8]

Less taxing commands preoccupied him for the next seven years, but he was eventually posted back to India in 1778, when the French entered the American War of Independence on the side of the Americans, thus reopening the subcontinent as an international theatre of war.

Coote managed to establish good relations with Warren Hastings, but with almost no one else. He then held together an ill-organized and poorly supplied army in the Carnatic, as he fended off the numerically superior Mysorean forces. The disastrous British reverse at Polilur in 1780 was gradually overcome, and Coote won a series of engagements with Haidar Ali, the most notable of which was the battle of Porto Novo in July 1781.

The Second Mysore War (1780–4) lapsed into stalemate over the next two years, but not without another series of disputes between Coote and civilian authority. The Governor of Madras, Lord Macartney, urged Coote to adopt a more aggressive strategy. Coote, outnumbered in the field and with constant problems of supply, refused to oblige. He then fell ill, and died of a stroke in April 1783.

Coote's successor, General James Stuart, also fell out with Macartney, and even fought a duel with him. However, Stuart pressed the Mysoreans more closely and this, along with the threat of possible Maratha attacks, brought about a ceasefire shortly afterwards.

The double war was then ended by two treaties—of Salbai in 1782, with the Marathas, and of Mangalore in 1784, with Mysore. These restored the status quo, except that the Company retained the island of Salsette, next to Bombay. The EIC owed its survival mostly to the unwillingness of the south Indian powers to coordinate their campaigns, thus losing probably their best opportunity to destroy it as a territorial entity.

When not fighting for survival, Warren Hastings spent most of his time in India working out the details of a new system of government for the massive population under his charge. He favoured a minimum of change combined with enlightened government, and he never expressed the intention of altering India in any profound way. In his own memorable formulation, he wished to rule the people with 'ease and moderation',[9] maintaining existing customs as much as possible. He tried collecting taxes by employing Europeans—to ensure honesty—and then Indians—to supply knowledge. Neither approach worked well; Europeans were rapacious and Indians opaque. He tried long tax assessments, then short. But corruption and lack of information frustrated him throughout, and he never managed to realize the levels of revenue he expected. As a consequence he was always short of cash.

In the legal field he realized that to enforce laws one must know what they are, so he commissioned translations of both Hindu and Muslim legal codes. Here begins the long, elaborate British involvement with Indian laws, which started out as an inquiry into what those laws might be, moved into a mission to preserve such laws as there were, and ended up as a project to provide new laws wherever it seemed necessary.

It was never the case that India had no laws or no respect for laws; it was always that there were too many, or that they were not fit for British purposes, especially in matters of commerce and finance. The *Code of Gentoo Laws* of 1776, a translation of the Vivadarnavasetu by Nathaniel Halhed, was the first result. Close involvement with law stimulated a wider interest in ancient Sanskrit literature, and the Asiatick Society of Bengal was founded in 1784, which acted as a centre for European interest in Indian languages, culture and history.

In 'foreign policy', Hastings's first important step was to stop the payment of tribute to the Mughal emperor, due under the Treaty of Allahabad (1765), which rendered a substantial saving. The tribute had always been essentially a voluntary act, but Hastings ended it because the emperor had moved to Delhi under Maratha protection.

More constructively, Hastings used instability on Bengal's northern borders to advance British interests. In 1773, raiding from the state of Bhutan allowed him to offer British protection to the Raja of Cooch Behar—the first of many such agreements. The Bhutanese were nominally under the protection of Tibet, and intercession from Lhasa offered an opportunity to open discussions about trade, and even a chance to open a back channel to the Chinese. Protracted till Hastings left office, these negotiations ultimately came to nothing, but the effects of the British presence had begun to ramify in ways that were hard to predict or control.

Hastings then sponsored a successful small war to expel the Afghan Rohillas from the territories of the Nawab of Awadh, hiring out Company troops to do the job. But his hands were then tied by the passage of the Regulating Act, which saddled him with a council which was happy to outvote him.

Disputes in the council led to accusations of corruption being thrown by both sides, and an unfortunate Bengali entrepreneur named Nandakumar was caught in the crossfire. He publicly accused Hastings of malpractice, only to be hanged shortly afterwards, in August 1775, on an unrelated charge of forgery. This convenient outcome touched off suspicions of judicial murder, and the exact sequence of events is still not clear. Hastings had no direct hand in the death sentence, but it was widely understood to have benefited him, and the judge in the case was Sir Elijah Impey, an old school friend of his.

Nandakumar had plenty of enemies besides Hastings, and although he may not have committed the crime in question, he was known as a man not above sharp practice. Nor did Hastings's chief opponent, Philip Francis, make any attempt to intercede for Nandakumar, so the matter can hardly be viewed as testimony to integrity on anyone's part. As many have pointed out, Nandakumar was sentenced to death for the same crime that Clive had committed in order to win Bengal.

By late 1780 the obstructive Majority had been depleted by death and desertion, and Hastings was allowed a free hand to pursue the Company's wars against the Marathas and Mysore. He lost control of the council again in 1783, but his conduct through these later years made his reputation as a great statesman and strategist. His expeditions to raise revenue in Benares and Awadh were successful, but his high-handed manner provided ample material to political opponents, who were more than ready to see government misconduct in India as a symptom of malaise in the British body politic.

The Company survived the two wars involving the junior Presidencies with its territories still intact, an improbable result considering the enormous Maratha power ranged against it and the military blows it suffered at the hands of Mysore on land and of the French at sea. But by 1784 Hastings had had enough; the directors in London were calling for his resignation, his own council in Calcutta was ranged against him again, and he was disturbed by the prospect of government intervention to reform the Company.

All this made for something of a natural break, and Hastings resigned and returned in 1785 to London, where party warfare had been raging about competing schemes of EIC reform. In this charged atmosphere, his record of unproductive wars and financial deficits was a serious liability, and he was to earn not recognition for his hard work, but impeachment for alleged 'high crimes' of tyranny.

In some ways Hastings was forced to carry the can for the failures of the Regulating Act. Long before his return, it had become obvious to London politicians that North's 1773 measures had not brought orderly governance to India; Hastings was even censured by the Commons in 1782. Demands for political and legal change were voiced on all sides, and Select and Secret Committees were formed in 1781–2 to examine the Company's affairs and make proposals for reform.

No less than four India Bills then appeared through the politically unstable years 1782–4. One, proposed by Henry Dundas, and two, by Charles James Fox, failed—but a fourth, sponsored by William Pitt the Younger, was passed in August 1784.

Pitt's India Act attempted to address the more obvious failings of the Regulating Act, largely by injecting more ministerial control in London and more executive centralization in India. It strengthened the office of Governor-General but made him subject to a six-member Board of Control in London, appointed by the government of the day, which was to have sight of all correspondence to and from India. Appointments within the Company were left with the directors, but the Crown was given the power to recall any Company officeholder. The Governor-General's Council in Calcutta was reduced to three members and given a purely advisory role, and a Secret Committee of three directors was to supervise important military and diplomatic orders passing between the Board and the Governor-General. The Bengal revenues, and all trading decisions, were left in the Company's hands.

The Act was a shrewd compromise. It maintained the distance between ministers and the India trade, but allowed much more government control of the Company's more state-like concerns. It aimed to achieve some sort of balance between necessary executive power on the ground in the East and effective accountability at home. By and large it worked. The system was good enough, in British political terms, to remain unchanged until 1858, when the Company was finally removed from all governmental responsibilities.

There was still to be a great deal of debate about the purpose and direction of British rule in India over the next half-century, but constitutionally the matter was now settled. The government would superintend the Company's affairs, while Indian patronage was left with the directors, ensuring that the government could not acquire any additional political leverage. The role of Governor-General was strengthened to permit more control from above, but this was balanced by the preamble to the Act, which disavowed any intention of acquiring further territory in India.

In a typically British fashion, much was left unsaid, and the political nation simply observed the agreed principles within its standard practices. The patronage issue was left poised, balanced between the Company's right to appoint its own officers, up to and including the Governor-General, and the Crown's right to recall any of those employees, up to and including the Governor-General. The common sense of the political nation was left to steer a course between these privileges. This was not a completely smooth process, but it was one in which the Board of Control consistently won out over the directors.

The theory was that important decisions about India would now be taken by directors in Leadenhall Street with the tacit approval of the ministry of the day. In practice, there were few prominent figures in Indian affairs. The most important was the president of the Board of Control, who after 1812 was, by convention, a member of the cabinet. The only others of significance were the three men who sat on the Secret Committee of the Court of Directors.

This all looked good in London, but severe limitations on the speed of communication meant that in practice the Company's servants in India were often free to chart their own destinies. The separation of ministers and directors in London was also to some degree illusory, because the smallness of the contemporary world of affairs precluded any rigorous isolation between them. What persisted was a potentially very large distance between policy-making in London and the day-to-day management of affairs in India.

British schoolchildren used to learn that Clive 'won' India at Plassey in 1757, but this was a gross oversimplification. Plassey was a Bengali affair, and it was the victory at Baksar in 1764 that really secured the British presence, by stabilizing the complex politics of northern India. Baksar was also central in persuading Emperor Shah Alam to hand over the diwani of Bengal, which represented real governmental responsibility. Clive was concerned, as were the merchant directors, to do things legally; trade, legality and orderliness go naturally together. The British search for legitimacy started here.

But more than battles or treaties, the truly irreversible step into imperial government was taken when, under increased scrutiny from politicians, the EIC's directors resolved in mid-1771 to end Clive's Dual System. This involved paying off the eleven-year-old nawab Mubarak-ud-Daula, dismissing Muhammad Reza Khan and Maharaja Shitab Rai, the Company's deputy diwans in Murshidabad and Patna, who had been in post since Clive's day. Hastings then 'stood forth as diwan', as the directors had instructed him, and the Company took the entire government of Bengal and Bihar into its own hands, nizamat and all. This represented a constructive step away from simply respecting legality to addressing issues of legitimacy. This momentous decision moved the Company into a position of complete responsibility for the governing of about twenty million people. It was also to bring much labour, confusion and a developing sense of moral burden.

4

1784–1813

LAND, LAW, EXPANSION, VICTORY

1784–93: Cornwallis, Hastings, Burke

By late 1784 the Company had ridden out a military storm in India and a political storm in Britain. It had managed to keep its charter, its monopoly, its patronage and its territories. The Company's 'military fiscal state' was in place, but its military side was in rather better shape than its fiscal. Detailed problems of administration had yet to be solved on the ground, and powerful enemies still bordered Madras and Bombay.

The Company's fate was now bound up not with trade but with government. Pitt's Act of 1784 clearly established that Indian territory was more than the private concern of stockholders, and the poor performance of the Company's first twenty years as sovereign in Bengal led to instructions from the directors that its affairs were to be thoroughly reformed. General Charles Cornwallis was dispatched to Bengal, with a remit to organize the Company's affairs in line with official thinking.

Lord Charles Cornwallis (1738–1805) was a soldier sent to India in a time of peace to set the Company in order. This he did to the directors' great satisfaction, and he also triumphed in the one war he fought—the Third Anglo-Mysore War against Tipu (1789–91).

Cornwallis holds a unique place in Indian history. He served twice as Governor-General of Bengal, from 1786 to 1793, and again from July to October 1805, making him the only man to take up the post twice. He was also the first of only three men to be Commander-in-Chief and Governor-General simultaneously, the others being the Marquess of Hastings (1813–23) and Lord William Bentinck (1828–35). It required a special Act of Parliament in 1786 to allow this seemingly dangerous step, but it actually worked out quite well. He was also one of only three Governors-General who died in office, the others being Lord Elgin, who succumbed to illness in 1862, and Lord Mayo, murdered in 1872.

Cornwallis has frequently been written down as a dull man of slow intellect. This does not quite accord with contemporary judgements of him, which focus on his impeccable integrity and considerable military ability. It was these qualities that turned him into a globetrotting troubleshooter, posted in turn to North America, India and Ireland. Although his command in America ended in surrender at Yorktown in 1781, no disgrace attached itself to his name, and Prime Minister William Pitt considered him a natural choice to succeed Warren Hastings in India.

As Governor-General, his task was to address the entire range of Company responsibilities, and to disentangle its various conflicts of interest. This led him to decree that the Company's various 'lines'—military, political (diplomatic), civil, mercantile—should be separated, and that Europeans henceforth were not to hold land. Whiggish unease about concentrations of power then led him to reform the lowest level of government, so that authority was balanced between two separate officials, a district magistrate, who was to preside over all civil and criminal matters, and a Collector, who would simply collect the revenue.

Police powers were taken away from the zamindars (subcontractors within the Mughal land revenue system), and were instead given to specialist officers called darogahs in rural areas. In the towns, police powers remained with kotwals (Mughal law enforcement officials). Both came under the supervision of the district magistrate. The criminal law was also addressed, to try to render it both more intimidating and less unequal in its outcomes.

Cornwallis excluded all Indians from administrative positions worth more than £500 per annum. Later critics have labelled this decision as racist, but it was simply a necessary step to ensure direct responsibility of the administrative machine to the Company in London. Similarly, it must be pointed out that although Cornwallis distrusted Indians as incorrigibly corrupt, his expectations of Europeans in India were little better. He deliberately selected soldiers, not trained civilian administrators, to 'settle' the lands won from Mysore in 1792, trusting to their higher standards of discipline and honesty—a decision that allowed Thomas Munro to switch from military to civil affairs.

Cornwallis tried to select honest and competent men, but he did not address the education of recruits—that would have to wait for Richard

Wellesley. Instead he tried to nurture honesty, by increasing salaries, and competence, by making administration a specialized career. He thus effectively set up an Indian civil service. This self-contained, meritocratic body, audited and supervised, had no counterpart in England. Cornwallis, the Whig pragmatist, accidentally created a liberal institution.

But the most important financial and political decisions that faced him concerned land law, because taxation, tenancy and the right to adjudicate disputes were all inseparably linked in India. The Company's ultimate welfare depended on this interrelated system, yet after more than twenty years as rulers, its servants had still found little reliable guidance in their efforts to understand and regulate it. Local advice was all to some degree financially interested. Cornwallis, less patient than Warren Hastings, was determined to simplify and innovate wherever necessary, in order to make the Company's task easier and its position more secure.

The result was the Cornwallis Code of 1793, whose most significant part was Regulation I—the Permanent Settlement. This revolutionary measure gave possessory rights in land to the zamindars, whose function had previously been simply to collect the land revenue. Regulation I effectively redefined the legal basis of landholding in Bengal, because until then there had been no local equivalent of the European concept of 'absolute possession' in land; Indian law only recognized a right to occupy and cultivate land in return for a 'king's share' of the produce. Having given zamindars secure possession, the Permanent Settlement also fixed for all time the amounts payable on zamindars' holdings.

Under the Permanent Settlement the government of Bengal could look forward to the exact figure of Rs 286 lakhs per annum, and it knew where to go for the money. Collecting a fixed income from a small cadre of grateful estate holders was an attractively cheap alternative to trying to cajole revenue out of the mysterious countryside. Along with financial certainty came political security: Indians were bound into the system by financial interest.

There were two further considerations that lay behind the decision. One was theoretical, based on Whig ideas about limited government. By fixing the revenue demand, state power was being taken out of society, not pushed further into it. The other was the expectation that by limiting the government's demands, landlords would now be encouraged to improve their holdings, and wider prosperity would follow. Any short-term loss of revenue could be recouped from raised taxation on non-agricultural sectors.

The Permanent Settlement thus seemed on several levels to be an ideal way to secure the Company's financial and political future—without the expense of fighting. The outcome, however, was rather different. Scope within the system for landlords to exploit their subtenants was enormously increased. With a fixed demand from government but no curb on rental demands, it was more in zamindars' interests to raise rents than to fund risky improvements. And because the government had no part in the landlord–tenant relationship, disputes now had to be determined in the courts, which was not easy for small tenants. What was intended to be a dynamic economic incentive structure turned into a static engine of extraction. Money did flow into the rural economy, but not into improvement. It went instead into a new market in land rights, which provided an attractively steady return on investment.

As a final part of his reforms, Cornwallis tidied up criminal and family law. The existing Mughal criminal code, which was basically Hanafi shari'a law, remained in force, but the more egregious punishments were abolished: amputation and impalement were replaced by flogging and hanging, while the various Islamic impediments to capital punishment were removed. In matters of marriage and inheritance, Hindu and Muslim customary law continued, as in Warren Hastings's time.

Cornwallis's objective was always to take discretion out of the hands of officials, in an attempt to guard against arbitrary use of power, and in this he succeeded. But his innovations, with the exception of the police reforms, were all based on experience of running Britain, and as such they were doomed to long-term failure. The main deficiency of the new system was lack of responsiveness, which was revealed in due course; the police reforms were retained but extensively modified over coming decades.

He created a bureaucratic machine designed to eliminate the perceived evils of contact with Indian society—unearned wealth, irresponsible decisions and bad governance. With the creation of a new class of landlords in Bengal, he refashioned traditional Indian legal and social relationships for British purposes. This was a complete abandonment of previous policy, which had been to respect Indian institutions wherever possible, as a prudent way of laying the lightest, most agreeable yoke on the population. Cornwallis had effectively been instructed to import British standards, and after a period of consultation and research into all legal aspects, he set out a reforming policy designed to ensure British control. In this he was certainly bolder than Warren Hastings, but he also faced less obstruction from his underlings, and enjoyed much firmer support from his political masters.

He gave the directors a very succinct rationale for why such extensive interference with established Indian legal practices was appropriate. He felt 'called upon by the principles of humanity, and a regard for the honour and interest of the Company and the nation' to reform 'cruel punishments' and to 'restrain the spirit of corruption' prevailing in 'native courts'. He also assured his masters that the expense incurred would be as light as possible.[1]

He was quite unembarrassed about rolling together the widest possible moral grounds for his actions with much less elevated motivations—the national interest and the economic health of Company rule. Yet he managed to set out, as early as 1789, almost the entire manifesto of imperial British India, with its themes of mission and feelings of obligatory action. The 'work' had begun.

It also fell to Cornwallis to reverse the military policy (and fortunes) of his predecessors since Clive. Clive had never tried to take territory outside the boundaries of Bengal and Bihar. The Company's subsequent wars, with Mysore (1767–9 and 1780–4) and with the Marathas (1775–82) had been largely defensive affairs that had not yielded any major territorial returns. By contrast, Cornwallis took on Tipu Sultan of Mysore and managed to defeat him soundly enough to carve off large chunks of his territory. The war ended in 1792 with Tipu tamed, his territories reduced and his two sons handed over as hostages to the victorious Cornwallis—the sentimental subject of a number of popular paintings of the period.

Cornwallis thus left behind a very different India from the one he had found. British arms were now going forward, and the governmental machine behind them was less an ad hoc adaptation of native practices and more a recognizably European-style bureaucracy, manned by clerks and officials who were responsible to codes of practice, and supervised by well-rewarded senior members who were themselves expected to follow constitutional principles laid down in London.

Pitt's Act of 1784 and Cornwallis's reforms were the government's responses to the various problems that India presented, but in the minds of opposition politicians the main cause of the troubles of the previous thirty years was believed to be excessive individual enthusiasm for power and loot, and Warren Hastings was easily represented as a man suffering from such vices. That was why, when he came home in June 1785, it was not in triumph, but to face charges of misgovernment and corruption.

How could such apparent success come to this? And what kind of a man was it who was about to endure such a humiliation?

Warren Hastings (1732–1818) held high office in British India from 1772 to 1785. Though he controlled no more territory than Clive, he shouldered a much greater burden of responsibility. Clive came and went; Hastings stayed. Clive hid behind puppet nawabs; Hastings 'stood forth' as diwan and had to wrestle with India's laws. Clive had responsibility only for Bengal; Hastings for Madras and Bombay too.

This wider remit, laid out in the Regulating Act of 1773, was really the source of the trouble. It was premature, and rather too optimistic; it assumed that the Company had only minor administrative problems of self-discipline and cash flow. Promotion to the new office of Governor-General was supposed to enable Hastings to direct the Company's affairs more centrally and wisely, but instead it offered opportunities for the junior Presidencies to draw the much greater resources of Bengal into local wars of their own making, which rendered the Company's fiscal position so precarious that Hastings was eventually forced to raise arrears of tribute in Benares and Awadh. This led him into autocratic acts that were to tarnish his reputation, and formed a large part of the indictment against him. For his contemporaries, these actions came to overshadow all the other things he had done, and it was left to later generations to appreciate his finer qualities.

Neither a soldier nor a merchant by background, he was more of a literary man. On his father's side his family were 'distressed gentry', reduced to making a living as clergymen. His mother died giving birth to him, and his father left for the West Indies when he was an infant. Brought up by an uncle, he was sent to Westminster School, where he excelled in languages. He left early to go to India as an EIC writer in 1750; here he spent six years at Cosimbazar in Bengal, trading largely in silk.

He was at the centre of the tumultuous events of 1756–7, and after the fall of Calcutta he ended up on a mudbank downstream from the town with most of the other refugees. Once British fortunes had recovered, he was made Resident at the court of the new nawab, Mir Jafar, where his principal function was to cajole the nawab into cooperating with his foreign masters. This was not too difficult a task with the aged Mir Jafar, but proved much harder with his successor, Mir Kasim. As relations deteriorated, Hastings argued for a conciliatory approach, but when hostilities broke out in 1764, his policy had very evidently failed. He resigned from the Council of Bengal and returned to England in early 1765.

Though not particularly wealthy at this point, he had done well enough to live in style. He spent the next four years promoting the learning of

Persian at Oxford, thinking about possible administrative reform of the Company, and scheming with Laurence Sulivan—Clive's great enemy—for a return to India. Eventually he secured a new appointment in 1769 as second on the Council of Madras, and did so well there that the directors sent him to Calcutta as Governor of Bengal in February 1772.

War, reform, law and finance occupied him for the next thirteen years—years of faithful service to the Company. But within two years of his return to London in 1785, he was facing impeachment at the hands of Edmund Burke.

Impeachment was an archaic procedure by which the House of Commons prosecuted an individual for high crimes before the House of Lords, sitting as a court of law. Burke revived this process, which had been in abeyance for sixty-three years, as a makeshift way of forcing Hastings to answer for crimes committed outside England.

After a trial of epic length and similarly epic rhetoric, Hastings was acquitted in 1795, partly because the prosecution case became so exaggerated and personally vituperative, but also because in most cases he had acted either within the bounds of contemporary practice or in ways that seemed reasonable to his judges. He had behaved no better and no worse than others entrusted with a similar degree of power, and many felt that his actions were ultimately beneficial to the country. The Lords rose above political and personal issues, and proved reluctant to convict him on what seemed like weak grounds, largely unproven.

Why did a man so evidently useful to the national interest ever come to stand trial? It was mainly because he had made enemies of both Philip Francis personally and Edmund Burke ideologically, but just as importantly, the prime minister, William Pitt the Younger, had no political motivation to support him. Indeed Pitt, who could have stopped any prosecution in its tracks, had at least two positive reasons to leave Hastings swinging in the wind. Firstly, it served his purposes to cultivate the impression that Indian affairs had been in need of reform before his India Act of 1784. Secondly, it made the management of his business easier if the attention of the main opposition grouping was centred on attacking an individual not only out of office but with no political connection to the government.

Even more ominously, standing behind Pitt was Henry Dundas, the most active member of the newly created Board of Control for India, who had a direct and personal interest in discrediting the one person in the British political firmament who could outrank himself in knowledge of

Indian affairs; it was Dundas who moved the censure motion of 1782 against Hastings.

Hastings had also made known his ambition to continue to serve his country in some capacity, and it may have been Dundas who persuaded Pitt to desert Hastings in a crucial 1787 Commons debate on the impeachment. Pitt was expected to support Hastings, but on the night he condemned his actions as 'disproportionate' and the fine levied by Hastings on Raja Chait Singh (of Benares) as 'shamefully exorbitant'. The mood of the House turned hostile, the motion was carried, and impeachment followed.

Politically, Hastings made the mistake of outlasting his patrons, Lord North and Laurence Sulivan, but not his enemies. As a consequence, he came home out of office and without influence, easy prey for political jackals. The one saving circumstance was that the king personally gave him unwavering support, and let this be known.

His trial rather unfairly highlighted Hastings's human weaknesses—irascibility, a tendency to autocracy, and lax personal accounting. British historians warmed only slowly to him. This was largely as a result of the hostile views of Lord Macaulay, whose Whig inheritance from Burke included an aversion to Hastings, which led him to write movingly about the slaughter of Rohilla children, an event he had not witnessed and which almost certainly never happened. And even when, in the 1830s, Macaulay found that many Bengalis held Hastings's memory in respect and affection, he was still reluctant to accept that Burke could have been wrong. But Macaulay was never a man of flexible opinions.

Since then, imperial historians have admired the way Hastings consolidated British interests, while liberals have praised his respect for indigenous customs and concern for the rule of law. By Lord Curzon's time Hastings was no longer a tyrant but a man 'ill used', revered by Raj apologists as the true founder of British dominion in India.

Through a dramatic life, Hastings enjoyed a curiously unfair mixture of occasionally good but mostly bad luck, and he emerged as a man with a remarkable capacity for enduring adversity. Though not a great virtue in itself, this did allow him to use the best of his talents and intelligence. He was as clever as Curzon and as literary as Lytton, but shrewder than both, if no luckier. His successes were primarily diplomatic and cultural, his failures mostly financial.

He wrote some sad lines in retirement, which sigh with dignified resignation:

... be this enough for me:
To bear contented my accomplished lot
Impeached, reviled, acquitted and forgot.[2]

He has not been forgotten by posterity, though he was something of an embarrassment to his contemporaries. The EIC were grateful enough to give him a large pension and to pay off his legal bills, which totalled an astronomical £70,000. Eventually, towards the end of his long life, he was listened to with respect in the discussions prior to the 1813 Charter Act, and was made a Privy Councillor. But he never received even a knighthood, let alone a peerage, and in this he stands alone. No other ex-Governor-General died a commoner.

Beyond Burke's mismanagement of his case, the House of Lords acquitted Hastings largely because of developments in India. During his trial, the Company fought its first successful war in a generation, against Mysore in 1790–2, after which he began to look less like a tyrant and more like the far-sighted architect of an emerging British dominion in India. Nevertheless, a clear warning had been sent out to future proconsuls, that they would be held accountable for their actions in foreign lands.

Hastings was essentially a conservative figure, but his activities in India stimulated new thinking in Britain, especially in the mind of Edmund Burke. Edmund Burke (1729–97) had a largely unsuccessful career in public life. He had only two short spells as Paymaster General, between 1782 and 1784, and his most important political role was as theorist to the small faction known, after their patron, as the Rockingham Whigs. Contemporaries admired him mainly as an orator, especially for his speeches in support of the American colonists' demands for liberty in the period 1770–83, but ultimately it was his fervent hostility to the revolution in France that defined his intellectual legacy.

His political touch may have been unsure, but his vision went far beyond that of most of his contemporaries. He was not a particularly methodical thinker—he distrusted abstract systems—but several of the ideas he outlined during Hastings's trial went on to become enduring ideals of empire, principally his insistence that there is no geographical limit to the domain of morality, and its corollary, that all rulers, no matter where, have obligations to those they rule.

Edmund Burke was first and foremost a Whig, meaning that he opposed the exercise of unaccountable royal authority, and preferred dispersed aristocratic power. This attitude led him to defend the EIC against the government in 1773 over the Regulating Act, because he wished to preserve the Company's chartered rights against the king's ministers, who seemed to him too greedy for the patronage of the East. But by 1782, and the motion of censure on Hastings, he had become not just an opponent of Hastings the man but also of the Company, and the way its affairs were being run in both London and India.

He argued against state intervention in 1773, yet he went on to be the chief author of Charles James Fox's two failed India Bills of 1783, which would have gone much further in terms of government control than either the Act of 1773 or Pitt's Act that followed in 1784. Why? This question is important because it was principally developments within Burke's political outlook that brought Hastings to trial.

After 1773, Burke decided to abandon his defence of the Company's rights in favour of promoting governmental accountability, a central theme within the issues then emerging in America and India. This represented a major shift of emphasis, from a Whiggish defence of 'property' to a general defence of subjects against state power. He began to see the British government through the eyes of American colonists and, eventually, of Indian peasants.

Gradually his worries about excessive Crown power were replaced by concerns about the evolution of national political institutions and how their 'ancient' foundations helped them to discharge their responsibilities. The trial of Hastings stands midway in Burke's ideological journey from supporting the American colonists as defenders of individual liberty, to condemning the revolutionaries in France as destroyers of traditional institutions. India fitted into this mental transit because he thought that the British were unjustly depriving the Indians of their traditional government by replacing it with an artificial, alien system. On the third day of the trial he said, of Indians: 'we must govern them upon their own principles, not ours'.[3] This is an extraordinarily statement for an eighteenth-century Whig, and demonstrates how far he was prepared to go to recognize universal principles—what he called 'morality enlarged'.

He appealed to the 'eternal laws of justice', and denied 'scholastic distinctions' between laws at home and abroad. Even though the trial was about alleged crimes in India, he asked their Lordships not to confine themselves to the 'narrow circle of municipal justice'. He wished to enforce responsibility 'as understood in our constitution', because a British subject in power should not be allowed to possess rights 'denied to allies and dependants'. He even talked of 'our fellow citizens in India'.[4] For Burke, the political world, and especially those parts of it under British rule, had to be seen as one entity.

This wider belief in political universality locates him firmly as a forerunner of modern liberalism. Though the word 'liberal' cannot be accurately attached to his views, he believed that rulers had moral obligations to the ruled, which is a liberal principle, though not originally liberal. He was suspicious of money and of monetized relationships, which is a distinctly illiberal view, as was his belief in the value of hereditary systems of privilege. But he was perhaps the first man to articulate very clearly the idea that any country that ignores liberty aboard while proclaiming it at home is on unsure ground, and may in the end be endangering its own freedoms. In this he was very liberal and indeed very modern.

Burke was also out of step with his contemporaries, in that he refused to see the Mughals as despotic. It suited his purposes to argue that there was an 'ancient constitution' in India, which the British had an obligation to respect and into which they should fit themselves. In an extraordinary leap of intellect he was prepared to assert that when the EIC took on the diwani as a vassal of the emperor, 'Great Britain made a virtual act of union with [India]'.[5]

By the early 1790s, it was clear to him that the British in India were destroying an ancient constitution for base motives, and that the French were about to do the same thing. Regardless of whether the Mughals had been good rulers, overthrowing their legacy had opened up the door to misrule and, in the person of Hastings, tyranny. Burke was convinced that Mughal government, whatever its defects, was better for Indians than Warren Hastings's version of autocracy. Worse, the Company's men were destroying the indigenous nobility and gentry, with unforeseeable but doubtless baleful results.

Burke was no radical, and the position he took on Indian affairs represents his desire to protect the interests of subject populations without using the new language of universal 'rights' that the French were developing. He was comfortable with the general idea of rights; he was, after all, a lawyer. But his conception of universal rights was not founded on any revolutionary theory of egalitarianism. He had an old-style Whig attachment to rights within a larger frame of inequality.

He was therefore not impressed by the 'rights of man', as set out in revolutionary Paris in 1789. He hated the whole package; it undermined 'property' and denied aristocratic privilege, two great bulwarks of his philosophy. Instead, he couched his arguments in terms of the trust reposed in rulers, passed down under God in the form of ancient institutions.

This was not a tenable position in the long term; it was swept away in France, and eventually in India. But this is the key to Burke's thinking, and explains how someone who is now regarded as the founder of modern conservatism could have ended up defending the rights of Indians against a colonial regime. The left–right polarity that seems to be out of place here is an anachronistic illusion. Burke, like a good Whig, feared unaccountable executive power, and his stance on behalf of American, Irish and Indian people stemmed from this basic outlook.

There was also possibly an additional personal undercurrent to his opposition to Hastings. Burke was connected by either blood or friendship to a man named William Burke, whom Edmund described as a 'cousin', although later researchers have struggled to substantiate this relationship. William Burke had close links with the Raja of Tanjore, who had been dispossessed in 1773 by Company troops sent from Madras, acting on behalf of the British-backed Nawab of Arcot. Twists and turns within the Madras Presidency meant that Governor George Pigot, appointed in 1775, supported the raja while most of his Council, for self-interested financial reasons, supported the nawab.

The infighting in Madras was even worse than in Calcutta, and the Arcot party eventually imprisoned Pigot in 1776. Warren Hastings, rather surprisingly, sided with the successful rebels, perhaps as the simplest way of restoring order. However, his leniency did not go unnoticed by a young Henry Dundas and was to cost Hastings dearly in the 1780s.

These events became politicized domestically because Pigot was a supporter of the Rockingham faction. So this whole complicated business eventually played out in London, with Laurence Sulivan and his allies pro-Arcot and pro-Hastings, while Philip Francis, the Burkes and the Rockinghams were pro-Tanjore and anti-Hastings.

As Burke drew up charges against Hastings over the winter of 1785, it seems that he never really believed that the trial would take place, so convinced was he of the corruption at the heart of the British state. His cause was unexpectedly helped, however, by Hastings himself. In a personal defence before the Commons in May 1786 Hastings made it clear that he considered he had no case to answer. This contrasted badly with Clive's 1773 appeal to the mercy of the Commons, and was a serious mistake. Hastings's decision to inform Honourable Members that he was above criticism was perceived as arrogance, and opinion hardened against him.

By May 1787 specific charges were ready to be voted on. The first, relating to the Rohilla War, was defeated. The second charge, concerning his dispossession of the Raja of Benares, might have failed too but for the late intervention of Prime Minister Pitt, who spoke vehemently against

Hastings. The motion was carried, and impeachment, on twenty charges, followed in February 1788.

But Hastings got away. Burke's language during the trial was consistently over-pitched; could the defendant's heart really have been 'gangrened'? To some extent Burke was also trying to put the whole British government in the dock, prompted by fears of a Crown–Company alliance that might prove fatal to the British constitution, a network of venality and rapacity he later called 'Indianism'. He felt he was saving the political nation from sinking into a morass of corruption, and one reason for his excessively long speeches may have been an attempt to read the dismal litany of Company misdeeds into the national record through press reports. Certainly he felt a sense of moral outrage, and he frequently used the language of debauchery and orgy.

By the end of the trial he went beyond rational fears and produced some quite hysterical accusations against Hastings, particularly in his last speech in 1795, delivered over nine days, during which he warned that to acquit was to invite Jacobin terror into the country from across the Channel, and with it the end of aristocracy.

As the trial dragged on Burke seemed to intensify rather than abate his fervour, possibly because the prosecution of Hastings remained his one hope of bringing justice to a world that seemed to him to be losing its way. But in the end Burke was holding the wrong man to account, for the wrong reasons. If he had wanted to find a destroyer of systems, he should have accused Clive. If he had wanted to expose corruption, there was a choice of at least three Governors of Madras. If he had wanted to arraign a foreigner for excluding natives from the government of their own country, he should have harangued Cornwallis for days on end.

Burke failed to secure a conviction, but subsequent generations have remembered him more kindly as the defender of ancestral institutions, and as a pioneer of the idea of the 'nation' as a framework for political rights, mediating between the individual and the state. A leading work on him written in 1929 does not even mention India in the index, though it does acknowledge that he played a role in developing 'colonial policy'.[6] His contemporaries, including Richard Wellesley, Thomas Munro and John Malcolm, admired him for all this and more. The list of later liberal devotees stretches right across the nineteenth century, from Thomas Macaulay to John Morley.

Burke belongs very clearly to an era when the priority was still the Whiggish objective of protecting India and Britain from each other, not the liberal intention of saving Indians from themselves. But the direction that Burke laid down for British rule in India proved surprisingly prescient. Not a modernist himself, or a conscious designer of systems, he envisaged maintaining Indian practices at local level. This 'Indian idiom' was exactly the way ahead discovered by men in the field after the second wave of conquests, between 1792 and 1818.

What he set out was less than an ideology, but its very looseness allowed for the relationship with India to feel comfortable at its British end. His insistence on morality seemed right to men of the executive class in Britain. It flattered them that they were doing no harm, and their adoption of high-flown moral norms meant that the failures of empire that followed were always of practice, not of principle.

British power in India was still unsure of itself in 1795, and Burke's arguments were far more general than should ever have been considered in any trial of criminality. And in reality, the intellectual positions of Burke and Hastings on India were not so different; it was the British political context that set the two men against each other. The key points of contention between them were perhaps more institutional than moral or political. Both men were concerned to preserve and protect the rights of Indians, but Hastings wanted Company men to have a free hand in India, while Burke thought that politicians should exert close control from London.

Hastings was certainly more interested than Burke in the specifics of Indian culture. This genuinely Indophile approach launched a sturdy tradition of British research into Indian languages, antiquities, religion and philosophy. Sir William Jones, who was heavily influenced by Hastings in person, was only the first in a long line of scholars, including Henry Colebrooke, James Tod, H.H. Wilson, William Hunter, Alfred Lyall, and Monier Monier-Williams, who put their minds to understanding India's past.

The name of Sir William Jones (1746–94) has become synonymous with the foundation of systematic Western studies of Oriental languages, and he remains one of the most interesting and sympathetic characters to emerge from the rough and tumble of the early British period in India.

His start in life bequeathed him brains but not wealth or status. He was born in London in 1746 to a Welsh father, a brilliant mathematician who died when William was only three. The quest for 'independence', in both thought and financial status, went on to determine much of the rest of his life.

His natural abilities earned him a scholarship to Harrow School, where he proved to be a linguistic prodigy, then carried him on to Oxford. By early adulthood he had mastered not only Latin, Greek and Hebrew, which formed a fairly normal classical education for the time, but also Arabic and Persian, which marked him out as unconventional. He moved easily into original scholarly work, translating Persian and Turkish classical texts, and writing a grammar of Persian in 1771, principally for the use of the EIC. Gifted though he was, he could not support himself as a specialist in such an obscure field without resort to aristocratic patronage, and his desire for independence led him to read for the Bar. He was admitted in 1774.

Legal practice took him to his ancestral homeland of Wales, where he appeared as an advocate on circuit throughout the late 1770s, frequently defending poor Welsh farmers against English landlords. During this period he developed a deep radicalism, which sustained him intellectually but also threatened him with a lifetime of exclusion from preferment. He sympathized with the cause of the American colonists and became politically close not only to mainstream Whigs like Edmund Burke, but also to more radical elements like John Wilkes. This counted against him when he first applied for a judgeship in Bengal in 1778—which he was refused—and also when he stood, unsuccessfully, in a parliamentary election for Oxford University in 1780.

Jones did valuable work with parliamentary committees on Indian affairs through the early 1780s, and worked closely with Edmund Burke on legal policy. Eventually, in March 1783, through the good offices of the prime minister, Lord Shelburne, Jones was appointed a judge of the Supreme Court in Calcutta.

He arrived in India that September to enjoy his salary of £6,000, a very large sum that had been instrumental in attracting him to the position. Here at last was a man in Calcutta who was sensitive to abuses of power, had a solid grasp of common law, and could understand Persian, the language of official business in Bengal at the time. Here also was a nominal ally of Burke arriving to work with the tyrant Warren Hastings.

Any potential tension was immediately dispelled by Jones's complete adoption of Hastings's attitude to government in India. Jones abandoned Whiggish distrust of executive authority, and accepted that, although unrestrained or unaccountable power was in theory a bad thing, nevertheless for British rule to survive in India—which was assumed to be beneficial to all parties—the ground rules of domestic Whiggism could be modified.

Jones became convinced that few Indians had any understanding of civil liberty, 'and those, who have, do not wish it'.[7] Governmental authority was not something that needed to be defended against in India, as long as the intentions of the rulers were benign. Introducing Indians to notions of British-style political liberty was to be avoided as inappropriate, potentially troublesome, and possibly even cruel. Jones effectively became Hastings's man, and this brought about a permanent breach with Burke, whose 'aristocratical' principles had already begun to repel him.

Jones began to make diligent inquiries into the traditional laws of India, as part of Hastings's research. He recognized that accurate translations were vital, and that, in order to escape the control of interested local parties, the British must learn Indian languages thoroughly for themselves. In 1785 he launched himself fully into the learning of Sanskrit, under the tutelage of a pandit named Ramalocana.

He also recognized within a few months that Sanskrit was not only a very ancient language, but that it bore unmistakeable kinship with the revered classical languages of the West, such as Greek and Latin, and that it probably had close affinities with Gothic and Celtic tongues, even Old Persian, a fact that had been only partially grasped by Nathaniel Halhed during his work on *The Code of Gentoo Laws* (1776). Jones then famously announced to the Asiatick Society in 1786 that Sanskrit was 'more perfect than the Greek, more copious than the Latin, and more exquisitely refined than either'.[8] This was, indeed, going native.

Jones also realized that familial resemblances between languages potentially implied that Greek philosophy and religion may have shared roots with Vedic teachings. He was imaginative and open-minded, but hardly infallible. His conviction that Devanagari script was the ancestor of all western Asian alphabets was mistaken. His work on ancient chronology was dominated by his insistence that all the world's peoples were descended from the three sons of Noah, which produced a stack of garbled notions that did little to illuminate history, though it helped support the idea of linguistic families. His attempts to unify the pantheons of India and ancient Greece have since been used to support fantastical theories about the development of world culture, but ultimately his attempts to reconcile Hindu cosmology and Christian theology led nowhere. For all his unprejudiced rationality, he could not bring himself to abandon his belief in the truth of the first eleven chapters of the Bible.

Jones was a founder member of the Asiatick Society of Bengal, which turned out learned papers on all aspects of Indian languages, culture and natural history. In 1789 he translated the Sanskrit play *Sacontalá*, by Kalidas, which caused a sensation in Europe and directly influenced Goethe's ideas about drama. Jones also threw himself into a project to compile a definitive edition of the Laws of Manu, or Menu as he unfortunately preferred to spell it, meaning that statues of Jones brandishing the book give the impression that he is in a restaurant. This was a massive undertaking that ran to nine volumes, and was only completed after his death. The man who finished the work, Henry Colebrooke (1765–1837), became the first of a long line of successors to Jones, who began to rediscover, edit and translate the enormous body of India's ancient literature that has come down to us today.

William Jones stood at a pivotal point in the cultural, political and administrative history of British India. It was largely thanks to him that indigenous Indian culture was studied on a permanent basis, for Warren Hastings's immediate successors expressed little interest in any element of Indian culture that stood outside direct utility. The virtues of his academic approach were instrumental in laying the early foundations for comparative studies in philology and religion. Jones is sometimes also credited with helping to lay the groundwork for the Romantic movement, with its interest in antiquity, national cultures, and personal sentiment.

But his legacy can be seen as very mixed. He was among the first Britons to be comfortable with authoritarian government aboard while advocating radical solutions at home. He wanted Indians to be ruled by their own laws, truly discovered and understood, but his thoroughness in the task helped to cut off indigenous legal development. The assumption was that India was somehow essentially ancient, and that Indian society had lost its dynamism; legal development, though real in Europe, could not be allowed in India. Hence the laws that he, Halhed and others were discovering became fixed for all time. While attempting to provide sympathetic governance, the scholars were also stealing India's future.

Jones died of a sudden liver complaint in 1794, when he was still only 47, worn out by hard work and the rigours of the unhealthy climate of Calcutta.

1793–1805: The Empire Comes Alive

As Cornwallis returned to London in 1793, his contemporaries believed that he had injected the right kind of Englishness into the Company's affairs. But the next phase of the Company's development showed that much of what he had put in place was too inflexible and ill-adapted to the Indian context. Men on the ground were soon to undermine his work, especially in the areas of Whiggish administrative practice and social engineering.

1793 also saw the passing of the first of four Charter Acts, which appeared at twenty-year intervals to revise the EIC's rights. The 1793 Act was the least momentous of the four. Principally it extended the Company's monopoly for another twenty years, while the free trade lobby was appeased by the requirement to reserve a small tonnage within the Company's ships for non-Company merchants. The powers of the Governor-General over his Council were increased, and the salaries of members of the Indian Board of Control were henceforth to be paid from Company funds, not the British exchequer. Most importantly, from a London viewpoint, was the fixing of the Company's dividend at 10.5 per cent, payable from the China trade, not government revenues in India.

By the time Warren Hastings was acquitted, the Company's commercial position had enormously improved. The Tea Act of 1773 never achieved its intended goals, but better luck attended the Commutation Act of 1784, which slashed the duty on tea sold in England to a tenth of the previous level. The resulting drop in price had a spectacular effect on sales, which tripled within a year, and continued to grow steadily. Smuggling was ended at a stroke. Duties rose again later, but in the short term the Company enjoyed a greatly enhanced income, as did the government, through customs duties.

The import of tea was part of a lucrative triangular trade in which the sale of Indian opium to China paid for the purchase of tea to be sold in Europe. In 1804 the China trade finally tipped over into India's favour, helped by the export of raw cotton from the west coast, and it remained highly profitable until the Company was deprived of its trading role in 1833; over the period 1793–1810 the Company made a profit of £17 million in China alone. The other success story of these years was the rise of the indigo trade, which grew rapidly after 1780. By 1800 Britain was the world's leading supplier.

But despite some patchy commercial success, overall the EIC continued to struggle financially. One issue was the insistence of the government that trade with India should not be neglected for the more lucrative China market. Imports of foreign cloth were certainly restricted, but the EIC always did a thriving trade in re-export to Europe. Henry Dundas, president of the Board of Indian Control from 1793 to 1801, publicly implored the directors of the East India Company to expand the import of Indian textiles, expressly in order to maintain Indian artisans in work.[9] It was never in British interests to destroy the textile industry in India, especially not when they were still buyers.

But with the land revenue fixed by Cornwallis, and trade hit by war in Europe, the Company struggled as military costs continued to rise inexorably. Its armed forces stood at about 70,000 in 1790, swelling to 100,000 by 1795, then to 200,000 by 1813. So, although from 1792 to 1811 British exports to India tripled in volume, over the same period the EIC ran up a deficit of £8 million. This was almost entirely due to the wars of Governor-General Richard Wellesley (1798–1805), which doubled the Company's territory but trebled its debt.

Warren Hastings managed to hold onto what he had—just—and Cornwallis fought one successful war that extended the Madras Presidency. Richard Wellesley's enterprise, however, was on an altogether different scale. He arrived with a definite ambition to secure Britain's presence in India, by diplomacy or force, and it was under his leadership that British expansion took on a momentum of its own.

In 1784, the Company's territory bordered three main powers in the south: Mysore, directly next to Madras (hostile), Hyderabad to its north (friendly under Nizam Ali), and the Marathas in a broad area from Gujarat in the west to Orissa in the east (unpredictable and divided). Although Bombay was to have a great future, its trade was still small by comparison with the other Presidencies, and expansion in that area was not a prime objective of British policy. The focus of attention was on supporting friendly buffer states around Bengal and maintaining alliances to protect Madras.

The two treaties negotiated in 1782–4 did not resolve any of the significant issues between the major southern powers, and peace was short-lived. By 1787 Tipu was at war with the Marathas, then in 1790 the Third Anglo-Mysore War began after Tipu attacked the state of Travancore, a British ally. It took two years for Cornwallis to defeat Tipu, after which he imposed harsh terms; portions of Mysore were divided up between the British, the Marathas, and the Nizam. Minor southern states, including Cochin and Tanjore, were suddenly keen to agree 'subsidiary alliances' with the EIC, under which they promised to maintain a force of Company troops for their own 'protection', and to conduct all their foreign relations through a British intermediary, or Resident.

War between the Nizam and the Marathas followed in 1795, with the Nizam suffering a significant defeat at the battle of Kardla (Kharda). This should have left the Marathas as the single most powerful force in the Deccan, but their leadership was then depleted by a series of deaths in the mid-1790s. Madhav Rao, the childless puppet Peshwa, committed suicide in 1795 and was succeeded by Baji Rao II (1775–1851). This coincided with deaths in the other main Maratha families: of Mahadji Sindhia (1794), Ahalyabai Holkar (1795) and Tukoji Holkar (1797). A vacancy even arose behind the peshwa's throne when the great Maratha politician and diplomat Nana Phadnavis (1742–1800) died, after being thrown into prison by Sindhia's adopted heir, Daulat Rao Sindhia, who at the time was also literally at war with his predecessor's three widows.

A new generation of inexperienced Indian leaders were thus in place just as an invigorated period of British expansionism was about to confront them. Richard Wellesley extracted a high price for their unpreparedness and disunity.

Richard, Lord Mornington, Marquess Wellesley (1760–1840), was unlike his predecessors in his background, attitudes and conduct, and his arrival as Governor-General in 1798 marked a new departure for British India.

Wellesley was not a Company man like Warren Hastings or his immediate predecessor, the saintly Sir John Shore (1793–8), who had taken not an inch of land from anyone. He was, instead, a Westminster politician and a close ally of Prime Minister Pitt. An MP since 1784, Wellesley had served at the Treasury, then from 1793 on the Indian Board of Control, where he worked harmoniously with its president, Henry Dundas. This meant that it was only in 1798 that British India finally fell into the hands of an experienced government insider.

Wellesley was also a man with a larger vision. Among Governors-General it was he who first began to use the word 'empire' in its modern sense, as opposed to the eighteenth century's looser usage, synonymous with 'dominion'. He was unencumbered by sensitivities to Indian traditions, and took little care to balance the accounts. He was also a believer in free trade, which put him in an embarrassing position regarding the Company's jealously guarded monopoly, which he was being paid to uphold. Above all, he came to India with concerns far wider than mercantile issues, knowing that Henry Dundas would fully support him in an expansionist policy and a determination to defeat Revolutionary France in all theatres of war.

As Governor-General he constituted something like an internal opposition to the EIC's traditional aims and policies, but his allegiance to Britain's national interests was never in doubt. In 1800 he wrote to the directors:

'We feel that it would not only be impolitic, but highly immoral to suppose that Providence has admitted of the establishment of the British power over the finest province of India, with any other view than that of its being conducive to the happiness of the people, as well as to our national advantage.' Bearing this dual divine–national mission in mind, 'increasing stability' was the sure outcome of carrying out these 'beneficent intentions'.[10] The core values and justifications of the imperial project are all here. Wellesley's distinct contribution was to add active expansionism to the mix and abandon financial restraint.

He went out to India with the title of Lord Mornington in the Irish peerage, a status he found barely sufficient. He was an egotistical and highly ambitious man, but despite his pomposity his subordinates generally adored him and referred to him as 'the glorious little man'. He conceived of his role as Governor-General in almost theatrical terms, and introduced a much more ostentatious and considerably more costly style of government than his predecessors. It was Wellesley who commissioned the building of the grand Government House in Calcutta.

Undaunted by expense, he founded Fort William College for the better education of the Company's recruits. Where Cornwallis had tried to control the Company's servants with rules and committees, Wellesley attempted to do it with education. He drove his plans for the new college through in the face of fierce opposition from the directors, who had their revenge when, after his departure, the whole project was scaled down in scope and ambition. However, the directors did take up his concern for the better education of Company men, and in 1806 they founded a specialist school in England, permanently established at Haileybury two years later.

It was never details that concerned Wellesley; he was always a man for grander schemes. From the first he set out to tame the five main powers—the Marathas, Mysore, Awadh, Arcot and Hyderabad—that threatened the British in India, either by overt hostility or internal instability. All received different treatment at his hands. Bellicose or diplomatic, Wellesley understood these manoeuvres to be an extension of the war in Europe against the French, a view forced upon him by the prominent presence of French commanders in the armies of Indian princes.

The fear of French influence had never left British minds, even after the French were decisively beaten in India between 1757 and 1761. There was a rumour in 1770 that the French were about to attack Bengal by sea, and the presence of talented French soldiers like de Boigne, Raymond and

Perron in the armies of the southern powers acted as a constant reminder that there was still an armed French presence in the subcontinent. The outbreak of war with Revolutionary France in 1793 had triggered the precautionary occupation of all French settlements in India, so if French influence were now to be found, it would be at native courts.

This vigilance was intensified following Napoleon's invasion of Egypt in July 1798, a move Wellesley considered as a direct threat to British interests in India, which is how Napoleon saw it too. The appearance of a small contingent of ill-trained French soldiers in Mysore not long afterwards was therefore taken as a sufficient pretext for war.

Wellesley was all too willing to take on Tipu Sultan. Tipu, like his father Haidar Ali, had been a long-term opponent of the British, and held a deep mistrust of their intentions. Quite rightly, as it turned out. But Tipu had a fatal flaw—impetuosity. He inherited a throne, military skill and great bravery from his father, but not patience. Haidar Ali had put in long years of service through the 1750s in the ranks of Mysore's army before staging the coup that brought him to power in 1761. Then, as ruler of Mysore, he repeatedly fought himself into winning positions in the first two Anglo-Mysore Wars. Tipu, by contrast, constantly found himself in situations where his deliverance lay only in the disunity of his enemies. His rashness was to prove his undoing, when confronted with the grim determination of Wellesley.

With Napoleon in Egypt, Wellesley viewed contacts between Tipu Sultan and the French governor on the Île de Bourbon (Réunion) as a provocation, and he attacked Mysore with deadly intent in the spring of 1799.

It was in some ways the weakness of Hyderabad that gave Wellesley the opportunity to overwhelm Tipu. Considering its size, the state of Hyderabad never exercised anything like the military muscle that might have been expected of it. The founder of the state, the great Mughal courtier and viceroy Asaf Jah, Nizam-ul-Mulk (1671–1748), was not succeeded by men of similar calibre, and by the late 1790s the state, under Nizam Ali, lacked force or direction.

In June 1798 Wellesley pressured the Nizam, who had recently survived a coup led by his son, into dismissing all his French troops and signing a treaty of subsidiary alliance. Then, when Tipu refused to sign a similar treaty the next year, Wellesley, with Nizam Ali as a junior partner, was ideally set up to attack Mysore. Driven back into his fortress at Srirangapatna, the Tiger of Mysore died a soldier's death on the battlements, cut to pieces in the final assault, sword in hand.

Letters subsequently discovered gave Wellesley the excuse to depose the Nawab of Arcot for treasonous correspondence with Tipu. This accusation was never fully made out, but Wellesley would not be thwarted, for there were two extra imperatives for the extinction of Arcot as a power. One was that it avoided the succession of the aged nawab's notoriously Anglophobic son. The other was that it offered a perfect opportunity to end the long-running scandal of the Nawab of Arcot's debts—a saga of mismanagement and corruption dating back to the 1740s, which had become so complicated and contentious that it had even become an irritant in British domestic politics.

With the south thus secured, in 1801 disorder in Awadh was used as a pretext to replace its ruler and to annex the southern, most prosperous part of his territory as payment for the maintenance of an increased British force in Lucknow.

Wellesley then moved on into the Second Maratha War, a neat label that covers a series of disparate events between 1803 and 1805, including two decisive campaigns and one prolonged stalemate, which between them ended in three separate treaties.

Maratha power had long posed a threat to both Madras and Bombay, so the five-headed Maratha Confederacy was sure to feel the power of Wellesley's hostility at some point. A chance presented itself when armed struggle broke out between Sindhia and Holkar in 1801, over control of the Peshwa, Baji Rao II. The eventual victory of Holkar so unsettled the peshwa that he fled to nearby British protection.

Wellesley used this circumstance to impose terms on his guest in a treaty signed at Bassein in late 1802. Its terms required the peshwa to submit to the presence of a Resident in Poona, and the payment of subsidies for British protection. Taking the peshwa's historical claims to leadership of the Maratha Confederacy at face value, Wellesley then demanded that Sindhia, Holkar and the Bhonsle of Nagpur should each agree similar terms. All three prevaricated, and open war followed.

The first phase of the conflict featured campaigns north and south. Northern operations were conducted by General Gerard Lake, who won a series of victories over Sindhia's forces at Aligarh, Delhi and—in a final, bloody showdown—at Laswari. General Arthur Wellesley's campaign in the south led to the decisive defeat of Sindhia and Bhonsle forces at Assaye and Argaum, and the capture of the Bhonsle fortress of Gawilgarh, after which Wellesley dictated his terms. In December 1803, the punitive treaties of Surji-Arjungaon and Deogaum were signed with Sindhia and Bhonsle respectively.

Jaswant Holkar managed to keep out of the first campaign. When finally confronted in 1804, he displayed skilful generalship in avoiding pitched battles, but he was gradually forced northwards, away from British territory, and the fire went out of the conflict.

This loss of momentum gave the directors an opportunity to rid themselves of the bellicose Wellesley. He had funded his wars with several million pounds intended for debt reduction, and the directors now openly charged him with a list of misdemeanours, including disobedience, making illegal appointments of his brothers, Arthur and Henry, and of 'profuse expenditure of public money'. Henry Dundas was no longer in a position to protect him, having stepped down as president of the Board of Control in 1801, and its new president, Lord Castlereagh, would not back him up. Wellesley was forced to concede defeat. He resigned and went home in July 1805.

Jaswant Holkar then took his own opportunity, and negotiated peace on lenient terms with Acting Governor-General Sir George Barlow.

The confidence and reputation that grew out of Wellesley's aggressive campaigns set up the British for the remainder of their stay in India. No native power was capable at the time of fielding such heavy infantry formations and disciplined artillery, although the Sikhs came close forty years later. It was also Wellesley who perfected the subsidiary alliance system, by which local powers were obliged to pay for the upkeep of British soldiers. The financial desperation to which this reduced many of them was a major cause of the collapse of princely regimes between 1799 and 1856.

Governor-General Wellesley gave Sunday as a day of rest to India, and educated an elite of young gentlemen officers, but it was the military juggernaut created by the efforts of his younger brother Arthur that truly secured the future of British rule in India.

Arthur Wellesley (1769–1852) spent eight years in India, from February 1797 to March 1805. It was during this tour of duty that he established his reputation as a master of logistics and a winner of battles. He did not personally create British India, but in the same way that it is difficult to conceive of a British Bengal without Clive, it is also hard to imagine a British India without Arthur Wellesley. It was he that pursued and defeated two of the best Maratha armies of their day in the campaign of 1803, with a rare blend of nerve and thoroughness, victories that opened the way for British domination of the whole of south and central India.

He came from Anglo-Irish aristocratic roots, and through his early life he remained rather in the shade of his older brother Richard. He showed no promise as a soldier, or indeed as anything at all, until sent to a military college in France, aged sixteen, after which he became a more serious character and began to develop the earnestness and intensity that marked out his career in public life.

Before India, his only active military service was in the abortive Dutch campaign of 1794–5 against the French, a miserable few months that he claimed later had only taught him what not to do. He was then sent to India with the 39th Regiment of Foot. On the voyage out he read a book that contained the disparaging remark that generals who had only commanded in India would come back to Europe like admirals who had only ever sailed on Lake Geneva. He was to prove this received wisdom quite wrong, for after his return to Europe he used his experience to win a long series of victories against the French, across Portugal, Spain and into France itself, a run that ended with the decisive defeat of the Emperor Napoleon at Waterloo in 1815.

The foundations of those epic victories were laid in India, principally in two major campaigns—against Mysore in 1799, and against the Maratha houses of Sindhia and Bhonsle in 1803. In the former, Wellesley played a subordinate role, but in the latter, he was responsible for planning and leading the entire undertaking, scoring victories in open battle, at Assaye and Argaum, and in sieges, at Ahmednagar and Gawilgarh. In seven years he rose from colonel to major general and developed into a superb soldier, combining the attention to detail of a quartermaster with the imagination of an inveterate worrier, mixing both of these with a strategic vision to match even that of the great Napoleon.

His sustained military success was not a matter of luck. It might be contended that he won so repeatedly in India because he had a better army than his opponents, but he had a better army because he took great pains to ensure that it was better trained, equipped and supplied. And it was not only better by design, it was also better led. Leadership was a massively important factor; European-led troops did not automatically outfight Indian troops. Lake and Monson's ineffective campaigns against Holkar in 1804–5 illustrate this, as does Baillie's defeat by Haidar Ali at Polilur in 1780.

India taught the young Arthur Wellesley a great deal. On the night that the British first reached Tipu's stronghold of Srirangapatna in April 1799, he lost several men in a running maul, fought in total darkness. This encounter has been over-promoted into the only 'defeat' he ever suffered. His second-in-command that night, a man named Elers, later published a highly critical book about the incident, including the observation that, had

Colonel Wellesley been a less well-connected man, he would have faced a court martial for his failure. Perhaps it is nearer the truth to say that if Wellesley had been a lesser man, then nobody would ever have heard anything about the engagement, and somebody else would have taken command of the next assault. In fact Wellesley was big enough to insist on leading the attack the next day, and carried the objective in quick time, without casualties.

This skirmish at Sultanpetah Tope did, though, teach Wellesley some very specific and valuable lessons. Firstly, he learned never to attack an enemy whose positions he had not reconnoitred by daylight. This was a maxim he followed throughout the rest of his time in India, and beyond. The second lesson was that, paradoxically, it was imperative to stay behind troops to lead them effectively; if ahead of them one cannot see both them and the enemy.

This idea of vision was central to all of Wellesley's subsequent battlefield activities. He rode dozens of miles in a day in order to keep a close personal eye on the progress of his own men and the enemy. This was how he spotted the ford at Assaye that gave him the advantage he needed, and it was also how he noticed the ditches running across the field at Argaum, allowing him to warn of their potential dangers. His obsession with reconnaissance and intelligence dates from that night in the tope (copse). Metaphorically at least, he never fought in the dark again.

After the fall of Srirangapatnam, Wellesley was appointed Governor of the city and then of all Mysore. These positions, combined with his duties as colonel, enabled him to bring about some important changes in the British military establishment. The type of force that had marched south to attack Tipu, composed of the slow, heavy units hitherto favoured by the British, was now replaced by a lighter, faster army more able to take on the highly mobile Maratha cavalry. Wellesley intended to fight wars that combined rapid movement, secure supplies and accurate intelligence. When the time came to face the formidable Marathas, he and his army were ready, aided by the acquisition of a very large number of white Mysore bullocks inherited from Tipu.

He evolved a system of rapid marching, starting at daylight and proceeding at three miles per hour till noon, using the coolest part of the day. This is why his infantry had already covered twenty-four miles before engaging at Assaye and eighteen before Argaum. They were used to it. The fact that these men then went on to distinguish themselves on both occasions is a tribute to their fitness, the toughness of their boots and the regularity of their meals. It was on these simple pillars that Wellesley erected the legend of British audacity and endurance.

By the time of the Maratha campaign of 1803, Wellesley had reassessed the relationship between his infantry, cavalry and artillery. Artillery had traditionally been seen as a separate, specialized arm, technical and slow. Wellesley developed a system under which all infantry units took at least two six-pounder cannons with them, as an integral part of the unit. The French had theorized about this approach and it was not original to Wellesley, but he was the first to employ it in India, where it conferred a massive advantage over the Maratha forces, who used heavier ordnance, deployed separately. It became a feasible technique once he had rejected the use of horses to draw cannon, which he was happy to do when he found that Mysore bullocks could walk as far and as fast as his infantry. Any of Wellesley's units of foot were able to take a position at marching speed, then turn two cannons on opposing infantry or charging cavalry, and spray them with case shot before they ever reached musket range.

In pitched battles Wellesley deployed his men two deep, in the famous 'thin red line'. Again, this was not a new tactic, but it was supremely effective in Indian conditions against massed charges, because it meant that every man could fire on the enemy—a vital factor in India where opposing numbers were often very large. Wellesley therefore never deployed men in column, which would vastly reduce their ability to return fire. A sustained fusillade from trained men, at about four rounds a minute, had a highly demoralizing effect on opponents. The success of this fusillade produced an enormous preponderance in his battles of death by bullet over death by bayonet. Wellesley's forces did not have to close with their enemies to beat them.

His Indian campaigns also impressed upon him the need not only to be adequately supplied but for the local population to think well of him, his men and the country he served. He therefore insisted on paying local suppliers properly for their goods. In some ways he was lucky because throughout his Indian career the Company had the wherewithal to fund his purchases. But as a philosophy, it contrasted noticeably with much traditional practice in India.

Although he used a rather more defensive approach in his European campaigns, for Wellesley Indian warfare was all about forward momentum. To go out against the Marathas only to sit on a well-chosen downward slope would achieve nothing, apart perhaps from inviting death by thirst or starvation, as marauding bands of horsemen intercepted his supplies.

Nor would this have been the way to deliver the knockout blows that his brother Richard's strategy required. Arthur's genius was to build a fighting machine both light enough to catch its opponents and powerful enough then to unleash heavy firepower upon them.

He left India with an aura of success, which he carried forward into his campaigns in Spain. By 1815 he was recognized as the greatest British soldier of the age, equal perhaps even to the great Bonaparte.

As Duke of Wellington, he then went into politics as an anti-reform Tory. He served as prime minister twice, between January 1828 and November 1830, and as a stop-gap, one-man administration for just under a month in late 1834. He remained a background presence in Indian affairs until his death, largely because in status and knowledge he outranked nearly all the men who served on the Board of Control. He followed Indian affairs closely and always with a primary interest in defence. Other Tory-minded Indian hands, including John Malcolm and Lord Ellenborough, looked to him for guidance, and together they incubated a deep suspicion of Russian intentions. He was, however, generally sceptical about the merits of the Afghan campaign of 1839, fearing that it would lead to a perennial commitment in the country.

He also had an abiding fear of provoking rebellion, and spoke vigorously against interfering with or reforming Indian society in the debates on the Charter Act of 1833.

Robert Clive was an adventurer, keen to stuff his pockets and get back to England in order to build up his personal political influence. Warren Hastings acted, and even thought, like a traditional Indian ruler. Cornwallis was a soldier-Whig who faced up to the realities of a long-term British presence in India, and stopped accepting limitations that others thought inevitable under Indian conditions. Finally, it was Richard Wellesley who saw wider reasons for conquest: expanded trade, the prestige of empire, and global advantage over the French. The breadth of vision was increasing throughout.

Clive held back from taking on territorial responsibilities but had no hesitation about making money. Hastings had no problem with the idea of government but had a great deal of trouble with the details. Cornwallis tackled the problems of government robustly but did so in an entirely non-Indian way. Richard Wellesley took both government and expansion as manifest destinies and a beneficial thing for both Indians and Britons. The shift from serving Britain's national interests to serving India's, a reversal implied in the rationale of high imperialism, was nearly complete. The missing elements, modernity and moral legitimacy, were soon to arrive.

1805–13: Supremacy, Hiatus

Richard Wellesley left India under a cloud, to be replaced by the old warhorse Cornwallis, who had continued his distinguished imperial career with a stint in Ireland as Lord Lieutenant from 1798 to 1801, years in which he suppressed rebellion, fought off the French and helped drive through the Act of Union (1801). Now he returned to India with instructions not to provoke the native powers any further, and to dismantle the harshest parts of Wellesley's post-war settlement. He had hardly begun the task when he died. There is a monument to his memory at Ghazipur, near Benares.

He was succeeded by Lord Minto (1807–13), who presided over a period of consolidation. The directors opposed further expansion as expensive and provocative, but there was still a war to be fought with France and her allies. The destruction of the French naval base on the Île de Bourbon in 1810 and an expedition to capture Java from the Dutch in 1811 duly followed. Looking towards the Asian interior, Minto also developed concerns about Russian expansion into Persia. After a Franco-Russian alliance was set up by the Treaty of Tilsit in 1807, he dispatched missions to Persia, Kabul, Lahore and Sind to shore up British support in the region.

Instability in Afghanistan first became a direct concern at this time, as the sons of Timur Shah (d. 1793) continued to dispute the succession. No attempt was made, however, to confront Ranjit Singh in the Punjab. Instead, the Treaty of Amritsar of 1809 declared that the Sutlej river was the Company's border, an agreement that held for thirty-six years.

One major though largely symbolic development at this time was the final eclipse of the heirs of Timur, as with the capture of Delhi in 1803 the British wrested guardianship of the Mughal emperor from the Marathas. By then, Shah Alam, at seventy-five years old, was a destitute and pathetic figure, blinded by an Afghan warlord in 1788, and robbed by his servants ever since. He commanded no armies and held almost no land. But withal he was the heir of Akbar, and he still represented the most venerated source of honour and political authority in the subcontinent. Wellesley held back from officially deposing him because it seemed more prudent simply to leave the old man as he was, and indeed to spruce him up a bit.

Shah Alam died in 1806, and the British allowed his son, Akbar Shah, to succeed him, but they only ever referred to him as 'the king of Delhi'. Gradually the British went further than the Marathas had dared, and began to act as if they were legitimate inheritors of the old Mughal 'paramountcy'.

The scope of British control continued to widen, and there was pressing work to do in south India, where the successful campaigns of 1790–1805 had delivered enormous territories into the Company's hands. Long considered a junior and highly corrupt Presidency, Madras was now forced to come of age, having accumulated a portfolio of lands that stretched from coast to coast, including territory taken from Arcot, Tanjore, Hyderabad and Mysore. These lands all had to be 'settled', that is, revenue and judicial arrangements had to be made. This presented very different problems from those characteristic of Bengal. In south India, much of which had never been under Mughal rule, there was no semi-official class like zamindars, only local landholder-warlords, or poligars.

It was in this administrative vacuum that Alexander Read and Thomas Munro developed the ryotwari system of direct settlement with the cultivator. Despite its high initial costs—the setting up of accounts and the surveying of individual fields—ryotwari settlement promised to increase revenues by eliminating intermediaries. It also encouraged productivity, by ensuring that increases in profits remained with the cultivator. Rising prosperity and an end to lawlessness were deemed likely to secure the loyalty of the peasant cultivators to their new British masters.

These expectations were a good deal more realistic than Cornwallis's distant hopes of creating improving Whig landlords in Bengal. Indeed, the ryotwari system had such an appeal in London that it became established as standard Company policy in south India, and thus became the second British attempt to create a new socio-economic class in India.

The other important point about ryotwari was that it involved the concentration of legal and fiscal powers in one man, the district officer. Munro realized that it was not possible, or desirable, to separate powers of judicial decision from revenue collection; rural India was no place for Whig scruples. Charles Metcalfe was to have the same insight during his time as Resident in Delhi between 1811 and 1819, and this streamlining of government, later also favoured by Lord Dalhousie, played an important part in determining how British India was eventually to be run.

Over the period 1784–1805 the Company grew enormously in strength, while all the Indian powers declined. They proved unable to withstand the constant pressure from the Company's well-funded armies, and even the very obvious peril they faced failed to produce political cooperation between the leading Maratha dynasties in anything like sufficient degree. Economically, however, outside Bengal and the major presidency towns, India was still largely unaffected by the British presence. British manufactures were not yet sufficiently cheap or plentiful to affect domestic markets in India, though Indian textile exports to Asia had begun to decline under British competition.

Wellesley's expansionist policies were to have one final political effect—in England. It was mainly because of the massive expense of his wars that the Company entered an acute financial crisis in 1808—the government forwarded loans of £4 million to the Company—just as political pressure was building for extensive reforms to be included in the charter revision, due in 1813. It was the Company's financial weakness that eventually allowed the Act to be rather more radical than the Company would have liked.

5

1813–1839

ROMANTICS, LIBERALS, EDUCATION, REFORM

1813–28: Christians, Liberals, Romantics

As the Company's domains expanded and its responsibilities diversified, a series of new questions had to be faced. What type of government should be set up in the new territories? What kind of political institutions would fit most suitably with Indian social structures? And what of the 'pacified' Indians? Should they be educated, or even converted to more acceptable forms of religion? Was the EIC really a fit organ of government? Should its monopoly be maintained? Distinct approaches to these questions emerged, each with its partisan advocates.

A loose free trade pressure group had been operating in British politics for some time and had tried, unsuccessfully, to have the Company's monopoly withdrawn in 1793. With renewal of the charter due in 1813, this alliance of manufacturers and exporters reinvigorated its efforts. But the first truly organized lobbying about India came from a religious direction. Evangelical Christianity had swept through sections of the educated middle classes in the last years of the eighteenth century, and had produced new sensitivities on a range of moral issues, such as slavery. The resulting clamour for missionary outreach in India became a serious political force in the run-up to the 1813 charter debates. Particularly influential was a pamphlet entitled *Observations on the State of Society among the Asiatic Subjects of Great Britain*. Originally written in the early 1790s by Charles Grant, it was now reissued as newly relevant.

Grant had become a committed Christian during his time as a Company servant in India from 1778 to 1790. On his return he rose to be a prominent and active director. His *Observations* detailed the most lurid aspects of Indian religion and advocated the conversion of the subcontinent, in order to enlighten and civilize its inhabitants, whom he considered to be lost in a trackless wilderness of spiritual darkness.

Grant's attitudes were not typical within the Court of Directors, and they were, frankly, rather confused. He advocated active conversion work in India but was strongly opposed to expansion of the Company's territory. He wanted increased trade with India but was also keen to maintain the Company's monopoly—not on economic grounds, but because he believed that free trade would unleash a wave of European colonization, which would undermine the Company's authority. How Indians could be left alone but also converted, and persuaded to buy more British goods while being protected from contact with Europeans, was never explained. Grant's views also set him against the powerful commercial lobby, which was bent on abolishing the EIC's trading privileges and was all in favour of further intrusion into India to open up markets.

Nor did all Christians share Grant's opinions. Dr Thomas Malthus, the famous economist-divine, who was a tutor at the Company's college from 1815, opposed Grant over expansion, about which he was more bullish, and over conversion, about which he was more cautious. He wished, like Grant, to see some effort put into formal education for Indians in British-backed institutions, but for different reasons. He wanted to instil a version of Western 'civic virtue' in selected members of the Indian population, to encourage moral and economic improvement, whereas Grant was only interested in stimulating and facilitating reading of the Bible.

In the end, both Evangelicals and free traders got some of what they wanted from the Charter Act of 1813, and the EIC was the clear overall loser. The religious lobby secured the right to send missionaries to India, against the Company's long-term opposition, and an Anglican bishopric was set up in Calcutta. The Company also lost its Indian monopoly, though it was allowed to retain its exclusive trade with China, which was chiefly in tea and cotton, and was the most profitable part of its business. One minor provision of the 1813 Act was the setting aside of a small sum—Rs 1 lakh per annum (£10,000)—for educational purposes, defined, somewhat vaguely, as for 'the revival and improvement of literature' and 'the introduction and promotion of knowledge of the sciences'. The precise meaning of this clause was only determined twenty-two years later.

Lord Moira (later Marquess of Hastings) succeeded Minto as Governor-General (1813–23). A career soldier, he was markedly more aggressive than his predecessor, and continued the job that Wellesley had started. While still a young man attempting to make his way in London politics, Moira had opposed Cornwallis's war with Mysore, but once in Calcutta he was more than ready to fight. Incursions from Nepal led to full-scale hostilities in 1814, and over the next two years the British gradually wore down the Nepalese in a series of difficult campaigns. The Treaty of Sugauli (1816) then brought a degree of stability to the Company's northern frontier.

Next, the ragged borders left by the Second Maratha War were tidied up, when in 1817 a series of military actions against freebooting ex-soldiers (pindaris) escalated into a successful campaign against the forces of the Peshwa, Baji Rao II. Victory in this Third Maratha War placed the Company in such a position of dominance that all the major central Indian states still outside the subsidiary alliance system then entered it between 1818 and 1821. The enormous area of Rajputana thus came into the Company's orbit, leaving only the Punjab and Sind outside it.

The final defeat of the Marathas ushered in an era of relative military security for the Company. This was the period in which British rule could most easily be represented (and accepted by many Indians) as a blessing. The end of local wars, of pindari raiding, of random and excessive land revenue demands, the establishment of relatively disinterested government—all these boons could be seen as real improvements in the living conditions of millions. This was counterbalanced by the fact that revenue assessments in the newly acquired British territories were often very high, and their punctilious enforcement tended to have a depressive effect on the entire rural economy. Increases in agricultural production to meet high assessments lowered prices, and there was a persistent long-term trend in the Madras Presidency for spare land to go unused. Many of the new assessments were revised downwards later, but regular collection enabled the British, in virtually all cases, to realize more revenue than their predecessors. A fluid society tainted by many incidental injustices was gradually replaced by a more rigid structure, with entrenched inequalities.

The wars of 1817–18 also marked the final emergence of the Bombay Presidency as a territorial entity. The conflicts of 1799–1805 had not added greatly to the area ruled directly from Bombay, partly because of the theatres of conflict involved, but also because Jonathan Duncan, Governor from 1795 to 1811, preferred to sign peace treaties with native states, no matter how small. The Company thus accumulated literally hundreds of small independent allies in the Kathiawar region. It was only after 1818 that large tracts of land came directly under Bombay's control, principally in areas ceded by the Peshwa.

Moira was succeeded by Lord Amherst (1824–8). Neither can be classified as a great thinker. The main difference between them was that Moira, a soldier, won his wars relatively easily, whereas Amherst, a callow diplomat, struggled to win a two-year war against the Burmese (1824–6). This First Burma War was eventually concluded successfully, after much expense, with the addition of territories from Assam down to Tenasserim. Amherst also intervened in a succession dispute in Bharatpur in 1824–6, removing the usurper, Durjan Sal, by force. This was the last native power of consequence in the immediate vicinity of Delhi, and its humbling left the British unchallenged in north central India. The next round of major wars did not start until the late 1830s. By then not only the map of India, but also the leadership of the Company's armies, looked rather different.

The last of the swashbucklers, the real soldiers of fortune who were attracted to India by the possibilities of the 'Wild East', was the victor of the Nepal War of 1814–16, Sir David Ochterlony (1758–1825). He was born in Boston, Massachusetts, his mother's native city, and lived there for his first twelve years. His father, a Scottish sailor, died when David was seven, and the family eventually moved to England. His English stepfather then managed to get him accepted as a cadet in the East India Company's Bengal army in 1777. He was one of the men who marched from Bengal to Madras in 1781 to help the Company's hard-pressed forces against Haidar Ali. There he was wounded and captured while fighting the French at Cuddalore, and was later released by Tipu under the terms of the Treaty of Mangalore (1784).

He fought with distinction in General Lake's northern campaign of 1803–4, through sieges and battles, including a heroic defence of newly captured Delhi against a Maratha counter-attack in 1804. In 1803 he was made British Resident in Delhi, becoming the keeper of the aged Mughal emperor Shah Alam, with whom he struck up a courteous and respectful relationship. After a stint in command of the fort at Allahabad, he was sent to the border of the Punjab in 1809 with a large force, in order to support the diplomatic mission of Charles Metcalfe to Ranjit Singh at Lahore. After the signing of the Treaty of Amritsar later that year, he remained in post at Ludhiana, just south of the Sutlej river, partly to collect intelligence from the north-west theatre and partly to serve as a deterrent to the ambitions of the Nepalese kaji, Amar Singh Thapa, who was threatening to expand his influence into the area. The borders between the Cis-Sutlej states under British protection and Nepalese territory to the north were not agreed, and after an incident at Butwal in 1814, open warfare began.

Ochterlony took command of one of four columns sent into Nepal, and enjoyed the most success. Although his troops, who were mainly Bengali, were not well adapted to mountain campaigning, he managed to contrive ways of using heavy guns against hill forts, thus avoiding the skirmishing at which the Nepalese were particularly adept. With the capture of Malaun, defended by Amar Singh Thapa himself, hostilities came to an end. But formal negotiations in December 1815 did not go well, with the Nepalese unwilling to reach terms. A second campaign followed, in which Ochterlony again distinguished himself, including a decisive victory at Sikhar Khati in February 1816. This led, in March, to the Treaty of Sugauli, which settled the border issues, ceded lands to the Company that included Simla, and allowed for the extensive recruitment of Nepalese soldiers (Gurkhas) into the Company's armies.

Ochterlony was also heavily involved in the Pindari–Maratha wars of 1817–18, in which he commanded a force protecting Delhi. After the war, he was appointed British Commissioner to the Rajput states, a post soon amalgamated with that of Resident at Delhi, making him responsible for relations with rulers over a very large area still outside direct British rule. He stayed in this demanding position for seven years. But his health began to deteriorate, and misfortune and loneliness marked his final years.

Though never officially married, he was known to have had at least six children by Indian mothers. His only son died in 1822, and his one grandson, named Charles Metcalfe Ochterlony after his great friend, sailed to England in the same year, aged just four. His stepfather also died in 1823, which deprived him of all his close family. Finally, he fell out with the new Governor-General, Lord Amherst, over the future of the Jat state of Bharatpur. Ochterlony was in favour of ousting Durjan Sal by storming his enormous fortress, a task that had proved beyond General Lake in 1805. Amherst was nervous of trying again, whereas Ochterlony was convinced, along with most of the Company's military men, that prompt and decisive action was the correct policy in such matters. He resigned, and died shortly afterwards, in July 1825, only to be vindicated when Bharatpur was taken in January 1826 by troops he had recruited and trained.

Ochterlony was one of the men who built the British Empire without ever having much imperialist feeling himself. He was well liked by his contemporaries, and a large monument, paid for by public subscription, was erected to his memory on the maidan in Calcutta in 1828. It has since been renamed the Shahid Minar (Martyrs' Memorial).

His passing marked the end of the era in which British statesmen and soldiers took Indian wives and adopted local dress. From then on, senior soldiers typically were Evangelical Christians rather than relaxed fortune hunters. Ochterlony is sometimes remembered for the apocryphal story that he used to take the air of an evening in Delhi accompanied by thirteen wives on thirteen elephants. Such a story could never have been believed about any of his successors.

All this fighting indicates that the 'Pax Britannica', conventionally considered to have begun in 1818, was an imperial misnomer—one among many. The EIC remained heavily militarized, and local rebellions continued within British India for decades, especially where tribal or nomadic peoples, such as Bhils, Mers, Khasis, Ramosis and Kols, encountered the tidy mindset of the British regime. Nor were all states peaceful within themselves. Disorder persisted in Awadh, where a weakened king was unable to control his taluqdars, despite his self-promotion to Padshah in 1820.

The Pax Britannica within India effectively operated at a state or provincial level, and marked not the arrival of profound peace in the countryside, but the demilitarization, even the collapse, of Indian self-government.

Around this time, there were also several important developments in Britain. One was the publication of James Mill's *History of British India* (1817), which, with its depiction of the depravity and backwardness of Hindu society, served as a liberal manifesto for a reforming mission in India. Another was the appearance of David Ricardo's *Principles of Political Economy and Taxation* (1818), which profoundly influenced land revenue policy in India, especially after James Mill, a convert to Ricardo's rational economic theories, became a senior member of the Company's London administration in 1819. This represented a kind of low-profile liberal-progressive coup within the EIC, with Mill now installed as Examiner of Indian correspondence, and Malthus as Professor of Political Economy at Haileybury. Both were perfectly placed to guide the Company's policy and personnel along new lines.

Through the years 1792–1818 the Company had exhibited something like a 'conquest reflex'—triggered by a persistent belief that its future was best secured by aggressive military action or diplomatic bullying. This mindset, which continued until the borders seemed, if not entirely secure, then at least defensible, was very much a view from on high. Away from

Calcutta, the Company's problems looked rather different. New machinery for the purpose of colonial government had to be designed, installed and operated—both to keep order and to raise the money required to pay for and equip the very large military establishment necessary to maintain the whole edifice.

It was these closely related purposes that produced the great names of early Indian administration, principally Thomas Munro, John Malcolm and Mountstuart Elphinstone.

Munro, the senior man, began his administrative career in districts won from Mysore in 1792, while Elphinstone was tasked with settling the western lands conquered from the Marathas in 1817–18. Malcolm was directly involved in the diplomatic and administrative aftermath of both the Second and Third Maratha Wars, particularly in settling central India (Malwa). All three eventually succeeded to governorships: Munro in Madras from 1820 to 1827, and Elphinstone in Bombay from 1819 to 1827, where Malcolm succeeded him from 1827 to 1830.

As the Victorian historian J.W. Kaye put it, this was 'the harvest time of fame'.[1] Such fame, in the eyes of patriotic Victorians, was attributed to the admirable character of these men, but a much more direct cause was the absolute minimum of political interference from Westminster. Senior appointments still aroused some interest at home, but after 1807 parliamentary debates on the Indian budget ceased. This benign neglect allowed the characters of senior men to flourish in the free exercise of power, which they all handled with restraint.

The Company then became reliant on its servants to define the details of its administrative policy. Broadly speaking, the question was whether to impose a new system of government or to adapt the old. The answer delivered by experienced men on the ground was to leave as much as possible of the existing legal and social institutions in place, while imposing a top layer of British supervision and administrative practice. This approach seemed both more efficient and more legitimate than adopting schemes of reform. The two-level Company machine came into being.

Munro, Malcolm and Elphinstone have been dubbed 'Romantics', but this is a misleading label that should be laid aside. The only one of them that was really Romantic was Malcolm, who had fuzzy-brained notions of glory and adventure, and was very much in love with the idea of aristocracy. The others were primarily pragmatists, and 'Romantic' only in as far as they appreciated Oriental traditions to some degree, and were generally free of the contempt for India's ancient culture that many of the more progressive (or fervently Christian) British commentators on India were beginning to express at this time. The 'Romantic' label came later.

These men were chiefly concerned with practical questions, such as how to maximize revenue or how best to recruit political support, both of which were, fundamentally, questions of security.

Sir Thomas Munro (1761–1827) has a strong claim to be the outstanding Governor of his era, and possibly the greatest theorist of government in all Anglo-Indian history. Much praised and respected in his own time, he has been unjustifiably neglected since. Strangely, he was not accorded a place in J.W. Kaye's *Lives of Indian Officers* (1867), the unofficial Valhalla for heroes of British India. Kaye's only explanation was in a footnote[2] claiming that an earlier biography by G.R. Gleig, published in 1830, had said all there was to say. This was an odd and unconvincing excuse, and it was not even true because, as we now know, Gleig had edited Munro's correspondence to portray the man he wished to see, tacitly removing Munro's kinder references to Indian culture and his sceptical remarks about the wisdom of importing English law.

Kaye's omission of Munro does, though, reflect a significant change in British attitudes. Munro was sufficiently famous for Gleig to publish a large biography of him within three years of his death, but his life was a bit short on derring-do, and many of his views were not fashionable by 1867. He was against the conversion of Indians, and was committed to their inclusion in their own (civil, local) government—to 'native advancement' as it was then called. He certainly caught the eye of Victorian writers rather less than Elphinstone or Malcolm, being neither gentleman-scholar nor action hero. But in many ways Munro was the most consistently intelligent and admirable of the three.

He was born in Glasgow, of respectable merchant stock, and was destined to join the family business until war with the American colonies caused a slump in the North Atlantic trade in the late 1770s. Instead, he obtained a cadetship in the Company's army in 1779, and saw extensive service during the Second Mysore War of 1780–4, where his talents in the areas of logistics and intelligence earned him approval. Afterwards his skill in local languages recommended him for the task of settling the Baramahal, an area ceded by Tipu Sultan after the Third Mysore War of 1790–2.

It was during this work, under the supervision of Captain Alexander Read, that his ideas on Indian administration took shape. His relationship with Read is not exactly clear, but it seems that it was Read who originally devised what was to become known as the ryotwari system of land tenure, with Munro only becoming 'converted' to the system around 1796–7. Munro may well not have been the original deviser of the scheme—based on direct taxation of individual cultivators (ryots) assessed on individual fields—but he certainly became its main advocate, and he successfully fought for its adoption at the highest levels within the Company.

After the final defeat of Tipu in 1799, Munro was given Kanara to settle, then in 1800 he was sent to the Ceded Territories, an extensive area made over to the Company by the Nizam of Hyderabad. This far-larger task was not completed till 1807, when he began an extended seven-year furlough in England.

At this point, his thinking on the problems of British rule had developed sufficiently to fill two extensive minutes, covering land revenue and judicial arrangements. These documents contain the substance of what would later become known as the 'Munro school' of Indian government, which emphasized two things: moderate land revenue assessments and the impartial enforcement of justice. In practical terms this meant direct dealings with the ryots as tillers of the soil, and the enforcement of law at local level through village tribunals or panchayats, adapting indigenous law as far as possible, to produce a speedy, understandable system of justice.

Ryotwari represented, for Munro, an attractive alternative to the zamindari system established in Bengal. Unlike zamindari, it was based on small owner-occupiers, directly responsible to the state, and it boasted several major advantages: it was efficient, involving the least possible number of middlemen, and it provided an incentive towards self-improvement for the peasantry, who would benefit directly from their own industriousness,

Munro also grasped a political point about ryotwari. It required local knowledge and custom to run it effectively, and this knowledge and expertise could only be found in 'native agency'. Thus ryotwari, by creating a bond between smallholders, local Indian magistracy and the Company, was a better guarantee of continuing British supremacy than the artificial creation of a class of wealthy, semi-independent landholders, as had been attempted in Bengal, or by trying to build an alliance with the poligars, the traditional larger landlords of south India.

Munro's articulate advocacy finally paid off when the ryotwari system was approved for the Madras Presidency by a parliamentary Select Committee in 1812, and was formally adopted for newly acquired territories by the Court of Directors in 1814.

In that same year he married, then sailed out to India again as a Judicial Commissioner. Over the next three years he reshaped local judicial practice, taking criminal magistracy away from district (zilla) courts, and giving it to the local Collector, who also took on the protection of the rights of subtenants. Village and district panchayats, presided over by Indian munsifs, were given responsibility for all other disputes.

At the end of the Third Maratha War (1817–18), in which he commanded a reserve contingent, he returned to England in 1819 because of ill health, but in 1820 he was persuaded to take up the governorship of Madras, where he presided over a period of relative tranquillity. After three years in the post, with no important business to transact, he tendered his resignation, while offering to stay on until a successor could be found, a task to which the Company's directors proved themselves unequal. With the outbreak of the First Burma War in 1824, Munro suddenly had plenty to do, and provided valuable help to Lord Amherst, whose conduct of the campaign was under heavy criticism. Still waiting to be relieved, he went on a tour of the Ceded Districts in May 1827 and died of cholera, at Puttecondah, in July.

Like Malcolm and Elphinstone, eight and eighteen years his junior, Munro was thrust into positions of extensive personal authority at a time when there were few guidelines, and men were expected to sink or swim. Unlike the other two, Munro managed not only to swim but also to develop a coherent approach to Indian governance that went beyond reliance on the assumed virtues of Englishmen.

The Munro school was paternalistic and practical, and stands in contrast to Cornwallis's system, with its Whiggish scruples and overmanned internal vigilance. Nor did Munro's version of the single officer system owe any part of its slimline efficiency to Utilitarian philosophy. It prioritized the optimum use of man hours and clear lines of responsibility, two elements not easily established through committees and boards. It also predated the Ricardian ideas of 'rent' that so preoccupied senior minds in Calcutta across the 1820s.

Munro believed that the soil of India belonged to the state, that ryotwari tenure had always prevailed in the country, and that it was the only system that could ever be 'permanent'. He decried the support for zamindars and their like, because they would always defend or misuse their rights, becoming either 'petty princes' or ryots themselves, depending on their abilities. No benefit could accrue to the public treasury through tax farming because any gain to the ryot could be viewed as a loss by the tax farmer, and under the zamindari system there was no incentive to improve the crop. All land revenue came ultimately from the ryot anyway, so what benefit was there in creating a system that was 'detrimental to the country' and 'dangerous to the government'?[3] Better to work with what was already there. In the Deccan, the ryot 'has no possessory right nor does he claim it'.[4]

The way to create ownership rights in land, he believed, was to tax moderately, at a rate of one-third the gross produce. This would allow the growth of a market in land in two ways. It would give cultivators an incentive to stay on their plots and improve them, and it left enough surplus income for non-cultivators to buy, then rent out, land at a profit. Higher taxation would make land unsaleable, which would mean that no 'rights' would come into existence.

This whole pragmatic package covered government revenue, law and order, moral self-improvement, economic growth, maximum social continuity and minimal legal disruption. It was definitely a great deal more self-consistent, intelligent and benign than Cornwallis's approach in Bengal. The directors thought so too, which is why the rest of southern India was settled in broadly this way, except in areas where coparcenary (collective) ownership was already immoveably established.

Victorian writers found some of Munro's views surprisingly 'liberal', principally in the area of Indian participation in government, but he was not a liberal in the modern sense. He absolutely believed in the benefits of British rule in India, for both rulers and ruled, and although he realized that British sovereignty could not be eternal, he believed that for the benefit of all parties it should be 'prolonged to the remotest possible period'.[5] However, he had recognizably liberal concerns for the moral and economic advancement of the Indian people, and was insistent that Indians should be included in civil government, believing that they should have the road 'to wealth, and honour, and public employment' opened to them. To exclude them was 'to pass a sentence of degradation on a whole people'.[6] Furthermore, it was imperative to include Indians in the 'estimating and apportioning' of taxation. In general, the British had to learn to treat 'the higher classes of natives as gentlemen'[7]—an entirely Whiggish sentiment, but with a liberal tilt.

He had a political imagination far in advance of his contemporaries. For example, he recommended that all Company servants should start their career in the revenue department. This was partly to give them a proper grounding in the system, but also so that 'they will see the natives under their best form, as intelligent and industrious husbandmen and manufacturers'.[8] That sort of language was doomed to disappear. Fifty years later, the standard British characterization of Indians was as slothful, fatalistic and devious.

Munro was also able to understand the imposition of foreign rule as a degrading process in a way that most other Britons seemed incapable. He imagined what the effects of an invasion of Britain would produce if its people were excluded from their own government for two generations. The result, he predicted, would be the creation of 'a low-minded, deceitful and dishonest race'.[9] Perhaps, as a Scot, he did not find this so difficult to visualize. But it was certainly very unusual, and frankly contrary to most other British pronouncements about how Indians were better off and *happier*, not being bothered with government.

As a man of his times, however, Munro was studiously illiberal in other areas. He resolutely opposed any inclusion of Indians in high military command, and he supported the Company's monopoly, attributing the British conquest of India to its existence; he doubted whether demand for British goods would expand in India, were it to be lifted. He was against state handouts in time of famine, and was in favour of strict censorship of the press. In 1822 he wrote a lengthy Minute calling for extensive control over all published opinion, from both Indian and British sources, because he feared that discontents among the native sections of the army might result from anti-government comment. 'A free press, and the dominion of strangers ... cannot long exist together.'[10]

His views combined a proto-liberalism with a streak of cautious conservatism, an eclecticism which perfectly matched the Whig–Tory fusion that had grown up in India. For him the government's 'ruling vice' was 'innovation'. There was no hurry; good government had to come first. He considered that Hindus were probably the same as they had been in Vasco da Gama's day, and would remain so for a long time to come. But he also appreciated, in a way that very few of his colleagues did, exactly how the traditional Indian social-economic-political system fitted together. He did not see India as an alien England; he understood her as herself, and worked out a simple, sustainable governmental approach. It was this humane and practical outlook that ensured he remained a hero for many British officials who followed him, especially John Lawrence.

How influential was Munro? Bluntly, not influential enough for the long-term benefit of the Anglo-Indian relationship. He got his ryotwari system, and Lord William Bentinck was shortly afterwards to authorize the appointment of Indians to junior government and judicial positions. But his opinions did not prove so influential in other areas. When it came to central government, and whether its powers should be increased, it was Utilitarians and domestic liberals that had a more prominent influence. The legal structures of India were slowly anglicized. Indian idiom was abandoned, and government became increasingly interventionist and centralized, while his views on press censorship were disregarded.

In spite of lifelong deafness, Munro managed to climb extraordinarily high within the Company on pure ability. He came from a provincial background and had no influential patron in his early years; had he had one then he might have won territory as a commander instead of merely settling it as a bureaucrat. He did not start out with influential friends, but he acquired them. He certainly could never have been appointed to a governorship without admirers in high places.

In his understanding of India he was unsurpassed by any of the more famous names in British Indian history. At the same time he matched any of them in personal integrity.

The post-1818 period saw the ryotwari style of settlement adopted in Bombay. As a system of tenure it proved robust and effective, though the use of panchayats was abandoned in the late 1820s as cumbersome and inconsistent. Meanwhile Holt Mackenzie was developing a slightly different approach in the Ceded and Conquered Territories (renamed the North West Provinces in 1835), which consisted of lands taken from Awadh, Sindhia and the Bhonsle of Nagpur. This area became distinct within British administrative practice because Mackenzie and, later, R.M. Bird and J. Thomason all favoured a revenue system based on collective ownership of land grouped into villages. This mahalwari system was a third variation within British practice, alongside ryotwari in Madras and Bombay and zamindari in Bengal.

Decisions on all these matters were ultimately approved in London, but the practical details were always sorted out on the hoof, in the light of experience, by men trying to run a country full of unfamiliar customs and quirks. By different routes, all the regions of British India (outside Bengal) came to recognize the merits of giving local officials extensive judicial, administrative and fiscal powers, concentrated in the figure of the district officer. Following the path of least resistance allowed the British to slip on native dress as governors, while retaining a uniquely British style of aloofness. Eventually, the Company's servants lived down the disgrace of their predecessors, and absolute trust came to be reposed in them as superior characters, wholly unlike the parasitical freebooters who had plundered Bengal in the early years.

This looser supervision goes some way towards explaining the durability of British rule in India. It represented the triumph of practical experience after a period of unconvincing theorizing based on British concerns. India essentially reprogrammed the men who went there to grapple with the complexities of government, and strength of character gradually replaced Whig principles as the most reliable protector of the Company's Indian subjects.

At local level, British rule took on all the characteristics of an ideal Tory government—paternalistic but accessible, firm but fair, socially concerned but fundamentally conservative and aligned with the landed interest. The roots of the rightward 'blue shift' lie here. Personal authority, once the great Satan, became newly attractive, as the key to efficient administration.

Having so thoroughly mixed up its two main domestic philosophies with each other, and with a generous dose of expediency, the later Raj was left only with principles of government, not theories. There was, however, little willingness to acknowledge this change. The British continued to talk liberal talk, while doing illiberal things.

All the officers of Munro's generation sincerely believed that Indians were better off being ruled by the British than being left to do the job themselves, and the result was that Indian participation in higher government was cancelled till further notice. No one in Britain at this time thought other than that it was wisest to leave power largely in the hands of men who were above the social and commercial fray, and who were trying to take decisions for the good of the whole community.

This conviction ended at a stroke most of the dynastic arguments that had preoccupied India for so long, which was undoubtedly a good thing. But the decision proved almost impossible to revoke, and from around 1880, after about sixty years of exclusion, the desire of Indians to overturn this policy drove the whole of the political narrative of the later Raj.

The practice of single-seatedness relied on men of a certain vigour and strength of character. There were few better examples than John Malcolm.

Sir John Malcolm (1769–1833) was the pin-up boy of imperial historians. They loved him because he represented everything that the British admired about themselves in India. He was athletic, good-looking and dauntless—a man of action rather than reflection. He was moderate in his personal habits and a lively companion. He was even a good friend of that doyen of British soldier-statesmen, the Duke of Wellington, under whom he served.

Unlike the tainted figures of early British India, Malcolm looked like the perfect, archetypal empire builder—energetic, honest, brave and not too brainy; a man who wrote books that were often more about what he did than what he thought, and what he thought was entirely conventional. But Malcolm came with a bonus. His comforting anti-intellectual straightforwardness was spread over a large body of historical works, including his *Life of Lord Clive*, the first biography of the man, published posthumously in 1836.

Like Thomas Munro, Malcolm was a soldier-administrator sprung from an aspirant Scottish family. In 1781, at the age of twelve, his parents took him out of school and sent him to London to seek a place with the Company's army. J.W. Kaye, the EIC's historian, tells us that at his interview one of the Company's directors patronizingly asked the diminutive candidate what he would do if confronted with Haidar Ali, the Company's bogeyman *du jour*. Young John enthusiastically replied in a thick Scottish accent that he would 'out with his sword, and cut off his head'.[11] This bravura performance secured the desired place.

He was then just fourteen when he fought in the tail end of the Second Mysore War, earning himself the nickname 'Boy Malcolm', a soubriquet that was to cling to him throughout his life.

He made himself fluent in Persian, a talent that opened up a career in the Company's 'political' service, and he went on to have the good fortune to come to the attention of Henry Dundas while on sick leave in England in 1794. Dundas got him attached to the staff of Sir Alured Clarke, Commander-in-Chief of the Madras army, where he remained until he was sent to Hyderabad as assistant to the British Resident. He was caught up in the abortive coup there in 1798 when the Company forced the nizam to dismiss his French officers, leading to a serious mutiny. Malcolm's life was in danger for a while but he escaped harm. He then served as liaison officer between EIC and Hyderabadi forces in the final campaign against Tipu in 1799, and was part of the settlement commission after the war.

Then, following Napoleon's landing in Egypt (1798), Malcolm was sent on a diplomatic mission to counter French influence in the Near East. Through 1799–1801 he visited the Sultan of Muscat, the Turkish Pasha in Baghdad and the Shah of Persia. Treaties were apparently agreed with the Shah, though nothing was heard of them again. On his return, Malcolm became Governor-General Richard Wellesley's right-hand man. He was deeply involved in relations with Indian states in the run-up to the Second Maratha War (1803–5), and undertook missions to Hyderabad and the Peshwa at Poona.

Illness prevented him from taking much part in the war itself but he recovered sufficiently to participate in the peace negotiations, during which he drew the Governor-General's severe censure for allowing Daulat Rao Sindhia to retain the fortress of Gwalior, a decision Malcolm had made with the support of the Governor-General's brother Arthur. This personal rebuke greatly distressed him, but the two soon mended their fences.

By 1807 he was British Resident at Mysore, and was sent to Persia again in 1808 as part of another British campaign to exclude French influence from the region, after the signing of a Franco-Russian alliance in 1807. The mission was unsuccessful, not least because Malcolm had to contend with a rival delegation from London under Sir Harford Jones, a circumstance that both confused and annoyed the Shah, who, quite understandably, chose not to deal with the apparently junior party.

The ever-busy Malcolm's next task was to talk down the 'white' mutiny within the Company's Madras army that broke out at Masulipatnam in 1809. He managed to negotiate the release of the commander, Colonel Innes, and dissuade the mutineers from a grand plan to unite with the army of Hyderabad and declare independence. He was sent to Persia yet again in 1810, and this time his mission prospered, so much so that Sir Harford Jones was recalled to London. Jones's replacement, Sir Gore Ouseley, was not acceptable to the Shah, who had taken a liking to Malcolm and wanted him to stay on as a military adviser. Malcolm declined, returning first to India, then eventually to London in 1812. This flurry of activity served as the basis for a series of books, including a *Sketch of the Political History of India*, a *History of Persia*, *Observations* on the Masulipatnam mutiny of 1809, and a *Sketch of the Sikhs*.

On returning to India in 1817 he helped to organize the Pindari campaign, later playing a distinguished role in the defeat of Holkar at Mahidipur in December 1817, though he exposed himself to danger rather too frequently for the liking of many on his staff. But this was the moment he had waited for—the opportunity to win personal glory in the heat of battle. This was his 'chance at fair fame as a soldier' as he put it in a letter home. 'I did not lose the opportunity afforded me,'[12] he confided. He was then involved in negotiating the peace, taking responsibility for the generous offer to the defeated Peshwa, Baji Rao II, of a pension of Rs 8 lakhs per annum. Under this agreement, the EIC was obliged to pay out for the next 33 years, at a total cost of over £2 million. Malcolm always defended this deal as the best way of bringing the fighting to a definitive end. His employers, however, did not repose enough confidence in him to promote him, and he missed out on the governorship of Bombay in 1819 and of Madras in 1820. Nor was he given charge, as he had hoped, of the newly won lands in central India. He resigned and went home in April 1822.

He was eventually offered the governorship of Bombay in 1827, but his time there yielded neither happiness nor popularity. Much of his term was taken up in a testy constitutional wrangle involving a Crown judge named Sir John Grant, who, as a result of a child custody battle between two Indians, claimed that his royal jurisdiction lay beyond that of the Company. The relationship between Company and Crown jurisdictions had been a long-running cause of friction after the Regulating Act of 1773 had set up a Crown court in Calcutta without precisely defining how it was to work in parallel with the Company's courts. Various attempts had been made to clarify the situation, but the two rival jurisdictions continued to run in the presidency towns.

Tempers became heated and the Commander-in-Chief of the Bombay army even threatened to intervene militarily, in support of Grant. But the home government backed Malcolm. Eventually Grant was replaced and the royal court's jurisdiction was limited to Bombay and its close environs—roughly the position that had been established in Bengal in the 1770s. Malcolm then returned home in 1831 to undertake yet more literary projects.

He entered Parliament in 1831 for the rotten borough of Launceston in Cornwall, on the 'interest' of the Duke of Northumberland. In English political terms, Malcolm, like his friend and hero the Duke of Wellington, was a 'red hot' Tory, and he spoke against the proposals for parliamentary reform then under discussion in the House. His constituency was one of those due for extinction, and his principal argument against reform was that by removing the small boroughs, gentlemen like himself would no longer be able to represent the interests of India, which, of course, had no seats. In the 'reformed' election of the next year he stood, and lost, at Carlisle.

He worked on, trying to finish his biography of Clive and preparing for the debate on the upcoming renewal of the Company's charter. But he died, weakened by cholera, in May 1833.

Genial, humorous, enthusiastic and vigorous, Malcolm was the man on the spot repeatedly in the years 1798–1820, so much so that in response to any problem Company officials would cry 'Send Malcolm!' Undoubtedly a figure of some importance to earlier generations of British writers, he seems curiously bumptious and insubstantial to modern eyes. He did a great deal, almost none of it enduring; he wrote a great deal, almost none of it memorable. Compared to Munro he was a lightweight, and compared to other military figures his fame is dim.

Despite all the stress his admirers laid on his robust and athletic constitution, it was clearly his sociability that served him best in all situations. His true vocation lay in diplomacy, where his skill in languages and personal charm made him a natural. As a writer he could turn the odd good phrase—he believed that the principles of British government gave 'grace to conquest',[13] and he once encapsulated the nub of his conservatism very neatly by writing 'how much better work is done, when it does itself, than when done by the best of us'.[14] But his prejudices as a romantic militarist have not served him well down the years.

His pen proved a fair bit mightier than his sword, but he was not a profound thinker. As a young man he laid out a code of conduct for the British in India, which amounted to the importance of being kind to the locals, and that the British must 'keep sacred their word' as the best means of exerting 'a constant superiority'.[15] In his mature years he developed a deep admiration for the 'fallen greatness' of India, which became almost a political credo, making him a convinced advocate of indirect rule. This can be seen as a manifestation of his essential Toryism, as this policy was designed to preserve existing social arrangements and support the reigning princes.

He also talked up the Russian threat years before it was remotely credible, so he can be considered either prescient or simply a fool in advance of many others.

It is hard to explain the veneration in which he was held, for his record of actual achievement is decidedly patchy: three missions to Persia and no permanent treaty; a mishandled settlement with Sindhia in 1805: the Pindari War which escalated far beyond his original intentions; the Peshwa's bounteous pension; and the one time he had proper administrative responsibility, as Governor of Bombay, he presided over prolonged chaos.

A statute of him stands in Westminster Abbey, which reflects the esteem of the British establishment, but more knowledgeable heads had their doubts. Mountstuart Elphinstone damned him with faint praise in his obituary, describing his 'ready though not always accurate insight into affairs'.[16]

His legacy, despite the encomiums of the Victorians, was minimal, except, perhaps, for his introduction of the potato to Persia.

The third great harvester of fame was Mountstuart Elphinstone—a somewhat nobler and more restrained soul than Malcolm but, like him, another Victorian hero who left little, beyond a college, by which he is remembered.

Mountstuart Elphinstone (1779–1859) was one of the men most often held up for admiration by Victorians as an architect and exemplar of British greatness in India. Macaulay awarded him a 'spotless glory', and he typified the calm, patriarchal British servant of empire abroad. This was not entirely a facade in his case, as he came from noble stock. His father was a Scottish baron, the eleventh Lord Elphinstone, who arranged for Mountstuart, his fourth son, to join the East India Company. The young man had plenty of EIC connections: his uncle was a director, and his brother was a serving soldier with the Company. As he sailed out in 1796, he was accompanied by a cousin on his mother's side, John Adam, who later served as Acting Governor-General in 1823–4.

Although typically grouped with Munro and Malcolm, Elphinstone was a man of a different mould, though closer to Malcolm than Munro. His basic attitudes to Indian government were more or less the same—authoritarian and paternalistic—but he expressed more approval of native aristocratic traditions, whereas Munro saw more virtue in yeoman cultivators. Wherever possible he made it his policy to find out exactly how Indians governed themselves before attempting to introduce changes to existing patterns of government. In general, he thought he could best 'serve the country [India] if I can prevent people making laws for it until they see whether it wants [needs] them'.[17]

He was educated in Indian policy at Governor-General Wellesley's Fort William College, which had a decidedly 'Orientalist' bent to its curriculum. Perhaps because of this, like Munro, he was keen on the administration of local justice through traditional village panchayats, and he did ultimately recommend the adoption of the ryotwari land revenue system.

He was also fiercely against Christian evangelizing in India and strongly in favour of the teaching of Indian languages—even traditional Indian science—in schools and colleges, and was thus in the most resistant ranks to the Westernizing of India in any form. Instead, he advocated a long, slow readjustment of Indian society and learning, a view that places him in polar opposition to the Bentinck–Macaulay project of the 1830s. It is somewhat ironic, therefore, that it is his name that decorates Elphinstone College, opened in 1835, which taught a Western-style syllabus.

On arrival in India in 1796 his first posting was to Benares, where he joined his brother, and only narrowly escaped death there in 1799, when the troops of the deposed Nawab of Awadh, Wazir Ali, attacked the town; several other British officers were killed. His next posting was to the staff of General Arthur Wellesley, with whom he rode through the Assaye campaign of 1803. After the Second Maratha War (1803–5) he was made Resident at the court of the Maharaja of Berar at Nagpur, where he stayed for four years, before being sent to Afghanistan in the frenzy of diplomatic activity which followed the Franco-Russian alliance of 1807. He never went further than Peshawar, but managed to agree a very short treaty of friendship with the amir, Shah Shuja—an alliance that was to lead to the First Afghan War thirty years later. This experience provided the basis of his first major literary work, his *Account of the Kingdom of Caubul* (1815). On his return he took up a long posting at the court of the Peshwa in Poona (1811–19).

He went on campaign again during the Third Maratha War of 1817–18, but he is better known for having suppressed the rebellion that followed it in Poona. He discovered and thwarted a plan to kill all the British occupants of the Residency, after which he had the plotters blown from the mouths of cannon. His superior, Evan Nepean, Governor of Bombay, wondered if he had not been a little too fierce, but Elphinstone was perfectly confident, and refused an indemnity for his actions, saying that if he had done wrong he should be punished, and if he had done right he needed no protection. The directors reposed as much confidence in him as he showed in himself on this occasion, and in 1819 he succeeded Nepean to the governorship of Bombay, where he served a largely uneventful term till 1827.

The keynote of his administration was the preservation in as large a measure as possible of existing institutions of government. Panchayats and village headmen had his support, as did the Raja of Satara, whose position he defended against Company encroachment. He also calculated that maintaining charitable support for Brahmans by means of the Dakshina festival was money well invested.

He perfectly represents the pragmatic-conservative policy of his generation of Company administrators, a careful line that enabled British rule to establish itself by a process of massive military expenditure, followed by a minimum of local interference. Such men had fewer qualms than their predecessors about using 'native agency' in their ideal system; it was cheap and socially less disruptive. To modern eyes this system of light-touch local government also distinctly resembles the way that England had been run for several centuries.

Elphinstone never became a Victorian hero, partly because his adventures were more prosaic, and possibly because he was a good deal less overtly Christian in his beliefs than men like Henry Lawrence. His apparent capacity for effortless administration and his avoidance of controversy have also pushed him further from the spotlight over time. He has, perhaps, paid the price of espousing dowdy conservatism as opposed to eye-catching reformism. This was a mildly surprising turn, because as a young man he had been a 'juvenile radical', having picked up a degree of revolutionary fervour from French prisoners held in Edinburgh Castle, when his father was governor there. But as an adult he was as cautious as anyone on the Company's payroll.

In character he was more reserved than the clubbable Malcolm, but he did complain of feeling isolated during his long spell as Governor of Bombay. Private friendships and intimate gatherings were officially discouraged, as likely to promote perceptions of favouritism, and he consoled himself with outdoor pursuits, principally pig-sticking, of which he was very fond. His tenure of the governorship was an unremarkable time in the history of western India and he registered no spectacular achievements during these years, devoting himself to studies that eventually bore fruit in his classic *History of India*. This was inspired, it seems, by the success of John Malcolm's own works on India, though Elphinstone thought it wise not to write of recent times and living men, as Malcolm had done.

The one remarkable quality noted by his contemporaries was his competitive nature when it came to 'manliness'. He was ever ready to outdo the exertions and physical accomplishments of his colleagues and subordinates. As a result, he could be drawn into strange and perilous activities, such as camel riding, or climbing daunting rock-faces. This trait combined once with his contempt for luxury, when he decided to dispense with a bed for several months. When he eventually resumed normal sleeping arrangements, he was asked why he had denied himself conventional comforts. 'Because I was a fool,' he replied.[18]

He left India in 1827, and returned to England to enjoy an extended retirement for a further thirty-two years. He never married and devoted himself to literary pursuits, finally finishing his *History of India: The Hindu and Mahometan Periods* in 1841. He was twice offered the governor-generalship of India, as successor to Bentinck, by two successive administrations in 1834 and 1835, but refused on both occasions. His official reason was fear for his health which, like that of so many British administrators in India, had suffered under the twin assaults of climate and workload. Many of his contemporaries, however, suspected either lethargy or a persistent lack of self-confidence to be the real cause. Perhaps a lack of ambition at the end of a career so dominated by the idea of service is not such an unworthy failing.

Munro, Malcolm and Elphinstone, and to a lesser extent Charles Metcalfe, were a kind of unofficial steering committee of early nineteenth-century British India. They were men who learned to wield traditional Indian authority with a distinctly British sense of fair play, thus adopting a kind of double legitimacy. Something they all shared—something very evident to their contemporaries—was absolute personal probity. This set them apart from a great many of their British predecessors in India, especially within the army, where men in charge of large military budgets often availed themselves of whatever booty or perquisites they could find. Those that survived battle and disease usually retired very wealthy: Robert Clive, Hector Munro, Richard Smith, Eyre Coote and the last of the line, David Ochterlony, all did very well out of prize money, 'presents', military contracting, and access to army payrolls. The soldier-civilian tradition represented by Munro and Malcolm was different, and was to become the norm.

However, it would be wrong to conclude that all these men were intellectually in lockstep. Elphinstone and Malcolm were the truer conservatives, in British terms at least. They knew aristocracy from their homeland and recognized that the maintenance of traditional hierarchy in India was an inexpensive and potentially helpful way of promoting political stability. While Resident at Poona, Elphinstone wrote to Charles Metcalfe of how he wished 'to prevent the destruction of the few old families that remain in this Empire'.[19] He was convinced that 'great families' should be maintained in their status, and that hereditary rights should be protected wherever possible. The practicality and attractiveness of this attitude ensured that a hierarchical social order was to survive in India.

Munro's views were quite different. He advocated direct contact between the British authorities and the Indian peasant, mostly because he believed that subtenants and small farmers were more likely to be exploited by larger landlords than by British officials. The choice of either privileging the interests of the upper classes, or of protecting those of the lower, has clear beginnings in this period. The two rival 'Punjab schools' of the Lawrence brothers thus have traceable roots in this Elphinstone–Munro distinction.

Munro, especially, used economic theory to determine the rate at which tax levels could be set, and all three were keen to use detailed technical data to relate taxation to the variables within Indian conditions, such as rainfall, irrigation, quality of the soil, crop selection and so forth. They all spent a good deal of effort attempting to understand the history of landholding in their various districts, inquiries that sparked off a whole tradition of British antiquarian interest in rural India, a subject in which James Tod came to excel.

James Tod (1782–1835) was yet another soldier-civilian-writer-scholar from a Scottish background, but he differed in several respects. He never rose to high position within the Company, and his writings were of a different tone, resembling Elphinstone's scholarly antiquarianism rather than Malcolm's attempts to justify and celebrate British rule or Munro's technical analysis of the problems of Indian government. Tod was a man who seemed interested in the physical geography and ancient history of India more or less for its own sake, and as such he prefigures the more dispassionate approach of Sir William Hunter. The detailed topographical work he undertook demonstrates the way in which British outsiders were frequently more interested in understanding India than were the inhabitants of the country, who had no need of such generalized knowledge to live their lives.

Tod obtained a cadetship through an uncle and reached India in August 1799. He arrived too late for the Fourth Mysore War of that year and played no active part in the Second Maratha War of 1803–5. In fact he never managed to find himself in the thick of the action, the nearest occasion being when he volunteered for an expedition to the Moluccas in 1801 which never actually sailed. Instead Tod became attached to the Resident at the court of Gwalior, from 1805 till 1817.

During this period he travelled extensively across north and central India, collecting geographical and political intelligence as well as historical and antiquarian information. This knowledge was put to direct use in the Pindari War of 1817, when the British finally mopped up the bands of freelance soldiers marauding across the region. He is reputed to have cowed the pindari chiefs by persuading the ruler of Kotah to seize their families and hand them over to the British.

After the Third Maratha War (1817–18), Tod was made political agent to western Rajputana, and it was his responsibility to supervise the peace that followed. His task was slightly different from those of Elphinstone and Malcolm at this time, for Tod was working with Indian regimes, exercising indirect influence, not direct power. Nevertheless he was credited with bringing peace and prosperity to areas within his remit. His knowledge of people, languages and customs, combined with a genuine care for and understanding of the local population, enabled him to counter abuses and resolve grievances.

According to Reginald Heber, Bishop of Calcutta from 1823 to 1826, who passed through the region, Tod's success prompted some to suspect that his popularity and his advocacy of the rights of local chiefs were the result of simple corruption. This was unfair, though forms of corruption in the outlying areas of British control were not unknown at the time, and several Residents and Agents were rightly suspected of it. However, in Tod's case there was no reason to believe that he was anything other than genuinely respected and admired by the local people, or that he was motivated by anything other than a genuine willingness to promote their welfare.

With Elphinstone, Tod became one of the first men to apply more rigorous standards in the study of Indian antiquity. William Jones read books, but Tod went out into the field. Others had been more credulous in their attempts to find confirmation of Bible stories or parallels with ancient Greek religion, and though Tod was not entirely free of speculative urges, he paid close attention to his sources and faithfully recorded what he found. In this he was perhaps modern, but in his willingness to see India as a land of ancient and unchanging tradition he was also establishing a distinctly imperial attitude, in tune with the paintings of ruined temples that became popular with the British at this time.

Writing about India's exotic past became yet another way of defining India's present, and effectively fossilizing it, accepting it as a true reflection of the country and its culture. Though this was not Tod's intention, Indian history, as written by the British, soon became an indirect confirmation of India's deep-seated backwardness.

Tod eventually resigned because of ill health in 1822, and after his return to England he spent the rest of his life writing up the enormous store of material he had accumulated. The results of this work were his classic *Annals and Antiquities of Rajasthan* (1829–32) and *Travels in Western India*, published posthumously in 1839. He also became a noted numismatist and is credited with founding modern scholarship on the Indo-Hellenic coins of north-western India.

He suffered a stroke while visiting his bank in September 1835, and died two days later. A village in Mewar was named Todgarh after him by the Maharana of Udaipur, and still bears his name today.

Looking closely at this cadre of celebrated early colonial officials and the problems they were trying to solve provides a mountain of evidence that Company rule in India was not all about profits and shareholders. It should also make clear that no single approach to India's governance, society or culture emerged among the men charged with understanding these crucial areas. It should also be clear that the essential nature of the solutions they found and the attitudes they formed was more practical than ideological.

1828–39: Reform and Retrenchment

By the late 1820s, the British had created a powerful central government in India, and had destroyed organized opposition to it. This Company 'state' was very unlike its counterpart in Britain; the EIC was far more ambitious to control the lives of its subjects. However, in line with domestic Whig theory, the senior men in India were quite willing to make alliances with influential Indian social groups.

The inconsistency between the views from home and abroad meant that the nearest thing to a consensus in Indian policy was that the new territories should be both defended and developed, with pragmatic concessions to Indian custom but theoretical aspirations towards reform. So, through the 1820s, the men on the ground had to address a difficult tangle of economic, legal and socio-political objectives. The older generation still favoured local idiom, but the rising cadre of Haileybury graduates tended to take a more liberal, reformist approach. The impatience of the Cornwallis era was about to return.

But liberalism itself was still very new and untried. It found no favour in British government circles during the long Tory ministry of Lord Liverpool (1812–27), and the more progressive ministries of the 1830s were described as Whig. Nor, in its original French form, did liberalism seem to have much relevance to British India. Indeed, the dominant strand in Indian policy after the Cornwallis reforms was conquest, not political inclusion. However, from the mid-1820s, the tendency was to move away from Whig orthodoxy and towards rational and Utilitarian approaches, which, though inspired by liberal ideas, were primarily authoritarian.

An influential figure in this process was Charles Metcalfe, who had a very pessimistic view of the British connection with India. His discovery of corruption in Hyderabad in the early 1820s disturbed him profoundly, because he believed that British authority was so naturally 'disgusting' to Indians that exceptionally high standards of honesty in government had to be observed, though even this might not be enough to sustain British rule. He was inclined to gloom throughout his life, and was not a man of action like Malcolm, who could easily lose himself in field sports or bonhomie.

Charles Theophilus Metcalfe, 1st Baron Metcalfe (1785–1846) was born in Calcutta while his father was serving in the East India Company's

Bengal army. As Acting Governor-General from 1835 to 1836, he is, therefore, the only native Indian ever to rule British India.

His father was a close friend of Governor-General Richard Wellesley, and Charles was the first pupil to enrol in Wellesley's new educational venture at Fort William College. The great man's favour then placed him in a series of important positions.

John Malcolm, a lifelong friend, succeeded in persuading him that the most promising opportunities in the Company's service were in the 'political' department, and in 1806 Metcalfe obtained his first senior post as assistant to the British Resident at Delhi. This placed him right at the centre of the diplomatic and intelligence traffic of north India, a particularly unstable region at the time, with two rising powers—the Nepalese and the Sikhs—and a plethora of small, independent rulers all jockeying for position, including the Jat Raja of Bharatpur, an Irish adventurer named George Thomas who had set up a small 'kingdom' for himself in one corner of the Punjab, the Begum Shumroo, and a number of independent states in Rajputana. Beyond all this lay Afghanistan, where dynastic struggles made the region both ungovernable and unconquerable.

There was even talk of a French or Russian invasion via Afghanistan, and it was concerns over this possibility that took Metcalfe as envoy to the court of Maharaja Ranjit Singh at Lahore in 1808, to try to negotiate some kind of defensive alliance. Metcalfe's persistence in the face of Ranjit's indifference was exemplary, and despite his inability to bring the maharaja into a close alliance with the Company, he did eventually manage to agree the short Treaty of Amritsar of April 1809, which defined the Sutlej river as the border of British India and declared a mutual non-interference pact across it. Though less than the British might have wanted, this treaty was respected by both sides till 1845, and effectively guaranteed peace with the Company throughout the rest of Ranjit's life.

In 1811 Metcalfe was appointed Resident at Delhi, and it was from here that he developed his own style of local administration, based on the village unit and the merging of powers in local officials. This was anathema to those of the Cornwallis school, but Metcalfe's 'Delhi system' seemed to work well in the area, which remained peaceful and prosperous, and it picked up admirers within the Company. As a slight variant of the Munro system, it confirmed that robust use of local authority was the way ahead for the British.

Metcalfe stayed in Delhi till 1819, when he was recalled to serve briefly on the staff of Governor-General Lord Moira (Hastings), before being dispatched to another important Resident's position, in Hyderabad. Here he came into direct conflict with entrenched corruption involving a malign alliance between the nizam's diwan, Chandra Lal, and a firm of British bankers, who between them were diverting a large part of the (very substantial) revenues of Hyderabad into their own pockets. The story ended badly for the leeches, whose schemes were exposed and dismantled. The diwan was dismissed and the bank, Palmer and Co., took a heavy blow to its reputation from which it never truly recovered. The affair also ended badly for Moira who, as patron of one of the bankers involved, found himself tainted, and had to return to England under suspicion of malpractice.

Metcalfe was back in Delhi between 1825 and 1827, by which time he had developed a distinct outlook on Indian affairs that was out of step with much British thinking. He was pessimistic about the prospect of continued British rule, and considered that the Company's hold on power was very slender; he likened the position of the British to sitting on a barrel of gunpowder. He identified two elements necessary to sustain British rule. One was what he called 'impression'—keeping up the illusion of strength—or, more baldly, bluff. The other was scrupulously fair government, and he was particularly sensitive to corruption and injustice, perceiving both as much greater threats to British security than rebellion.

He was resigned to the likelihood of more territorial expansion, which seemed the surest way to guarantee British dominance, but he insisted that this should go along with enlightened social policy. He strongly supported the landowning peasant, believing that distributed landholding was more equitable and politically advantageous than the system of large estates that characterized the Cornwallis settlement in Bengal. Unlike Thomas Munro he believed that the cultivator, not the state, owned the land, and that what the peasant was being asked to pay was a tax, not rent. Admiration for the simple, timeless world of the peasant that he came to know in the Delhi region led him to talk of India's 'village republics', a concept, indeed a phrase, that Munro had touched on as early as 1806.

Differences of opinion about India's villages were to continue for decades. Were they ultimately the source of India's social strength? Were they a good basis for administration? Was landholding truly a village enterprise, and if so, should village tenures be broken up, because they were holding back the development of property rights and enterprise in the Indian economy? Metcalfe was in no doubt that they were a good thing.

His general opinions, though, are more difficult to characterize. He combined a traditional Whig dislike of ambitious government with a liberal belief in self-improvement. This tended to put him on the smallholder's side, and led him to believe that non-interference was best for Indian society, but at the same time he was patriotic enough to want British rule to continue indefinitely. He somehow managed to reconcile social conservatism about British society with a willingness to express criticism of India's social institutions. Men like Metcalfe remind us that British officials in India had to form their opinions within a double-ended system, in which government by Britons spanned two very different environments.

By the late 1820s Metcalfe was one of the Company's most senior servants, and during the governor-generalship of Lord William Bentinck (1828–35) he was centrally involved in all the chief affairs of state. But the directors regarded him with some suspicion, and he was passed over for the governorships of Madras and Bombay, both of which fell vacant at this time.

Official disfavour was also to deny him the top job in India. His temporary appointment as Acting Governor-General in 1835 was not made permanent, partly because his pro-Indian sympathies, guided by the more genuinely liberal instincts of Thomas Macaulay, led him to push through the Press Act in September 1835. This measure was not quite a charter of freedom, but Metcalfe supported it because he felt that India's path to self-improvement lay through free speech and the unhindered dissemination of modern knowledge. The Act itself did not lift all government controls, but it required that all printed matter had to carry the name of its publisher—yet another way of enforcing responsibility.

Charles Metcalfe was the last of the Company's servants to run its affairs in India, and his departure marks the end of anything resembling independence for the EIC. His successor, Lord Auckland, was yet another London politician, as were all the men that followed him, with the exception of John Lawrence, who was viceroy from 1863 to 1869. Lawrence was a Company man, but only held office after the end of Company rule.

On leaving India, Metcalfe was appointed, in succession, to the governorships of Jamaica and Canada, and managed to shine in both. He eventually returned to England in 1845, and was made a baron in recognition of his long and meritorious service. He died the next year, having suffered a protracted and very painful illness—probably some kind of cancer of the jaw.

Although earlier accounts of his life claimed that he never married, it is now known that he had a long-term relationship with an Indian wife, probably a Sikh he met at Lahore in 1808–9. He is believed to have had as many as three children with her, and in his will he named a 'James', to whom he left the very large sum of £50,000, but without acknowledging him as his son.

All these famous early administrators were, in a sense, heirs to Warren Hastings in their engagement with Indian languages and their sensitivity to local custom. Like Hastings they wished, as far as possible, to leave the existing institutions of the country in place; British interests had to come before abstract British principles. In this they were all also heirs of Burke, and were like a transplanted aristocracy by appointment, a better match for the conditions than Cornwallis's zamindars. As a group, they shared Burke's distrust of abstract political theorizing. Malcolm, in his *Sketch of the Political History of India*, was quite specific on this point. 'The most prominent error' of British legislators was to be guided by that 'dogmatical principle' of attempting 'to fix that which is constantly changing'.[20]

But there was never a truly unified approach to the problems that India posed. Even men who agreed on many practical solutions, such as Munro and Metcalfe, had important theoretical disagreements. Munro, a soldier, always favoured civilian predominance over the military arm, whereas Metcalfe, a civilian, preferred to think of the civil power as a kind of military structure.

These disagreements should warn us against over-enthusiasm in identifying the political typology of early imperial government. However, the collective bewilderment of the men deputed to cope with the exotic problems of India was a key factor in causing the disparity in the system between its higher and lower reaches, a mismatch that was undoubtedly intensified because of the separate audiences, colonial and domestic, that the system was designed to placate, and by the multiple purposes—administrative, financial, military and judicial—that it was intended to fulfil.

Under the loose leadership of men such as Lords Moira and Amherst, the fame harvesters were free to leave alone or interfere, admonish or supervise as they wished. But this cosy partnership was soon to come under threat with the rise of a younger generation of political reformers who thought that the English language, English social norms and sometimes even Christianity were the best ways forward for India.

This new liberal generation thought they knew better than their elders, and better than Indians too. The reformers threw aside the caution of the respecters of Indian tradition. Within the debate on education, the two groups were labelled Anglicists and Orientalists.

The conviction that Indians should not only be educated but also reformed or converted took hold in both Evangelical and liberal circles in

England. The idea of education in English appealed to both these groups; the significant difference between them was that most of the Evangelicals were outside the Company, and most of the liberals were inside. Evangelicals wanted Indians to be able to read the Bible, while liberals believed that Indian social practices had to be reformed on principle. Both tendencies looked back to the 1813 Charter Act, which set aside funds for education.

This provision had been allowed to drift, largely because no one in the Company had much idea of what it meant and therefore what to do about it. Lord Moira submitted a minute in 1815, but his recommendations were vague and confused. With such a small amount of money available, he saw no point in setting up a school system. He also felt that there was little demand for one. In India, education at lower levels was very much a private function, and decisions about what to teach, to whom and how left Moira stymied. Munro and Elphinstone both set their minds to the same problem, but neither came out with anything like a coherent or large-scale scheme. Problems of funding, curriculum, and a lack of teachers remained serious obstacles.

Education was not yet a high priority. Warren Hastings had founded the Calcutta Madrasa in 1781 and Jonathan Duncan the Sanskrit School in Benares in 1792, but neither of these was a great success. The duties laid down by the 1813 Charter Act were therefore unwelcome as well as unclear, and their appearance was prompted almost entirely by domestic British concerns. But education was shortly to become a key issue, because irreversible social and economic changes were under way in Bengal.

The most important of these was the flowering of Calcutta. The town had grown enormously in size and sophistication from the small trading settlement of a century before. Its large population was becoming increasingly wealthy, with a steady growth in commercial activities after the ending of the Company's monopoly in 1813. The requirements of finance, insurance and banking had spawned a cluster of Agency Houses in the town, and several Indian dynasties, such as the Tagores, Debs and Days, had made substantial fortunes supplying the EIC with managerial and financial services. By the 1820s these families were running large operations, on their own account or in partnership with Europeans. The city seemed destined to become a thriving, cosmopolitan place.

There was also a rapid growth in demand for English-language education, supplied by the circle of teachers and experts gathered round Fort William College, and by the Protestant mission based in the Danish enclave of Serampore. This demand lay behind the creation of the new

Vidyalaya, or Hindu College, set up in 1817 by Indians, to teach modern subjects in English to Hindu boys. The College, which was independent, catered to the demands of a new class of Indians eager to absorb Western education, primarily as a qualification for employment.

The Company had declined to involve itself in the founding of the Hindu College, but in recognition of the changing circumstances it set up a General Committee of Public Instruction in 1823. This body, however, proved itself no more able than Moira to form clear views about the future of British-sponsored education, and it was the arrival of new men and more forceful opinions that resolved the matter a decade later. This contrasts with the situation in Maharashtra, where Mountstuart Elphinstone decided to approve the setting up of the Poona Hindu College in 1821, which taught an entirely traditional curriculum, in line with the demands of the local population, who had less desire or opportunity to take up employment in the Company's service.

With peace and prosperity in Bengal, aspirant Indians now began to imagine ways to modernize Indian society, which led many of them to criticize or reject conservative social and religious practices. Most prominent and most brilliant among those that called for religious reform was Ram Mohan Roy (1772–1833). Organized opposition to modernizing and Westernizing tendencies also appeared, led by Radhakanta Deb (1784–1867) and Ramkamal Sen (1783–1844), who opposed Roy over several issues, including the practice of sati. In 1828 Roy set up the influential religious and social reform movement called the Brahmo Samaj. Deb and Sen replied with the creation of the Dharma Sabha.

Meanwhile, outside these two streams, which historians have dubbed 'liberal' and 'orthodox', there was a third radical tendency, whose most prominent member was the brilliant young Anglo-Indian teacher and poet, Henry Derozio (1809–31). This grouping was more confrontational than either Roy's reformers or Deb's conservatives, and was more modernist and critical of government than anyone else in contemporary India. Derozio taught at the Hindu College for only five years, till he died in 1831, aged just twenty-two, but his legacy was the loose movement known as 'Young Bengal'. He pointed the way beyond rational reformism and into modern radical ideas, like those of Thomas Paine, translations of whose works were by then appearing in Bengal.

This fertile and dynamic situation gave Indians new choices, and many took their open-mindedness very seriously. One Kartik Babu wrote in his autobiography: 'How shall we Indians be civilized, and how will our country be free from the tyrannical sway of error and superstition, if we abstain from wine?'[21]

The other great indicator of social and intellectual change in Bengal was the growth of a popular press. In Calcutta there was a large population of perhaps 250,000, easily enough to support an active fourth estate. Journals and newssheets in English proliferated, although none of the regular papers had circulations above about 1,000. Rival loyalist and radical titles soon emerged, with the *Oriental Herald* as an anti-establishment voice, and *John Bull* as the organ of loyalism. Opposing Indian periodicals also appeared, with *Sambad Kaumudi*, published by Roy, up against *Samachar Chandrika*, edited by Bhawanicharan Banerji (1787–1848), the secretary of the Dharma Sabha.

From the earliest days of the press, in the 1780s, the effect of free opinion passing among the population had disturbed Company high-ups, but the exact relationship of government and press remained unclear. The first Bengali-language publications, which appeared from 1816–18, were largely non-controversial. Sections of the English press, however, were deliberately provocative. Officialdom avoided censorship, preferring direct action against journalists. Matters came to a head in 1823 with the imposition of official restrictions and the deportation of James Silk Buckingham, editor of the radical *Calcutta Journal*. A small group of Indian notables, led by Ram Mohan Roy, submitted a petition to have the new restrictions reversed. The appeal was refused, and the press carried on under government licence.

But change was inexorably coming, and from around 1825 a new crop of men appeared in India, imbued with a sharper political consciousness. Most of them had formed their views in the light of new political thinking in Britain, and it was not the details of Company rule that interested them so much as its purposes. They were also the first to be concerned about how to justify British rule in a land without political inclusion, which meant going beyond narrow legality—the Company's preferred strategy—or armed force—the Company's actual practice. From here on we can detect a new, more explicitly liberal desire to earn legitimacy, which developed into a concern for law and order, public works, social reform and education.

This shift in attitude was representative of a larger, more important change in the political dynamic of British India. The most prominent feature of this change was the loss of autonomy of the EIC and the rise of London's political influence. After about two decades of self-absorbed reflection, the Company entered a new era.

The EIC had been a vulnerable and fearful state when it began, but by the late 1820s it had grown into a government with something of a conscience. By 1819 its sole import to England was tea. As its trading role fell away, there was no other reason for its existence than ruling and, conscious of its distance from the people it ruled, it turned its thoughts to education, health and welfare. A case in point was the Company's attitude to language and education. In Richard Wellesley's time, it was considered necessary that Company servants should learn Indian languages to deserve advancement. But this attitude was now reversed; through the 1820s it became a requirement that Indians should learn English to deserve advancement.

There were other significant changes in attitude. The new men emerging from the Company's school at Haileybury believed that if India did not possess rational laws and institutions, she should be given them. The attitudes expressed in James Mill's *History of India* reflected this shift, and make a stark contrast to Malcolm's writings. Malcolm wrote of heroes and glory, and wished that India could be run like Tory Britain. Mill analysed social forces and government structures, recommending reform and intrusion, with a yearning for benign authoritarianism in line with Utilitarian desires for rationality, order and security. This coincided with a widespread acknowledgement that the efforts of Munro and Elphinstone to adapt the panchayat system had failed. Out with the old, in with the new.

Thus liberal ideas promoted by men with little experience in Company service began to gain ascendancy. Once such was Charles Trevelyan, who had been taught by Malthus at Haileybury. He reached India in 1826, and went on to have an extraordinarily long and influential career in both British and Indian administration—as did his friend and future brother-in-law, Thomas Macaulay, who arrived in India in 1834.

But there was also a large political question hovering in the background. The Company's charter was due for renewal in 1833, and opinion among liberals, free traders and Evangelicals was hardening against the Company. And with the EIC carrying a debt of £40 million, politicians were about to start asking searching questions about its conduct and future role. All this pressured the directors into accepting the need for new approaches.

The concentration of political power in London won out over the more dispersed administrative power within India, and this produced the reforms of the 1830s. But there was one further, personal factor, which was slightly more fortuitous. The Governor-General who went out in

1828 was Lord William Henry Cavendish Bentinck (1774–1839), appointed to that post in 1828, who for his own reasons was disinclined to argue with the directors. For the first time in a generation, British India fell into the hands of a politician who was all too ready to listen to them—a man who wanted to repair a career, not forge one. There were no more conquests or dreams of expansion during Bentinck's time. His remit was reform and retrenchment. This was a perfect way in which to streamline government on modern lines.

Lord William's mission, as defined by the directors, was to put the Company's affairs in order, and to balance the books before the review of the Company's charter. Whatever else Bentinck achieved, he succeeded in this, by turning an annual deficit of about £2 million into a surplus of £500,000.

He was extraordinarily lucky to land the job of Governor-General. Several well-qualified candidates had turned it down before it was offered to him, and it was something of a surprise that he was offered the post at all, because trouble was known to follow him around. He had undertaken a variety of important missions overseas but had under-performed in all of them, most notoriously during his stint as Governor of Madras from 1803 to 1807, when he was thought to have made a poor job of putting down a mutiny among the sepoys at Vellore in 1806. Until then he had been a career soldier, serving in the Low Countries, Ireland, Italy and Egypt, but without ever seeing much action. After being recalled from India in 1807, he campaigned in Spain, where he actually led troops in battle, before moving on to become Commander-in-Chief of the Mediterranean.

This involved him in a series of semi-diplomatic missions to Italian states, where his enthusiasm for upsetting the French by promoting Italian nationalism got the better of him; he set up a parliament in Sicily, and declared a republic in Genoa. When he started subversive schemes in Piedmont he was finally recalled, replaced by a diplomat less imbued with reforming fervour. Back in England he re-entered Parliament, where he served from 1816 to 1826, but spoke little and held no offices. Increasingly he spent his time in attempts to improve his Norfolk estate, while sliding slowly into debt. The second call to India saved him financially, and allowed him an opportunity to restore his reputation.

How did a plum job, worth £25,000 per annum, fall to him after a career such as his? The answer lies in what contemporaries called 'connection'. He was the second son of the third Duke of Portland, a senior Whig grandee, who was twice prime minister for short spells, in 1783 and

1807–9. Family influence was absolutely central to Bentinck's career. It was his father that got him the governorship of Madras in 1803 through the then prime minister, Addington. Another important link was his elder brother's wife's sister. She was married to George Canning, a Tory politician who became prime minister in 1827, and it was Canning who, despite party allegiances, persuaded the directors to appoint Bentinck as Governor-General.

Bentinck's term in India stands clearly apart from the quarter-century that preceded it, as he conducted a very broad review of policy in areas that included the law, education, social reform, finance and administration. Sati was prohibited, internal customs were abolished, the language of government and the high courts was changed from Persian to English, the currency was standardized as the Bengal silver rupee, the emperor's head was taken off the coinage, and Indians were more closely involved in the structure of Company rule, especially in the lower ranks of the judiciary.

Some of these policies were prompted by the reforming attitudes becoming prevalent in Britain, but most of Bentinck's activity was closely controlled by the EIC's directors, and amounted to an exercise in public relations, aimed at presenting a more efficient and socially concerned image to the Company's critics in England. This was certainly true of the prohibition of sati. It cost nothing and had been vociferously called for by the Evangelical lobby, which had gone to considerable lengths to exaggerate its prevalence.[22] The Christian cohorts were also greatly pleased by the adoption of English-language instruction, after Macaulay's Education Minute of 1835.

Bentinck dutifully followed his instructions throughout, liaising closely with John Ravenshaw, a prominent director. He pleased his London masters by resisting pressure from within his own Council to allow freedom of the press in India, despite his own sympathy for the measure. Deep cuts in the military budget were similarly well received in Leadenhall Street, although they made him unpopular with the Company's senior soldiers, who derisively named him 'the Clipping Dutchman', a reference to his family's seventeenth-century Dutch roots.

He was the first Governor-General since Sir John Shore (1793–8) to avoid fighting a major war, which greatly helped him with his budgets. What Bentinck and Shore had in common was that they were more directly answerable to the EIC's directorate than the intervening politicians had been, though in Bentinck's case this did not mean an absolute avoidance of territorial expansion.

By 1828 the EIC had become the policeman of India, and was entangled in affairs all across the subcontinent. Disorder in nominally independent Mysore allowed the British to impose direct rule in 1831. Bentinck considered similar measures in Jaipur and Gwalior, while Kachar (1832), Coorg (Kodagu) (1834) and Jainta (1835), were annexed, all to restore orderly government. He also concluded a treaty with the amirs of Sind to open up the Indus river to trade.

Bentinck's intellectual make-up is a favourite subject for historians. He has sometimes been represented as a great liberalizer, especially by commentators keen to establish reforming credentials for the British Raj, but this is a misplaced description. He certainly flirted with Benthamite Utilitarianism, and there is a well-attested story that at a dinner to mark his departure for India, Bentinck kindly remarked to James Mill, the most Benthamite of the EIC's senior London staff, that it would be he, Mill, who was about to become Governor-General.[23] This may have been nothing more than man-management dressed up as politesse, but better and cheaper government was just as acceptable to the directors as it would have been to Bentham.

But Bentinck cannot be so simply labelled. He was an Evangelical Christian, an admirer of Burke, a critic of British rule, and a reader of Bentham. More prosaically, he can equally plausibly be presented as nothing much more than a wayward soldier who had finally learned the value of obeying orders.

There is no doubt that Bentinck personally espoused views of a liberal nature, but his 'liberalism' fitted very neatly in many cases with a drive for economy, especially in the employment of Indians within the administration and judicial system. In dismantling the old Whiggish system of boards and committees, Bentinck gave ordinary Indians speedier justice, but also saved a great deal of money. The 'single officer' style of government that resulted was more Utilitarian than liberal, but with proper supervision and esprit de corps it was considered reliable and appropriate in India.

Similarly, the drive for English education was part of a long-term strategy to expand the Company's administration at low cost. This was even true of medical services. The Calcutta Medical College was opened in 1835 to increase the supply of Indian doctors trained in Western medicine; a school opened earlier, in 1822, had only trained assistants.

But Bentinck spent money too, and in new ways. He provided funds for canal building, improvement of the Great Trunk Road, and river works in south India, with anicuts by Arthur Cotton on the Cauvery and

Coleroon. He also conducted a costly campaign against highway robbery (thagi). All these initiatives, along with the prohibition of sati, can be seen as an attempt to legitimize British rule in a land without representative government. With the Company under no credible threat, Bentinck's choice of priorities marks a definite move away from the narrow pursuit of legality and security to a clear quest for legitimacy. This should not be confused with mature liberalism, but a clearly liberal concern for the rights of subjects can be seen all across his policies, as in his abolition of flogging for sepoys.

The whole idea of the liberal Bentinck is to some degree a matter of guilt by association. At exactly this moment, the first raft of truly liberal legislation was being enacted in Britain, with the emancipation of non-Anglican Protestants in 1828, of Catholics the next year, the selective enfranchisement of the middle classes in 1832, and the abolition of slavery in 1833. It would be more accurate to see Bentinck as a weak figure, and his efforts as a faint reflection of this domestic activity, with a distinctly imperial perspective.

But even with a balanced budget and a list of creditable administrative and social reforms accomplished, Bentinck was unable to save the Company's trading rights, which were completely abolished by the Charter Act of 1833. From then on, the Company was simply an administrative body, charged with government in India. All the Company's territories now came under the direct authority of Calcutta, which itself implied more political control from London.

The duties of the Governor-General of India still involved the government of Bengal, but his legislative powers were extended to the whole of British India. In his capacity as legislator, he now sat on an extended Council, augmented to four by the addition of a Legal Member. The Governors of the two junior Presidencies were each given an executive council of three; they lost their independent powers of expenditure, but retained the right to conduct separate correspondence with London. The Bishop of Calcutta was also provided with two junior bishops, based in Madras and Bombay.

The greatest liberal triumphs in the 1833 Charter Act were the termination of all the EIC's trading rights, and the declaration in Section 87 that no person should be denied administrative employment on grounds of religion, 'descent' (race), place of birth or colour. These two provisions apart, the 1833 Act was the most realistic and practical yet in terms of facing up to the problems of governance in India. It also marked the high point of the concentration of powers at the centre. By the time of the next Charter Act, twenty years later, concerns had arisen about the wisdom of placing so much executive and legislative power in the hands of such a small, centralized group of individuals.

Under Bentinck's direction, the suppression of thagi (ritualized highway robbery) used a degree of administrative and judicial muscle that would have made any true liberal shudder. The prime mover of the campaign was Sir William Henry Sleeman (1788–1856). William Sleeman won enduring fame for the way he penetrated, documented and eventually destroyed the network of gangs engaged in thagi, the murder of travellers by strangulation as a prelude to robbery. This campaign, from 1830 to 1839, which he conducted virtually single-handedly, has since regularly been held up as proof positive of the benefits of British rule.

Sleeman went out to India as a soldier, but did very little actual fighting. He took part in the Nepal War of 1814–16, but spent much of it ill with fever. The fact that he eventually attained the rank of major general in 1854 was purely a matter of survival and rulebook seniority.

He joined the EIC's political service, and was first posted to Sagar (Madhya Pradesh) in 1820, where he began to investigate the activities of gangs of thags (deceivers) in the region. Eventually he persuaded a number of captured thags to become 'approvers' (informers). By careful listening, and a process of detailed cross-referencing, he learned of a network of disciplined gangs that were responsible for the murder of thousands of travellers.

British officials had been aware of thagi since 1815, but by the 1830s gangs had begun to target two particular types of cash-rich victims—sepoys returning to their homes on leave, and runners carrying cash for banks between large mercantile centres. The loss of these important travellers was of more than ordinary interest to both the Company and the business community, British and Indian. Sleeman thus had no problem finding friends in high places to back his costly operation. Bentinck blessed his work in 1830, and in 1835 Sleeman was made general superintendent of a department specifically charged with suppressing thagi and dacoits (bandits).

A thag murder was almost the perfect crime, and the process of disrupting the gangs was slow and laborious. The victims had no prior connection with their murderers, whom they met purely by chance. Gangs chose their targets by a process of falling in with them and conversing, while pretending to share a destination. The decision to strike and the precise timing of the kill were determined by a combination of instinct and superstition, so there was never a pattern of repeated incidents to unravel. Nor were there any witnesses, because a thag gang would meticulously kill every last member of the party they set upon, strangling them rapidly and noiselessly with scarves. Their bodies were then dismembered and carefully buried so that no traces remained, and wild animals would not disturb the graves. The trail, therefore, was always cold; suspicions were only aroused when victims did not appear at the end of a long journey, weeks or even months later. And without bodies, there was no proof that a crime had ever been committed.

Sleeman was thus obliged to bend the rules of justice a little to get his convictions. As a crime without witnesses it was almost impossible to convict anyone of a thag murder under the modified shari'a law that the Company enforced in its territories, because under Islamic jurisprudence co-defendants could not testify against each other. It was also a matter of some dispute as to whether a scarf counted as a deadly weapon, the use of which was another important requirement to secure a conviction for murder. So Sleeman, who absolutely depended on informants' evidence, usually chose to try suspects in what was known as a Non-Regulation Territory, outside the Company's direct jurisdiction, where common law could be applied. Eventually Sleeman hanged over a thousand of the worst offenders and ringleaders. This left around 3,000 of the minor players to serve terms of life imprisonment in a specially constructed jail at Jabalpur.

Sleeman's own devout Christianity coloured the British view of thagi for at least a century, during which it was common to represent the thags as a secret religious sect, driven by a fanatical devotion to assuaging the bloodlust of the goddess Kali. This was both a vast exaggeration and a deep misunderstanding. The gangs generally came from poorer agricultural areas, where they would do deals with local rajas to split the loot in return for protection. Their secret language was no more than lower-class slang, unfamiliar to Sleeman.

Thagi was not a religiously motivated activity, though it was elaborately superstitious; Sleeman seems to have ignored the fact that about a third of the thags were Muslims. It was a hereditary profession more than anything else, and one that required a pitiless streak. The act of befriending strangers in a convincing way over several days, knowing that they were to die, and then mutilating their warm corpses must have required a form of psychological conditioning that no religion would be likely to instil. They killed for money and found a perfect way to bind the whole gang to the deed, while justifying it in a chillingly callous way.

Sleeman was hailed as a hero for his work, and moved on in 1842 to investigate unrest in Sagar and Nabanda. His report found that the principal cause of the trouble was a lack of respect shown by the British towards local Indian notables. He was then rewarded with two plum postings as Resident: in Gwalior (1843–9) and Lucknow (1849–54). From the latter he wrote extensively about the disorderly state of government in Awadh to Lord Dalhousie, but opposed the annexation of the province, believing that reform could be achieved without disrupting existing social and political arrangements. Sleeman was thus thinking along the same lines as Henry Lawrence in the Punjab, being more than happy to argue for the maintenance of the rights of native elites. But like Lawrence, he also lost his case. Awadh was annexed in 1856, two years after his departure.

Worn out by a lifetime of overwork, Sleeman headed for home to recuperate, but died on board ship off Sri Lanka in February 1856 and was buried at sea.

Another important reform during Bentinck's time was the order from the directors in 1833 that the EIC had to divest itself of the various responsibilities for temples and religious charities that it had accumulated on an ad hoc basis since the 1760s. The way that the Company had drifted into becoming a patron of mosques, temples and religious festivals was disturbing to some on principle, but it was also considered politically undesirable in terms of its potential to drag the Company into local disputes. The prevailing view in London was that the British should remain neutral in religious affairs, although a small group, led by Lord Glenelg (Charles Grant junior), wished to adopt a more active missionary role.

A strong streak of Evangelical Christianity emerged among both soldiers and civilians in India through the 1830s, and not always among the younger men. Sir Peregrine Maitland, Commander-in-Chief of the army of Madras, resigned his post in 1838 rather than punish a Christian sepoy for refusing to attend a parade in honour of a Hindu deity. The senior command condemned him, though he garnered some support within the Evangelical lobby in Parliament. Other notable evangelizers included Lord Tweeddale, Governor of Madras from 1842 to 1848, who was censured and recalled for his indulgence towards missionaries and his use of the term 'heathen' in public communications.

The directors were generally consistent in their caution in religious matters. Tweeddale's predecessor, John Elphinstone, had displayed the traditional aversion to religious interference, yet had still incurred the wrath of the directors for his reluctance to disengage with local religious establishments.

There was never any uniformity in policy among the Company's senior Christians, but they were fully aware of the need for caution. None was more devout than John Lawrence, who ran the Punjab from 1853 to 1859, but he was opposed to active proselytizing in the army. He would only countenance the conversion of those who were not part of India's major faith traditions.

Nor was there ever a 'growing band of Evangelicals'[24] within the directorate, as a well-known British writer has claimed. Between the two Charter Acts of 1813 and 1833 there were only two who merited the description—Charles Grant senior and Edward Parry. Grant died in 1823 and Parry in 1827. After 1833 there was only one—Sir James Rivett-Carnac, who served as chairman from 1836 to 1837. Alone among the directors, he supported the religious provisions of the 1833 Charter Act, but then changed his mind about permitting proselytization when in 1838, as Governor of Bombay, he faced rioting from the Parsi community over the activities of missionaries.

The Company did come under increased pressure from the Evangelical lobby after 1834, but it resisted adopting conversion as a policy. It chose instead to speed up the severance of its links with religious institutions, a long and complicated process not completed till 1863.

Through this period the traditional policy of neutrality and non-interference became increasingly fuddled. Politicians such as Sir Charles Wood insisted that wider provision of education was a proper government aim, and steps to fulfil this ambition were taken through the 1850s, to elevate standards, acculturate Indians to British rule, and expand economic activity. Indians, however, became increasingly unable to distinguish between the different segments of the Christian church and their relationships with government. All Christians seemed much alike to them, as did the schools they provided, whether independent (religious) or government-funded (secular).

The EIC's chaplains were banned from conversion work, but the situation on the ground was never very clear to either the godly or the heathen. This was duly acknowledged in 1847 when all Company servants were explicitly forbidden to engage in missionary work as part of their official capacity. Some claimed that this order was confusing and lacked detail, but the intention behind it was clear. The EIC always declined to be the instrument of any concerted Christianization policy.

Nor did Herbert Edwardes, often held up as a heedless and determined advocate of conversion, demur from this policy. 'It is not the duty of the

Government, as a Government, to proselytize India,' he wrote. He believed it was the 'duty' of 'private Christians'. And he absolutely forswore the use of 'anything like compulsion'.[25]

The most momentous positive work of this period was in education and the law, and it was accomplished not by Bentinck, but by Charles Trevelyan and Thomas Macaulay. These two liberal minds were behind the famous Education Minute of February 1835, later approved by Bentinck, which insisted that Indians be drawn into the British sphere by learning Western subjects, in English.

Considering that he was only in India for four years from 1834 to 1838, and that he never held a position of executive power, Thomas Babington Macaulay (1800–59) had a remarkably lasting impact on India. This was partly a matter of timing, in that he arrived at the climax of a period of government reorganization, but also because of his genuine capabilities as a polymath. He was an aspiring politician, a qualified barrister and a superb writer, which allowed him to leave his mark in three distinct areas: education, the codification of law, and the writing of Anglo-Indian history. In return, four years in Calcutta at £10,000 per annum meant that, financially, India set him up for life.

Macaulay was a complex and sometimes exasperating individual, frequently brilliant, but pompous and immoveable in his views. Usually shy in company, he could also become animated and pugnacious, with a capacity for partiality and exaggeration. Contemporaries often found him hard to take at full tilt. Sydney Smith, the noted wit, once said of him that 'He had occasional flashes of silence, that made his conversation perfectly delightful'.[26]

He was unmistakeably gifted, and stories of his precociousness abound. One has it that when, aged four, his legs were scalded by a misdirected stream of coffee, he replied to a kind enquiry after his welfare with the words 'Thank you, Madam, the agony is abated'.[27] His reputation as an adult encouraged these sorts of stories and this one may well be spurious. Better attested, and more believable, is the account of the occasion when a housemaid removed some oyster shells he had placed in the family garden to mark a flowerbed. His Bible reading enabled him to express his anger in a uniquely devastating manner. 'Cursed be Sally,' he raged, 'for it is written: "Cursed is he that removeth his neighbour's landmark" [Deuteronomy 27:17].'[28] While still only ten, an indulgent elder famously said of him: 'I wish I was as cocksure of anything as Tom Macaulay is of everything.'[29]

Though he grew up to be associated with strongly liberal opinions, Thomas was born into a high Tory family. His father Zachary was a fervent Evangelical and an active anti-slavery campaigner, whose commitment even took him to Africa to provide health care for escaped slaves.

Thomas went to Trinity College, Cambridge, in 1818, and became a Fellow in 1824. He then qualified as a barrister in 1826, and was elected a member of Parliament in 1830. His speeches on the Great Reform Bill of 1832 got him noticed, leading to a place as secretary to the Indian Board of Control. He spoke extensively on the renewal of the EIC's charter in 1833, and in 1834 he was sent out to Calcutta to fill the newly created position of Legal Member of the Governor-General's Council, a job he seems to have taken, like Bentinck, partly to mend his own and his family's finances.

After Bentinck's departure in 1835, he drafted a new Code of Criminal Law and Codes of both Civil and Criminal Procedure, to run throughout all British India. Despite some revision, the substance of these Codes has remained almost unaltered to this day. It was this remarkable work that led the Indian historian K.M. Panikkar to hail Macaulay as a 'second Manu'.

His other great work was his review of education policy in India, as set out in the famous Education Minute of 2 February 1835, which he wrote in his capacity as chairman of the Committee of Public Instruction. This document contains most of Macaulay's well-known derogatory pronouncements about Indian culture, and it clearly spells out his views of the purposes and prospects for British rule in India. Broadly speaking, Macaulay asserted that the most enlightened and useful options open to the Company were, firstly, to educate Indians rather than leave them ignorant, and secondly, to educate them in English and local vernacular languages as part of an overall syllabus that should include English literature and European science, as opposed to an education in Sanskrit, Persian or Arabic classics. By implication, such an education would be secular and Anglophile, not theological and conservative. This overall scheme, it must be emphasized, was not intended to produce radical social change or to promote Christianization. Macaulay's intellectual hinterland in this matter was secular liberalism, not any kind of Christian conviction. He was much more concerned with finding ways of running a viable British regime in India, supported by compliant and capable Indian subjects, than with winning souls for Christ.

Macaulay kept very quiet about his own religious beliefs. He was probably not a believing Christian, unlike most of his contemporaries, and very unlike his friend, the devout Charles Trevelyan, who married his sister and whose views on Indian education and anglicization he adopted. Macaulay is generally regarded as having had an aversion to religious enthusiasm, and he may have lost his seat in Edinburgh in 1847 partly because the pious Scottish electors suspected him of godlessness.

His mature political and intellectual views were all from the Whig-Radical-Liberal areas of British life, not the religious. In the Education Minute itself he specifically rejects missionary and conversion work: 'We abstain, and I trust shall always abstain, from giving any public encouragement to those who are engaged in the work of converting the natives to Christianity.'[30] Attempts by Indian nationalists to paint Macaulay as a soldier of Christ are unjustified.

His recommendations, however, were not disinterested; he certainly intended that any Indian product of his proposed system should be loyal, English-speaking and of practical value to the British regime. For him, the purpose of education was to produce a local supply of administrative staff imbued with Western habits and values, 'a class of persons, Indian in blood and colour, but English in taste, in opinions, in morals, and in intellect'[31]—the notorious 'brown Englishmen' of a later phrase.

Bentinck approved the minute wholeheartedly, on 7 March 1835, and its subsequent adoption marked the permanent defeat of the Orientalists, such as Thoby Prinsep, who wished to give full respect to the ancient traditions of all sections of the Indian population. The results of this victory were slow to appear, and Macaulay does not bear responsibility for the future of all Indian education; he merely laid down aspirations and guidelines about higher education.

The minute's only immediate practical effect was the gradual appearance of public schools—one per district. It was a combination of Thomason's work in the North West Provinces (1843–53), Sir Charles Wood's Education Despatch of 1854, and recommendations from later commissions that shaped education in India over decades.

Macaulay also played a small part in advancing the equality agenda in India, when in 1836 he revoked the privilege, accorded to Europeans, to have cases heard in the Supreme Court in Calcutta, rather than in the Company's Sadr Adalat. This measure, dubbed the Black Act, was resisted vigorously, but unsuccessfully, by the European population of Calcutta, in the first large-scale outburst of anti-government feeling in favour of white privileges. The promotion of equality under a uniform legal system was at the very centre of Macaulay's mission in India—an impeccably liberal aspiration, but one that was not always popular. Measures towards its achievement were resisted by Europeans again in 1849 and 1882.

After returning home in 1838, Macaulay had a political career of no great distinction, sitting as MP for Edinburgh, and serving short periods as Secretary at War and Paymaster General. More notably he resumed writing criticism and essays for the *Edinburgh Review*, the most prestigious organ of the liberal classes. In this capacity he reviewed Malcolm's *Life of Robert Lord Clive* in 1840, and G.R. Gleig's biography of Warren Hastings later the same year.

It is in these lengthy reviews that Macaulay clearly sets out his considered views on India. In them he was prepared to admit that early British rule was indeed corrupt and unsavoury. Clive was a doer of deeds that were 'of evil example' and Warren Hastings was accused of 'great crimes' and of being 'deficient' in elements of 'social virtue', such as sympathy for his fellow man. These criticisms, however, are laid out only to create a contrast with the times in which he was writing, in which everything was much better, and honesty and humane government had become the norm. In particular, he strongly and consistently disagreed with Malcolm about Clive's actions, which Malcolm refused to condemn in any great degree, defending Clive's deception of Omichand as the merited deserts of a practised deceiver, and his acceptance of vast gifts from Mir Jafar as no more than a personal offering prompted by gratitude.

Less creditably, Macaulay's writings on India include his extravagantly expressed contempt for Bengalis, listing a set of monumentally insulting prejudices (weak, servile, effeminate, deceitful, etc.) that remained fresh in the minds of his targets for at least a century. This went along with his considered belief that Oriental people were different from Europeans. Indians, he said, were 'a people who have much in common with children'.[32]

Equally disappointing in a man of such intelligence, Macaulay chose to revive and embellish the story of the Black Hole of Calcutta. It was Macaulay who first called the defence of Calcutta 'feeble', surely a misjudged description of a fight that lasted four days, cost the lives of at least 200 defenders, and was only ended by treachery. It was Macaulay that first sought to condemn the Nawab of Bengal directly for the death of 123 prisoners in an overcrowded cell.

Macaulay's great reputation seems to have established his version of these events as sacrosanct, ensuring its inclusion in school books for more than a century after 1840, so that John Z. Holwell's personal account of his night in the Black Hole, a transparently exaggerated and self-serving telling of the tale, peppered with inconsistencies, inventions and absurdities, became a sort of holy writ, under the imprimatur of Britain's greatest historian. That no one saw fit to challenge this account meant that someone as well educated as Lord Curzon was prepared to swallow the Holwell–Macaulay myth almost whole. Curzon even felt it necessary to erect a new monument to the (long-forgotten) victims of the tragedy in 1902.

So it was that Macaulay's buoyant patriotism and his unshakeable convictions about the justice of Britain's mission to India passed unquestioned into a Victorian tradition of high piety and cultural chauvinism. So it was that Macaulay unwittingly not only called into being an education system, he also provided it with a central part of its didactic, historical content.

Macaulay's time in Calcutta only overlapped with Bentinck's for a few months, so their collaboration was necessarily brief and was confined to the education issue. Once Bentinck had left, Macaulay did what he had originally been sent out to do. He drafted rational, unified legal codes for British India, finishing the job in two years of intensive work. This was not only a novelty to India but also to Great Britain, which still boasts no such foundational document in its legal system. His codes underwent a leisurely process of review and revision, but were finally introduced in 1860–2.

6

1839–1858

DISASTER, SUPREMACY, MODERNITY, MUTINY

1839–49: Five Wars

The peace that Bentinck bequeathed was not to last. Over the years 1839–49, the EIC fought five major wars. The first two, in Afghanistan and Sind, were loosely connected by a perceived threat from Russia, the third was fought in Gwalior to enforce the Company's claims to paramountcy, and the last two determined who would rule the Punjab.

Since 1800 the British had been wary of Russian influence in the region, fearing that Tsarist troops might suddenly appear on India's border backed by a friendly shah of Persia or a compliant Afghan amir. Russia fought victorious wars with the Persians in 1826–8 and the Turks in 1828–9, which set nerves jangling. There was then much talk about the best way of defending India in the north-west, with occasional changes of mind about supporting Afghanistan or Persia, and discussions about where the 'natural' (i.e. most defensible) border lay. None of the five rivers of the Punjab nor the Indus was seriously considered as defensible, so the search was always on for another potential line of defence beyond or behind the Indus, which in turn brought up the question of who ruled the Punjab, and how friendly they were.

Afghanistan was under the rule of Dost Muhammad Khan after 1826, but the British were sheltering a long-time Afghan ex-amir, Shah Shuja, who had been expelled from Kabul in 1809, and had unsuccessfully challenged Dost Muhammad for the throne as recently as 1834. Shah Shuja's main redeeming quality was neither his ability as a ruler, which was deficient, nor his popularity in Afghanistan, which was non-existent, but the fact that he had signed a treaty of friendship with the Company shortly before his ouster three decades before. He was also acceptable to the Sikhs, who had supported his recent bid for the throne.

A British mission to Kabul in 1836 broke down over the issue of Peshawar, lately seized by the Sikhs; the amir wanted it back, and asked for British help to get it. The British, however, were not prepared to antagonize Maharaja Ranjit Singh, and demurred. The last round of the preparatory game was the appearance of a Russian mission to Kabul in 1837, and an attack by the Shah of Persia on Herat in mid-1838. Tensions rose, but then the Russians withdrew from Kabul and local forces drove the Persians from Herat. Peace should, by rights, have followed too. But Governor-General Lord Auckland (1836–41) thought otherwise, as he shared the fear of Russian intentions that afflicted Foreign Minister Palmerston in London. Plans were made to march on Kabul in order to replace Dost Muhammad with Shah Shuja.

Afghanistan did not share a border with British India, so any invading force was obliged to cross foreign territory. Cooperation was therefore required from Ranjit Singh, and a Tripartite Treaty was signed in June 1838 between the British, the Sikhs and Shah Shuja. The amirs of Sind, to the south, were bullied into paying a large subsidy towards the campaign, but as war approached Ranjit Singh held back, leaving the adventure entirely in British hands. A large British-led force then set off for Sind in December 1838, in order to attack Kabul from the south via the Bolan Pass. Sir John Keane was in nominal command, but the real power lay with William Hay Macnaghten, secretary to Governor-General Auckland, and chief 'political' officer on the expedition.

Progress was swift. The Bolan Pass was crossed in March 1839, Kandahar fell in April, Ghazni in July, and Kabul in August, by which time Dost Muhammad had fled. But this was hardly the end of the story. It was a relatively simple matter to proclaim Shah Shuja as amir, but much more difficult to make his writ run, and resistance continued in the uplands. Almost a year of peace followed in Kabul, during which the main body of the soldiery was sent back to India, and the families of those that remained were allowed to join them. Meanwhile unavailing attempts were made to enforce loyalty from the surrounding areas, including an ill-judged assault on the Khan of Khelat, who was considered to have been insufficiently helpful to the invading force.

The situation was unstable, and withdrawal was not considered prudent, so the British army stayed, encamped on the plain close to Kabul.

Dost Muhammad was finally captured in November 1840, but this still left a British garrison in Kabul supporting a puppet amir, isolated amid a resentful population.

The cost of the occupation was running at well over £1 million per year, but Macnaghten and his number two, Alexander Burnes, could only sit in Kabul and try to pretend that Shah Shuja was running the country. Both Macnaghten and Burnes had misgivings, but neither saw any other option than to continue the occupation. By November 1841, Burnes thought it time to retire from the country, while Macnaghten was keen to leave and take up the post of Governor of Bombay, which he had recently secured. They were preparing to withdraw when Burnes was murdered. The population of Kabul rose up, took control of the strong points in the city and massacred every European they could find. The British force remained in its camp outside the city—the first of a series of tactical blunders—and the initiative was lost.

The British camp came under repeated attack, and although it managed to hold out, the situation was clearly untenable. Macnaghten signed a humiliating treaty with Dost Muhammad's son, Akbar Khan, on 11 December, under which the British undertook to leave, to take Shah Shuja with them, and to release Dost Muhammad, who was being held in India. Having signed this document, Macnaghten then unwisely plotted with other Afghan leaders to undermine Akbar Khan, who caught wind of the conspiracy and shot Macnaghten dead at their next meeting, on 23 December.

The senior British officer, General Elphinstone, then had no choice but to sign another treaty, and a full-scale withdrawal of all troops, families and camp followers began on 6 January 1842. It rapidly turned into a massacre, a hideous drawn-out retreat under fire, in the coldest part of the year. Out of around 16,000 souls who left Kabul, only one man reached the safety of Jalalabad, on 13 January 1842.

Such a military catastrophe would put any imperial power at risk in a distant country, and the British leadership in Calcutta understood this very well. Auckland tried to pretend that it was only a minor reverse, but in February 1842 he was replaced by Lord Ellenborough (1842–4), a man whose pugnacious and independent character stood in stark contrast to Auckland's lassitude.

Ellenborough had opposed the war, but now accepted that the best way to retrieve the situation was through further fighting. He therefore sent General Pollock to punish the Afghans at the head of an 'Army of Retribution', which Auckland had already assembled. Pollock retook

Kabul without difficulty, freed prisoners and hostages, and demolished the city's bazaar, where the dismembered remains of Macnaghten had been displayed. Ellenborough then announced, by a proclamation of 1 October 1842, that the Afghans would be left to run their own affairs.

Rather less shrewdly he also announced, a month later, that the doors of the temple at Somnath, taken to Afghanistan as booty 800 years before, had been recovered by Pollock. He was mistaken; the trophies were obvious fakes and were never heard of again. Dost Muhammad was finally released in January 1843, after which he returned to Kabul and continued to rule until 1863, in almost perfect amity with his erstwhile captors.

In purely military terms, the First Afghan War was short and not particularly interesting. The fighting lasted less than six months, and was entirely successful for the British. The reason that this war has remained a subject of fascination for historians is almost entirely because it sent out unheeded warnings about Afghan conditions to generations of future strategists. It showed that while heavy firepower could win pitched battles in lowland areas, fighting over broken country in smaller formations was likely to be open-ended. The sheer hardiness of the resistance showed that while it was relatively easy to 'conquer' Afghanistan by taking its towns, it was murderously difficult to enforce obedience outside them.

Military incompetence played a part too, but the real flaws in the campaign were primarily political and diplomatic. There were no firm foundations for the original policy of 'defending' Afghanistan against the Russians, and even weaker ones for the return of Shah Shuja to Kabul. Predictably, Dost Muhammad played the British against the Russians, but the British never tried very hard to accommodate him. Overconfidence took hold of Macnaghten, who was well placed to influence Governor-General Auckland, and an early decision was made that a friendly face had to be installed in Kabul, and the military wherewithal was then assembled through 1838. The historian J.W. Kaye maintained that the whole enterprise was conceived in a fit of 'political insanity' brought on by isolation in Simla.[1]

Kaye had a point, but it wasn't the thin air of Simla that was the problem. It was the flawed logic of alleviating diplomatic tension by military preemption, which led inevitably to expansion up to India's outermost borders. Imperial powers are always prone to paranoia. Any neighbour, if strong, can be seen as a direct threat or, if weak, as potential prey to other powers and thus an indirect threat. The prevailing logic is always expansionist.

In the aftermath of defeat, Ellenborough had a simplistic recovery strategy, which was to continue to display the strength of British arms in the region. His unfortunate targets were the neighbours of the defiant Afghans and surly Sikhs—the feudal Sindis. In a brief campaign, General Charles Napier then conquered the province, for no other reason than minor infringements of treaty obligations and alleged hostility during the Afghan campaign.

Sir Charles Napier (1782–1853) was the most untypical of British soldiers in India, and his haphazard blend of freethinking, self-justification and reckless autocracy defies classification. In general he was suspicious and resentful of authority unless he himself was wielding it, and in this he reflected some of the Raj's worst hypocrisies. Of all the generals who added to the British domain, he was the most individual, eclectic and intellectually arrogant.

Born in London, eldest of eight children, he grew up in Ireland. He liked to pretend that he was of obscure social origins, but his mother was the daughter of a duke and once turned down an offer of marriage from King George III; his father was a career soldier, but also the son of a baron. Charles followed his father into the army, enrolling at the age of twelve, and it was in defending his family's estate against the Irish uprising in 1798 that he had his first taste of real fighting. Typically, he found himself sympathizing with the rebels. This mirrored his generally flexible outlook, which was able to square a long career fighting the French with a deep admiration for Napoleon, and self-styled 'radical' views with extending colonial rule in India.

He gained his principal military experience in the Peninsular War, where he was wounded, captured and wounded again, returning to England in 1811, whereupon he saw fit to criticize Wellington's conduct of the war. In 1812 he was sent to the backwater of Bermuda, but still managed to cause uproar by hatching a plan to free plantation slaves and attack the American mainland, as part of the war then in progress with the former colonies.

His next prominent posting was to Cephalonia, an island off the west coast of Greece, which had for centuries been part of the Venetian state. It fell into British hands during the Napoleonic Wars, and became part of the United States of the Ionian Islands, a British protectorate from 1815 to 1864. Napier ruled the island as virtual dictator from 1822 to 1830, rather as Minto ran Corsica from 1794 to 1795, and Bentinck Sicily from 1813 to 1814. During this time he scrupulously avoiding traditional imperial policies, which he listed as 'robbery, oppression, murder and extermination of natives'.[2]

He was then put in charge of the northern domestic command in England, where his self-confessed sympathy with the Chartist protest movement helped to keep the peace. In all this he remained very distant from the classical Whig views of soldier-aristocrats like Cornwallis, who had led the suppression of the Irish in 1798.

Nevertheless he was dispatched to India in 1841, where he continued to criticize British policy unremittingly. He was capable of writing: 'Every shilling ... has been picked out of blood, wiped and put into the murderer's pocket ... We shall yet suffer for the crime as sure as there is a God in heaven,'[3] but at the same time he openly confessed that he had gone east himself to secure the financial future of his two daughters.

Napier reached India at a time when the EIC's quest for a secure northern border had started a war in Afghanistan, and had raised tensions with the independent Sikh state in the Punjab. The arid region of Sind to the south of the Sikhs seemed to present a strategic opportunity to strengthen the Company's position, as it commanded the Indus river and was ruled by a loose confederation of feudal amirs.

Napier disliked the amirs; he viewed their rule as oppressive, and called for annexation. This view was opposed by his subordinate, James Outram, who advocated setting up a protectorate. Guarantees of friendship were demanded by the Company, but the amirs remained evasive. Napier's views carried the day, and war followed.

The Sind campaign, which began in August 1842, was brief and victorious. The battles of Miani in February 1843 and Dabo in March ended resistance, after which the territory was placed under Company rule. The subject of money immediately raised its head again, with Napier locked in a long-running argument with the directors over prize money.

Two famous stories came out of the annexation. The first concerns the entirely apocryphal one-word telegram that Napier is alleged to have sent to the directors after his triumph. The message is supposed to have read 'Peccavi', Latin for 'I have sinned' (Sind). Napier did no such thing, nor could he have. There were no telegraphs in India for another ten years. The whole story is based on a humorous cartoon that appeared in May 1844 in *Punch*, satirizing his supposed guilt and reluctance. But the cartoon was not so wide of the mark: 'We have no right to seize Sind, yet we shall do so, and a very advantageous, useful, humane piece of rascality it will be!'[4] he wrote in his diary.

The second story concerns a deputation of local Sindi leaders to Napier, after he had extended the Company's prohibition of sati to the newly conquered province. This story may actually be true, but it exists in several versions. The shortest is that the amirs told Napier that sati was a customary act of piety. Napier replied: 'My nation has also a custom. When men burn women alive, we hang them and confiscate all their property ... Let us all act according to national customs.'[5]

As holder of supreme authority both military and civil, Napier set about reshaping the country he had won. But his quirky nature asserted itself in a string of unrestrained opinions about the mercilessness of his justice. Ever the critic of power, he was always keen to back the peasant against oppression, and often preferred to punish officials first and find out the truth afterwards. However, his introduction of a disciplined police force, loosely based on the contemporary Royal Irish Constabulary, was considered a success, and it was adopted as a model in other parts of British India.

The unnecessary and incompetently conducted Afghan War was therefore followed by the annexation of Sind, the most nakedly aggressive and unjustified conquest of the entire British period. This left Governor-General Edward Law, 1st Earl of Ellenborough (1790–1871) in a position of unshakeable dominance within India, which suited his character very well.

His father had been a successful barrister who defended Warren Hastings, acquired a peerage, was the last judge to sentence a man to be hanged, drawn and quartered, became Lord Chief Justice, and sat in cabinet from 1802 to 1807. Ellenborough junior was therefore born into privilege, and was more or less propelled into politics.

His background and connections were thoroughly Tory—the Duke of Wellington appointed him president of the Indian Board of Control in 1828 and 1834, and Sir Robert Peel sent him to India as Governor-General in 1841—but there was always a maverick aura about him.

His opinions on Indian economic and foreign policy were thoroughly Tory too, especially in terms of the need to make a strong alliance with India's existing ruling classes. Tories thought Britain should be run by a hereditary landed elite, and believed that this prescription was good enough for India too. Ellenborough was the first proconsul to see the problem of Indian governance in such clearly 'party' terms, and his ideas were later picked up by Canning and Lytton.

He believed that change should not be brought to India unnecessarily, because it risked unsettling the population, and might undermine the authority of the 'natural' leaders of society. Thus legal reforms, and especially religious proselytizing, were frowned upon, as was settlement by colonists.

A successful British India would be a quiet place, where prosperity could grow slowly and naturally under benign government. The British would rely on the loyalty of the army and on a mutually beneficial alliance with the landholding classes. In all this he would have concurred with John Malcolm, but he arrived at the same place by conviction, not experience.

Ellenborough remained an active advocate of such attitudes in Anglo-Indian politics for thirty years. The pinnacle of his career was his time as Governor-General from 1842 to 1844, but he also served as president of the Indian Board of Control on four occasions, in 1828–30, 1834–5, 1841 and 1858.

It was during his first stint as president that the tone of the next two decades of the Company's foreign policy was settled. The old strategy of reliance on Persia was rendered redundant after 1828, when the Russian defeat of the Persians opened the possibility of further Russian designs on Afghanistan. At that time, British access to Afghanistan relied on the cooperation of other powers—Sind under its amirs, and the Punjab under Maharaja Ranjit Singh—which was a precarious state of affairs.

It was under Ellenborough's leadership that preparations for solving this problem first took shape. It was he that sent Alexander Burnes (later killed in Kabul) on an expedition up the Indus in 1831, officially to deliver a present of horses to Ranjit Singh but unofficially to spy out Sind, strategically, economically and politically.

Ellenborough served as president again in 1841, then accepted the post of Governor-General as successor to Lord Auckland. The two met briefly, and Auckland came away convinced that his successor was actually mad. The directors, the cabinet and Ellenborough himself had all opposed the Afghan War, and he was offered the post before news of its disastrous second phase arrived in London. By the time he arrived in India, the story of the calamitous retreat from Kabul was fully known, and he immediately dispatched General Pollock to exact revenge.

But despite Pollock's victories, the north-west region remained insecure, with the amirs of Sind still independent, and an unstable Sikh regime descending into faction. So, despite his professed opposition to expansionism, it fell to Ellenborough to preside over the invasion of Sind, which was duly added to the Company's domain, again despite the opposition of the directors and the cabinet. In the end it was thought better to keep Sind than to give it back—a familiar decision, taken for familiar reasons, and one that would shortly be repeated in the case of Punjab.

Soon after the Sind campaign there was trouble in the Maratha state of Gwalior. Its maharaja died in early 1843, leaving a young adopted heir, whereupon an anti-British faction, led by Dada Khasgiwala, took over the government. The new regime harassed the British Resident, William Sleeman, to such an extent that he fled to nearby Dholpur, after which the Gwalior army, around 40,000 strong, threw out its Eurasian members, in violation of treaty commitments. Ellenborough responded by asking that Khasgiwala be handed over. Then, conscious that the Company's paramountcy was at stake, he further demanded that the Gwalior army be disbanded. Refusal to comply led to war.

Two British armies marched on Gwalior, and in a swift campaign both inflicted bloody but decisive defeats on the Sindhia forces, in the north at Maharajpur on 29 December, where Ellenborough himself was present, and in the south at Panniar, on the same day. Khasgiwala was captured, and a council of regency set up, led by Ram Rao Phalke, a long-time ally of the British. Under a revised treaty, the Gwalior army was then reduced in size, given British officers, and augmented by Company troops, which were paid for by grants of land. The fort of Gwalior was retained under a British garrison (until 1881), and guarantees of friendly relations were extracted from Jayaji Rao, the young maharaja.

This sent an unmistakeable message to all other Indian states—that the British position would be defended at whatever cost. Indeed, by 1843 there was no way in which the British could reasonably expect to avoid maintaining an active 'foreign policy' within India. Paramountcy could only operate if it was seen to be enforceable.

Both of Ellenborough's military ventures were thus completely successful, and the only major problem that remained was the Punjab. But it did not fall to Ellenborough to resolve it, because by the middle of 1844 the directors in London had tired of his disobedience and impudent dispatches. Eventually it was his determination to exclude the Legal Member from his Council that brought about his downfall. He was recalled—the only man of his rank ever to experience that indignity. 'Under an Indian sun, Ellenborough's fatal defects of character flourished like rank weeds.'[6]

His dismissal was at least partly the result of his persistent refusal to accept the established system of patronage that drove appointments within the Company. Instead, he preferred his own coterie of soldier minions, while expressing undisguised contempt for both the directors in London and their civilian protégés in India. This was both ill-judged and somewhat hypocritical, for he had been a beneficiary of straightforward nepotism himself, having been appointed chief clerk to the Court of King's Bench at £8,000 a year while his father presided there.

In the end his insistence on standing outside networks of personal 'interest' proved his undoing in domestic politics as well. His heedlessness and vanity earned him two nicknames: 'the Elephant' and 'the Peacock'. It was rumoured that Queen Victoria, like Auckland, also believed him to be mad.

He was certainly a strange creature intellectually. Like many Tories he seemed unsure of how abstractions were meant to join up. For instance, in foreign policy, he believed India should be protected strongly, but not too expensively or rashly, and that deliberate expansion was not worth the risk of unsettling or endangering the existing estate. Yet he ended up sending armies beyond the boundaries of British India twice, at considerable expense, and at some risk. This might come as less of a surprise if we consider that, privately, he once had the temerity to write, 'Asia is *mine*'.[7]

Somewhere in his complex psyche he also had a degree of sympathy for 'nationalist' sentiments. Earlier in his career, like Bentinck, he had supported Italian aspirations to nationhood. He recognized, though, that the formation of an Indian nation was likely to bring an end to British rule, and his solution to this dilemma was also typically arrogant. He felt that he should somehow take control of this incipient national feeling, in order to guide and shape it himself. This is why he made repeated references to ruling like Akbar, or 'coming the Aurangzebe'. If India were to be a nation, then he would embody it and lead it. His rather clumsy appeal to Indian patriotism through his mistaken claim to have recovered the gates of Somnath can best be understood in this light.

Of the Governors-General before 1857, he was in temperament by far the most despotic. He listened to no one; he thought of himself as a ruler and would not be treated like 'a clerk'. In this strong-headed independence he came to resemble the kind of man that an earlier generation had feared India might produce—a ruler of millions, beholden to none, a true Oriental autocrat. What many thought Clive might become, Ellenborough actually was.

He ranks as the first of the four most high-handed rulers of British India—the others being Dalhousie, Lytton and Curzon—all of whom were Tories. Of these four, Ellenborough and Lytton were the keenest to woo the upper classes in India, while Curzon felt a particular responsibility to promote the interests of the peasant. Dalhousie had little time for anyone, and consulted his masters back home as little as Ellenborough, but always managed to have rather more to show for his efforts.

Ellenborough can perhaps be considered the last man of the Company era who felt tempted by the possibilities of the East. He prefigured the ambitions of Curzon, but by Curzon's day the security of the Raj, and its heavily bureaucratized nature, meant that his style of despotism and independence did not alarm in London so much as irritate.

Other moves towards securing what might now be called 'broad spectrum dominance' were taken at around this time. Slavery was indirectly abolished throughout India in 1843, when the right to own slaves was no longer recognized in law, and the Lex Loci Act of 1845 extended common law to all of British India wherever there was no clear legal provision. The settlement of the North West Provinces was completed in 1843 on a basis of mahalwari or village tenure, and the last large area of British territory to be fully settled was the Bombay Presidency, where in 1847 the report of the Bombay Revenue Survey determined rules and regulations for the whole region. A small rebellion was suppressed in Kolhapur in 1844, while territorial acquisition continued, with the purchase in 1845 of the Danish possessions at Tranquebar, Serampore and Balasore, at a knock-down price.

By 1845 the independent Sikh power was the last loose piece in the strategic jigsaw. The Company had maintained friendly relations with Ranjit Singh throughout his reign, and wisely never considered taking on his powerful army. But after he died in 1839, the Punjabi state suffered from chronic instability. Intrigues at court and within the leadership of the army led to a series of short reigns, which brought Ranjit's youngest son, the five-year-old Duleep, to the throne in 1843. In late 1845, for reasons that are still not clear, a Sikh force crossed the Sutlej and full-scale war ensued.

There were two fiercely fought campaigns, in 1845–6 and 1848–9, both of which the Sikhs eventually lost. The veteran Sir Hugh Gough (1779–1869) held command throughout, despite the lack of faith his superiors had in him.

Gough had first seen action forty years before as part of the expeditionary force that captured the Cape of Good Hope from the Dutch in 1795, and he is reckoned to have commanded in more pitched battles than any other British soldier except the Duke of Wellington. Colleagues criticized his heavy-handed approach on the battlefield—what they called his 'Tipperary tactics', a slighting reference to his Irish roots.

Gough was appointed Commander-in-Chief of India in August 1843, after which his first task was to deal with the situation in Gwalior. He defeated the Sindhia forces, but his victory at Maharajpur did him no good in the eyes of Lord Ellenborough, who thought he lacked 'grasp of mind' and 'prudence'. Whatever his limitations, Gough kept his job and it was the autocratic Ellenborough who was sacked.

Ellenborough's successor, Lord Hardinge (1844–8), did not have much more faith in Gough, but was forced to rely on him when the First Sikh War broke out in December 1845. Hardinge, who was also a soldier, took the unusual step of opting to serve as Gough's second in command, the only time this reversal of political and military precedence occurred in British India.

Gough saw the job through with victories at Mudki, Ferozeshah, and Sobraon, hard-fought battles in which the Sikhs gave a valiant account of themselves. A treaty was then concluded that stopped short of annexation but imposed a fine, and placed the young maharaja under a British-controlled Council of Regency. Kashmir was taken as compensation, and then sold to Ghulab Singh, a former ally of the Sikhs.

The situation, however, was not stable and war broke out again in late 1848. Battles at Ramnagar, Chilianwala and Gujrat then put an end to Sikh resistance. The new Governor-General, Lord Dalhousie, was shocked by the high casualties suffered at Chilianwala and attempted to replace Gough with Sir Charles Napier, but Gough finished off the job at Gujrat before Napier could arrive.

As Commander-in-Chief, Napier, ever the malcontent, then clashed with Dalhousie over allowances for sepoys, which Dalhousie had withdrawn. Napier insisted they were prudent and just, and reinstated them. But Dalhousie was the senior man. He censured Napier, who resigned and retired to England.

Napier's instinct was always to side with the underdog, and he expressed genuine concern for men under his command. This made him another of the generals with a reputation as a 'soldier's friend'.

Still critical of British rule, Napier died three years later. As a postscript to his life he left not a memoir, but a sharply observed volume entitled *The Defects, Civil and Military, of the Indian Government* (1853).

For the Sikhs, this second defeat brought a definitive end to Khalsa government. The Koh-i-noor diamond was gifted to Queen Victoria, about half the Sikh army was absorbed into the Company's forces, the system of sardars (large landholders) was dismantled, and the Punjabi peasantry was brought into direct contact with a new British Board of Commissioners.

The Lahore state was the last fully independent Indian power of any size, and its demise represented a milestone in Indian history. All that remained of indigenous government was now dotted haphazardly across the subcontinent, consisting of isolated small states, none of which was capable of standing alone against the Company's enormous war machine. This marked the high point of British military fortunes.

The years 1839–49 had seen nearly continuous warfare, almost all of it successful, which had cleared up the major outstanding issues in northwestern India. The glaring exception remained Afghanistan, whose status was as unclear in 1849 as it had been ten years earlier. As a country it always looked unstable, and though it remained outside British control, it lurked within the British imagination.

The Punjab now had to be absorbed, and the challenges this presented created a new school of settlement. It also set up a famous argument between the Lawrence brothers, Henry and John. Sir Henry Lawrence (1806–57) became one of those British heroes whose career would scarcely have been remembered but for the circumstances of his death, which rendered him immortal. He was considered one of the 'martyrs' of the Uprising of 1857, and became a staple of Victorian hagiography, held up for special veneration because of his devotion to duty and his strong Christian faith. Putting this to one side, his career demonstrates a number of important elements in the rise of the British in India.

He was an average pupil at Addiscombe College, the EIC's cadet school, but he later excelled at Indian languages and this put him onto a parallel career path, enabling him to combine military command with political responsibilities. Though nominally a soldier all his life, like Malcolm and Sleeman he did very little actual fighting, and his rank of lieutenant colonel was the reward of persistence not brilliance.

He saw action early on in the First Burma War (1824–6), but was then side-lined by malaria and dysentery, from which it took him two years in England to recover. After his return in 1830, accompanied by his younger brother John, he threw himself into acquiring languages, and was appointed to a series of positions in land and revenue assessment.

Posted to Peshawar after news of the trouble at Kabul in November 1841, he then accompanied Pollock's force in 1842, commanding a Sikh contingent through a series of small engagements as the avenging army made its way to Kabul. Once there, he was reunited with his brother George, who had been held hostage for eight uncomfortable months.

His conduct earned him further promotion, and in April 1843 he took charge of the lands of the Raja of Kaithal, which had lapsed to the British for want of an heir. His success in 'settling' the area led to an appointment as Resident in Nepal, where he spent two fairly idle years, during which he wrote articles for magazines and founded an asylum, the first of many, for the children of Europeans.

After the outbreak of the First Sikh War in 1845, he was attached to Gough's army, and as the Governor-General's Agent for the Punjab he negotiated the treaty that ended the war. Here his political opinions surfaced for the first time; he was keen to support the existence of the Sikh state, and opposed its annexation. This restraint, however, did not extend to Kashmir, which the British took from the Sikhs as reparation and then sold to Ghulab Singh, the Raja of Jammu. When the incumbent, Sheikh Imamuddin, proved reluctant to quit, Lawrence persuaded him with a show of force.

Lawrence's relations with the Lahore Durbar were not entirely smooth, and he had to make himself virtual ruler of the kingdom; he pensioned off Lal Singh, regent to the under-age maharaja Duleep, and installed himself at the head of an eight-member Regency Council. He left local administration in Sikh hands, only requiring the easing of taxation and a reduction in numbers of the old Khalsa army. He also gave fifty Sikh 'greybeards' the task of collecting a corpus of Sikh customary law. But the strain of government reduced him to ill health, and he sailed to England on sick leave in 1847.

He returned to India in time to participate in the Second Sikh War of 1848–9, and was present at the indecisive battle of Chilianwala, where he reputedly persuaded General Gough to stay on the field to give at least the impression of a British victory.

After the war, Lawrence resigned over Dalhousie's decision to annex the Punjab, but was eventually persuaded to remain, whereupon he was created president of a three-man Board of Administration, set up to control the newly acquired lands. Henry took on the 'political' aspects of the annexation, his brother John handled the land settlement, and Charles Grenville Mansel was placed in charge of judicial matters.

But things did not go well. Though both devout Christians, the Lawrence brothers were temperamentally very different, with Henry decisive, quick and sociable, and John deliberate, cautious and sober. Henry disliked Dalhousie's modernizing ambitions and had a taste for princes and rajas, while John was a great defender of the peasant cultivator. Henry hoped that traditional social structures could be made a bulwark of British rule, while John thought that good government was a better foundation. Henry was prepared to commute cash demands into payments in kind; John insisted on cash, believing payments in kind to be an open door to abuses.

These were classic 'colonial' disagreements, of a kind visible all across British policy in India, but it was unusual to find the split so heavily personalized. That there could be such disagreements between brothers tends to emphasize that 'imperialism' was developed on the ground, not taught in books or schools.

Eventually the friction became sufficiently intense for Henry to offer his resignation. Dalhousie accepted it, abolished the Board, and put John in sole charge of the region. Henry was compensated with a senior diplomatic post, as Agent in Rajputana, but his influence lived on, in a cadre of 'Young Men' he had nurtured, including John Nicholson, Herbert Edwardes, Harry Lumsden, William Hodson and Neville Chamberlain. These were men that dispensed informal governance in remote regions, secure in the knowledge that their principles were sound and that their superiors would back them up. Many played important parts in suppressing the Uprising of 1857. Nearly all of them preferred Henry to his more stolid brother.

The heart of colonial society remained in the presidency towns, where many Indians continued to absorb and adapt alien influences and ideas. There was nothing yet like modern politics to address public concerns, and what would later become political energies found a home in intellectual inquiry and social causes. The new Indian bourgeoisie developed intense curiosity about modern scientific developments, and loose associations were formed to promote social improvement or to represent particular interest groups. This was very much how the fringes of domestic politics had worked all over eighteenth-century England in the heyday of the Whig system, when direct political representation was not considered necessary by the governing classes. Informal liaison was enough; the political climate remained restrained and moderate.

This was the context of the formation of bodies like the Society for the Acquisition of General Knowledge or the Landowners' Society, both established in Calcutta during 1838. A small roster of Calcutta intellectuals appeared in similar bodies right through to the end of the century, with members of the Tagore family prominent among them. In that same year, Prasanna Kumar Tagore, writing in his own journal, *The Reformer*, foresaw a time when Indians would be treated as fellow subjects under the Crown and would be accorded appropriate privileges.

Criticism of British rule was not absent, but it was generally muted, and tended to be directed at specific legal or economic issues. One notable exception was the series of letters that appeared in 1841 in the *Bombay Gazette*, written by Bhaskar Pandurang Tarkhadkar (1816–47), under the pen name 'A Hindoo', which were highly critical of colonial rule, and anticipated many of the economic arguments that Dadabhai Naoroji was later to take up. After eight such letters the paper's editor resigned, and the anonymous correspondent was silenced.

In general, the Indian intelligentsia was reluctant to criticize British political norms, because the aspirations of liberal England were their aspirations too. Criticism was more often addressed to contemporary Indian practices, and a vanguard group of reformers appeared in Bengal, soon replicated all over India, advocating modern education (even for women) and opposing caste distinctions and child marriage.

Calcutta remained to the fore in all these areas, with a stream of energetic intellectual pioneers figures emerging from Hindu College and Sanskrit College, founded in 1823. Most famous among these was Ishwar Chandra Sharma (1820–91), better known as Vidyasagar, who studied at Sanskrit College and later became its principal. He took up a variety of social causes, including widow remarriage, female education and the admission of non-Brahmins to Sanskrit College. Over all these issues he faced opposition from traditionalists. Ishwar Chandra Gupta was a vocal opponent of widow remarriage, and Rasamoy Datta, secretary of Sanskrit College, fought to restrict the College's intake.

It is easy to overstate these disputes, but fundamentally they were not about the rejection of all Western influence, which had evidently come to stay and had brought a range of benefits. They were part of a wider discussion about the pace and degree of modernization and the management of foreign influence, not its total rejection. The questioning of social norms was an important part of this, but similar debates were going on all over Europe at this time over very similar issues—social inclusion, scriptural authority, access to education and personal liberty.

The spread of new ideas, however, did not mean that India's more ancient traditions were neglected or rejected. Akshay Kumar Datta (1820–86) embarked on a critique of Indian philosophical traditions, not to discredit them, but to show how much within them was rational and valuable. As part of his investigation he challenged the authority of Vedic literature and succeeded in drawing the Brahmo Samaj away from literalism. He also strove to popularize scientific ideas and to place them in an Indian context.

Another evident side effect of British influence was the growth of international trade. In Calcutta, Madras and Bombay, Indians were involved in prosperous domestic enterprises, though they tended to stay out, or were kept out, of the export trade with Britain. Calcutta boasted the closest relationship between British and Indian commercial interests. Dwarkanath Tagore (1794–1846) left the Company's employ to build a business empire with active British partners, which encompassed banking, coal mining and shipping. Unfortunately for the future of Indian industry he went too far too fast, and shortly after his death the whole edifice collapsed under the weight of overextension and undercapitalization. But others built on more solid foundations. Ram Gopal Ghosh (1815–68), another alumnus of Hindu College, managed to amass a considerable fortune, and to live down his rebellious youth as a Derozian.

Similar developments were taking place in western India, where forward-thinking businessmen were moving towards industrialization. Bombay soon built a solid prosperity on cotton and opium. Both Jagannath Sunkersett (1803–65) and Jamsetjee Jejeebhoy (1783–1859) made fortunes in trade and became noted philanthropists, funding a range of cultural and educational projects. A new class of intellectuals also appeared, promoting education and social improvement. Balshastri Jambhekar (1802–46) set out to popularize Western science, and founded two popular newspapers, *Darpan* and *Digdarshan*. Another periodical, *Prabhakar*, carried a series of articles in the late 1840s, written by Gopal Hari Deshmukh 'Lokahitawadi' (1823–92), which were critical of Indian social norms. He had passed through the Poona English School, and was one of the early generation of writers who recognized the benefits of British rule, such as orderly government and consistent legal standards, while also retaining an ambition towards self-government at some future, as yet unspecified, date.

1849–56: Dalhousie, Paramountcy

The annexation of the Punjab in 1849 was one of the first acts of Governor-General Lord Dalhousie (1848–56), and it was a portent. Over the next seven years Dalhousie enormously increased the area of British India and, with the exception of the Second Burma War in 1852, he did it with paperwork, as part of the relentless logic of paramountcy.

The Company was now claiming a range of rights—essentially feudal powers—over subordinate princes, including the right to refuse recognition of an adopted heir, if the direct line of succession failed. On this neo-feudal basis, the EIC 'inherited' Satara (1848), Jhansi and Nagpur (1854), plus several smaller states. This 'Doctrine of Lapse' flouted the time-honoured recognition of adoption within Indian ruling families, and ran counter to Mughal practice. Widespread resentment followed in the states affected. Dalhousie was also prepared to use paramount power to sanction two other grounds for annexation—insolvency and misgovernment. Under the first of these he took Berar from the Nizam of Hyderabad in 1853, and under the second he annexed what was left of independent Awadh in 1856.

But there was much more to Dalhousie than land grabbing. James Andrew Broun-Ramsay, 10th Earl and 1st Marquess Dalhousie (1812–1860) was certainly high-handed, but he was as enlightened as any other British ruler of India. An affable, quiet man, he had a long-term vision of India 'improved' by railways, telegraphs and canals, and modernized by education and better treatment of women. His political views, however, were not easily defined. In domestic British terms he was a fairly mild Tory, but he described himself in 1856 as 'a curious compound of despot and radical'.[8] As such, he was one of the very few British politicians who effectively moved leftwards as he travelled east.

He was a Tory appointed by a Whig administration as the best man available, and he did not disappoint. His term as Governor-General, from 1848 to 1856, was one of the longest, and the enormous workload is generally considered to have killed him. His achievement consisted not only of a welter of treaties, annexations and military expeditions that tidied up nearly all the outstanding territorial issues within India; he can also be credited with a sheaf of social legislation, administrative reforms and technological introductions that mark out his governorship as perhaps the most pivotal of the British period.

A sincere believer himself, he was determined that the British should show that they were 'not ashamed of being Christians'.[9] This kind of aggressive confidence set him at a distance from both Company policy and Tory attitudes, and it made him more accommodating to missionary activity than any of his predecessors. In 1854 he supported a mission to the Khasi Hills, with a grant of Rs 50, declaring in a letter to London: 'I am of opinion that for these days we carry the principle of neutrality too far; that even in a political point of view we err in ignoring the agency of the ministers of our own true faith.'[10]

This left him open to accusations that he had provoked the Uprising of 1857 with insensitive intrusions, but the story is somewhat subtler. Like many others, he was in favour of conversion work in the tribal tracts of India, where a fair amount of success followed, including with the Khasi people. But like many senior officials he was cautious about the army, and when blanket statements are made about missionary work, it is necessary to be very clear about where and by whom that work was carried on, how successful it was, and where revolt later appeared.

For instance, Dalhousie's father-in-law was Lord Tweeddale, Governor of Madras from 1842 to 1848, a keen proselytizer who blessed mission work across his Presidency. Riots in Tinnevelly followed in 1846, but the region was completely quiescent during the revolt of 1857. There was trouble in 1858, but it was about the use of a road for Christian funeral processions and had nothing to do with active conversion work.

Dalhousie has also been blamed for provoking the Uprising of 1857 by annexations and social reforms, and there is a grain of truth in this, as his general attitude took little account of local feeling. And apart from religious and social sensitivities, a good deal of his more technological reforms actively put Indians out of traditional lines of business, principally in transport and news gathering. But paradoxically he can also be seen to have ensured the rebellion's defeat, by the installation of telegraphs, and by his settlement policies in the Punjab, which reconciled the mass of the Sikh population to British rule.

He was a confident man directing an apex predator organization, unafraid of competition. Such self-assurance came naturally to an ambitious young man, born to wealth, privilege and political expectations. From an ancient Scottish noble family, he was a third son, and was not expected to succeed to the family earldom. But his two older brothers predeceased him without issue, and when his father died in 1838 he entered the House of Lords. He declared himself a Peelite Tory, and in 1843 was made vice-president of the Board of Trade. Here he took responsibility for railways, and developed a good understanding of their construction and the benefits they brought. The capacity and application he showed at the Board recommended him for the demands of government in India, and at the age of only thirty-five he became the youngest-ever Governor-General.

He arrived in India in January 1848, and within just over a year he had fought and won the decisive Second Sikh War. The Punjab was annexed and had to be settled. Conscious of previous mistakes, he recruited as many Sikh veterans as he could into Company service, to avoid the problem of unemployment and banditry that had plagued other regions after conquest.

He then had to act as referee between Henry and John Lawrence. Dalhousie favoured John's view, that the British ought to back peasants against landlords, and disempower or bypass the sardar landholding class. Thus the so-called 'Punjab school' was born, characterized by the rough-and-ready, rule-of-thumb governance of men on horseback, who spoke local languages and did their utmost to understand local custom and respect it, wherever it did not cross certain moral lines, such as female infanticide or burying lepers alive.

Dalhousie then went on to add further territory to the Company's domain by provoking and winning the Second Burma War, in 1852. This cleared up a number of long-standing issues left by the earlier war of 1824–6. Most importantly it brought the area of Lower Burma (Pegu), which included Rangoon, under Company control.

Meanwhile the Doctrine of Lapse was regularly deployed across central India, where British holdings were rather patchy. The first opportunity arose in the state of Satara, home of the heirs of Shivaji. With the failure of the senior line of the Chhatrapati, and despite protests from Bartle Frere, the Resident, the territory was annexed in 1848. Smaller states followed: Mandaul, also in 1848, Jaitpur and Sambalpur during 1849, Baghpat in 1850, and Udaipur in 1852—though these last two were restored after the Uprising.

Then came the most notorious cases. First was Berar in 1853, taken from the Nizam of Hyderabad to pay for the contingent of British troops stationed in his state to support him. Next was the annexation of Jhansi, a small state that Dalhousie himself felt was scarcely worth the trouble of taking on, but which became famous four years later when its dispossessed rani, Lakshmibai, rose up in revolt. Finally, in 1854 the cotton-rich state of Nagpur fell into British hands—a major coup. The territory was large and prosperous, and lay in a strategically important position, straddling lines of communication from Bombay to Calcutta.

Paramountcy fulfilled so many positive purposes for Dalhousie that he never questioned it. Privately he admitted that resorting to the protection of the welfare of the people was essentially 'humbug', but the short-term advantages to the Company were persuasive. And because his actions were generally viewed in London as expedient, prudent or economically beneficial, he was allowed to continue.

There were few appreciable downsides. Politically, he was rationalizing anomalies and restoring good governance; strategically, he was filling in blanks and rounding out corners; financially, he was swelling the Company's revenues without the expense of war (though costs also went up). Nor did he always resort to annexation. The treaty he negotiated in 1854 with the Khan of Khelat, to secure the frontier with Baluchistan, was a standard subsidiary alliance.

But for Dalhousie, all this was only one leg of the project. Just as important were his canal schemes in the Punjab, and the new railways out of Calcutta and Bombay; the first lines were approved in 1851, and operating by 1853. He also overhauled the postal system, and soon telegraph lines were appearing all over the Indian landscape.

Around 1853–4, Dalhousie also explored ways of setting up a more broadly based government in India—not directly responsible to Indians, but involving a wider circle of consultation than had ever been envisaged before. In an extremely important constitutional development, Dalhousie asked for, and received under the Charter Act of 1853, the power to expand his Council into a larger body specifically tasked with drafting legislation for all India. However, his plans to introduce a more parliamentary form of proceeding in this expanded Council were vetoed by Sir Charles Wood, president of the Board of Control, who was horrified by the prospect of posturing and oratory in a subsidiary administrative body. Had Dalhousie managed to get a little further down this road, by creating a proto-parliamentary or ministerial system in India, history might have been different.

Dalhousie was also particularly concerned to promote social change through new initiatives in education, and the London government eventually responded with the famous Education Despatch of 1854, which bears Wood's name, but to which Dalhousie made substantial contributions.

This despatch made five major recommendations. Dedicated education departments were to be established in all provinces of British India; universities modelled on the new, non-residential London University were to be founded in the presidency capitals of Calcutta, Madras and Bombay; a minimum of one government school was to be provided in every district; approved private schools would be given grants-in-aid (subsidies); Indian students were to be given instruction in vernacular languages. This all went much further than Macaulay had dared nineteen years before, and there was much greater political will to act. The three presidency universities opened in 1857, though the rest of the package took longer to appear.

Many of these ideas originated in the schemes of the great missionary Alexander Duff, who wanted Indians to be able to read the Bible, and thence to question their traditional patterns of life. But these were essentially liberal measures, and the overall reforming direction of the proposals was to be one of the most visible elements of British liberal policy to survive the Uprising of 1857, as the drive to bring Western-style education to Indians carried on through to the Hunter Commission of 1882 and beyond.

There were several other socially sensitive pieces of legislation on Dalhousie's watch that are sometimes credited with provoking the

Uprising of 1857. Converts to any religion were permitted to keep their rights to inherit property after conversion by the Caste Disabilities Act of 1850, while widows were given the legal right to remarry in 1856. The first of these may have been genuinely unsettling, because of its effects on family property, but the second had been called for by influential Indians for many years in several parts of the country, including Balshastri Jambhekar and Gopal Hari Deshmukh in Bombay, and Ishwar Chandra Vidyasagar in Calcutta.

Less often mentioned, however, are Dalhousie's prison reforms, after which the appalling death rate in custody began to subside. He also abolished the branding of convicts, and reformed the state of the lunatic asylums.

Yet despite his apparently irresistible power, Dalhousie did not have everything his own way, and he had to face his share of the traditional problems that accompanied British rule. There was violent unrest among the Mappilas of Malabar in 1849–51 and 1854, while the Santals of Bengal, driven to desperation over debt serfdom and the loss of their lands, sustained a serious rebellion through 1855–6.

The last great issue addressed by Dalhousie was the governance of the state of Awadh. Because of its proximity to Bengal, Awadh had been one of the first Indian powers to come under close British control, and a series of treaties had gradually taken away substantial portions of its territory and income. By 1856, stories of depravity and misgovernment in Lucknow were common, coupled with reports of anarchy in the countryside, where taluqdars were waging private wars and evading their revenue obligations. Dalhousie, somewhat reluctantly, announced the annexation of what remained of independent Awadh in February 1856, when its king-nawab, Wajid Ali Shah, refused to sign a treaty agreeing to his own deposition. There was no resistance; the self-styled Padshah had long ceased to have any effective armed forces of his own.

Direct British rule was imposed, with a major restructuring of landholding and revenues. Under the new arrangements, the taluqdars fared badly, and their tenants did little better, as the new revenue assessments were frequently very high. This was to be the last British land grab within India, and it was handled as badly—after Dalhousie's departure—as the annexation of Punjab had been handled well.

Eventually the ceaseless work exhausted him, and he would have left office sooner, had the home government not requested him to stay on after the outbreak of the Crimean War in 1854. Finally, he handed over to Lord Charles Canning in March 1856, and returned home, never to recover his health. He died, aged only forty-eight, in 1860 at his ancestral family home in Scotland. He had always harboured high ambitions in domestic politics, and his death deprived Britain of one of her more capable sons.

He had no great regard for historical precedent, and his mind was filled with the benefits of rationalization, centralization and technical progress. But there is an important point to be made about modernization here. What modernization meant to a mid-nineteenth-century Tory like Dalhousie was very different from what it came to mean later. To Dalhousie, it was a package of better governance, increased social equity, and economic growth. A modern India would be a more productive place than a 'backward' India—and easier to rule. From around 1870, however, modernization began to represent a potential loss of control over India.

Enlightened, hard-working, paternalistic and almost reluctantly 'liberal'—Dalhousie, in many ways, was the substance of what Bentinck was thought to have been, and the model that Curzon later attempted to emulate.

During Dalhousie's time, the future of British India was significantly shaped by the 1853 Charter Act, which both he and Sir Charles Wood helped to draft.

Most importantly, the Act introduced competitive examinations for entry to the Company's civil service, thus finally ending the old system of patronage that had caused so much concern seventy years before. Entry by examination was perceived to be both fairer and more likely to introduce young men of talent into Indian service. The Act also increased the size of the Supreme Council in Calcutta, which had been functioning as the legislative body for all of British India since the 1833 Act. Concerns had arisen that this body, with its Bengal bias, was too small and too ill informed about other provinces. In future, the Governor-General would be joined by representatives from the two other Presidencies, the North West Provinces, and two judges.

One other significant aspect of the 1853 Act was its failure to grant another twenty-year extension to the Company's privileges. After 1853, the EIC held India at Parliament's pleasure. Wood already foresaw a transition to Crown rule, but the time was not yet right.

The prospect of a new Charter Act also stimulated political activity in the presidency towns, as prominent Indians bestirred themselves to lobby Parliament in their own interests. This was the principal motivation behind the formation of the British Indian Association in 1851. The appearance of this body, based in Calcutta, represented a distinct advance over previous attempts at political organization in several significant ways. It was composed entirely of Indians; it included a broad cross-section of opinion—its leading lights included conservatives like Radhakanta Deb and progressives like Peary Chand Mitra; and it became part of a nationwide network of affiliated bodies, including branches in Bombay, Poona and Madras.

Although essentially a pressure group rather than a disciplined political body, its significance lay in the template it created for future organizations that would be more expressly political, and in the way that it was an autonomous Indian creation, born of the growing realization that partnership with Europeans in political ventures was a mixed blessing. European voices made it easier to be heard within government circles, but there were distinct conflicts of interest, both economic and political, that only separate Indian representation could avoid.

1856–8: The Second Conquest

As Lord Charles Canning sat down at his desk in March 1856, there was no military power to resist British arms, no political opposition to speak out in any public forum, and no reason to suppose that the subcontinent would not continue to move forward gratefully into prosperity. British rule was also still largely excused detailed supervision from home.

But challenges and changes were about to come. Forces of resentment and reaction had been maturing across all levels of Indian society for some time. Though there were a substantial number of influential winners under British rule, there were also many who felt no better but more threatened in their traditional way of life. Many, especially among the soldiery, feared a wave of Christianization. All this was known. Sir Henry Lawrence had reported a frank conversation with a sepoy who had warned him of widespread unrest in the ranks.

Perhaps these disaffections could have been overcome, had they been taken seriously at the highest levels and been addressed in some manner. Perhaps they would have eased if the spread of enforced modernity had brought rapid prosperity. But neither of these things happened. Instead, as Munro had feared, violent insurrection broke out among those against whom the British had no defence. The army finally turned on its paymasters.

There are several discernible reasons for this that do not require the detection of 'nationalism' in the ranks. By the mid-1850s, officers were taking less interest in the welfare of their men than previous generations, and there were numerous specific grievances, such as the introduction of compulsory overseas service under an Act of 1856, which obliged soldiers to cross ocean water, thus causing them to lose caste, while also denying them extra payments for doing so.

Then there were the notorious new cartridges for the Enfield rifle, which needed to have the end removed before use. There were strong suspicions, which a British investigation later considered to have been well founded, that these cartridges had been greased with pig or cow fat. The reason, however, was not a deep plot to break the caste of the troops, but cost-cutting by contractors. The British had no reason to antagonize their own soldiers. Interfering with their ritual purity was of no conceivable use to the high command.

There had been some willingness among senior officers to promote Christianity within the ranks, but this was more often a matter of practicality, related to sobriety and discipline rather than personal conviction. This factor has been overlooked since and may have been misinterpreted then. But in 1857 tensions were high, and by the time the new ammunition appeared, relations had deteriorated beyond the issue of animal fat. The sepoys would not accept compromise solutions, and refused either to tear the cartridges, which did not in fact need to be bitten, or to grease them with concoctions of their own devising. In the event, none of the new cartridges was ever distributed to serving men, yet still they mutinied.

And beyond grievance there was opportunity; the European section of the Indian army had been severely depleted to provide men for the Crimean War (1854–6). There was also direct provocation. Many of the sepoys came from Awadh, and the recent deposition of their king-nawab was considered by many as an offence to their personal dignity, and by others as a threat to the safety of their families, which were struggling with the new land settlement's heavy burdens.

In January 1857, an entire regiment, the 19th Native Infantry, was disbanded for refusing to use the new cartridges, but the first mutinous shot at a British officer is attributed to Mangal Pandey of the 34th Native Infantry, at Barrackpore on 29 March 1857. Pandey was hanged for his actions, which he did not seek to excuse. His comrades had made no attempt to protect the officer, so the 34th was disbanded in disgrace that May. Discontent was rife, but nothing seems to have unduly disturbed senior commanders, who had experience of discontents in the army and considered them manageable.

Concerted violence finally erupted during the evening of 10 May at Meerut, after eighty-five troopers of the 3rd Bengal Light Cavalry were found guilty of insubordination, for refusing to accept the new cartridges. Heavy sentences—ten years' imprisonment—and the public humiliation of these men in front of their comrades proved too much. Most of the garrison—three regiments—then rose up and killed their officers that night. This was a point of no return, and the mutineers immediately set off to Delhi, about thirty miles to the south-west, for safety, and to seek leadership from the octogenarian Mughal emperor, Bahadur Shah Zafar.

They reached Delhi the following day, killing its British garrison and any European civilians and Indian Christians that fell into their hands. The British defenders managed to blow up most of the magazine there, and staff at the telegraph office raised the alarm with a short, desperate message to the Punjab.

There were about 5,000 insurgents in Delhi, but they were soon joined by thousands of others from all over north India. News of the revolt travelled quickly, and the violence spread across the Gangetic plain, but not a great deal further. This was an important factor in allowing the British to stay ahead of the wave in the more distant provinces, and a number of small regional mutinies were put down across the country, from Benares to Peshawar.

Reinforcements were swiftly called in from everywhere available—South Africa, Malta, Burma—and were even diverted from an expedition to China. With substantial numbers assembled, Brigadier General James Neill then marched up from Calcutta, hanging anyone he thought deserved it; this, it must be emphasized, was before news of any massacre at Kanpur had ever reached him. Meanwhile in the Punjab, John Lawrence undertook several less drastic actions that contemporaries considered to have 'saved the empire'. He disarmed Bengal army units in the area, then raised irregulars among the Sikhs and sent them south to retake Delhi.

All this effectively confined the first wave of the revolt to central north India, and by 8 June there was a large British force stationed on the ridge to the north of Delhi, with perhaps 30,000 sepoys in the city. Delhi then became the rebellion's defining trial of strength. A loose siege dragged on for three months, with the rebels too poorly supplied to drive off the British, and the British too weak to take back the city.

As this central stand-off continued, two other striking scenes were played out over that terrible summer. The first was at Kanpur, where the last Peshwa's adopted heir, Nana Sahib, led an attack that lasted three weeks from 6 June. On 27 June, General Wheeler finally surrendered with assurance of safe conduct by river to Allahabad, but the troops were shot down as they embarked, and the women and children recaptured. About a fortnight later, on the approach of a relieving British force, these 211 hostages were murdered and their bodies thrown into a well. This may have been a form of reprisal for the widespread lynching that was going on all along the Ganges, but when news of it became widely known, the ferocity of the fighting, and of reprisals, was greatly increased.

Nana Sahib later claimed that this atrocity was not conducted on his orders, and it was certainly not committed by his disciplined troops. In his defence, it might be pointed out that he had not initially wanted to join the rebels, and had only done so under threat, so he may have felt unable to stop the massacre. But such an extended and undoubtedly noisy act of slaughter was carried out within a few metres of where he was lodged, and it is not credible that he knew nothing of it.

Further north in Awadh, a rebel army reached Lucknow on 1 July, trapping a small British force in the Residency there. In command was Henry Lawrence, who had been sent as Resident to Awadh just a few months before, a job he had only accepted reluctantly, having been about to visit England on leave.

At the outbreak of the revolt in May, Lawrence expected an attack on Lucknow and had prepared to defend it, but the insurgents were preoccupied elsewhere. After the fall of Kanpur, rebel troops moved towards Lucknow, and Lawrence chose to meet them in open battle—a disastrous mistake. On 30 June, his small unit was outnumbered and soundly beaten at Chinhat. The remnants of his force made it back to Lucknow, but in numbers sufficient to defend only the Residency. The famous siege then began the next morning.

Within hours Lawrence was severely wounded by a shell splinter in the thigh and lower abdomen. After two days of terrible pain he died, and his body was buried as the battle raged around the beleaguered Residency. His last act, which won the hearts of every sentimental Victorian, was to suggest a modest epitaph for himself, asking only for the words 'Here lies Henry Lawrence who tried to do his duty. May the Lord have mercy on his soul'.

Henry Lawrence lived on in legend, but of him it might indeed have been written that nothing in his life became him so well as the leaving of it. As a deeply pious Christian, he sincerely believed that the British had divine work to do in India, and should do it with the highest moral probity, while doing the least damage to existing Indian systems of social organization. All the misapprehensions about India that this attitude betrays were not obvious to men like him, and it would probably never have occurred to him that the ghastly wound that killed him was in some degree a comment upon his mission, a small token of what the Indians he was trying to save actually thought of his efforts. Nor did the manner or fact of his demise deter his many admirers from seeing his death as an act of noble sacrifice in a worthy cause.

Delhi was the last great tableau, and provided another celebrated deathbed scene. Brigadier General John Nicholson (1821–57) was fatally wounded during the final storming of Delhi, and took nine days to die. This made him one of the great icons of the high British Raj, and earned him a great deal of uncritical adulation from the nineteenth-century British public, both on account of his fervent Christianity and his extraordinary bravery. Sir Henry Newbolt, the bard of imperial heroism, even wrote a poem about him.

He was often grouped with Henry Havelock and Henry Lawrence as a great Christian 'martyr' of the Uprising, but he fits less certainly into modern categories, somewhere between a hero and a monster, a paragon and a dreadful warning. Though admired at the height of empire, much that he did is more likely to evoke shame in an era of colonial guilt. He was, after all, the man who declared that being flayed alive was too good for the mutineers he was slaughtering at the time.

Born to a respectable Ulster family, he was physically very large and had enormous personal courage. He liked to hunt tigers single-handed on horseback with only a sword; he once undertook a solo punitive expedition in which he tracked down a fugitive offender and personally cut off his head. These attributes won him an extreme form of devotion among his Indian troops, who would have followed him anywhere. He was also perhaps insane, and there is a school of modern psycho-writers that insists he was a repressed homosexual, consumed with self-loathing.

Nicholson arrived in India as a cadet in 1839 and fought in the First Afghan War, ending up besieged in Ghazni between December 1841 and March 1842. A surrender and safe conduct were arranged, but the terms were not respected, leading to a period of desperate fighting in the town, in which Nicholson played a prominent part. He was captured and taken to Kabul, but managed to escape and rejoin Pollock's relieving force that September.

In the First Anglo-Sikh War he was at the battle of Ferozeshah, then served in Kashmir to help its new owner, Maharaja Ghulab Singh, to take possession of his recent purchase. He started the Second Sikh War as a captain, and after distinguishing himself at the battles of Chilianwala and

Gujrat he was promoted to major. Upon the annexation of the Punjab in 1849 he was made Deputy Commissioner under the Board of Administration, having repeatedly impressed its president, Henry Lawrence. He then took leave to England in 1850, and enjoyed a tour of Europe in 1851.

On his return to India he was posted to the troublesome border area of Bannu, where he proceeded to administer a highly personal version of the rough-and-ready justice favoured by John Lawrence's 'Punjab school'. Lawrence believed that the peoples of the Punjab liked their government firm and fair, and that the British should avoid the introduction of time-consuming bureaucracy. The idea was to preserve traditional forms while injecting them with British consistency and impartiality. Lawrence himself managed to find a popular and enduring way of doing this, but Nicholson seems to have been a more enthusiastic despot; Lawrence warned him to use courts wherever possible and not to hang men without evidence. Nevertheless the local population responded well to Nicholson's firm rule, and crime virtually disappeared.

The legend that he was worshipped as a god—Nikal Seyn—seems to spring from a particular incident when a local fakir erected an image of him to curry favour. Given that the devout Nicholson had a horror of idolatry, this was one attempt at toadyism destined for sure failure. The fakir and his fellow votaries received a sound flogging.

When mutiny broke out in May 1857, Nicholson was Deputy Commissioner in Peshawar, where eight native regiments of the Bengal army were stationed. He instantly took steps to disarm suspect units, then actively pursued and wiped out a body of mutinous troops at Hoti Mardan. For a month or so he quelled resistance in the area, including hanging a group of regimental cooks who tried to poison him. In mid-June he was promoted to brigadier general and took command of a 'movable column' of royal troops, Sikh regiments and Punjabi irregulars, with whom he marched south towards Delhi, arriving in mid-August. The final assault on the city took place on 14 September, and he was fatally wounded in the escalade.

His death prompted an outpouring of praise from his comrades, and an outburst of generosity from his employers. He never married, and in the absence of dependants, a pension was granted to his mother. She had the ill luck to send four sons to India, none of whom returned.

Delhi was retaken in an orgy of plunder, murder and destruction. The emperor was taken prisoner, and several members of his close family were killed out of hand.

But this did not signal the end of the rebellion. Lucknow was still besieged, and although its garrison was reinforced when James Outram and Henry Havelock fought their way into the city on 25 September, the relieving force proved too small to lift the siege.

The tide, however, was turning. The rebels suffered day-to-day problems of supply and finance that rendered them too static to press for victory, and they found it impossible to strike sufficiently hard at the head of British power. The presidency towns, solidly loyal, remained beyond their reach.

Although the fall of Delhi removed much of the focus of the rebellion, fighting carried on across a large area of northern and central India. Newly reinforced by 30,000 fresh troops, Sir Colin Campbell was able to relieve Lucknow on 25 November, but he was then immediately called away to defend Kanpur, which was again under attack from a force, including the famous Gwalior Contingent, led by the elusive rebel commander Tantia Topi. This force inflicted a defeat on a British army led by General Windham outside Kanpur, and Lucknow was surrounded yet again. It was only relieved, for a third time, in March 1858.

By then the main fighting had switched to the native states of central India, particularly Jhansi, where the dispossessed rani was earning herself an immortal crown as a warrior queen. She joined forces with Tantia Topi and defied the British through several engagements, till she was killed on 18 June 1858 in a cavalry action outside the fort at Gwalior, which was retaken by Sir Hugh Rose two days later.

In a symbolic final act, Bahadur Shah Zafar, the last Mughal emperor and the Company's acknowledged feudal overlord, was deported to Burma in October 1858, having been found guilty of treason to his own vassal, the EIC. He lived out his days as a prisoner in Rangoon, and was buried in an unmarked grave in 1862.

The bitterness of the fighting resulted in widespread cruelty and massacre on both sides. Governor-General Canning took a conciliatory line throughout, and was much criticized for it by fellow Britons.

Charles, Earl Canning (1812–62) was a fairly typical member of that small pool of British aristocrats who, by the mid-nineteenth century, were deemed exclusively fit to wield supreme authority in India. Like Lords Bentinck and Ripon he was the son of a prime minister, George Canning; like Dalhousie he succeeded to his father's title after the death of two older brothers; like Cornwallis, Wellesley and Ellenborough he had been educated at Eton; like Dalhousie, who preceded him, and Elgin, who followed him, he had studied at Christ Church, Oxford. Also, like these last two, his work in India effectively killed him.

He was derisively dubbed 'Clemency Canning' by hardliners in Calcutta who wanted to extirpate the rebellion in ruthless and exemplary fashion, but over the years this epithet has done him more honour than his original detractors could possibly have foreseen. Indiscriminate executions horrified him on grounds of justice and humanity, but also as a kind of political insanity, being less likely to pacify the country than to destroy any prospect of continued British rule. He was always perfectly clear about the situation. Acts of murder were punishable by death, but summary executions and collective punishments were not acceptable, principles he set out in his 'Clemency Proclamation' of July 1857.

He was an unspectacular character, judicious rather than timid, and his political rise was slow. He became a Tory MP in 1836, but only attracted attention after he was appointed Postmaster General in 1853 by Lord Aberdeen, leader of the Peelite faction after Peel's death in 1850. He filled the position very capably, and in 1855 Palmerston thought him fit to succeed the ailing Dalhousie in India.

His first major undertaking was the settlement of Awadh, annexed by Dalhousie in February 1856. This was not well handled, and caused a range of resentments that were soon to lead to open revolt. Then in November 1856 he sent troops to push the Persians out of Herat, precipitating the short, successful Anglo-Persian War of 1856.

Canning was not a soldier and took little direct part in the military suppression of the Uprising, but as Governor-General, then Viceroy, it was his responsibility to pick up the political pieces. Canning's real importance lies in the way he did this, because he made several momentous decisions relating to the revolt.

The first was to abandon social reform as a positive British policy. There were two main reasons for this change of attitude. Firstly, the hereditary princes had mostly remained loyal—they had been 'breakwaters' against the storm, in his oft-quoted phrase. Second, the peasantry, whom the British believed they had been protecting, showed absolutely no sign of rallying to the British cause against their landlords, particularly in Awadh, where Canning considered he had recently helped them throw off the oppressive demands of the taluqdar class. The lesson was clear: if the peasants would not accept the help the British were giving them, then the British were better off backing the landlords.

Profound changes followed. With the princes now regarded as allies, Dalhousie's policy of annexation was permanently abandoned. Adoption was henceforth to be permitted, and Canning granted a flood of sanads (edicts) authorizing adoptive heirs over the next two years. The pacification of Awadh, a main centre of the resistance, then took on a particular character. By a decree of March 1858, Canning confiscated all the land held by taluqdars, with only five named individuals excepted. Estates were then gradually re-granted, after suitable professions of loyalty. A grand durbar for this purpose was staged at Lucknow in 1859.

By setting up this relationship between princes, landowners and the Government of India, Canning set colonial rule on a course that gradually directed the Raj away from active government and into stasis. Unwittingly, perhaps, this also closed the door on economic development.

The Uprising stimulated great political concern in London, and the EIC, widely believed to have been guilty of mismanagement, now faced its final days. The compromises that the Company represented had clearly now outlived their usefulness. But the difficulty, as so often in British politics, was how best to replace a venerable institution at a stroke. In this case the problem lay in constructing a new system that might govern India better than the Company, yet still provide the various safeguards within British politics that it had supplied.

Lord Ellenborough, who in early 1858 had again been made president of the Indian Board of Control, introduced a bill for the creation of a Council of India in London, with elected members from British and Indian interest groups. But it was soundly defeated, mainly because the principle of election was deemed unacceptable in Indian policy. Ellenborough then made his final exit under something of a cloud. He openly criticized Canning's policy of dispossessing the taluqdars of Awadh, but spoke without first consulting his colleagues. This characteristic act of autocracy cost him his job, the last public office he held, and he left politics under something of a cloud. His successor as president, Lord Stanley, then saw through the Act for the Better Government of India, passed in August 1858, which introduced direct Crown rule. It took much from Ellenborough's bill, but reduced the Council to fifteen and removed elections.

What were the causes of the widespread, violent insurgency that swept across India in 1857? Despite the efforts of some historians to turn this into a deep and puzzling question, the causes of the revolt were clearly understood at the time by those who took up arms. Several rebel 'manifestos' have survived, such as the Azamgarh Declaration of September 1857, which lists grievances related to the unfair, unresponsive, oppressive and socially corrosive effects of colonial government, including heavy taxation, distraint of real property for arrears of land revenue, hardship among the merchant classes, and the enforcement of equality before the law.

There were other strands of discontent. Sayyid Ahmad Khan, scion of an old noble family in Delhi, explained that the traditional Muslim landed classes felt dishonoured by exclusion from government, while William Howard Russell, special correspondent of *The Times* who witnessed the later stages of the revolt's suppression, specifically cited 'the arrogant and repellent manner in which we often treat natives of rank'.[11] Sleeman had said precisely the same thing fifteen years before, and Thomas Munro had foreseen the dangers of doing this even earlier.

An important point here is that the reason often adduced for the rebellion—the perceived threat to religion—was only one of many grievances. We should also be wary of too simplistic an understanding of the frequent citation of 'religion' in the complaints and petitions of the insurgents. The central words 'din' and 'dharma' can be translated crudely into English as 'religion', but both carry layers of meaning and association beyond that simple word, including proper conduct, social order, tradition and the world as it is. The rebels were protecting not just their denominational faith, but their sense of status and their traditional way of life. The description of the British as 'destroyers of all religion' is the correct context for their fears.

It must also be questioned whether the Rani of Jhansi or Nana Sahib or the Emperor's children were primarily motivated by fears for their religion. Conversion, by force or stealth, was certainly a matter of concern for those lower down the social scale, especially in the army, but those higher up were dealing with personal issues of status, wealth and political power.

Despite attempts in some quarters to prove that there was a plan for the Christianization of India, the fears of sepoys and peasants were not well founded. Until the more cavalier days of Dalhousie, the Company had always resisted mixing Christianity with ruling, and Dalhousie only did so under the pretext that he was not attacking Indian religion but amending abuses in the area of personal property. Dalhousie's predecessor, Lord Hardinge, had specifically stated that British rule rested upon 'the fidelity of this native army',[12] and he would have no truck with ideas of conversion. Nor did the home government ever have a policy to promote Christianity in India beyond the provision of Anglican clergy to supply the needs of the British expatriate community.

Missionary work was always primarily the preserve of non-official, 'low' church bodies, and there were only around 400 missionaries in India in 1851. Taking the missionary conference survey's own figures from 1850, fewer than 15,000 Indians regularly attended Protestant Holy Communion that year, and only twenty-one Indians were ordained as priests.[13] Government pressure was only ever placed on the EIC under three religious headings: to remove disabilities from Christian converts, to disengage from the active patronage of temples, mosques and festivals, and to stop collecting the pilgrim tax.

Fears for religion may have seemed reasonable in a changing world shaped by foreigners, but they were essentially a way of trying to preserve a familiar past. Indigenous concepts of justice and good governance had always been couched in religious language, because there was no other political vocabulary available. Similarly, the insurgents had no other terms in which to express their very wide-ranging discontents.

There were plenty of things to complain about in 1857, and plenty of people in high places ready to nourish fears, grievances and resentments. The depth of the discontent and the mixed social character of the rebels attest to this, and attempts to simplify the issues either introduce distortions based in current prejudices or serve to open up yet more questions about why the rebellion failed.

In truth, the rebels never had much chance of success with the strategy they employed; they had no central command or coherent war aims. Apart from Tantia Topi, they stayed static and showed little ambition beyond defending the strongholds they had taken. This passivity allowed the British to take back the initiative as soon as they had recovered their strength, and left them unmolested while they did so. Politically, the rebels' message was simple—the foreigners must go—but beyond that they seemed to be heading either for the past or for anarchy. They hitched their star to the Mughal emperor, the least modern symbol available, and one that was probably too specific to north India. Crucially, wealthy and educated Indians in the presidency towns remained aloof throughout.

The rural–urban split is remarkable. If the revolt is characterized as 'anti-colonial', we need to ask why none of the modern towns—which would have experienced the most dramatic foreign impact, and therefore might be expected to have harboured the fiercest resentment—joined in the rebellion. They declined to do so.

In Calcutta, the editor of the *Hindu Patriot*, Harish Chunder Mukherjee (1824–61), kept up a running commentary on the fighting, and repeatedly condemned the actions of the sepoys, while also reminding his readers that there were 'grievances inseparable from foreign rule'.[14]

Ultimately, for reasons of self-interest, and for the future of India as they wished to see it, the Indian modernizers backed the winners, even if only by standing aside. But the victorious British did nothing in return.

This was not immediately apparent; modernization continued in several areas, but not in the crucial area of political development. The post-revolt settlement certainly marked a conservative shift in British thinking, but it was eventually domestic developments in Britain that unhitched the two countries politically.

The Uprising might perhaps have succeeded with more dynamic leadership and a lot more money. But it had neither, and it came to grief. It did, however, ensure the ultimate downfall of the Raj, not in military terms, but because the introduction of Crown rule made India part of a self-serving, self-preserving imperial system. This ultimately tore out the weak roots of British rule in India, leaving it unable to mesh into Indian society in any adequate way. Force of arms restored control, but the prospect of ever creating a legitimate, British-led government virtually disappeared.

And, what was worse, Indians lost the chance to design their own version of modernity.

THE GREAT BETRAYAL

remained very difficult when there was no established forum in which to do so. Nor was the Congress really a suitable instrument for such a purpose. Without any permanent national organization, and lacking popular support, it remained merely an annual gathering and its demands could easily be represented as self-interested.

The government, though, was not entirely devoid of a capacity for self-criticism. In such problems some expert complaints led to the setting up of a number of important investigative bodies, with the Aitchison Commission in 1886–7 on the 'Indianization' of places held [illegible] Commission on [illegible], and the Welby Commission (1895–1900) on the equitable distribution of financial burdens between India and Britain. William Wedderburn and Dadabhai Naoroji both [illegible] Wacha and Gokhale spent two days giving evidence to the [illegible].

The Aitchison commission brought about some [illegible] and the allocation of government posts, but its overall impact on [illegible] was minimal. Welby's five-year effort managed to secure a refund of only £250,000 for India. [illegible] government [illegible] the fact that [illegible] was [illegible] standard [illegible] the Fowler Committee [illegible] fixing a standard [illegible] India was thereafter living on a gold standard [illegible] sterling [illegible].

In 1896–8, the Government of India entered two years of [illegible] famine [illegible] across [illegible] The famine [illegible] of 1896.

Plague [illegible] in western India, [illegible] political pressures increased. The British authorities were desperate to inspect, fumigate and disinfect persons and premises, and did not seem to care whom they offended, while the civil servants [illegible] were not [illegible] and men of low caste were frequently used to do the job, both [illegible] deep offence.

A particularly virulent outbreak in Poona in 1897 led in June to the murder of two British officials, Walter Rand, Chairman of the Bombay

7

1859–1885

RECOVERY, INVESTMENT, DEBT, DEVOLUTION

1859–64: Settlement, Recovery, First Partition

The Uprising swept away the thin veneer that had humanized the Company's rule. In practice, officials had been able to stand in for representative institutions with a personal touch that mitigated the absolute nature of British rule. This sort of system was not unfamiliar to the Indian population, who had lived under a version of it for centuries. Now, under direct Crown rule, India was to have an elected government, though not elected by Indians. Instead, India was granted a second-hand style of political accountability, rooted far away in distant institutions. Personal connections were replaced by formal political responsibility in Westminster.

The British thought they were improving matters, but over time an amended Company system, with its looser grip, might have had more chance of accommodating Indian aspirations, because individuals could have been admitted to it, and run it in much the same way. This would not have been 'modern', but it might have been inclusive.

Instead, the one intermediate body that had effectively protected India from the most naked of British interests, the EIC, was removed, leaving India at the mercy of British national economic forces, with only British politicians to protect her. The seeds of high imperialism were sown, as the flimsy restraints that conscience had once exercised on individuals were now removed, replaced by the massive self-confidence of a venerable Parliament which believed axiomatically that it could do no wrong.

After 1858, British politicians held firm to the narrow belief that Indians wanted jobs, not political responsibility. Indians could be trained as employees, but responsibility would remain solely the business of the

British political classes. As Abraham Lincoln delivered the Gettysburg address, there were no concerns in London that government of the people, by the people, for the people need ever exist in India. No matter how well meaning it may have been, the introduction of Crown rule was, conceptually at least, disastrously demeaning.

In standard histories, the Uprising is assumed to have derailed the British modernization project in India, but this is not true. The damage that 1857 did was primarily to the *Indian* project of modernization, by changing the political climate of the country, with consequences well understood by Harish Chunder Mukherjee.

'The Widows' Marriage Act [of 1856] is an instance to prove the advanced position which the legislature had taken in respect to social matters. A law to restrain polygamy ... merely awaited a few formalities to have effective penal force throughout the country. Other abominations live [on], which it were unpatriotic to expose to the gaze of idle curiosity. All these have gained a long lease of existence. All hopes of their extirpation lie for the time dashed to the ground.'[1] Despite an attempt by Raja Deo Narayan Singh of Benares to revive anti-polygamy legislation in 1863, the situation remained unchanged till 1955.

The British project to modernize India was not halted so much as deflected, and 1858 marked the beginning of several new strands—the expansion of public works, the restructuring of Raj finances, judicial reform, a whole raft of civil and commercial legislation, and the admission of Indians to high-level political consultation.

As part of this, there were major changes all through the administrative system. In London, the president of the Board of Control was replaced by a Secretary of State for India—a government minister, advised by a Council of fifteen experts on Indian affairs. In India, more Indians were co-opted onto governing bodies, as spelled out by the Indian Councils Act of 1861. Although the Viceroy's Executive Council remained a bastion of British privilege for another forty-eight years, his Legislative Council was now to include nominated Indians. In 1861 there were three, but they were not picked from the ranks of vanguard modernizers; all were from princely India.

The Indian Civil Service replaced the Company secretariat, and all the top jobs in Indian administration were reserved exclusively for its members. Indian candidates were now permitted to sit the entrance examination, and the first successful applicant was Satyendranath Tagore in 1864. But his admission proved a false dawn. No matter how able, it proved extremely difficult for Indian candidates to compete, for a variety of reasons, most of which were incidental rather than directly discriminatory. However, the number of Indians in the service was to stay very low until well into the twentieth century, because prevailing British attitudes remained unconcerned to remedy the deficiency. It was potentially embarrassing to have Indians in superior positions to Britons, and there was an abiding fear that admitting Indians at all would concede a species of 'right' to employment in positions of trust that might have unfortunate consequences.

There were major changes in the military. The prevalence of Bengali and Awadhi Brahmins among the mutineers led the British to change their recruitment policies. After 1858, preference went to Sikhs, Pakhtuns, Jats, Dogras and Gurkhas, all from areas further to the north-west. Two other responses were notable. The overall proportion of Europeans in the Indian army was increased. It had fallen to about one in six on the eve of the Uprising, so confident were the British in the loyalty of their sepoys. Now the proportion was kept somewhere between a half and two-fifths. As a final lesson learned, the artillery wing became a white preserve.

It was also abundantly clear that social alliances had to be remade. Princes and large landowners had played prominent roles in the revolt, and Canning was predisposed to appease and support the 'natural leaders' of Indian society. So he conditionally reinstated the taluqdars of Awadh, and allowed the sardars of the Punjab to reconsolidate their landholdings. He was also in favour of permanent land revenue settlements throughout India, which would have benefited large landholders. Sir Charles Wood, Secretary for India, recommended the idea in July 1862, but concerns about the financial implications eventually saw it dropped.

The most obvious conciliatory step towards the indigenous aristocracy was contained in Queen Victoria's Proclamation to the Indian people, of November 1858, which included a promise to respect the rights and beliefs of all her Indian subjects. In this she remained largely true to her word, but she was truest of all to the Indian princes. Most, and the most prominent, had stood firm at the height of the danger, and were now rewarded.

Canning confirmed their existing rights, and permanently renounced the Doctrine of Lapse. The British finally concluded that the hundreds of small, relatively powerless princes no longer presented a military threat, and could be recruited as a political bulwark. Support from conservatives was thus met with public gratitude and a grant of security, while support from modernizers was passed over in silence.

The decision to leave the princes alone effectively constituted a first partition of India, and it was the single most conservative decision that the British ever made. It attached a sheet anchor onto Indian cultural life, and condemned the country to a political future of irreconcilable conflicts of interest. This was not the intention; no one could have been so prescient. What drove the decision was prudence, a desire to bring peace and settlement in the immediate short term, and in this it was effective. The princes were generally well satisfied with the new regime, under which they were left to manage their own domestic affairs. All that was required of them was that they did not have dealings with each other, that they did not keep large armies, and that they ruled their domains well.

The political benefits were apparent to both parties, and the deal stuck. Not one princely state lapsed or was annexed under the Crown Raj, despite multiple occasions on which either of these things could have happened. Maharajas were deposed, in Baroda in 1875, and Indore in 1905 and 1926, and rebellion was suppressed in Manipur in 1891, but in all of these cases, and many others, due succession was observed. Self-government returned to Mysore in 1881, and Sindhia got the fort of Gwalior back in the same year.

This enduring settlement was partly the work of Canning, but the real brains behind it belonged to Sir Charles Wood. Sir Charles Wood, 1st Viscount Halifax (1800–85) was an old-fashioned, mildly liberal Whig with a landowning background. Never an ideologue, he was a practical man, who held senior political offices in Britain over the period 1846 to 1874, including six years as Chancellor of the Exchequer (1846–52). He also held two positions from which he had an important impact on modern India; as president of the Indian Board of Control from 1852 to 1855, and as Secretary of State from 1859 to 1866.

While at the Board of Control he supervised the passage of the 1853 Charter Act, and submitted the Education Despatch of 1854 that bears his name. After 1859, as Secretary at the new India Office, he was the co-author of what might be called the post-reconquest settlement in India. The details of this are interesting in themselves, but especially significant is the fact that the settlement's two architects, Secretary Wood and Viceroy Canning, owed allegiance to different political parties in Britain. The new policy was, in fact, a triumph of conservative, Whiggish pragmatism.

By the time Palmerston invited Wood to return to Indian affairs in June 1859, the discussions of the Munro–Elphinstone era, about whether to rule India directly or indirectly, were redundant. Elements of all classes had united to eject the British—rajas, zamindars, taluqdars, ryots—even sepoys. Where were the British to look for allies now?

Together, Wood and Canning came up with a compromise. As a Tory, Canning would naturally align with the landlords, but he had to find ways of securing their loyalty. Wood was a conservative Whig, and had not entirely welcomed the Great Reform Act of 1832, which he had reluctantly accepted as an expedient measure to accommodate new interests. He now brought a similar approach to India. There were more peasants than landlords, and the only way to keep the whole British Indian edifice in place was to find ways to control them. A modified Whiggism was the answer, but one flavoured with economic manipulation. Simply to deliver the ryots unprotected into the hands of newly strengthened landowners would be morally indefensible, so tenancy legislation became one of the Raj's new obsessions. In this, Wood was impressed by the parallel of Ireland. The shadow of Irish discontents, and British policies to combat them, lay across the next six decades of British India.

The new policy was not based on an exact position within British politics; India allowed some latitude to London politicians. It was premised on a recognition that the pessimism of Charles Metcalfe was right, that the British would never earn a legitimate place in India by good government alone, and would certainly never be either loved or thanked for any good they did. The late imperial sense of dogged duty starts here.

It was clearly now not possible to make reliable, permanent social alliances within India, so the British fudged the issue by backing both upper and lower classes in an ideologically inconsistent but politically pragmatic way. The strategic objective was to stay on, by walking a line between the interests of landlord and tenant, backing neither to the disadvantage of the other. Traditional social arrangements would be left in place. The sugar on the pill was that investment in public works would increase, in the hope that the general level of prosperity would rise, to the benefit of all.

This was the theory—a hybrid concoction of economic dogma and political nous—but in practice public investment was never a great success. Debt accumulated, and optimism withered; political and economic paralysis was the result. The quest for legitimacy carried on, propped up less by economic success and more by a permanent sense of moral superiority, bolstered by memories of Kanpur.

Wood was at the India Office for nearly seven years; Lord George Hamilton (1895–1903) stayed longer, but he was far less influential. Wood worked with three viceroys—Canning, Elgin and Lawrence—all different in their political outlooks, but the policy track was firmly set. Wood preferred to have the people of India guided by their 'natural chiefs', rather than leave them to 'the seduction of upstart leaders';[2] this meant propping up large landholders. Wood was determined not to have to face down an 'agrarian movement',[3] and he and Canning agreed that all subordinate rights had to be protected too. Social engineering was replaced by social balancing—'equipoise' as it came to be known. As Wood wrote to Elgin in 1862: 'we have maintained our power by playing off one part against the other, and we must continue to do so'.[4] He was specifically referring to castes and regional identities in the army, but the general approach held for social classes too.

Here again was the perennial Whiggish striving for balance, driven by the idea that good government sprang from recognizing important social interests and accommodating them in appropriate ways. It is important to stress that this was not a new way of thinking specially designed for India. In 1861 John Stuart Mill included a passage in his *Considerations on Representative Government* that referred to the desirability of designing representation in Britain that was 'equally balanced' so that no class or combination of classes would be able 'to exercise a preponderant influence' within government.[5] The policy later demonized as 'divide and rule' was thus firmly rooted in current domestic practice. To men like Wood it seemed sensible to follow similar principles in India.

By the time Wood stepped down, it was conventional wisdom that India was not a party issue, which remained true for at least another forty years. India could not easily be drawn into Westminster politics during this time, because Parliament voted no money for India's government. India sat uneasily as a non-political ministerial responsibility, but one bereft of choices and resistant to initiatives. There was no easy way forward. Pacification was the main objective, with a long-term aspiration that this would somehow nurture prosperity.

After 1858, absolute rule from London through a non-political viceroy was the new model. The tempering effect of parliamentary supervision would act as a safeguard; the alternatives were all much worse. Allowing India to go her own way was clearly not permissible, and any attempt to set up representative institutions in India, or to give any British institutions a base in Indian opinion, would not only create potential problems of control, it would also set up a rival legitimacy. Parliament was always very jealous of its supremacy, and it was exactly this issue that had brought on war with America in 1775.

The high Raj therefore continued as a withered arm of Britain's internal political processes. Ruling India fairly while ruling Britain accountably was deemed sufficient. This arrangement seemed perfectly acceptable in a pre-democratic Britain, and it was only the franchise extensions of the next thirty years that made British rule in India into an anomaly within British political thinking. It was at precisely this point that 'high' imperialism first appeared, rooted in ideas about India's political immaturity—the certainty that representative institutions and political responsibility could not be extended to India.

Charles Wood's decisions made at this time were to have a huge influence on the nature of India's final entry into modernity. He pursued a mixed policy, conscious of costs and wary of innovation, taking pessimism and practicality from Toryism, elite inclusion from Whiggism, and social conscience from liberalism. The aspiration to leadership that had inspired so many earlier officials ebbed away, and the 'civilizing mission' became an increasingly passive affair, of waiting for better behaviour, if and when prosperity might appear. The most powerful forces in the land were soon doing the least to embrace the possibilities of modernity; India's future was silently stolen.

Wood's influence was not always obvious, but three of his Under-secretaries rose to be viceroys—Lords Northbrook, Ripon and Dufferin—and a fourth, Lord Kimberley, was Secretary of State for India three times. Wood was also the grandfather of the Tory viceroy Edward Wood, Lord Irwin—the Irwin of the Gandhi–Irwin Pact of 1931—a kindly, devout man, who had no more intention than his grandfather of letting Indians rule India.

The British were deeply shocked by both the ferocity of the insurgency and the fact that so many millions of Indians had apparently been able to keep such a terrible 'secret' so well. This seemed so devious as to be unimaginably wicked, or if not wicked, it betrayed the enormity of the gulf that had opened up between rulers and ruled. At lower levels there was undeniably an increase in hostility among the ranks of the British army, and a great deal of violent, racist behaviour under the later Raj, from planters and lower military ranks, may well be traceable to attitudes cemented at this time.

It is not, however, entirely correct to characterize the British as frightened after 1857. They were shocked and chastened, but the economic behaviour of the British community does not betray fear. Two of the main features of the early post-Uprising years were an influx of foreign investment into industrial projects and a great upsurge in expenditure on public works. Roads, bridges, harbours and dams were planned, and Sir Bartle Frere, Governor of Bombay (1862–7), poured as much public money as he could into the development of the city.

But the main area for investment was railway building. This was intended to connect inland resources and markets with seaports, but it was also an aid to military deployment. Railways dramatically increased the swiftness with which troops could be moved, meaning that smaller garrisons could hold larger areas of territory. The only drawback was the enormous expenditure involved, but this was solved by offering private investors a guaranteed minimum return, underwritten by the government. This did make for slightly more expensive construction than might have been the case under direct government control, but the result was a rapid expansion across the network after 1857, without the necessity of finding large capital sums from the public purse.

The idea that the British refrained from interfering with Indian life after 1857 is also misplaced. As soon as peace returned, Canning began a wide programme of legislative and judicial reform. The High Courts Act of 1861 unified the appellate jurisdiction within the whole country, while Macaulay's Penal Code was finally introduced in 1862, in an attempt to place all Indians and Europeans under the same laws. In fact the legislative programme undertaken after the Uprising was on an altogether more ambitious and extensive scale than anything envisioned by Dalhousie.

Several hundred new Acts were passed, especially concerning contracts and financial transactions. One element of this was the long string of tenancy protection laws, such as the Tenancy Act of 1859, which may have salved the British conscience about siding with landlords, but also did a great deal to restrict the potential for modernization and capital investment in the rural economy.

All this post-1857 energy shows that the lesson the British took from the Uprising was the one they had preferred all along—that the job of the British in India was to rule well. The violence was understood as a warning that standards had slipped. A lesson not yet ready for the learning was that imperial rule, of no matter what quality, was in itself a grievance beyond remedy.

The post-1857 settlement brought the Indian ruling classes back into British plans, as closer allies than ever before. Organized resistance to the Company had always been most formidable from that quarter, but the new alliance was rewarded with abiding loyalty. What was much less clear after the Uprising was where exactly the Indian peasant fitted into the picture. 1857 dragged the ryot to centre stage, as an insoluble political problem.

Much of the previous fifty years of British policy had been based on Munrovian ideas of protecting and nurturing the agricultural sector from the roots upwards, and if 1857 was taken as a comment on this policy, it could only be seen as violent rejection. A kind of despair now set in about the peasantry. Aspirations to create a sturdy yeomanry were replaced by a new analysis of the peasant's problems—trapped by caste, misled by religion, persecuted by moneylenders. Feckless, ignorant and incorrigible, childlike and primitive, the peasant became the *cause* of Indian poverty.

Here now was the essential Raj dilemma—that the British could change relationships with the princes and bhadralok, but not with the peasantry. With them nothing worked, nothing changed. The genesis of the special ethnography and social analysis of India's lowest classes begins here, and led to all kinds of intellectual rambling across the new terrain of Victorian bioscience. One practical result was the discovery of 'hereditary' criminality, expressed in the Criminal Tribes Act of 1871.

After 1857 India remained a permanently alien place to the British. Bafflement became an acceptable response to Indian problems in a way it had never been before the Uprising. After 1857, incomprehension was less an admission of British weakness and more an assertion of India's exotic backwardness—another key ingredient of high imperialism.

Nor did violence end when the British finally declared the rebellion over in 1859. Resistance continued for several years in the area around Poona, and in Bengal the Indigo Rebellion (1859–60) broke out among ryots forced to grow the crop under highly unfavourable conditions. More worrying in the short term were attacks from the Wahhabi movement. Although a concentration of 'fanatics' around the border area of Sitana was dispersed by a campaign in 1863, further military expeditions had to be mounted over succeeding years.

Suppressing the revolt was ruinously expensive. Government debt increased by over 70 per cent, swelled by three consecutive yearly deficits of £10 million. This left the Indian exchequer in a parlous state, and Secretary Wood immediately laid down political priorities. The budget had to be balanced, and indeed more than balanced, to recover lost ground. He dispatched James Wilson, a prominent politician and economist, to review the situation.

James Wilson (1805–60) made only a brief appearance in Indian history, but he exerted a considerable influence, and stands in a unique position as the first man to take charge of India's national finances in a modern manner.

By birth a Scot, he was educated in England and showed promise in mathematics. His studies, though, were cut off by his family's Quaker beliefs; at the time, non-Anglicans were barred from the universities. Wilson therefore became apprenticed to a milliner in the Scottish borders. Shortly afterwards his father bought the business and James became his own boss. This started him on a successful career in hat manufacture, and by the late 1830s he had made a large fortune, which he then lost by investing in indigo.

All this left him with wide practical experience in financial matters, which informed his more academic interest in the 'classical' economics of the Ricardian school. He published a series of pamphlets through the late 1830s and early 1840s, which attracted the attention of politicians, and in 1843 he founded a magazine, *The Economist*. Having converted to Anglicanism in 1832, he was welcomed into higher social circles and moved to a house in Mayfair.

His political career blossomed; he became an MP in 1847, Secretary to the Indian Board of Control in 1848, and then Secretary to the Treasury from 1852 to 1858. In July 1859 he was offered a place on the Viceroy's Council, to run the Indian exchequer under the new Crown administration. With high ambitions within British politics, the prospect was irresistible. He accepted, and sailed east in October 1859.

His first budget, in February 1860, was revolutionary, designed not only to balance the books but to reform the entire fiscal structure. His proposals included the introduction of systematic auditing and accounting, funding for a major expansion of public works, a general import tariff at 10 per cent, the imposition of an income tax on higher earners, and a licence tax on people whose incomes were difficult to monitor. The objective was to escape the awkward reality that the Government of India relied very heavily on the land revenue, which was 'inelastic', and the opium monopoly, which was far too elastic—it yielded hugely varied sums from year to year, depending on growing conditions in India and demand in China, where it remained illegal. He also declared his intention to introduce a paper currency. Drastic military economies completed the package, with a cutback in sepoy regiments from 146 to 72—which would also help to adjust the ratio of Indian to European troops.

These proposals proved deeply unpopular in many quarters. The Lancashire cotton lobby protested about the 'protective' tariff, but

Secretary Wood faced them down. In India, opposition came not just from the business community but also from Charles Trevelyan, an India veteran, now returned as Governor of Madras.

Sir Charles Trevelyan (1807–86) had one of the longest, most distinguished records of Anglo-Indian service, through a career in which he involved himself in multiple aspects of British rule, including education, administration and finance. He spent all his working life in the British and Indian civil services, both of which he helped to shape. He was also the grandfather of the eminent social historian G.M. Trevelyan.

From respectable gentry with roots in south-western England, he entered the Company's service in 1826 as a clerk. His aptitude in languages marked him out, and in 1827 he became assistant to Charles Metcalfe, then the Judicial Commissioner at Delhi. It was while in this post that he brought down Sir Edward Colebrooke, the Resident, by accusing him, correctly, of corruption.

In 1831 he was transferred to Calcutta as Deputy Secretary to the EIC's political department. There, in 1834, he teamed up with Thomas Macaulay; the two men found that they shared a commitment to liberal schemes of 'improvement'. Shortly afterwards Trevelyan married Macaulay's sister, Hannah, who had accompanied her brother on his travels, and the three spent a great deal of time together. Trevelyan was the experienced man in Indian affairs, and his views on education were to have a strong influence on Macaulay's famous minute. Later, Trevelyan expanded his views further in a work entitled *On the Education of the People of India* (1838), in which he explained that education was not only about 'improving' Indians, it was also a matter of British self-interest—the best way of turning the Indian population from subjects into 'profitable allies'.

Lord William Bentinck, the Governor-General under whom he spent much of his Indian career, had a high opinion of him, but despite this and his obvious capacities, he was not rewarded with senior office. He therefore returned to England in 1838, where he became Secretary to the Treasury under successive governments from 1840 to 1858. While there he was heavily involved, or as it turned out not involved, in the Irish potato famine of 1845–9, during which two million people starved to death.

As a firm believer in laissez-faire economics, Trevelyan considered that government interference in the mechanism of supply and demand would do more harm than good, especially in the long term. This attitude prefigured the reluctance of the British authorities to intervene during famines in India through the 1860s and 1870s. As a rather priggish Protestant, Trevelyan also felt that the Irish potato blight was the work of God, a divine lesson that should be learned in its awful entirety by the 'selfish, perverse and turbulent' (i.e. improvident and irredeemably Catholic) Irish.

As part of his work at the Treasury, Trevelyan conducted a review of the British civil service. The result, known as the Northcote–Trevelyan Report (1853), recommended that the time-honoured system of aristocratic patronage should be abandoned in favour of entry by competitive examination. This reform, which became enormously important in the modernization of British public life, had already been adopted by Parliament as part of its renewal of the EIC's Charter in 1853, due in large part to the advocacy of the Trevelyan–Macaulay team.

Trevelyan kept up a close interest in Indian affairs all through the middle of the century. He was consulted as an expert in the run-up to the 1853 Charter Act, and made clear his support for the expansion of education and railway construction. He also took an important part in the public debate after 1857, during which he regularly wrote letters to *The Times* using the pseudonym Indophilus. Both he and the Orientalist scholar Max Müller, who was writing as Philindus, considered that mutual misunderstanding had been the root of the trouble, and that greater knowledge of languages was essential to avoid a repeat. Trevelyan, though, believed Indians should learn English, whereas Müller recommended that the English should learn Indian languages.

Years of solid work at the Treasury and his continued interest in India finally earned him the governorship of Madras in 1859, but the posting did not go well. He was deeply opposed to Wilson's reforming budget of 1860, disliking its centralizing tendencies, and he was uncomfortable about introducing general taxation in the absence of representative institutions. English-style budgets should only be introduced if India were also given English safeguards, he believed. He was not alone in his objections but, more skilled perhaps in administration than politics, he chose to express his hostility by means of an open telegram, which was leaked to the press. Private opposition was acceptable, but public dissent was not, especially in the highly sensitive atmosphere after the Uprising. He was forced to resign.

James Wilson died of dysentery, on 11 August 1860, and the position he had held became formalized as Finance Member of the Viceroy's Executive Council.

The establishment then forgave Charles Trevelyan fairly swiftly, and in some degree even vindicated him, because in 1862 he returned as the

Viceroy's Finance Member, replacing Samuel Laing, Wilson's successor. Once in control he preferred to balance the books through reduced spending rather than increased taxation, and he picked up a reputation for having anti-commercial attitudes. But in two and a half years he nursed the government into surplus, paid off a large amount of debt, phased out the income tax, and was able to finance a cut in the import tariffs set by Wilson.

But by then, as he approached sixty, he was out of step with official Indian policy in a number of areas. He had always been one of the few minds prepared to contemplate Indian self-government, and he continued to do so, even after the Uprising. As a very classical liberal he was also fiercely opposed to intrusive or 'political' taxation, even though this was becoming a necessity to sustain the Raj in its wider ambitions to 'improve' the country. Only in his support for greater local self-government was he moving in the same direction as the 'official mind', and this largely by coincidence, for he was not so much concerned to promote administrative efficiency as to recognize India's diversity, and to include Indians in their own government as a matter of political morality. He would have preferred to see a supreme supervisory executive at the centre with extensive local autonomy—a structure that was way in advance of its time, and not unlike the Cabinet Mission's plan of 1946.

Had James Wilson lived longer, the entire course of India's economic development might have been different. As it was, the impetus to modernize India's finances, in particular to adjust the taxation system to address the country's principal sources of liquid wealth, was lost and never truly regained. The prevailing alliance between the most conservative forces in Indian society and the most cautious elements within the British government produced a passive and impoverished executive, and an entrenched economic elite whose earnings remained largely beyond the government's reach.

Charles Trevelyan, despite his passionate liberalism, was unintentionally party to this development. As Finance Member, his political purism about taxation helped to ensure that the Indian tax system was not used in a constructive way. His refusal to levy taxes in an illiberal manner was popular in some quarters, but it also highlighted the linked nature of the two most insoluble weaknesses of the later Raj—its indigence and its unrepresentative nature.

Wilson, Laing and Trevelyan had the Raj back in the black on its current account by 1862. The speed of this recovery was greatly helped by a large expansion in international trade, stimulated by the start of the American

Civil War in 1861, after which the unavailability of US cotton provided a stimulus for Indian growers. Trade with Europe doubled in the decade 1865–75, which gave the Government of India an expanded economic base. But, in a pattern that Trevelyan set up and that was to recur, a surplus in the government's accounts encouraged not activity, but passivity. Income tax was reintroduced after a downturn in 1869, but remained in place only until a surplus reappeared, in 1873.

1864–76: Better Government, Public Works, Devolution

Peasant and adivasi (tribal) unrest was an recurring theme of the later Raj. There were uprisings across Orissa in the late 1860s, riots in the Deccan in 1874, and sustained unrest in Bengal until 1883, including the Pabna movement from 1872 to 1876. It was hard to suppress this kind of disorder by police action in such a large country, so the authorities tried to respond by means of more structural policies. These consisted principally of reforms to tenancy legislation, which stretched over the next sixty years.

The other main cause of the unrest was indebtedness, so yet more legislation followed to regulate moneylending, while forms of credit or loans in kind—taccavi—were made available to small farmers. Yet despite all these attempts at amelioration, the Indian countryside remained an arena of conflict, not only between social classes, but between the Raj, settled farmers and tribal peoples.

Although much recovered in financial health, by the mid-1860s the Raj still faced the familiar question; how could better government be delivered? The favoured solution was to 'push on' with public works, which would both enhance India's prosperity and open up financial opportunities for British investors and traders. But finding the money to pay for it had its attendant risks. There was a deep reluctance to increase taxation, on both economic and political grounds. Borrowing remained an option, but this was also a daunting prospect. Where could the extra income be found to support loans? And what of the danger of default?

The way out was a ruling, made in 1867, that government borrowing would be authorized for 'productive' public works, meaning those that could cover their running expenses and interest charges, and thus not make demands on current revenues. Loans were then raised for a range of projects, primarily large-scale irrigation schemes. However, over-sanguine projections and inaccurate costings meant that, in practice, many of the ventures did not actually pay for themselves. Undeterred, Raj officials tried, whenever possible, to label the cost of public works as 'productive debt', in order to open India up as an economic proposition, and to earn the gratitude of the subject population. In accountancy terms they succeeded, and by the turn of the century the government's debts were largely of the productive type. The overall economic effects, however, were discouragingly slight.

Meanwhile shortfalls in ordinary revenue still had to be covered by borrowing, and in the twenty years after the Uprising, the Government of India's debt doubled, from £69 million to £140 million. Here was a government desperate to buy approval from its subjects, yet terrified to tax them at a level that might produce noticeable differences in everyday life. The 'chicken and egg' problem of how to create a prosperous and contented India that was also still British was not easily solved. Investment in public works was a gamble, and investment in irrigation was a particularly slow and low-yielding gamble. Even customs duties turned into a dilemma. Free traders were keen to abolish them, but the resulting loss of revenue had to be replaced somehow. Principles in London and practicalities in India began to conflict.

Daily governance was problematic too. Despite Wilson's reforms, the Raj's accounts remained muddled; some loans were raised in Britain in sterling and some in India in rupees, and the military budget—the largest head of expenditure—was a ramified affair across three Presidency armies. Meanwhile there was no great pressure from London to clarify the situation. Parliamentary supervision of Indian finances remained loose, because there were no votes in the Commons on Indian expenditure. Although permission had to be obtained for borrowing, debates on the Indian budget were poorly attended; by convention there were no formal divisions.

Nevertheless, India remained of great interest to senior politicians. Before 1858 there was a Company to take the blame, but after that date no one wanted to have to carry the can for misgovernment or revolt. Ministerial involvement also increased, because daily supervision of Indian affairs was made possible by the introduction of overland, then direct oceanic, telegraph lines between 1865 and 1873. General communication too was enormously speeded up by the opening of the Suez Canal in 1869.

These developments helped foster the impression that ministerial responsibility in London was somehow enough to ensure good government in India. But this kind of supervision relied heavily on the centralization of government in India itself, and by the late 1860s it was clear that this was not the best way to run the country. Ellenborough had foreseen this in the 1840s, but Dalhousie had preferred to ignore the potential difficulties, attracted by the simplicity of central control and reassured by his own capacity for hard work.

Centralization and provincial devolution offered rival possibilities. Centralization made control of India seem easier from London, whereas devolution made India easier to run from within India. The constant juggling of these purposes, and especially the financial details, kept the administrative structure in a constant state of revision throughout the later Raj.

Meanwhile a range of less theoretical problems were solved by military methods. A border war with Bhutan lasted several months in 1864–5, a rebellion by Naikda tribals in Gujarat was suppressed in 1868, an expedition was mounted across the north-east frontier against the Lushai in 1871–2, and there was a serious outbreak of violence among the Kukas, a sect of militant Sikhs, which peaked in 1872.

All the while, the senior leadership of the Raj remained becalmed in mediocrity. Canning was followed as viceroy by the forgettable Lord Elgin (1862–3), who died in post shortly afterwards. This left an awkward vacancy, as there were no obvious candidates to succeed him from within the privileged gubernatorial class that had provided the previous eleven Governors-General. Trouble on the Afghan border then prompted Wood to choose John Lawrence, for his knowledge of the north-west and his reputation as the man who had saved the day in 1857. The choice was not a good one, however, and Lawrence proved unable to cope with the leap from running the Punjab as a one-man government to chairing his own Executive Council.

The respect with which contemporaries regarded John Lawrence (1811–79) is reflected in the way he became the most written-about proconsul since Robert Clive. This was mainly because, like John Malcolm, he personified qualities that the British liked to admire about themselves. He was a dutiful man of great personal integrity, full of Christian virtue and humility. *Lord Lawrence* (1888), by Sir Richard Temple, another Raj luminary, is crammed full of praise for Lawrence's outstanding devotion to duty, enormous appetite for work, fine judgement, temperance and humanity, all repeatedly endorsed as seldom equalled and never bettered. But despite possessing admirable qualities of character, in truth he was a man promoted beyond his abilities, at a time when the Raj needed first-class leadership.

John Lawrence's career spans the middle segment of British rule in India, and illuminates its passage from youthful dynamism to premature senescence, the retreat from close personal contact to remote paperwork. He was one of the East India Company's best 'settlement' officers, but went on to become one of the Raj's least successful viceroys, thus personifying the switch from the horseback government of the early 1800s to the 'office Raj' that succeeded it. He was the last of the Company's men to rise to the top in India, and his departure in 1869 marked the end of an era.

One of twelve children, he joined his two older brothers, Henry and George, in the Company's service, but unlike them he entered its civil, not its military, arm. Arriving in Bengal in 1830, he moved up-country to Delhi, where a highlight of his time was his detection and capture of the murderer of William Fraser, the Company's Resident there. He then took charge of a succession of districts until 1838, when he was transferred to the North West Provinces (now Uttar Pradesh). In 1840 he was forced to return to England on sick leave, and took two years to recuperate.

He returned to Delhi and stayed there till 1846, when he was given the job of settling newly ceded Sikh territory between the Sutlej and the Beas. He also served, during his brother Henry's absences, as temporary Resident at the Lahore durbar. This drew him inexorably into Punjabi politics. After the Second Sikh War, he had constant disagreements with his brother over policy towards the former regime and the Punjabi peasantry. In 1853 Lord Dalhousie gave John sole charge of all seven districts of the Punjab, with the title of Chief Commissioner, a new rank created specially for him.

Thus empowered, John built up his 'Punjab school' of energetic regional administrators, who dispensed justice and collected taxes in a highly personal style, characterized by informality, decisiveness and a facility in local languages. Firm and swift justice administered by men who knew their area and its people was the ideal; his hero was always Sir Thomas Munro.

He was not in favour of social revolution, and his policies were not designed to promote it. He simply believed that an alliance of trust and care with the poor was a better way of prolonging and securing British rule than an alliance with the landowning rich—the strategy favoured by his brother Henry.

John also developed the view that, although a fervent Christian himself, conversion work was inadvisable and potentially hazardous, especially within the ranks of the army. It was best to develop the population socially and economically, while waiting for the manifest benefits of Christianity to suggest themselves to the more discerning. 'Example' was always the key. Later he was to sum up this approach as 'Christian things done in a

Christian manner'.[6] Nothing undertaken in this spirit, he believed, could be offensive to Indians or harmful to British rule.

Ideally, he wanted to see India 'thickly cultivated by a fat, contented yeomanry',[7] and under his regime taxes were kept low, civil order was enforced, canals were built and basic schools set up. These developments produced general contentment in a historically turbulent region, and the placidity of the Punjab during 1857 is frequently attributed to two things: good harvests and Lawrence's style of government.

He was credited by his colleagues with saving north India for the British in 1857, but this was too kind to him and overlooked the vital role played by the officer corps, whose initiative and bravery disarmed the Bengal regiments in the region or fought them to the death. It also ignored the fact that he was keen to cede the Vale of Peshawar to Dost Muhammad temporarily, as a way of securing the neutrality of the Afghans to his rear. His subordinates, to a man, opposed this idea and it was abandoned. Treaties with the amir, negotiated and amended in 1855 and 1857—which Lawrence had considered unnecessary—held good, and did as much as he did to preserve British rule in India.

As the rebellion faltered, Lawrence was prominent in urging clemency and proportionate responses. He was not averse to hanging rebels, but only in small, exemplary groups of the most violent offenders. It was also his personal intervention that halted the vengeful destruction of the centre of old Delhi.

Once the amnesty of November 1858 was secured, he left for England and took up a place on the new Council of India. He was not considered for the post of viceroy when Canning came home in 1862, but when Canning's successor, Lord Elgin, died unexpectedly in 1863, Lawrence seemed a popular choice.

Hopes that a man who knew India so intimately would rule her well proved unfounded, and his term was dogged by disputes over taxation policy and tenancy reform. Between 1864 and 1866, during discussions over the shortcomings of the 1859 Tenancy Act, he was keen to establish fixity of rents, while others, including Henry Maine, the Legal Member, and Charles Trevelyan, the Finance Member, were convinced that security of tenure was the answer. The Act remained unaltered.

Lawrence was generally hostile to the business community in British India, mainly because he found them difficult to control, and he especially disliked the indigo planters, notorious as a law unto themselves. He also distrusted railway companies and preferred to encourage irrigation projects. And rather than any commercially slanted investment, he proposed to spend £2 million on the provision of new barracks for the extra European soldiers stationed in India after 1857. By this stage, like many others, he had some difficulty in working out for whom exactly he was supposed to be working.

In his person, John Lawrence contrived to sum up and live out many of the contradictions and conflicts of mid-nineteenth-century British India. He was convinced of the superiority of his Christian faith, yet he had a genuine respect for Indians under his charge, and was keen to leave them unmolested in their traditional ways as much as possible. He consistently advocated government investment, particularly in canals, yet he opposed increased taxation, unless it was upon the wealthier classes, both British and Indian. He was not a soldier, yet he was instrumental in the military decisions that suppressed the revolt of 1857–9.

Through all these attitudes ran an unshakeable belief that it was the destiny of the British to govern in India. He was convinced that this had not come about by chance. 'We are here by our moral superiority, by the force of circumstance, and by the will of Providence,'[8] he wrote. He had no doubt that the British should stay in India, though preferably as peace-makers and paternal guardians.

The core of this philosophy was graphically represented in a statute raised to him in Lahore, which portrayed him with a pen in one hand and a sword in the other. Under it was carved: 'Will you be governed by the pen or by the sword? Choose!'[9] Forty years after the statue was erected in 1887, the inhabitants of the town did exercise a degree of choice in the matter; they broke the sword.

As a younger man, John Lawrence led by example and inspiration, but in the more calculated politics of the bureaucratic Raj, he was hobbled. His moment had passed. What made the British successful in India, and what had been most admired by Indians, was exactly his sort of commanding presence in the field, his responsiveness and genuine empathy. 'Where have we failed when we acted vigorously?'[10] he asked his superiors in May 1857. But the new Raj managed only to serve up a stiffer, slower style of government, turning in upon itself and gradually coming to doubt its own purposes.

He had been a natural leader in the Punjab, but he became a brooding presence on his own Council. As a one-time outdoor autocrat, he found sitting on committees frustrating. He had no experience of dealing with political opposition, and he struggled when faced not with subordinates but with near equals, men with influence in London who had political views and agendas of their own. The worst example of this came in 1866 with his unwillingness to overrule Bengal officials and intervene in a severe famine in Orissa. The failure to provide adequate relief or to control food prices may have cost as many as a million lives. Lawrence personally carried the guilt of this disaster for the rest of his life.

Never a politician, he was frustrated by the increased politicization of the Raj's machinery after the Indian Councils Act of 1861. His inability to exercise power at the centre prefigured the way the Raj was outgrowing its strength. Lawrence's successor, Lord Mayo, accepted that the new structures were too big and too detached from ground level. The phrase 'masterly inactivity' was coined by a journalist to describe Lawrence's policy towards Afghanistan. The phrase was a prescient description of the fate of the later Raj itself.

One of the best of the regional single executives, Lawrence as viceroy was especially keen to centralize authority into his own hands, and thus to hamper men in his former position, but the system of central supervision did not suit him. Others thought that it did not suit India either.

Bartle Frere, a long-standing opponent of his in Council, criticized him from the safety of retirement, writing in 1867 that India could not be run from Calcutta like a province newly won, and warning that autocratic centralization was a poor solution to the new problems the British were facing.

Of all the famous provincial administrators, Sir Bartle Frere (1815–84) was perhaps the most perfectly restrained and clear-minded about what he was doing; realistic, honest and humane. As such he probably represents either the best of empire or the worst, depending on your point of view. M.G. Ranade was prepared to praise him for his 'generous ambition to help the native population to elevate themselves'.[11]

His approach to government in India was a mixture of the old-school ideas of Malcolm and the vigorous firmness of Ellenborough. He was as convinced a Christian as John Lawrence, but rather quieter about his faith, and he differed with Lawrence on a range of issues, including the best way to 'settle' native populations and the defence of the north-west border region, where he wanted to uphold a policy of advanced defence based on Quetta, while Lawrence wanted to stay out of Afghan affairs altogether.

He was a bright boy, from a liberal Tory background, who passed out first in his year at Haileybury. Preferring to go out to India overland, he arrived in Bombay in 1834, and by 1838 he was Assistant Revenue Commissioner for the entire Bombay Presidency. Based in Poona from 1842, he was Secretary to the Governor of Bombay, Sir George Arthur, and by 1844 he had married his boss's daughter. After ten years he was fluent in local languages and entirely familiar with the machinery of regional government. At this point he fell ill and went home in 1846 to recuperate.

On his return he was posted as Resident to the state of Satara, the small Maratha principality ruled by the descendants of Shivaji. Though political authority in Maratha affairs had deserted Satara in the eighteenth century for Poona and the Peshwa, the royal line of Satara was still held in high regard within the Maratha confederacy. It was this residual status that led Frere, as Resident, to protest vigorously when Dalhousie decided to annex the state in 1848. Frere was convinced that this was a mistake. He felt no benefit would accrue, and that great offence would be given. But in the case of Satara he was proved wrong; no trouble resulted. He was, however, generally right about the offence caused by Dalhousie's annexations.

Frere was appointed Commissioner for Sind in 1851. This was a position ideally suited to his talents, and he set about settling the region in his personal style, in much the way that John Lawrence did in Punjab at around the same time. Frere, though, was working with a more rudimentary government system, in which political and military responsibility overlapped, allowing him a more flexible range of responses.

Both men were keen on improvements in infrastructure, and Frere made it his business to expand and modernize the port of Karachi. A network of roads, railways and canals sprang up across Sind, along with village schools and nascent municipal bodies. He is even credited with overseeing the transliteration of Sindi into a written language. By the time he took home leave in 1856, revenues from the area had doubled.

He was not a soldier, but he worked closely with General John Jacob to pacify the western borders of Sind where the countryside was rough and the tradition of feuding was strong. Between them they worked out a policy of trusting the local tribes and forging good relations with neighbouring rulers not under British control, a tactic that came naturally to Frere, who was always a great supporter of indirect rule.

Frere insisted on the apprehension of individual malefactors and their trial for specific crimes. This contrasted directly with policy further north on the Punjab–Afghan border, where collective punishment was the standard practice. The methods of the 'Sind school' worked well, and border warfare and feuding were reduced enormously in Frere and Jacob's time, a success seen as a direct rebuke to the rougher 'Punjab school'. The standard reply from the north was that Afridis and Pakhtuns were very different from Sindis and Balochis. It was certainly true that Pakhtun culture held entire tribes responsible for crimes, so the collective punishment that Frere so disliked was actually written into the social fabric further north.

During the events of 1857 Frere was kept busy. The region remained calm, but there were constant fears about intervention from Afghanistan and the loyalty of the Punjab. Frere dispatched men where necessary and quelled discontent wherever it appeared. He insisted that Peshawar should not be abandoned, and sent troops to reinforce the garrison at Multan. His conduct was noted and approved, with a motion of thanks for his work passed in Parliament. Recognition brought him promotion to the Viceroy's Council in 1859, then the governorship of Bombay in 1862.

He got on well with Viceroys Canning and Elgin, but after 1864 he struggled to work with John Lawrence. Lawrence's 'levelling' proclivities came between them, and Frere, ever the champion of regional autonomy, disliked Lawrence's centralizing instincts. There was also the matter of Afghanistan. Lawrence wanted to leave alone as far as possible, but Frere was always looking to extend British influence westwards and northwards as a matter of strategic security. Lawrence's views won the day.

Frere treated the Bombay Presidency as he had treated Sind, pouring money into public works, including the demolition of the walls of Bombay Castle in 1862. He was greatly aided in this programme by the 1861–6 cotton boom across western India. But when the crash came, Frere was criticized for insufficient attention to regulation of the banking sector. He resigned and returned to England, where he spent the next ten years on the Council of India. His last contact with India came in 1875–6, when he accompanied Edward, Prince of Wales on a tour.

Frere was another of the men lauded by the Victorians but now largely forgotten. His first biography appeared in 1895, but it was more than a hundred years before the next, and modern interest in him is almost exclusively related to his degree of responsibility, as High Commissioner to South Africa, for the outbreak of the Zulu War of 1879.

In India he cut a less spectacular figure than many of his contemporaries, and his achievements were all of a quiet, unmilitary sort. But his kind of restrained despotism, founded in practical experience and flecked with beneficent Christianity, typified the standard conservative approach to the governance of India, an approach that worked well enough in the mid-nineteenth century, but was never entirely abandoned in the changed circumstances of the twentieth.

Lawrence was replaced by the Conservative Lord Mayo (1869–72), who tackled several issues his predecessor had sidestepped, including the first serious attempt to decentralize the financial affairs of the Raj.

The business of running India from Calcutta had become increasingly unsatisfactory. Responsibility for taxation and spending was not properly integrated; regions that contributed most to the treasury were not the ones that demanded the most expenditure, and men at the centre generally had only a poor idea of how money should best be spent at local level. In sum, there was too little incentive towards economy in the regions and too much ignorance at the centre. Mayo therefore devolved responsibility for expenditure under a range of headings, including roads, education, policing and prisons, to be met from fixed grants. The money still came from central funds, but the decisions about spending it were henceforth made locally. Deficits were to be met by local taxation, under the Local Rates Act of 1871. From these small beginnings, a new system grew up with responsibility for taxation increasingly handed to the provinces, while fixed proportions of tax income replaced fixed grants. Five-yearly revisions of these arrangements, known as the Divided Heads of Revenue, continued until central, local and shared responsibilities were permanently allocated in 1912.

In the long run this sophisticated system improved the handling of details, but in the short term it distributed the effects of taxation in a way that officials were aware would avoid the creation of 'national' grievances. Here again we can detect the spectre of 1857.

Meanwhile discontent continued at local level all over India. Violent Muslim extremism persisted, and in two spectacular coups a senior judge was assassinated on the steps of the High Court at Patna in September 1871, and Lord Mayo himself was murdered while inspecting the prison on the Andaman Islands in February 1872. The assassin was not a member of an organized movement, but the killing further fuelled the suspicion of Muslims among Raj officials, who were still very ready to blame Muslims for the Uprising of 1857, for no better reason than that the mutineers had acclaimed the Mughal emperor as their leader. This somewhat circumstantial evidence inclined many to see the rebellion as the result of a Muslim plot, despite the fact that the majority of the mutineers were actually Hindus. The word 'conspiracy' was freely used for decades, and it was only a conscious effort by Viceroy Dufferin in the 1880s that began to reverse this prejudice.

The Muslim 'problem' remained a serious public policy concern. Why did they shun public service? How could they be more closely bound to the Raj? Were they in some fundamental way to be permanent enemies of British rule? For Mayo this was a problem of mutual comprehension, and he set the brilliant William Hunter to unpick it.

Sir William Hunter (1840–1900) typified a certain kind of intelligent British involvement with India, and his enormous published output comprised a great deal of what the contemporary British thought and knew about the country they were ruling. His tone was certainly imperial, but his personal priorities were scholarly.

He was an extremely bright student, and joined the Indian Civil Service in 1861, coming top of the list of applicants. He was not the idealized 'English gentleman' that the founders of the new Indian Civil Service had hoped to attract—he never shook off a reputation for parsimony—but he possessed many fine qualities. He had a solid higher education from Glasgow University, he had travelled and studied abroad before sitting the examinations, and he had even picked up a working knowledge of Sanskrit. On arrival in Bengal in 1862 he was made an assistant magistrate, but his future did not lie in running the Raj; he was destined to analyse it, and to compile historical and statistical data about it.

In 1868 he published *The Annals of Rural Bengal* to some acclaim. At the same time he issued a more speculative work on the comparative philology of India's non-Aryan languages. As an attempt at a rigorous work, however, the book's many failings were soon pointed out by scholars, and were duly acknowledged by its author.

His new prominence brought him to the attention of Viceroy Mayo, who asked him to write a book about the ongoing Wahhabi resistance to the Raj. The result was *The Indian Musalmans* (1871), which took the view that the Muslims of India were a permanent threat to British rule. He reached this conclusion based on the scale of the bloodletting in 1857, combined with a conviction that many Muslim grievances, about education and employment, were actually justified. He was prepared to blame the Raj, persuaded by the 'want of sympathy' between rulers and ruled. His solution was to use education to draw Muslims out of medieval beliefs and make them as placid and pliable as Hindus had seemingly become. This did not have to be an expensive undertaking, and though he knew it would take at least a generation, it seemed the only way to draw active loyalty out of India's Muslims, instead of enforcing reluctant obedience. In this he can be seen as a second Macaulay, trying to do to Muslims in particular what Macaulay had wanted to do to Indians in general—to bring them into the Raj's ambit through modern education.

The book provided a very different perspective from that of *The Loyal Mohammedans of India* (1860), written (in Urdu) by Sayyid Ahmad Khan as an attempt to dissociate Muslims as a body from the violence of 1857. Khan wrote a long review of Hunter's *Musalmans* in 1872, regretting its conclusions, and complaining that its suggestions were more likely to widen the sympathy gap than to narrow it. Nevertheless, Hunter's ideas took up a niche in colonial thinking, and *The Indian Musalmans* is considered by some historians to have been influential in the creation of a wider self-consciousness within the Indian Muslim community, a factor in the growth of later 'communalism'.

Hunter meanwhile was developing another major interest—statistics. In 1869 Mayo commissioned him to compile a Statistical Survey of India, and he spent most of the next twelve years on this task, sporting the special title of Director-General of Statistics. This was a rather more political appointment than it first seemed. Statistics were designed to take the guesswork out of government, and Hunter, now in charge of a vital political resource, soon found himself on the front line of government defence.

Debates about levels of income and the burden of taxation relied upon the government's own statistics, and there was always a feeling in certain quarters that they were inaccurate or biased. Post-colonial writers have tended to see all data collected by the Raj in this light, but Hunter would not have been aware that he was collecting 'colonial' knowledge. For him and his colleagues, the vast amount of data they were collecting was simply raw material to enable responsive governance.

In the course of his work Hunter had to travel extensively all over the subcontinent, and this made him more closely acquainted with India's diversity than any other official of his generation. One side effect of this was his standardization of the English spelling of Indian place names. By 1877 he had personally compiled the twenty-volume *Statistical Account of Bengal*, while supervising the production of over one hundred other provincial gazetteers. His next task was to condense and compile all this information into the *Imperial Gazetteer*, which first appeared in 1881, in nine volumes, soon expanded to fourteen.

Hunter's own introduction to the work later appeared under separate cover in 1895 as *The Indian Empire: Its Peoples, History and Products*. This still serves as a summary of a great deal of the standard thinking among Britons who ran India at the top level. Very much in the same vein, he also published a proud Raj manifesto, *England's Work in India* (1881), which contained everything a British person needed to know about how

India was being run by her guardians, and how much 'work' still remained to be done.

He sat on the Viceroy's Executive Council from 1881, as an additional member, and in 1882 he chaired a commission on education set up by the liberal-minded Lord Ripon, who wished to standardize the educational system. The Hunter Commission recommended a substantial increase in the provision of primary education, while accepting the rights of Indian parents to withdraw their children from religious instruction. But the projected expansion never appeared, and when twenty years later Lord Curzon looked at education again, almost nothing had been done.

Hunter retired from the Indian Civil Service in 1887 and returned to England, where he poured out articles and books on Indian subjects from his house near Oxford. Notable among these was his editorship of the *Rulers of India* series, of which he wrote two himself, on Dalhousie and Mayo. These short books are gems of later imperial thinking, in which every British high-up is a hero, and no shadows fall across the Raj's good intentions. Despite his prodigious output, which included one novel, *The Old Missionary* (1895), he only ever completed two volumes (of a projected five) of his own history of India.

The general calm across the years 1859–76 afforded the Raj a good deal of time to contemplate its own failings, yet by and large it remained happy with itself, or at least happy enough not to undertake major reform. After all, the biggest challenge it had yet faced had been seen off successfully. British moral self-assurance swelled to fill the vacuum at the heart of India's political life, and high imperialism was born. The successful suppression of the revolt furnished the best proof ever that the British were fit to govern, their legitimacy blessed by providence.

The first two historians of the 1857 rebellion could not have been clearer about how adversity had brought out the superior nature of the Anglo-Saxon. J.W. Kaye, in the preface to his *History of the Sepoy War in India, 1857–58*, wrote that the rebellion provided 'the most signal illustration of our great national character ever yet recorded in the annals of our country'.[12] His collaborator, G.B. Malleson, later wrote: 'there is no epoch in the history of Great Britain in which the men and women of these islands shone with greater lustre'.[13] Here was the first finest hour, and its power to move supporters of empire should not be underestimated.

But small changes were afoot that would soon grow into big ones. There were British critics at home and aboard—Sir Henry Fawcett in London and Allan O. Hume in India, for example—while Indians began organizing in the regions and travelling to see the imperial metropolis for themselves. In 1866 Dadabhai Naoroji founded the East India Association in London, beginning a conscious strategy of compensating for the lack of representation in India by talking to the British at the imperial centre. Many other Indians went west in the next decades to study law, and the ideas that many of them picked up there began to spill over into consciousness of political rights—and wrongs.

Three parallel processes were now in train that were to exert a significant influence on Anglo-Indian history. In Britain, there was the extension of the parliamentary franchise, while India experienced the increasing pace of modernization, and the rise of political activism.

The process of electoral reform in Britain is important in the Indian context because it placed the basis of government in Britain on a different footing from that in India. Before the extension of voting rights, and with it the introduction of modern notions of accountability, the two countries were run on a roughly similar rationale—that voting rights did not have to be universal, because the system accommodated political interests indirectly. The limited British franchise of the eighteenth century was justified by the idea that the whole nation was 'virtually' represented within the House of Commons, because of its organic interconnectedness.

There were obvious objections to this idea, with its hand-me-down medieval corporatism and its lordly social paternalism, but it remained orthodox constitutional theory in Britain even after the Great Reform Act of 1832. That Act slightly modified the political structure, by a small franchise extension and the removal of 'rotten' boroughs, but it was still assumed that individuals did not need a vote to have their grievances attended to. The subsequent Reform Acts of 1867 and 1884, which together expanded the electorate to nearly half the adult male population, were rather different. They tacitly acknowledged that the wider population should have a voice in national politics, through elections. The recognition that it was right and proper to respond politically to shifts in popular mood was an irrevocable step into modernity.

After this quiet liberal revolution, there had to be some reason why political reform could not be introduced to India. If political rights were to be granted to all, then why not Indians? Perhaps Indians were not wealthy or educated enough—the only grounds for exclusion still tenable in Britain. Poverty and ignorance could therefore now act as reasons why Indians should not be enfranchised; the side effects of colonial rule could then neatly become its main supports. Or perhaps Indians were simply not ready for self-government, and this remained the moderate position within imperial philosophy. High imperialism thus became, at best, a circular argument attempting to justify why political rights and popular representation were not necessary in the colonies.

The system of ruling through a small elite was perfectly coordinated in Britain and India before 1857, but electoral reform drew a line between the two countries. Electoral reform in Britain was matched in India by the idea that ruling was actually a burden that ordinary people should be grateful not to have to shoulder. After this, government in India was always represented as a personal imposition—work—not a right or a liberty.

The way forward now was to insist that India, in a multitude of ways, was different from Britain, not potentially the same, as so many had pretended to believe until that point. Instead, the theory of political—and even racial—superiority appeared in full force, and mature forms of imperial justification emerged in the writings of men such as James F. Stephen and John Strachey, who shared an intimate acquaintance with India and a deep uneasiness about the democratization of Britain.

Their collective view was that India was not capable of self-government of any kind, and that British rule was the only solution to India's problems. Meanwhile vigilance had to be maintained at home, to prevent the ignorant and selfish masses from wrecking the fine edifice that had sent forth men to win an empire for the benefit of all. Stephen, who served as Law Member from 1869 to 1872, particularly voiced the opinion that Britain should be run more like India, not the other way around.

The practical impact of these attitudes was that such concessions to representation as were made in India were highly restricted, and had much in common with the pre-1832 system in Britain, featuring small, special electorates, using appointment and nomination, and stressing the priority of status and interests over numbers.

Once the basis of political power in Britain and India became fundamentally different, the ornate rhetoric of high imperialism followed on, with all its post-rationalizations and special pleading. This, not a narrow capitalist imperative, was the basis of denying to Indians the fundamental political rights that Britons enjoyed. Here is the key to understanding how imperialism could find a welcome within a nation that was becoming a liberal democracy.

The other great factor for change at this time was the progress of modernization within India. Modernization was a delicately balanced process. Initially, technical progress made India easier to control, and potentially more profitable to run. But somewhere in the 1870s the balance shifted, and India gradually became less easy to govern, precisely *because* of modern conditions. From then on, even some of the most traditional Indians began to adopt the characteristic ideas and devices of modernity that led towards increased literacy, internal dialogue, self-discovery and, ultimately, political mobilization.

Printing presses, railways, universities, English-language schools and liberal political ideas now helped stimulate and coordinate criticism of colonial government. Had that government been clever enough to create economic growth at the same time as accommodating local demands for political inclusion, then those demands might have been controlled and directed, much as Canadian demands had been managed in the 1860s. But in India the government chose to fight foreign wars, spend money on self-aggrandizing durbars, and sit by while famine ravaged the land. This was the greatest betrayal: that the newly educated, aspiring middle classes could not find adequate reward for their skills or sufficient inclusion in the political life of the emerging garrulous, interconnected India.

The period 1866–80 was a time of turbulence in domestic British politics, featuring a wide range of constitutional and social reforms, a series of difficult foreign questions, mostly involving Russia, and frequent changes of administration. Unusually, this was reflected in Indian policy, which oscillated more widely through the 1870s than in any other decade. Mayo's successor, Lord Northbrook (1872–6), was appointed by Gladstone's Liberals in 1872, but after the election of Disraeli's Conservatives in 1874, Northbrook ran into disputes with London over Afghanistan, tariffs, public works, and the constitutional relationship between the viceroy and the elected government in London.

The early 1870s also featured the work of Henry Fawcett's committee, set up by the Liberal government of 1868–74. Although he never visited India, Sir Henry Fawcett (1833–84) holds a special place in the Anglo-Indian story. At a time when there was no effective representation of Indians in either Calcutta or London, Sir Henry spoke up for Indian interests at Westminster in such a persistent and persuasive manner that he earned the sobriquet 'the Member for India'.

Along with this extraordinary pioneering quality, we can also marvel at the fact that Sir Henry was completely blind, having lost the sight of both eyes, aged twenty-five, when his own father accidentally shot him. This disability daunted him not at all and he continued as a Fellow of Trinity Hall, Cambridge, and published his *Manual of Political Economy* in

1863, five years after the accident, by which time he was the university's professor in the subject.

Politics then called him, and after several failed attempts to enter Parliament, he was elected as Liberal MP for Brighton in 1865. He was in opposition from 1866 to 1868 and again from 1874 to 1880, but his political life was never strictly bounded by the Palace of Westminster. He constantly toured the country, speaking at public meetings to rally support for women's suffrage, university reform, the preservation of ancient common lands, and the demand for what would now be called 'transparency' in all aspects of the finances of the Government of India.

He believed, as an article of liberal faith, that Indians should have more of a say in their own government, although he never advocated self-government for India or even Ireland. Nevertheless he repeatedly called for detailed reform of such matters as the admission of Indians to the civil service and the holding of simultaneous entrance exams in London and India. In these causes he was virtually a lone voice.

He sat as a very active member of the parliamentary Select Committee on Indian finance between 1871 and 1874, which has since conventionally carried his name, and his questions and interventions are quoted at length by Romesh C. Dutt in his classic *Economic History of India* (1902–5). Awareness of how little protection India was afforded by government from Westminster drove Fawcett to try to educate the wider British public about Indian issues, which he did through speeches and articles. Although formal opposition could not be mounted, he hoped that pressure from the public might bring the legislature and government to treat India's needs more fairly.

His most influential contribution was a set of three essays, published in 1880 under the title *Indian Finance*. He repeatedly demanded economies and responsible expenditure, a stance that serves to illustrate that supporters of the political rights of Indians in Britain at that time were mostly calling for the government to spend less money within the subcontinent, not more. An exception to this rule was John Bright, who thought that increased expenditure on public works, coupled with military economies, was the only remedy for India's ills.

There were other voices speaking up for India at the time, such as the East India Association, founded in 1866, but Fawcett was different. He was forceful, expert, consistent and, crucially, he was inside the House of Commons, where he made himself the leader of a small ginger group. Its concerns were wider than India, but Fawcett persistently returned to the subject. Attempts were made to put together an Irish–Indian connection, with Irish members sponsoring pro-Indian motions, but the process never worked well, and apart from Fawcett's Finance Committee, the government remained untroubled.

Fawcett also did whatever he could to promote the employment of women, especially as doctors. An echo of this feminist streak has come down to us today through the Fawcett Society, which campaigns for women's rights. Originally known as the London and National Society for Women's Service, it was renamed after his wife, Millicent.

Throughout his life Fawcett was a radical with a strong social conscience, but he was a convinced anti-socialist. He believed that social progress was to be found in individual self-improvement, self-reliance and cooperation, not state intervention. This once-fashionable position lost ground as a later generation of more socialist critics, such as H.M. Hyndman, entered the debate. Fawcett's voice also became less distinctive as Indian issues were taken up by a stream of British figures such as Allan O. Hume, William Wedderburn and Sir Henry Cotton.

Charles Bradlaugh (1833–91), an atheist republican, was later also to earn the mantle of 'Member for India' for himself through his efforts. He attended the 1889 Bombay Congress, and introduced a parliamentary bill that year inspired by Congress demands for the introduction of elections to India's higher councils. It failed, but some of its provisions eventually reappeared in the 1892 Councils Act nursed through by Viceroy Lansdowne. Like Fawcett, Bradlaugh was deeply opposed to socialism, but it was Fawcett who had a greater impact and left a stronger legacy.

Henry Fawcett died in 1884, at the age of fifty-one, after a prolonged series of illnesses, commencing with diphtheria and ending with pleurisy. There is a small monument to him in Westminster Abbey.

Sir Charles Trevelyan, in his last significant contribution to British India, told the Fawcett Committee in 1873 that subsidiary representative institutions should be set up in India. He saw this as a logical and appropriate step, politically and educationally. He never lost his faith that representative government would come to British India in time, but he remained an isolated figure. To the end, he preferred education and cheap, inclusive government to expensive public works as the best way forward for India. Ironically, as an old-school liberal, his 'small government' leanings in 1862–5 did a great deal to prop up the forces of conservatism in India.

1876–84: Lytton and Ripon

After two years struggling as a Liberal under Tory masters, Viceroy Northbrook resigned early, citing family reasons, though many observers believed he objected to the government's aggressive Afghan policy, particularly its insistence on maintaining a diplomatic presence in Kabul, which he considered unnecessary. As his successor, Disraeli chose Edward Bulwer-Lytton junior, who seemed the perfect candidate—a comparative political lightweight, with high Tory opinions, and a love of pomp and poetry. Of all viceroys, Lytton had the least political experience, and was the most politically dogmatic—two qualities that may not have been entirely unrelated.

His administration falls into two sections; the first, from 1876 to 1878, ran relatively smoothly, when Lord Salisbury, with whom he enjoyed good relations, was Secretary for India. The second, from 1878 to 1880, saw him working with Salisbury's successor, Lord Cranbrook, who was less able to control him. The controversies of Lytton's term almost all sprang from the later period.

Edward Bulwer-Lytton (1831–91) was the only son of the highly successful Victorian writer, also named Edward Bulwer-Lytton—the first and last to begin a novel with 'It was a dark and stormy night ...' Until 1876, Lytton junior had been simply a career diplomat and part-time poet with a penchant for romantic atmospheres, but after the untimely departure of Northbrook, his father's friendship with Disraeli and his own cordial relations with Salisbury suddenly put the viceroyalty within his reach. After three others had declined, it was offered to him. Slightly reluctantly, he accepted.

A pleasant, mildly flirtatious man, his sociability enabled him to maintain some unlikely relationships across the boundaries of his opinions; he counted both the radical poet Wilfrid S. Blunt and the liberal intellectual John Morley among his close friends. He was urbane and cultured, and had spent much of his young life writing verse, to some acclaim, under the pseudonym Owen Meredith. He also made one of British India's few vice-regal jokes. Taking as a model the well-known dictum that Russia was 'a despotism tempered by assassination', he opined that British India, in his experience, was 'a despotism of office boxes tempered by occasional loss of keys'.[14]

His first major task was to organize the Durbar of January 1877 to mark the elevation of Queen Victoria to the imperial crown of India, a move he had discussed and agreed with Disraeli, who felt that the gap in India's public life created by the removal of its Mughal centrepiece needed to be filled—by the British. Lytton threw himself into the task, inventing a scheme of Western-style heraldry for the princes who were about to pledge their loyalty to their far-off empress.

Disraeli and Lytton between them came up with a carefully designed imperial vision of British India as a venerable institution rooted in the distant past, despite the fact that the British had been paramount power in India for hardly more than a generation. The magnificence of the Durbar was also offensive to many Indians, who blamed extravagant British government expenditure for India's poverty. Although Dadabhai Naoroji's protests about the injustice of the 'drain' of Indian wealth to Britain were not entirely convincing in economic terms, something as lavish and wasteful as the 1877 Durbar made his point for him better than dozens of articulately argued and minutely detailed pamphlets could ever have done.

Lytton was a tad over-enthusiastic about the Indian aristocracy, and considered forming an Indian Privy Council to include native princes. The idea was firmly stamped on by Salisbury in London, much as Wood had stamped on Dalhousie's plans for Indian inclusion in the 1850s. Lytton also tried, without much success, to attract the sons of the Indian nobility into the administration by creating a special, elite corps of Indian civil servants—the Statutory Civil Service (SCS). But the SCS was always a rather sorry body and was quietly done away with in the late 1880s, having never remotely justified Lytton's faith in the willingness of privileged Indians to undertake a life of pen pushing.

Lytton did not believe in the John Lawrence school of ruling well to earn the respect and affection of the Indian masses. In a much-quoted letter of 11 May 1877, he stated that it was a 'fundamental political mistake of able and experienced Indian officials ... that we can hold India securely by what they call good government; that is to say, by improving the condition of the ryot, strictly administering justice, spending immense sums on irrigation works, etc.'.[15] He was inclined to believe that a great show of strength coupled with firm rule was a better policy.

This attitude was essentially what marked Lytton out as a Tory, and set him against the more populist Bentinck–Dalhousie tradition of benign improvement. As the highest Tory who ever ruled India, he was the least convinced about the legitimization strategy, as far as it related to mass support. He was certainly keen to cultivate political alliances, but he concentrated entirely on wooing the aristocratic classes.

He was more classically liberal in economic terms, and held that free trade was the single most important policy available to the British to bring prosperity to India. This belief produced two notable outcomes. One was his abolition of the duties on coarse British cotton goods imported into India, a measure pushed through in 1879 against the united opposition of his own Council, all of whom wished to retain the duties—not to protect Indian industry, but because of the large sum that the duties yielded, which would have to be replaced from some other source if spending levels were to be maintained. Lytton was not concerned about keeping up levels of public spending in order to buy loyalty from his subject population.

The other outcome was much less theoretical. Lytton's term coincided with a devastating famine across south India from 1876 to 1878. His belief in free trade meant that he would not sanction government import of grain to the stricken areas, or the fixing or capping of prices. Free market forces were the best way to resolve the problem, he thought, and India, notoriously, continued to export grain during the famine. Lytton stuck to the classical argument that grain supplies would ultimately be drawn towards areas of famine—i.e. high prices—and that to interfere would simply make matters worse.

He was also against the distribution of funds directly to the affected population, partly for free market reasons, but mostly because he did not wish to burden the Government of India with an open-ended obligation to relieve hunger whenever and wherever it appeared. The bill for this would, of course, be astronomical, and there was a risk that the country's entire wealth would be committed to supporting a universal dole. Relieving famine was one thing; banishing hunger was quite another.

His determination to leave matters alone resulted in a very high mortality rate, as his favoured policy—the provision of waged work in public construction projects—was too unresponsive to meet urgent needs. This inhumane pedantry led to a bad-tempered exchange with the Governor of Madras who, despite his lofty rank as Duke of Buckingham and his quintuple-barrelled surname, was actually more liberal than the viceroy.

A storm of local press criticism over wasteful expenditure and threadbare famine relief pushed Lytton into passing the Vernacular Press Act of 1878, which allowed him to gag any Indian-language publication to which he took a dislike. This followed on from the suppression of 'seditious' theatre performances, enacted by Northbrook under the Dramatic Performances Act (1876). To some it seemed that India was in danger of losing her self-expression piece by piece. When Lytton reduced the tariffs on imported cotton goods, under pressure from the home government, it seemed that India's manufactures were in peril too.

But the main focus of Lytton's attention was always Tsarist expansionism. He pursued an aggressive 'forward policy' in Afghanistan, with the intention of whipping in the amir and pushing British influence to the far edge of the country in order to deter the Russians or, if necessary, to fight them well beyond Indian soil. This policy was also a little forward of his political masters in London, who were unable to restrain him over the telegraph. The Second Afghan War was the result.

Though Afghanistan had stayed quiet for decades, the British were always aware that Russian influence was creeping across Central Asia. John Lawrence remained unruffled about the Tsarist menace; he actually thought that Russia was a better neighbour for Afghanistan than the local Muslim rulers. He also placed no trust in Afghans, and had no wish to tie up valuable resources on the border, believing that Russian ambitions could best be controlled by diplomatic pressure. But by Lytton's time, Conservative politicians in London were in a panic about Russia's expansion into the Balkans and the approach of new railways to the western and northern borders of Afghanistan. The possible Russian capture of the oasis at Merv led to extended bouts of what became known as 'Mervousness'.

Nor did the chaotic state of Afghan politics help to calm the situation. After the death of Dost Muhammad in 1863, there was a series of succession disputes, which by the mid-1870s had produced three rival amirs in Afghanistan, based in Kabul, Kandahar and Herat. Picking a winner was not easy, nor was it agreed that Afghanistan was better united than divided.

There was much negotiation in the years 1869–74 between Russia, the Raj and the strongest Afghan ruler, Sher Ali in Kabul, all to no purpose. The British tried to avoid backing one party against another, but this diffidence naturally opened the way for Afghans to make approaches to the Russians and Iranians instead. The atmosphere changed with the arrival of a Russophobic and belligerent Conservative government (1874), and darkened with the outbreak of war in the Balkans between Russia and Turkey (1877), in which Britain strongly backed the Turks. Treaties and conferences occupied much of 1876–8; the British withdrew their Agent from Kabul, and occupied Quetta as a precaution.

Events took a serious turn with the arrival of a Russian mission in Kabul in August 1878, but Sher Ali did not receive the Stolietoff deputation kindly, and the Russians withdrew shortly afterwards when told of the signing of the Treaty of Berlin, which brought an end to the Balkan crisis.

Here was a natural breakpoint. The Russians had shown no willingness to go to war to oblige the Afghans, and Sher Ali had shown no great favour to either side. But as in 1838, the Government of India abhorred a vacuum, and Lytton could not resist attempting to impose close British control over parts, if not all, of Afghanistan.

The viceroy dispatched his own mission to Kabul in late 1878, only for it to be detained at the border. This he took as a provocative act and sent an ultimatum on 2 November. Sher Ali replied later that month, accepting the mission, but without an apology. His insolence was taken as sufficient cause for war. Military plans already in train were expedited, and three British columns marched into Afghanistan, where they met with minimal resistance. Sher Ali fled the country and died soon afterwards. His son and long-time rival, Yakub Khan, was then proclaimed amir, and was forced to sign the humiliating Treaty of Gandamak in May 1879. This installed a British Resident in Kabul, subordinated Afghan foreign policy to British approval, and gave the British control of the Khyber Pass. In return Yakub was to receive £60,000 a year.

This all seemed very straightforward. There was no military problem, and no diplomatic objection from St Petersburg or London, where the prospect of Afghan independence was always considered a risk. An Afghanistan securely dominated by British arms was, in Lytton's view, by far the best option. Major Louis Cavagnari was sent to Kabul as Resident, and the situation seemed settled. But the combination of a weak amir and an overbearing foreign impostor proved too much for the underpaid Afghan army. They slaughtered Cavagnari and all his staff on 3 September 1879.

Prime Minister Disraeli favoured an immediate military reaction, but regretted that the senior commanders available to him were 'utterly worthless', except General Frederick Roberts, whom he considered 'gifted'. Roberts repaid Disraeli's faith by retaking Kabul on 12 October 1879 after winning a battle at Charasiah. Yakub Khan fled, but this left an untenable situation, with the British stuck in Kabul and Kandahar, ruling in his name. Worse, British commanders considered that the insurgent Afghans should be treated as criminals and traitors, and they hanged too many men rather too enthusiastically to have any chance of pacifying the country. Roberts was forced to retreat from Kabul to Sherpur, where a relieving column from Kandahar came to rescue him.

A crowning humiliation followed in the shape of an acute financial crisis, the result of a serious miscalculation in the military estimates to the tune of £13 million. But it was not the British who left Afghanistan at this point, but Lytton and Disraeli who left office. The general election of May 1880 brought Gladstone's Liberals back to power on a strongly anti-imperialist platform. Gladstone then immediately sent out Lord Ripon to reverse Lytton's work.

Lytton resigned on the same day as Disraeli, and returned home to be given an earldom. In 1887 he was made ambassador to Paris, a posting that, as a confirmed Francophile, he had long coveted. The lack of business in Paris contrasted starkly with his hectic years in India, and his poetic output resumed. He was amused by the contrast between the vicious criticism he endured for his frenetic activity in Calcutta and the adulation he received for doing nothing in Paris. He died there in 1891.

One of Lytton's last acts in India was to open negotiations with Abdur Rahman, Yakub Khan's nephew, in exile in Russian Turkestan. Abdur Rahman skilfully managed to avoid associating himself too closely with the British, while getting them to fight his main rival for the throne, Ayub Khan, who was based in Herat. It was Ayub Khan who delivered the worst British defeat of the war, on 27 July 1880, at Maiwand, but he was himself beaten by Roberts a few weeks later outside Kandahar. The British withdrew, and Abdur Rahman managed to defeat Ayub Khan for a last and decisive time. The country was then left to its own devices—again.

Lytton was a wilful and occasionally eccentric man. He picked up a reputation for laziness and loose living in India. Photographs show him slouching on his throne, but this was probably due not to a lack of moral fibre, but to the painful piles that afflicted him. His legacy, however, was undoubtedly sparse. He set out the entire negative Raj agenda, of no constructive change. He gave India an empress, and would have gone further, by introducing an appointed Privy Council, selection for service by patronage, and English-style feudal titles and heraldry. All this would have made India into a medieval–Hanoverian crossbreed. He was as much of an anti-modernizer as any Indian maharaja who traced his descent from the Sun. Such men were his natural allies, and he courted them assiduously.

He was a great wielder of power, but he ran up against two important limits. One was the extent to which the British could control events in the north-west. No British ruler of India was ever tempted to try aggression on such a scale again. The other was the disappointing unwillingness of the Indian hereditary elite to engage with government. From then on, it was going to be a question of how the Indian middle classes, the new intelligentsia, would fit into the wider political picture.

By 1880 the earlier policy of 'low taxes and good laws'—essentially the Utilitarian prescription of James Mill—was not going to be nearly enough to satisfy the Indian population. Two areas of unavoidable significance in the future would now be education and its relationship to employment, and the growth of large bodies of organized, coordinated opinion.

As Lytton and Disraeli left office, so too did Lord Salisbury, a man closely associated with the development of late Victorian conservatism. A rare philosopher of the right, he was sometimes well ahead of his time. 'No lesson seems to be so deeply inculcated by the experience of life as that you should never trust experts,' he wrote to Lytton in 1877.[16] Less well known is his deep involvement in the construction of the high Raj, and he remains one of its most interesting and least studied figures.

Best known as a three-time Conservative prime minister (1885–6, 1886–92, 1895–1902), the aristocratic Robert Cecil (1830–1903) served twice as Secretary of State for India; from 1866 to 1868, when his title was Lord Cranborne, and from 1874 to 1878, by which time he was Marquess of Salisbury. He was also Foreign Secretary from 1878 to 1880, when, in tandem with Viceroy Lytton, he supervised the build-up to the Second Afghan War.

Salisbury's two terms at the India Office were very different. The terrible Orissa famine of 1865–6 fell during the first, and the loss of life so shocked him that he insisted on the future provision of generous government aid. During his second term, he was confronted with the very real danger that the Government of India might be bankrupted by the combination of further famines and a steep decline in the value of the rupee. This led him to revise the Raj's policy on funding famine relief and public works, including a ban on raising loans on the London money market.

His earlier policy—that none should starve no matter what the cost—was motivated by humanity; there had been no guidelines during previous famines, such as that of 1860 in what is now Uttar Pradesh. In 1865–6, the failure to react quickly, compounded by the lack of either a grain dole or relief employment, led to a massive death toll in Orissa. Salisbury was highly critical of the local administration in Bengal, claiming that the education in political economy of the Lieutenant-Governor of Bengal, Sir Cecil Beadon, had cost half a million lives.

The principle that all should be helped against natural calamity seemed a fine thing to Salisbury and his colleagues in 1867, but it began to look an extremely expensive commitment over the next run of famines, in Bengal and Bihar (1873–4), and especially in the Madras Presidency (1876–8), when the government found itself supporting literally millions of starving people. This extra expenditure, and the possibility of its indefinite extension, threatened that charity might be more likely to topple the Raj than revolt. Salisbury's comprehensive earlier ruling was then abandoned and a new policy, proposed and implemented by Lytton, took a much harder line, restraining the local authorities from buying grain stocks, and lowering the wages paid on government relief works.

Famine was not the only troubling expense. Salisbury was an enthusiastic proponent of public works in 1866, and launched a new era of irrigation projects, financed by loans. But the expected return on these various projects had fallen short of expectations, and by 1874 the situation looked very different. He was, though, reluctant to abandon the idea of public investment, and came up with several strategies to continue the works without increased taxation.

The first was to insist that only truly remunerative projects were taken on, which meant closer supervision of the works—making the money go further. He therefore insisted on the appointment of a Public Works member to the Viceroy's Council, a development fiercely but unsuccessfully resisted by Northbrook—another example of the frequent reversal of 'natural' liberal–conservative polarities in Indian affairs.

The second was to force the Government of India to raise loans in India, which was more difficult and expensive than in London. This, again, was designed to enforce discipline in spending, but as a principle it proved difficult to maintain strictly, because of the very urgent financial situation through the late 1870s.

His last initiative was to suggest that public works should be funded out of local taxation, and this led to a further decentralization of Raj finances in 1877, overseen by John Strachey. Schemes of national taxation tended to summon up the spectre of national rebellion at this stage in Raj thinking. Local taxation, on the other hand, allowed benefits to be experienced by those who were paying, while resentments would be concentrated in particular areas. Ideally, local levies would make the Raj fiscally more responsive and politically more secure.

In his various roles, Salisbury made a number of other decisions and interventions that affected India in important ways. He pressed for the repeal of tariffs in 1874, which was successfully achieved under Lytton in 1879; he lowered the qualifying age for civil service examinations in 1874, in order to catch applicants after they left school, which also made it more difficult for Indian candidates to compete; in 1878 he tried, unsuccessfully, to redistribute military costs between Calcutta and London; and he pushed through further tariff changes in 1895–6, which disadvantaged the Indian cotton industry.

The one thing he had nothing to do with, although it was done on his watch, was the elevation of Queen Victoria to Empress of India in 1877. He knew nothing of the plan, and did not greatly approve.

After the famine and war of Lytton's time, Lord Ripon's viceroyalty (1880–4) came as a pleasant contrast, and he has always been remembered more fondly in India than any other viceroy.

George Frederick Robinson, 1st Marquess of Ripon (1827–1909) was perhaps the most sympathetic character ever to rule British India. He was a man of genuine liberality and a lifelong supporter of forms of what would now be called 'inclusion'. His uncynical approach to the government of India should serve as a caution against dubbing all 'imperialism' as of the same stamp.

He was literally born into politics, at the distinguished address of 10 Downing Street. His father, Viscount Goderich, was prime minister at the time, at the head of an obscure and short-lived Tory ministry that lasted from August 1827 to January 1828. The wonder is not, then, that the young George went into politics, but that he grew up to be a man of unswerving and imperturbable radicalism, in contrast to his staid, conservative father.

George was tutored at home, so the source of his views remains obscure. His religious convictions, however, he certainly obtained initially from his mother, who was a pious and saintly Protestant. But even in this he managed a degree of rebellion; after her death he converted to Catholicism in 1874. The last element in his make-up was the extraordinarily privileged life he entered. He inherited earldoms from his father and his uncle, adding a marquessate of his own in 1871, which he earned for services to Gladstone's first ministry.

His political views were profoundly influenced by a visit to Europe in 1849, at twenty-two years old, where he observed the aftermath of the wave of revolutions that had swept the continent the previous year. On his return to England he joined the Christian Socialists, subsequently setting out his convictions in a pamphlet entitled *The Duty of the Age*, published in 1852. In it, he declared himself against privilege and in favour of self-government—hardly a promising grounding for a future viceroy of India.

Bearing the courtesy title of Lord Goderich, he entered Parliament for Huddersfield the next year and represented the town until 1857, when he stood successfully for the West Riding of Yorkshire. During these years he led a small phalanx known as the Goderichites, and pursued a number of radical causes, including extension of the franchise, taxes on inheritance, and support for the implementation of the Northcote–Trevelyan Report of 1853, which recommended the adoption of competitive examinations for recruitment in public administration. This last was part of a wider desire to stimulate education and to associate more people from humbler backgrounds in the running of the state.

In 1859 he inherited his father's peerage, which took him into the House of Lords as Earl of Ripon, and when his uncle died the next year he adopted the senior title of Earl de Grey. Public office in Liberal administrations followed, and in 1866 he was made Secretary for India, a position he held until the Conservatives came briefly back to power in 1868. When the Liberals returned to power in December 1868, Ripon was promoted to Lord President of the [Privy] Council, and oversaw a stream of reforming measures. He also successfully negotiated a commercial treaty with the United States. However, the strain of the workload and an increasing distance from Gladstone in policy terms led to his resignation in 1873. With leisure to reflect, he then decided to announce his conversion to Roman Catholicism, in September 1874.

As if being a privileged radical, a Catholic freemason, and a wealthy egalitarian peer was not confusing enough as an ideological mind-map, Ripon then became the first anti-imperialist viceroy of India when Gladstone returned to office in 1880.

Lord Lytton left him a string of problems to resolve. The first was the Second Afghan War, which he ended successfully, establishing friendly relations with the new Afghan amir and initiating a peace that lasted till 1919. The second was the issue of import duties into India on cotton, which he completely abolished. In practical terms he had little choice, because Lytton's piecemeal reforms of 1879 had left the tariff regime in a state of chaos. But Ripon was an instinctive free trader, and supported Lytton's policy, though not his motivations. He managed, though, to make the abolition a popular measure by representing it not as a sop to Manchester's cotton barons but as part of a general reduction of taxation related to budget surpluses. With the reduction in military spending after the war, he was able to remove the duties without imposing new taxes elsewhere. His third action was to reverse the policy on press freedom, and repeal the Vernacular Press Act of 1878. An attempt to modify Lytton's Arms Act of 1878, under which Indians but not Europeans needed a licence to possess weapons, was, however, vetoed in London.

Ripon then introduced a package of reforming measures in local government, which were designed to 'educate' Indians in Western-style self-government. Municipal bodies had been appearing in Indian towns since the 1850s, but a system of elections was now introduced for membership, which included separate electorates based on religious identity, to ensure diversity of participation. Corresponding Rural Boards were also set up to bring responsible lower-level government to the vast areas of India that lay outside the towns.

He also passed the 1881 Factory Act, which set a maximum number of hours for workers—another of those measures with a dual economic and humanitarian agenda in which the Raj specialized; though Indians were protected from long hours at work, British manufacturers were protected from goods made by cheap labour. It was also under his administration that the Famine Commission set up by Lytton delivered its recommendations, in July 1880. These were written up into provincial Famine Codes, which ensured that starvation remained at bay until the very serious droughts of the late 1890s.

He then pushed ahead with judicial reform, and in the process provoked the loudest and most strident protests ever mounted by Britons in India against the colonial government. He sponsored what became known as the Ilbert Bill, named after Courtenay Ilbert, the Law Member who introduced it. The bill provided that a magistrate sitting alone, whether Indian or British, could try any European in areas outside towns. This was a matter of basic equality before the law, but also a timely and logical step, as there were now Indian judges available to preside in these courts.

On both counts the reform recommended itself to Ripon, and indeed to the government in London. However, Anglo-Indians set up a howl of protest at the contrived thought, and unlikely circumstance, that a brown judge could try a white woman. The vehemence, persistence and intemperance of the protest forced Ripon to substitute the proposed new powers with an option for trial by a majority white jury. This retreat marks a particularly low point in the history of collective British courage in India.

Ripon was another proconsul who touched Indian history several times. As well as his four-year term as viceroy, he helped lobby for civil service entry for Indians in the 1850s, and he pushed through the Indian Councils Act of 1861, which added Indian members to the Viceroy's Legislative Council. But his hopes for a more representative government were never fulfilled.

He was always keen to change the political culture of India, to foster the aspiration for self-government, but he was swimming against the tide.

Many of his own officials disliked the local government reforms, and his attempt at judicial modernization was scuppered largely by the settler whites. There were about 16,000 European residents of Calcutta in 1881, and they knew how to make their voices heard in defence of their privileges. The example was not lost on politically conscious Indians, who wished to raise their own voices to promote what they were coming to perceive as their own rights.

The rest of Ripon's career in England was distinguished but almost entirely uninteresting. He died in 1909, describing himself to the last as a 'radical'. The Indian public liked and even loved Ripon, but he had no political heirs or imitators, except perhaps the liberal Lord Reading (1921–6), who ruled India in less trying circumstances.

Across the years 1867 to 1880, several strands of indigenous political and social activism began to coalesce under new cultural pressures—global markets, railway travel, newspapers, higher education, vernacular literature, provincial drama—in ways that were to shape India's emerging political agenda.

Standard histories of this period tend to focus on the birth of the Indian National Congress (INC), sometimes in an attempt to show how the political awakening of India was a unified and progressive phenomenon, but this is not strictly true. The growth of political activism in India was more complex and broader than the appearance of the INC, which originally represented a fairly narrow type of secular, socially conservative, middle-class nationalism. The Congress was strong in Bengal and Bombay, but other provinces nurtured a variety of movements, secular and religious, based on support from either higher or lower social strata, and pursuing aims varying from progressive to conservative. Concentration on the INC also makes the growth of religiously inspired activism more difficult to understand. While those within the Congress were keen to submerge religious differences, other movements were growing up that actively sought to emphasize them.

This was all part of the anticipation of democratization and the kinds of permanent, institutionalized competition that accompany it. This meant not just the competition for employment and preferment that all governments create, but also the broader rivalry between interest groups within society, which were often, though not always, religious.

In late colonial India, numbers now began to matter, especially for any self-identifying minority that perceived its own weakness. The growth of 'communal' feeling in the upcoming decades had an intimate connection with the consciousness of majorities and minorities, local and national, and how they could be defined and represented—or used. Hindus, as a generalized body, were always in a majority and so were less concerned about numbers, but there were many social subgroups that could be labelled 'Hindu'.

Some of these subgroups began to pursue their own social agendas, touching on religious traditions, but largely avoiding modern politics, such as the Advaidananda Sabha (1876) in central southern India, led by Iyothee Thass Pandithar (1845–1914). But the most famous was the anti-Brahmin Satyashodak Samaj, founded in 1873 in western India by Jyotirao Phule (1827–90). Phule was not strictly a modernist, but his grievances about the status of Untouchables (Dalits) were based in liberal principles of equality, expressed as a strong anti-Brahmin stance.

In 1870, a core group of Maharashtrian Brahmins formed the Poona Sarvajanik Sabha, which became a platform for a series of outstanding political and social reformers. The first was Mahadev Govind Ranade, who took a moderately pro-British line as part of a general modernizing agenda. Like many of his generation, his criticisms of British rule were more economic than cultural; he was critical of Indian society and was religious without being unduly traditional. His political heir, G.K. Gokhale, explained how Ranade wanted to pick out what was 'noble' and 'vigorous' from alien influence while keeping what was 'good and noble' in his own heritage.[17] Gokhale was less religious, but took a very similar line, while developing an advanced economic critique of colonial rule.

Other, more specifically religious movements appeared all over India. Some were in sympathy with modernization of various hues, such as the National Mahommedan Association (1878), formed in Calcutta under the leadership of Amir Ali, but others among India's Muslims had different ideas. The Deobandi movement (1867) took on the challenge of visualizing a future for India's Muslims as a distinct and separate bloc, while a more progressive Muslim identity was promoted by Sayyid Ahmad Khan, who advocated Western-style education as a way of coping with the political realities of British rule.

Among the Hindus a leader of vision and genius appeared. Swami Dayananda Saraswati developed a new and radical Hinduism, inspired by a return to the most ancient of India's scriptures—the Vedas. Whatever was in the Vedas was true, said the Swami, and only those things. This happened to exclude both idol worship and the idea of caste, which he regarded as later accretions. He considered himself to be the only person qualified to judge what was and was not ancestral Hindu dharma, and in 1875 he founded a movement called the Arya Samaj (Noble Society). He then set out his vision of a purified, revitalized Hinduism in a book titled *Satyarth Prakash* (The Light of Truth) written in 1882. In it he managed to reduce his fundamental beliefs to a list of fifty-one items. He died, or was perhaps murdered, the next year, but his influence was (and remains) enormous.

Militant feelings were also brewing in western India, where V.K. Chiplunkar launched a Marathi literary and educational movement, which attracted young men of high calibre, chief among whom were B.G. Tilak and G.G. Agarkar, both products of Deccan College, formerly the Poona Hindu College, which taught a Western syllabus. These two set up their own school in 1880, with Chiplunkar on the staff. A traditionalist and more militantly anti-colonial movement then emerged, centred on Poona, as a rival to the more urbane, business-friendly politics of Bombay.

This serves to emphasize that anti-colonial feeling in India at this time did not somehow lead naturally or inevitably to the formation of the Congress. Instead, the disparate and distributed nature of that feeling actually prevented it from coalescing into a 'national' movement.

Open rebellion, of course, remained the most direct political option, and in 1879 Vasudev Balwant Phadke (1845–83) led an armed insurrection around Poona. But his dream of re-erecting a traditional Maratha state found no takers outside some lower-class groups with their own grievances. Political action was now the way ahead, and armed rebellion henceforth was confined to India's tribal peoples and groups of dedicated revolutionaries.

National political organization was still a little way off for India, but national political issues were already very present. Of these, the most persistently troubling and centrally influential was the matter of the army, which was to take an increasingly important role in Indian life and politics, as the Raj's most indispensable support, its principal expense and, potentially, the greatest threat to its existence.

Lord Lytton was quite realistic about these conflicting roles, and appreciated that the solution was to make the army smaller or cheaper, while designing it so that it worked well with British officers, and badly without. In 1879, he asked Sir Ashley Eden, Lieutenant-Governor of Bengal, to address a long list of specific questions about the army's future structure. The Eden Commission delivered its report to Lord Ripon in 1881, and the various recommendations it contained were implemented only slowly over the next fifteen years. However, its two most important priorities—economy and efficiency—were never fully realized.

At this point the middle classes were still not entirely opposed to colonial rule; they were expecting it to morph into something else in due course. Publicly at least, major figures accepted British rule as a providential opportunity, a vehicle for improvement. Men such as M.C. Ranade in western India and W.C. Bonnerjee in Bengal began to criticize British rule rather in the way that Indians and Britons criticize their own governments today—without necessarily wishing them away.

It is not accurate to depict the whole Indian nation as straining at the leash from 1857 onwards. But it is true to say that from around that time the aspiring classes slowly began to recognize that the equality agenda, so clearly influential in Britain, was a sham in India.

A succession of light-bulb moments propelled the growth of nationalist feeling through the 1870s, such as adjustments to trade tariffs, changes to the entrance criteria for the civil service, the Dramatic Performances Act (1876), the Arms Act (1878) and the Vernacular Press Act (1878), all of which unmistakeably demonstrated that Indians were not being treated as the equals of Europeans. The organizations that emerged in response to these cruel and largely unexpected blows were more widely based than ever before. Mostly, though not always, they were liberal in nature.

8

1884–1905

CURRENCY, CONGRESS, COMMISSIONS, CURZON

1884–92: Congress, Stasis, Pessimism

After the turbulent Lytton–Ripon years, British India settled back into a tranquil period that was probably the least politically contentious of the century. High imperialism, as a philosophy of secure achievement, stood unchallenged in 1884, while in domestic British politics the hard truth remained that there were no voters in India and few votes to be had in Britain for doing good to Indians. Prevailing agreement about imperial objectives meant that the Conservative prime minister Salisbury was happy to appoint the nominally Liberal Lansdowne as viceroy in 1888, encouraged by Lansdowne's break with Gladstone over Irish policy. A degree of stability filtered through to India. But the situation was calm rather than static.

At this point, beneath the unruffled exterior, the political balance of the Raj shifted, and the British permanently lost the initiative. The post-1857 situation, with the Raj allied to the two most influential elements in Indian society—the rural landowning elites and the urban middle classes—slowly realigned. The landowners remained supportive, as long as the government either facilitated or did not actively threaten their aspirations. But the newer, educated, urban classes were increasingly adrift in a Raj that seemed incapable of finding any place for them. As their hopes for employment, inclusion and modernization were betrayed, they slid into hostility. In earlier years the babus had always been seen as potential allies; now they became the enemy.

Overall, the range of political activities open to Indians expanded while colonial purposes and policy did not. The political and financial structure of the Raj was almost too well established by 1884, and it lost its ability to adapt at roughly the same rate as Indian political self-consciousness grew. British leadership was complacent and slow, under a series of uninspired viceroys: Lords Dufferin (1884–8), Lansdowne (1888–94) and Elgin (1894–8).

While formal oppositional politics was still off-limits, the government's most persistent problem remained finance, and its heaviest expense was always the army. By the mid-1880s there were around 75,000 European troops stationed in India, 30,000 more than in 1857. But the massive scale of this commitment was determined solely by guesswork among senior military figures. Whether the Raj was genuinely under threat from the Russians, as they penetrated the central Asian plains, or from the French, as they courted the kingdom of Upper Burma, was purely a matter of opinion. The way that officials so often took a gloomy view of security matters imposed a constant strain on finances, drawing between a third and a half of government revenue into the military budget.

Early in his term, Dufferin had to deal with the Panjdeh Crisis of 1885, triggered by a Russian incursion over the Oxus, which threatened to escalate into full-scale war. The Russians withdrew, but finally got their hands on the oasis at Merv. Dufferin then fought a short, successful campaign in Burma against King Thibaw of Ava in 1886, and was able to impose terms after about ten days of fighting. In this last major expansion of the eastern borders, an area roughly the size of France was added to British India.

Military concerns persisted both internally and externally, but it was in the realm of politics that the most serious long-term challenges now had to be faced. Indian political demands were still manageable, but the small European community in India presented problems too. Many expatriates considered that the colonial regime was not protecting their interests sufficiently. The anti-equality protests of 1836, 1849 and 1882 stemmed from this feeling, and they often felt themselves in keen economic competition with Indian interests too. But for the Raj, accommodating Europeans politically was in some ways as difficult as accommodating Indians. The idea of setting up a local representative body as a rival to either the imperial Parliament or the Viceroy's Legislative Council was deemed too risky; the white community was considered too transitory and too selfish. Salisbury was clear on the point, if a little gloomy: 'the only enemies, I believe, who will ever seriously threaten England's power in India are her own sons',[1] he wrote to Lytton in 1876.

It was easier to have no representation than to contemplate listening to planters and traders, and this left very little room for manoeuvre on the British side of the colonial divide. Offence was likely to be taken in almost any scheme of either political or economic reform. But the pressure was not going to go away. By the 1880s the Indian intelligentsia was keen to engage fully in national affairs.

Since the 1840s there had been a variety of regional groupings involved in semi-political activity, including the British Indian Association (1851), the Indian League (1875), and Surendranath Banerjea's Indian Association (1876), but the Indian National Congress, founded in 1885, was different. Though not a political party proper, it was conceived on a much broader scale than previous pressure groups.

It was national in outlook, and membership was not restricted by region, class or religion. It relied heavily on landowning Hindus, but its leadership boasted a sprinkling of wealthy Parsis, a few Muslims, and the occasional European sympathizer. The membership was essentially the rising professional classes of urban India, educated within British institutions, speaking English, espousing shades of liberalism, and working mostly in law, education and journalism. Of the first seventy-two delegates who met in December 1885 in Bombay, the majority were from Madras and Bombay, because a conference with similarly national ambitions was being held at the same time by Banerjea's Indian Association in Calcutta. But the two bodies harmonized their plans, and the 1886 Congress, held in Calcutta, attracted 500 delegates.

Co-ordinating the new organization was Allan Octavian Hume, an ex-civil servant with radical views.

Allan Hume (1829–1912) was the gamekeeper-turned-poacher who was largely responsible for organizing the first Bombay Congress of 1885. After a long career in British officialdom, Hume decided to work for Indian self-government, not as a moderate conciliator, but as a fervent advocate.

Some Indian nationalist historians have tried to minimize his role, or to depict him as exercising an inhibiting influence on the national movement, but this is hardly borne out by the evidence. Hume's contemporaries—the 'greats' of Indian nationalism—were happy to accord him full credit for his coordinating role within the movement.

In the period 1884–94 it was Hume that was consistently at the forefront of demands for constitutional reform in India. His relative lack of success was due to three things: his own erratic behaviour, division and lack of interest among Indians, and the studiously reactionary line taken by the Government of India.

Born into a political family, he espoused the cause of social justice throughout his long life. His father was the MP Joseph Hume, a fierce parliamentary critic of government, and among his childhood friends he numbered John Stuart Mill, the great liberal thinker. Allan opted for a career in India, and duly passed through the Company's school system at Haileybury. He arrived in India in 1849 and took up his first important posting in 1856, as magistrate in Etawah in the North West Provinces, and remained there until 1861, when ill health forced him (as so many others) to recuperate in Britain for two years.

It was in Etawah that he developed his general approach to Indian affairs. He was passionately keen to improve all aspects of life, particularly education, agriculture and public infrastructure, and he developed a coherent critique of British rule, becoming an advocate of a fuller Anglo-Indian partnership in government. He was in Etawah during the revolt of 1857, and he raised and led native troops against the insurgents with distinction.

Hume drew his own lessons from the Great Uprising, seeing it as a direct response to misgovernment, oppression and exclusion. His first public statement of opposition, a criticism of the use of flogging, earned him a reprimand, and he was forced to retract his opinions before being allowed to resume his duties.

Once forgiven, he was promoted to Commissioner of Inland Customs in 1867, which put him in charge of the great customs hedge of north India. He took trouble to improve its general condition and effectiveness, and was rewarded with a position at the head of a new department of Agriculture, Revenue and Commerce. He was keen to stimulate agricultural growth, and pressed for the creation of model farms to improve husbandry. More controversially, he lobbied against indentured emigration, and in favour of land tenure reform. But his superiors were more interested in revenue than agriculture, and his outspokenness cost him his job again; in 1879 the Government of India abolished his department and sent him back to revenue administration. Unwilling to be silenced, he published *Agricultural Reform in India*, which was critical of a range of Raj policies.

He also diverted some of his energies into summarizing his extensive study of Indian bird life, issuing *The Game Birds of India, Burmah and Ceylon* in several volumes between 1879 and 1881, a work that earned him the title of 'the Pope of Ornithology'. The draft of a second book was stolen in 1882, leading him to abandon the project and donate his enormous collection of specimens to the Natural History Museum in London.

Ornithology was one diversion; another was mysticism, and from 1879 onwards he became interested in Theosophy. He had never been a Christian of any sort, but he found a congenial home in the jumble of occult and rehashed Oriental spirituality offered by Theosophy. The founders of the new syncretic faith, Madame Helena Blavatsky and Colonel Henry Olcott, had recently arrived in India, and Hume took to their teachings enthusiastically. His own exploration of Indian religion then drew him away from the charlatan wiles of Blavatsky, and he became a devotee of a genuine mystic, Swami Ramakrishna Paramahamsa.

This package of old disillusionment and new enthusiasm led him, after more than thirty years' service, to resign in 1882. The agitation over the Ilbert Bill then convinced him that Indian political opinion had to be focused, and that if Indians were too constrained to do it, he would do it himself. He tried to rally the students of Calcutta University in 1883, asking them to come forward to demand a share in their own government. Finally, in 1885, after giving due notice to the authorities, he organized the first Indian National Congress, which opened on 28 December in Bombay. This he managed by personally contacting prominent Indian leaders all over the country through the previous year. The first meeting was very much of his making, and he remained the movement's secretary until his return to England in 1894.

The British authorities were ambivalent about this new body, and its birth coincided with the start of a period of Tory rule in Britain, which did not augur well for reform. Viceroy Dufferin, a liberal by party affiliation, did not oppose the project, though he discouraged Hume from discussing political issues. These conditions led the early leaders into extravagant professions of loyalty, and attempts to set a tone that would, in the words of Dadabhai Naoroji to the 1886 Congress, 'prove ourselves worthy' of self-government 'by showing that we are never unreasonable, never violent, never uncharitable'.[2] Naoroji's faith in British fair play proved misplaced, but much of what followed over the first twenty years of the movement conformed to this approach.

Speaking as president of the first Indian National Congress in 1885, W.C. Bonnerjee was prepared to list the benefits British rule had brought to India: public order, railways, and Western education. Similarly placed, in 1890 Pherozeshah Mehta was happy to concede that India had been 'assigned to the care of England' by 'the inscrutable dispensation of Providence'; in 1895 Surendranath Banerjea asserted that 'India was a trust committed by Providence to the care of Parliament'; in 1898 Ananda

Mohan Bose talked of 'the loving help and the ardent sympathy of the great Nation, into whose hands Providence has entrusted the destinies of this land'.[3] Even as late as 1905, G.K. Gokhale felt able to write into the constitution of his Servants of India Society that British rule was ordained by 'the inscrutable dispensation of Providence, for India's good'.[4]

Hume, on the other hand, was much more impatient and a good deal more outspoken. He insisted on stirring up Indians to speak for themselves, and conveyed a subtly seditious message, which was that the British despised no man more than one who bowed down to them, and respected no man more than one who stood up to them. This was playing with fire, and not strictly true either, because the British were quite prepared to shoot people who stood up to them. But the political cause was clear: make your voice heard, puncture the ignorance of the government with your views, demonstrate that improvements can be made.

British officials, long suspicious of him when he was still one of their own, were not slow to impugn his motives and his honesty. By 1886, Dufferin was prepared to describe him as 'a mischievous busybody ... a little cracked, vain, unscrupulous, and, I am told, very careless of truth'.[5] Hume was similarly unkind to Dufferin in a pamphlet of that year titled *The Rising Tide*. Relations between the men then improved, only to worsen again. Hume did not believe that India was ready for self-government but, haunted by memories of rebellion and visions of future bloodshed, he passionately believed that reform and improvements had to be made. Faced with indifference or hostility from the government, and a good deal of apathy among eminent Indians, his tone became increasingly shrill.

Dufferin's successor, Lord Lansdowne, kept his distance from Hume rather more cannily, and accepted the Congress as part of the Indian political landscape. He doubted that 'it could, upon the whole, assume a more innocuous shape than that which it now takes'.[6] Despite Hume's apocalyptic blustering, Lansdowne held firm against the Congress, refusing to accept a House of Commons motion allowing simultaneous Indian Civil Service exams in London and India. But after repeatedly rebuffing Congress demands about inclusion of Indians in government councils, he eventually lent his support to a measure of reform, with the Indian Councils Act of 1892.

Finally, the lukewarm support from sections of the Congress for the Age of Consent Bill in 1891 convinced Hume that he was too far in advance of the movement, and that his labours would remain unrewarded. After a period of farewell touring and speaking, he sailed home in 1894, but remained involved on the London end of Congress affairs for the rest of his life, which he mainly devoted to collecting specimens of the plant life of Britain.

The Indian National Congress of these early years only distantly resembled the mass movement shaped by Gandhi and led to power by Nehru. The original Congress was only one pressure group among others, and met for three days a year. The 'microscopic minority' it represented in 1885 included about 5,000 university graduates, while the vast majority of Indians were illiterate and worked on the land. Early Congress demands therefore were not for mass democracy, but for small adjustments to the running of the Raj, such as increased employment of educated Indians in government jobs, the promotion of Indians within the army, reduction of government spending, especially on the military, and the inclusion, by appointment or election, of more Indians in the legislative process. At this point, laws in India were made either centrally in the Viceroy's Legislative Council or in similar provincial bodies in Madras, Bombay or Agra.

'Council entry' was the limit of the Congress's political imagination in its first years, and the one area in which it could lay claim to have made progress. The 1892 Indian Councils Act, which provided for a larger degree of 'non-official' participation in all the Legislative Councils, was the result of a combination of Congress pressure and Lansdowne's conciliatory instincts. Some members could now be 'nominated' by partly elected local bodies, including municipalities and Lord Ripon's Rural Boards, then 'recommended' by the viceroy or provincial governors. This added a small amount of indirect election to the system, and politicians in London congratulated themselves that they had introduced 'the elective principle' into Indian affairs, while avoiding the 'representative principle'. Here again was the Whiggish idea that it was acceptable to include prominent Indians in the process of government, but not to admit that they had a right to that inclusion by virtue of any status as representatives.

There was no mass popular backing available to pressure the government, and there was no obvious way to ask for institutional change. This, therefore, was the era of 'moderate' Congress opinion, an era typified not only by modest demands and elaborately loyal language, but also by a profound faith that the British would play fair by Indians, that to ask was to be granted, and that the case for Indian emancipation was so self-evident that the gradual concession of freedom to India was a certainty. This era continued until 1905 and the partition of Bengal, the most egregious act of betrayal to date.

Organized discontent during these twenty years remained largely under the mantle of religious bodies, though it was sometimes also expressed verbally in provincial journals or more violently in inter-communal confrontations. Trouble was slowly brewing in Maharashtra and the Punjab, among politically aware people who considered that the polite gradualism of senior Congress leaders amounted to 'mendicancy'—begging.

Among national political issues, the most emotive that emerged were not Congress issues at all. The greatest popular agitation was over the Age of Consent Act in 1891, which raised the minimum age at which girls could be married, from ten to twelve. This measure had long been advocated by socially conscious Indians, prominent among whom was Behramji Malabari (1853–1912).

But traditional piety was offended and took to the streets to say so, particularly in Maharashtra. The protests did not stop the Act becoming law, but they propelled Bal Gangadhar Tilak to national prominence for the first time. Tilak's objections, like Radhakanta Deb's sixty years before, were not specifically to the provisions of the Act, but to the idea that the British should be passing laws about such matters, which rightly were the preserve of Indians alone. Tilak was a gifted, energetic demagogue, and began to forge a new aggressive Maharashtrian political identity, featuring reverence for the seventeenth-century warrior chief Shivaji and the elephant god Ganesh, in honour of whom he invented festivals that became major public occasions.

Another important issue was cow slaughter, which set Hindus against both Muslims and the British. Cow Protection Associations were formed, and in 1893 violent disorder broke out in the North West Provinces. The government again remained unmoved, and the law stayed as it was.

This agitation accompanied an extended period in inter-communal religious violence, with riots in Delhi (1886), Madras and Calcutta (1891), Bombay (1893) and Poona (1894). This disturbed and baffled the British, who had no ready answer to this kind of popular disorder. The immediate response, familiar from modern dictatorships, was to discredit the agitators. Clichés about Muslim fanaticism and Hindu backwardness were polished up, and ultimately contributed to a sense of depression among the British, driven by the inescapable feeling that all Indians were incorrigibly unruly, and would never be suitably grateful for the hot, hard work the British had taken upon themselves. To some, confronted with revivalist ascetics, ancient Vedic learning and protests against cow slaughter, there seemed little evidence that there was much enthusiasm in India for entering the twentieth century in any different style from the fifteenth or even the fifth.

This apparent reluctance to move on was, however, taken by some as a valid excuse to stay and continue to rule the vast land that made Britain a great power; the 'work' clearly needed to continue. Sir John Strachey (1823–1907), a senior civilian for thirty years, cared little whether Indians appreciated their good fortune as subjects of the British Crown. He simply believed that Britain had a right, and even a duty, to rule in India. His prescriptions, as set out in his 1888 book *India*, were akin to imperial castor oil, administered by a nanny whose liberalism was of the most starchy and domineering kind. Strachey did not use the word 'imperialism', though he did make constant references to the 'noble' work of the British in India.

Strachey was pragmatic; others were more intellectual, but also more damning. J.S. Mill had laid down in the 1850s that India was not a candidate for self-government, and in the mid-1880s Henry Maine developed a view of India as a land becalmed. Among societies, the general rule was immobility, he announced, and it was only superior societies that shook themselves into transition. This, of course, did not include India. This wave of scarcely concealed contempt represented another, subtler betrayal of Indian aspirations.

With so little to hope for from such 'liberal' thinking, Indians began to look elsewhere for inspiration, and many found it in the ideas of Giuseppe Mazzini (1805–72), the great nationalist democrat and architect of Italian unification. Surendranath Banerjea translated his works, Lala Lajpat Rai wrote an account of his life, and V.D. Savarkar translated his autobiography. Mazzini believed that nationality is the individuality of a people. This idea lay some way outside the British tradition of universal liberalism, which was beginning to seem inadequate for the purposes of Indian nationalists, and it found ready acceptance in India. Mazzini's passionate advocacy of national unity and moral regeneration through suffering and sacrifice appealed to high-minded types, like Surendranath Banerjea, while his association with armed struggle in the cause of liberation, from armies to secret societies, found more radical admirers, Aurobindo Ghosh among them. There was no such British philosopher of nationalism to call upon; national self-discovery in the British tradition did not address the problems of throwing off foreign domination.

Some Indians began to admire countries other than Britain, principally Japan, which had absorbed Western influences without enduring colonial government. Indigenous styles of nationalist thought began to fill this vacuum, with Swami Vivekananda the most advanced and coherent among them. The import of radical left-wing ideas was soon to follow.

The Strachey tradition remained dominant among British officials, and lived on in a robust line of civilian writers and thinkers, including Sir Reginald Craddock, Herbert H. Risley and Harcourt Butler. Butler developed an enthusiasm for the taluqdars of Awadh through the 1890s in much the same way that James Tod had loved the rajputs seventy years before. Through his career, Butler stood by the classic, late-Raj view that Indians were not actually interested in politics at all, and wanted only good government and the impartial enforcement of law and order. It was men like Butler that were the true Romantics, rather than Munro or Elphinstone.

Meanwhile, the false urgency of military priorities persistently warped the institutional framework of British India. The paths of warfare were trodden too avidly and too often for genuine politics to grow, as the Raj's guardians brushed aside the seemingly less pressing business of building a viable political base. And the military problem was always delicate; memories of 1857 persisted longest in military circles. The army never mutinied again on a large scale, but its officers always remained wary of over-training or over-equipping it. The main objective was to stop individual units having too strong a regional or religious identity.

The recommendations of the Eden Commission were taken up very slowly, and it was only at the end of General Roberts's long stint as Commander-in-Chief (1885–95) that the Indian army was finally taken out of the presidency system and reformed into four regional corps. However, Eden's original objective—economy—was spectacularly ignored. Military expenditure doubled between 1885 and 1907.

At home, the British public enjoyed exotic images of India, such as the rumbustious tales and satirical poems of Rudyard Kipling or 'Mutiny' novels, such as Flora Steel's *On the Face of the Waters* (1897), but the intractable nature of so many Indian problems—the army, the finances, the peasantry—fostered a pervading pessimism among senior Raj staff.

There was not only confusion about what to do with India. The whole question of empire—whether to have one, what it was for, whether it was making or losing money for the country, etc.—fed into the wider debate about Britain's exact place in the world. Was Britain part of Europe? Or was she destined to stand alone, astride an empire? How much responsibility to take, and where? How much democracy to promote, and how? As a small island, Britain could not advocate democracy on too wide a platform within the imperial structure without the risk of being outvoted. But running an empire autocratically from one imperial Parliament was an impossible task, given the constraints of time, information and manpower. Such questions remained live issues for decades, and were only resolved finally by the devastating effects of two world wars.

The great philosopher of late imperial ennui in India was Alfred Lyall. Sir Alfred Comyn Lyall (1835–1911) was one of the most gifted and perceptive of Britain's imperial administrators, but also one of the least convinced about the staying power of the imperial project. Though he described himself as a radical, his intelligence and his experience both led him to pessimistic viewpoints. He worried that education would make Indians less governable; he thought the Bengal press was permanently hostile; he had severe doubts about the entire 'civilizing mission'. Like a number of later civilians, he was also well known for his unhappy marriage, and it remains a temptation to speculate as to the exact relationship of his opinions and his personal misery.

He was born into a well-off family in suburban south London, and became one of the very last to go through the EIC's old system of recruitment by patronage, taking advantage of the fact that his father's brother, George Lyall, had been chairman of the Company. This secured him a place at Haileybury in 1853, and he entered the Company's service in 1856. His first posting was as assistant magistrate in the Bulandshahr district (North West Provinces). This was shortly to turn into a very hot spot, and he was lucky to escape with his life in the Uprising of the following year. His horse, shot from under him, was not so lucky.

The Uprising served as a formative experience for the young Lyall. It exhilarated him—he fought in an irregular European cavalry force and killed a man—but it also left him with a lasting sense of fatalism about British rule in India. For him, the ultimate legacy of the violence of 1857 was the feeling that the British Raj was probably not sustainable, no matter what it did.

Like many contemporary British officials, he was always convinced that Muslims were primarily responsible for the Uprising. This left him with an abiding conviction that they had to be carefully handled, though he never went as far as W.W. Hunter in wishing actively to conciliate them. Lyall accepted that no amount of reform or degree of prosperity was likely to reconcile the Indians to alien government. He was not an active reformer, and believed that 'all the English need do is to keep the peace and clear the way'; 'the rising tide of intellectual advancement' would do the rest[7]—a thoroughly liberal view that could have been voiced in the 1830s.

He was against interfering with Indian customs and religion, though he believed there was 'one gospel which the English can preach and practise in India, the gospel of high political morality', which was, he maintained, a 'complete novelty' among 'Asiatic rulers'.[8] He was entirely convinced of the superiority of Western ways, and for all his doubts about the Raj he was certainly an imperialist; 'if ever the imperial system was necessary and fitted to a time and country, it is to India as we now see it,'[9] he wrote.

After a posting in the Central Provinces, he was promoted in 1867 to Commissioner of West Berar. While there, he compiled the *Statistical Account or Gazetteer of Berar* (1870), a forerunner of many other such volumes of 'colonial knowledge'. With its interest in local tradition and culture, this work put Lyall very much in step with W.W. Hunter, in terms of disciplined methodology. But over the next few years Lyall went much further into Hinduism than Hunter had into Islam—recording, classifying and interpreting it. This new interest chimed with the views of Henry Maine, who had detected links between ancient Indian legal texts and current practice.

Lyall took a similar approach to the content and customs of contemporary Hinduism, and recognized that it was a living thing. But it baffled him; he called it a 'tangled jungle of disorderly superstitions'.[10] Maine approved of Lyall's work and promoted his cause among the British intelligentsia, specifically introducing him to a future Indian player, John Morley, editor of the *Fortnightly Review*. Lyall returned the compliment by adopting Maine's view that India had not yet passed 'from status to contract', and was therefore still in an earlier stage of legal and social evolution, a condition that required the British to be especially careful in matters of reform.

Lyall's qualities won him favour with all the period's viceroys, which was a remarkable feat considering that Northbrook, Lytton and Ripon were very different, being cautious, authoritarian and radical in turn. Northbrook made Lyall Home Member in 1872, then sent him to Rajputana in 1874 to take up the important post of Agent to the Rajput states, as a sort of apprenticeship for the foreign portfolio. Lytton appointed him Foreign Member in 1878, but then rode roughshod over his advice all through the events that led to the Second Afghan War. Ripon retained him as Foreign Member but then sent him back to provincial administration in 1882, as Lieutenant-Governor of the North West Provinces, assuming he would be an ally in the introduction of reforms in local government. In this he was mistaken, for Lyall preferred to continue the older British habit of informal consultation with elites rather than to introduce new forms of local election. He was convinced that British influence—even if it brought prosperity—was more likely to destroy existing institutions in India than to create workable new ones.

He favoured two main policies within British India, both recognizably Whiggish. One was to promote provincial autonomy; he disliked central control and considered that the best way of preserving British rule was to recognize India's diversity, which meant working through alliances with large landowners, not by rule from above or the creation of local representative bodies. Like many other officials, he worried that British despotism was becoming top-heavy and rootless. The other policy was 'pushing on the native', meaning promoting Indian talent into British administrative systems.

His outlook is usually labelled as 'liberal authoritarianism'. Though to some degree a contradiction in terms, such a philosophy could find a natural home in the atmosphere of late British India, with its bevy of benign social and economic aspirations, its distaste for electoral politics and its dependence on existing social hierarchy. Another way of describing Lyall's viewpoint might be as a 'pessimistic imperialist'. British rule was a fact, and it could not be wished away, with all its faults—a very post-1857 view. Once the British had fought so hard to restore their rule, they could not then lightly abandon it, for this would raise the question why they had made such efforts to support something insupportable.

This is where the interest in Lyall's views lies. Not because he was original or consistent—he was neither—but because he, as a highly intelligent man, and one well able to empathize with Indians, could see no alternative but to continue on the path already set. Can't stay, can't leave, can't reform.

Faced with these stark options, Lyall chose to write. His later years saw a prolific output of articles, books, history and verse. He wrote a weighty biography of Lord Dufferin, the last viceroy he served. Neither book nor Dufferin is much remembered. He also wrote *The Rise and Expansion of the British Dominion in India* (1894), which refused to use divine destiny as a motif, or to mention God at all, and thus avoided the languid superiority of much Victorian writing on India. Ironically, the poetry he wrote is almost totally ignored in works on literature but remains widely quoted in history books.

His thirty-one years in India were followed by a further fifteen serving on the Council of India in London until 1902. He hoped to succeed Lord Lansdowne as viceroy in 1894, but his well-known reservations about the Raj and his habit of seeing both sides of any question disqualified him in the eyes of the Liberal Secretary for India, Lord Kimberley.

Lyall's final contribution to Indian history was the advice he gave to John Morley, by then Secretary for India, in the run-up to the reform package of 1909. Lyall strongly advised him to treat the Muslims as a separate entity, and Morley seems, albeit reluctantly, to have taken his advice.

1892–9: Currency, Activism, Commissions

The Raj developed a crippling guilt complex about running a budget surplus, and did little to put itself permanently in the black. This was partly liberal economic theory, but also a matter of political expediency. There was no way to expand government revenue without high political risk. This limited the Raj's ambitions and placed its more enlightened objectives, such as the development of education, constantly at the mercy of events. Its main income was still the 'inelastic' land revenue. But shifting taxation away from landholding remained impossible without significant growth in the wider economy.

The post-1857 Raj learned, with some difficulty, to live within its means, as long as events ran smoothly. When crisis struck, such as a severe famine, short-term deficits were funded by emergency taxation and the use of credit. But more insidious problems were lurking that would imperil the whole fiscal health of the Raj. India had a silver coinage and was therefore vulnerable to changes in the value of silver, especially because her economy was shackled to a gold-based currency—sterling. When, for a number of reasons, the world price of silver began to fall after 1873, imports from Britain became more expensive and the costs of the colonial government's sterling debt went up. Meanwhile the land revenue rose only slowly, income taxes remained highly sensitive politically, and levels of customs and excise duty had to be set with regard to the wider flows of imperial trade.

The currency problem was addressed repeatedly from the 1880s onwards, but could never be resolved without restructuring much of the Indian economy, or major changes in the imperial system. A metallic currency was much more difficult to manipulate than paper money, and the perils of either overvaluing or undervaluing the rupee were very serious. Too low a value and the Raj's foreign debt would be unaffordable; too high and there was a danger that not only would India's exports become too expensive, but the system of selling rupees in London to fund the Home Charges—government expenses paid in sterling—might collapse for lack of buyers.

The situation deteriorated rapidly in the early 1890s, and when the rupee hit a record low against the pound in 1892, the Government of India found itself facing a deficit of more than £2 million. Lansdowne's Finance Member, David Balfour, proposed a list of remedial measures in June 1892, after which a committee was set up to look at the problem. Chaired by the Lord Chancellor, Lord Herschell, it agreed with Balfour's proposals. The Indian Currency Act (1893) then ended public access to the Government of India's mints, which until then had, on request, turned silver bullion into currency for a small fee. The object of the closure was to constrict the amount of coinage in circulation and to push up the value of the rupee. The Act also permitted the Government to exchange gold for silver at a rate of 16d (1s 4d) per rupee, and to accept gold in settlement of public debts at the same rate. This, it was hoped, would draw gold into the public treasury and prevent the value of the rupee rising above 16d, at which point it was thought gold would flood into the country to be exchanged at a profit. But the measures were ineffective, and despite the efforts of the Secretary of State in London to support a minimum gold value for the rupee, by May 1894 it fell to 12½d, though it rallied a little afterwards.

The only long-term solution that attracted widespread official support was to peg the rupee to gold, but public resistance to this course was very strong, and the Government of India had to limp along as it was. An official committee reviewed the situation again in 1898, and made broadly the same recommendations as Herschell. There was a subsequent attempt to introduce gold coinage, but rupees were not made convertible into gold, and the gold sovereign and half-sovereign failed to find favour with the Indian public. Political will to make radical changes was never sufficient in London, and Raj officials found it impossible to make headway, because they were unable to exercise sufficient control over their own economy's exchange rates and the cost of public debt.

This point was illustrated the year after Herschell's report. In March 1894, the cash-starved Raj imposed a 5 per cent duty on imports in order to raise extra funds, but cotton goods were exempted on the insistence of the Secretary of State, Lord Kimberley. This exemption was very unpopular in India, and Viceroy Elgin, fearing for his revenues, pleaded with London to let him include cotton goods. Such a move was unacceptable in Britain as a 'protective' measure. Viceroy Elgin and Sir Henry Fowler, Kimberley's successor, then agreed that certain British cotton imports, defined by the gauge of yarn they contained, would carry a duty of

5 per cent, if a countervailing excise were levied on the Indian equivalent, in order to remove the disadvantage in price that the duty would cause. Though seemingly fair, the details proved difficult, and arcane arguments proliferated about quality of cloth, gauge of yarn and technical processes, in an attempt to weed out 'protective' tendencies.

At this point Rosebery's Liberal government fell, and Lord Salisbury's Conservatives returned. Salisbury was the man who had insisted on the removal of cotton duties in 1879, and the new Secretary for India, Lord George Hamilton, unsurprisingly took a harder line than his Liberal predecessor. Hamilton insisted that the import duty be reduced, using a slight improvement in the Raj's finances as pretext. In the end, the force of free trade dogma and the interests of Lancashire's manufacturers ensured that duties and excise were removed from all yarns, while the Government of India got the benefit of duties placed on all woven goods, imported or Indian, at a rate of 3.5 per cent.

It was unfortunate that India's cash crisis coincided with a depression in Lancashire, and doubly unfortunate that India was saddled at the time with probably the most ineffective viceroy she ever endured. The one beneficial effect was that India went on to become a massive exporter of coarse yarn. But the dispute left no doubt as to where the power lay in the making of commercially sensitive decisions, and whose interests ultimately were most likely to prevail.

Potential insolvency was thus the context for all the major economic and political decisions made in Calcutta over the period 1884–99. Who to tax, and how much, are questions that all governments face, but lacking a modern, consultative political system, the British in India had few alternative answers. Shifting the tax burden from the rural to the urban population, and from the richest and poorest to the middling earners, became the least unpalatable courses, but also the most difficult administratively. One sure device was the salt tax, but this notoriously weighed most heavily on the poor and could not be raised without distress.

It was considered necessary to reintroduce income tax in 1886, when military expenditure shot up again because of the war in Burma. This was a step towards modern governance, but rates were set low, agricultural incomes were exempted, and only 300,000 out of 180 million Indians actually paid it. The proportion of state revenue that the tax generated was therefore small, and remained so until after the First World War. The government still had to hope that the economy expanded or that emergencies did not arise.

The 1890s saw Afghanistan make a small-scale return to Raj thinking. Abdur Rahman had proved be a strong and largely friendly ruler, but one day he would be gone; meanwhile the Russians were most definitely coming. Binding diplomatic agreements were always considered easier to make with tsars than amirs, so efforts were made throughout the 1890s to demarcate British, Afghan and Russian territory in the mountains. A desire to make agreements about these unproductive and extremely inaccessible areas eventually produced a fully surveyed border settlement, laid out in 1893 and signed off in 1895. This established the Durand Line to mark the British–Afghan border, while the Pamir Agreement of 1895 drew the northern borders of Afghanistan, creating the long panhandle on the country's eastern end, as part of a deliberate policy to confine Russian influence to areas beyond the Oxus.

But the complex and unstable political world of the uplands constantly drew the British into policing the border areas. Close control proved impossible, so a system of 'butcher and bolt' was developed, to keep order by use of punitive raids. All through the 1890s the main military focus remained the north-west. There were campaigns on the Black Mountain in 1891 and 1892, in Chitral in 1895, and in Tirah two years later. The romance of the frontier inspired numerous British writers, especially Kipling, who had seen its chivalrous barbarians for himself, and the young Winston Churchill, who came to India in 1897 to fight in Malakand.

It was only with the signing of the Anglo-Russian entente of 1907 that this whole phase of border skirmishing was demoted from a global chess game into the petty raiding that it really was. But the inflated military expenditure of these years played a crucial role in reinforcing the Raj's military identity, and diverting public funds from more constructive purposes.

With the official mind steadily closing to criticism at the same rate that it ran out of constructive purposes, and while the government continued to run short of cash with which to make itself popular, the power to shape the future of India was slipping out of British hands. In the new century it was to be the British who proved timid and the Indians who came up with radical proposals for change—not all of them forward-looking. But the commitment required to transform the subcontinent was no longer coming eastwards in sufficient force. As an institution, the Raj was becoming more of an obstruction than a force for change.

Yet no matter how Indians organized themselves, and no matter what they asked for, the hard reality was that the Raj felt no pressing need to develop a true political dialogue in India. Wringing concessions from it remained very difficult when there was no established forum in which to do so. Nor was the Congress really a suitable instrument for such a purpose. Without any permanent national organization, and lacking popular support, it remained merely an annual gathering, and its demands could easily be represented as self-interested.

The government, though, was not entirely devoid of a capacity for self-criticism. Internal problems and external complaints led to the setting up of a number of important investigative bodies, with the Aitchison Commission in 1887–8 on the administration, the Herschell and Fowler Committees on currency, and the Welby Commission (1895–1900) on the equitable distribution of financial burdens between India and Britain. William Wedderburn and Dadabhai Naoroji, both MPs, sat with Welby, and Gokhale spent two days giving evidence to them.

The Aitchison Commission brought about some reforms in recruitment and the allocation of government posts, but its overall impact on either government efficiency or interracial fairness was minimal. Welby's five years of effort managed to secure a rebate of only £250,000 for India. Even the two currency inquiries failed to produce significant government action, despite the fact that money was the very lifeblood of the Raj in a way that education or Indianization of the civil service was not. The gold standard was adopted after the Fowler Committee of 1898, but the coinage remained the same and the gold element was confined to the fixing of a standard exchange rate. India was thereafter living on a gold standard while using silver coins—a situation that was never satisfactorily resolved. India retained the silver rupee until the end of the colonial era, and it was a constant concern for the authorities in both London and India to juggle the three-way equation of the rupee, sterling and gold.

In 1895–6, the Government of India entered five years of trauma. Famine, at bay since the early 1880s, reappeared across southern and western India with a vengeance. The Famine Codes worked out in the 1880s were scarcely able to cope, and millions died in the sharp dearth of 1896–7. Plague then appeared in western India, and as it began to take lives, political pressures increased. The British authorities were desperate to inspect, fumigate and disinfect persons and properties, and did not seem to care whom they offended while they did so. Women's quarters were not sacrosanct, and men of low caste were frequently used to do the job; both caused deep offence.

A particularly virulent outbreak in Poona in 1897 led in June to the murder of two British officials, Walter Rand, chairman of the Bombay

Plague Committee, and his assistant Lt Charles Ayerst. Three brothers named Chapekar were apprehended and accused of the killings. All three, plus an accomplice, were hanged, and Tilak was prosecuted for sedition, because his newspaper *Kesari* was held to have provoked the murder. Despite a thin prosecution case, he was convicted and served eighteen months in prison.

In the last two decades of the nineteenth century, India generated a wide range of new ideas that were religious or political, or sometimes both, which began to guide Indian society into new modes of thought and action. Distinctly modern Indian literature began to appear, written in vernacular languages—especially Bengali—which explored specifically Indian narratives and concerns. Bankim Chandra Chatterjee (1838–94) blazed a trail in poetry and fiction that was soon followed by Rabindranath Tagore (1861–1941). Indians found themselves looking at these role models of achievement, while they recognized themselves, their lives and their dilemmas portrayed in sympathetic forms.

The growth of nationalism also stimulated interest in ancient Sanskrit philosophy and science. Vedic learning was rediscovered and glorified by a raft of new writers. These including Pramatha Nath Bose (1855–1934), whose *A History of Hindu Civilization* (1896) was unapologetic in its praise of ancient Hindu knowledge and achievements, and Prafulla Chandra Ray (1861–1944), who claimed to have recovered a body of neglected ancient knowledge in his *History of Hindu Chemistry*, which appeared in two volumes, in 1902 and 1908.

And as Hinduism re-formed and mutated in dialogue with or rejection of the West, the Muslims of India faced their own range of options. Broadly, they could retreat into traditional piety or engage with the modern world. The Deobandis remained traditional and aloof, Sayyid Ahmad Khan continued to advocate modernization in political isolation, while a small band of Muslims, including the young Muhammad Ali Jinnah, preferred secular nationalism and joined the Congress.

Nationalist politics also developed a presence in the West. The Congress set up a London committee in 1889, followed by a breakthrough in 1893, when Dadabhai Naoroji became the first Indian to enter the House of Commons, elected as Liberal member for Central Finsbury. With a real Indian finally inside the precincts of the Palace of Westminster, an Indian parliamentary subcommittee was formed that year.

A second Indian, Sir Mancherjee M. Bhownaggree, was then elected in 1895 as member for Bethnal Green, but his arrival did nothing to aid the nationalist cause; he stood as a Conservative, hostile to the Congress's objectives. Nevertheless his appearance in British politics was a sign of changing times, as was the stream of Indian lawyers making their way to London. As Bhownaggree took his seat, Jinnah had nearly finished his studies at Lincoln's Inn.

This London connection illustrates an important shift across the period. At the start of the 1880s, political Indians still felt that London was the best place to pursue their purposes. Yet despite the formation of committees and the maintenance of permanent agents by the Congress, these efforts completely failed to engage British political leaders with Indian issues. This was a final confirmation that the future of Indian politics lay in India. From this protracted failure, Congress 'extremism' was soon to arise as a force within India.

1899–1905: Curzon

In 1899–1900, the last famine of the nineteenth century coincided with the arrival of a new young viceroy. Lord George Curzon was a highly intelligent man with more energy than the previous three viceroys put together, but he was fated to burn out that energy to little avail in the cause of an alien government almost past reviving. Some of the most perceptive men in the service of the Raj were already losing faith in the civilizing mission; nor was there great willingness apparent among many Indians, both high and low, to embrace change. The small Congress coterie were seemingly the only ones to share Macaulay's dream of a politically aware, Western-educated class of Indians willing to take on national self-government. Yet the Congress was dismissed by Curzon as 'tottering', and he boldly declared that he hoped to assist it to an early demise.

Viceroy from 1899 to 1905, George Nathaniel Curzon (1859–1925) was high-minded and humane, but also stubborn and deeply insensitive. His voluminous speeches served as a beautifully articulate manifesto for the Raj and its style of government, but his actions as viceroy merely underlined all the failings of that very government. What others had built up he intended to preserve and perfect, but he only managed to raise discontents that terminally loosened the British hold on India. He was like the fairy on top of the Raj's Christmas tree—the most glittering of ornaments, yet somehow faintly absurd.

His biographer, Lord Ronaldshay, who served as his private secretary in India, wrote freely of his 'perversities' and described an extraordinary man who possessed both noble virtues and banal weaknesses. Curzon's arrogance frequently led him to make statements that seem outrageously offensive, yet these were balanced elsewhere by much more modest and sympathetic sentiments. For instance, he repeatedly denigrated Indian politicians in private, but he believed passionately in fair treatment for all, and often stood up very publicly for the lowly in India, especially against violence meted out by the army. Above all, he understood the British mission in India to be the provision of good governance in all its aspects, and in this he was no hypocrite. He dedicated seven years of his life to this ideal—quixotic or wrong-headed as it might have been—and he never consciously did a mean-spirited thing. Indeed, his conduct was suffused with a kind of self-righteousness that made it very difficult to deflect him from his chosen course.

This massive self-assurance, however, made it all too easy for him to view any opponent as a scoundrel. And buoyed by imperial selflessness, it was not difficult to convince himself that being busy was the same as being useful.

The young Winston Churchill thought him an insufferable prig, of a typical Oxford type—until, that is, he met him in India, after which he reversed his opinion, confessed he had entirely misjudged him, and declared him a great man.[11] This, too, after Curzon had used their meeting to lecture the loquacious Churchill on the dangers of garrulity. In some ways the two men could easily have found common ground. Both were brilliant manipulators of language, political mavericks, dedicated patriots and profoundly Romantic imperialists.

George Curzon was born to privilege, but he was not from the top drawer of the aristocracy. His family was old but undistinguished, and despite owning a large neoclassical house, Kedleston Hall, and extensive lands in Derbyshire, the Curzons had only been noblemen for about a century. His recent ancestors were stout Tories, and his father was an Anglican clergyman, having been born a younger son and thus not expected to inherit the family's title and estates. Young George had an elder sister and nine younger siblings. As an intrepid child of around eight years old he is reputed to have led a party to look for the gooseberry bush under which his many brothers and sisters had been found.

He shone at Eton, but scarcely had he become a student at Balliol College, Oxford, when a damaging and highly memorable squib was penned: 'My name is George Nathaniel Curzon, I am a most superior person'. This seemed so apt that it stuck to him all his life and is still probably the best-remembered thing about him. The Master of Balliol, Benjamin Jowett, thought him overconfident and verbose, and was proved right when Curzon only achieved a second-class degree, not the first he craved and had expected. This failure may have worked as a permanent spur to his ambition, though that ambition was so powerful that it was hardly in need of second bidding.

Curzon became MP for Southport in 1886, and held junior office twice in Conservative governments, as Undersecretary for India from 1891 to 1892, then as Undersecretary at the Foreign Office from 1895 to 1898. He also spent a considerable time exploring central and south Asia, and received a medal from the Royal Geographical Society for discovering the source of the Oxus. He wrote up his travels to much acclaim, and between 1889 and 1894 he published three books that interlaced his adventures with his thoughts on British foreign policy. All this was quite conscious preparation for the high offices he intended to secure, the first of which was given to him in 1898 when he was made viceroy by Lord Salisbury.

As he sailed east, Curzon was already exceptional. He was the best-prepared, most widely travelled man ever to take on the supreme government of British India, and at thirty-nine the second youngest. But he was also unusual in that he was determined not to be daunted by detail or obstructed by his own civil servants. He had already formed a specific set of policies, which he laid out immediately in his first budget speech, under twelve heads of proposed action, from education and law reform to economic stimulation, departmental restructuring and relations with Indians.

The keyword was 'efficiency', and the next seven years saw an intensive programme of administrative reorganization. He set up a central body to coordinate government policy, and carved the North West Frontier Province (NWFP) out of the far end of the Punjab. Archaeological preservation was prioritized, and famine relief reviewed. More contentiously, university education was reformed, and local government in Calcutta reined in, both of which impinged upon the privileges of the Indian middle classes. Eventually he proposed to partition Bengal, allegedly for reasons of administrative efficiency, but the move was widely suspected by Indians to be an attempt to undermine the vocal Bengali bhadralok.

He also organized the great Delhi Durbar of 1902–3, an occasion that neatly sums up much of his administration. It was a gigantic affair, held rather belatedly in honour of the accession of King Edward VII in 1901, and it symbolized the subjugation of the Indian princes to the King-Emperor, in the most public manner possible. All this appealed enormously to Curzon, who loved the big occasion and the chance to glory in his status. As a civilian it was probably the only time he could wear a uniform and feel in no way inferior to the military men around him. But the display also involved calling upon soldiers he had recently disgraced over the notorious murder of one of their Indian cooks.

Curzon had publicly censured the 9th Lancers, yet as they paraded, the public cheered them wildly, which he took as a personal humiliation. Such are the dangers of combining personal ego and imperial pride. If he did not want to see the Lancers cheered, he should have confined them to barracks—yet he did not, because he needed their sparkling swagger to make a show for the Raj. Curzon knew how he wanted people to react, but he was consistently unable to foresee that they might fail to oblige him. This proved to be his Achilles heel in politics.

There are two rather less reputable achievements to chalk up against Curzon's name. Firstly, he spent considerable time and effort in reviving the story of the Black Hole of Calcutta; he commissioned a new collection of relevant documents, and erected a monument to the victims. As a scholar himself he would have known, had he read the documents collected at his behest, that the story had serious flaws and that the classic horror story narrated by J.Z. Holwell in 1758 was extremely unlikely to be true. Curzon either took the myth at face value, carried away by its poetic heroism, or he simply valued its didactic utility in reinforcing the imperial civilizing mission. Either way he became party to a fiction, and it is hard to excuse his wrong-headedness in the face of easily accessible truth.

The other great blot on his record was his sponsorship of Sir Francis Younghusband's invasion of Tibet through 1903–4, which resulted in the death of a great many monks and failed to discover a single malevolent Russian.

Ultimately, despite all his reforming energy, his time in India brought little improvement in the state of the Raj. His administrative changes were, essentially, an extended exercise in window dressing. In some ways he squandered a golden opportunity, because his arrival in India coincided with an upturn in world trade and an enormous improvement in the Raj's finances. In his time plague retreated, famine disappeared, there was peace on the north-western border, and the rupee stabilized against the pound. The resulting fiscal surplus could have allowed him to do many useful things, but as a natural Tory he chose to pass the benefits to the richest in India through tax cuts. He had a rare chance—probably the only chance—to launch the Raj into the paths of modern government, and he squandered it.

But the most serious damage Curzon did to British rule was to drive through the partition of Bengal against the clear opposition of Bengalis. Reform was indeed overdue; the province of Bengal contained some 80 million people, and had grown to include parts of Assam as well as the heavily populated heartland of Bengal proper. Schemes for breaking up this large territory had been mooted for fifty years, and the appointment of a separate Lieutenant-Governor for the province in 1853 was an early attempt to address the chronic oversupply of government work. Nor was Curzon singling out Bengal particularly. During his time he also created the entirely new North West Frontier Province, added Berar and parts of Bengal to the Central Provinces, and renamed and reorganized the old North West Provinces, which became the United Provinces (now Uttar Pradesh).

But Curzon's plan for Bengal was different and altogether more objectionable. He proposed to split the mostly Hindu west of Bengal from the mostly Muslim east, then add the western section to Orissa and Bihar, while adding the east to Assam. This seemed both insensitive and overtly political to many of the people affected. Curzon himself wrote that on top of the plan's administrative merits there was a bonus in that the partition would 'dethrone' Calcutta from its place at the centre of 'intrigue'. Foremost in the opposition to the scheme were the inhabitants of Calcutta, who faced a new life in West Bengal outnumbered by Biharis and Oriyas. The riots and repression that followed were materially important in connecting the elite Congress with a mass following.

Curzon's years ended in conflict with his Indian subjects, but by then he had managed to fall out with his fellow Britons too, as a result of his invitation to Lord Kitchener, the greatest imperial hero of the age, to come to India to reform the army. Kitchener arrived in late 1902 and immediately began to make demands of his own, specifically concerning the fact that he was only an 'extraordinary' member of the Viceroy's Executive Council, whereas the Military Member—his subordinate—had a permanent seat. The argument was arcane but it set up a very clear power struggle between two autocratically inclined men. Curzon appealed to London for support, but found that the cabinet, though sympathetic to his constitutional points, was politically behind Kitchener.

Curzon contributed enormously to his own isolation by a long series of wheedling complaints to London, especially over his fears about Russian influence in Tibet. His relationship with Lord George Hamilton, Secretary for India from 1895 to 1903, had been easy and affable; Hamilton was no enthusiast for hard work or arguments. But the appointment of St John Brodrick to the post in 1903 changed matters—Brodrick and Kitchener had worked closely and harmoniously for the previous three years while Brodrick was Secretary of War. Curzon may have held the theoretical high ground in the dispute, but in political terms Kitchener had the numbers and the heavy weapons. Curzon was forced to resign in August 1905, two months before the partition of Bengal finally went through.

He left in November, after giving a valedictory speech at the Byculla Club in Bombay, in which he summed up all his favourite themes of duty, sacrifice, progress, and kindness to those less fortunate than himself. The contrast between his stirring rhetoric and his political naivety is still jarring.

Despite this political debacle, Curzon managed to recover and go on to higher office, becoming one of only five returning Governors-General who climbed further in domestic British politics. He served as Foreign Secretary from 1919 to 1924, a post that Richard Wellesley and Lord Lansdowne had filled, and that yet awaited Lords Reading and Irwin. Yet despite his late promotion, and despite acquiring no less than six titles in addition to the one he inherited, Curzon's career was more failure than success. He desperately wanted to be prime minister, and when he missed out in 1924, pipped by Stanley Baldwin, he is reputed to have burst into tears.

George Curzon was the last of the great imperialists, fully comfortable in the exercise of untrammelled imperial power. The fact that the design of Government House in Calcutta was on exactly the same plan as his family seat at Kedleston must at the very least have allowed him to feel at home as viceroy, even proprietorial. Churchill, the other great late-imperialist, was by contrast pessimistic, knowing full well that the Second World War presaged the end of the imperial era.

Curzon sincerely believed it was the destiny of the British to bring civilized ways and enlightened government to the world. He shook up every part of the Indian administration and worked his subordinates as hard as he worked himself. But for all his high-mindedness he was a man of limited vision. His constant tinkering with the details of British Indian government rather missed the point that by 1899 India did not need a more efficient version of British autocracy; she needed more inclusive ruling practices, economic self-determination, and more government spending.

Curzon was dedicated to the precise opposite of all these policies and was absolutely deficient in the kind of political instincts that might recognize the need for them.

Despite the persistent weakness of the Raj, Curzon's term marked the true imperial high noon, higher than the early 1820s or the mid-1850s, which had both witnessed unchallenged periods of British confidence. In 1905 things looked much the same. The 'work' continued largely unhindered, and the British still thought of it as their own, shared, at most, with God alone. It was difficult to imagine who or what might emerge to challenge British supremacy.

It was going to be a man that operated outside British institutions, who commanded a new, entirely indigenous moral authority.

9

1905–1920

COUNCILS, WORLD WAR, GANDHI, MASSACRE

1905–14: Swadeshi, Terror, Reform

Curzon refused to accept that there was any role for political activism in India, and did his best to prevent its appearance. But in the thirty years after his departure, national politics came to India from two directions: from the bottom up, through increased Indian awareness and organization, and from the top down, through British reform packages.

There is a standard way of viewing these developments, which emphasizes the reality of the new national consciousness apparent in Indian political life, and sees the British as conducting an extended rearguard action, during which they reluctantly appeased Indian demands for inclusion in government. From this standpoint the reforms of 1909, 1919 and 1935 can be seen as ways not to nurture but to subvert and dilute Indian political ambitions—in 1909 by the establishment of separate religious electorates, in 1919 by deliberate decentralization of power that left the Raj unchallenged at the centre, and in 1935 by proposals for a federal structure in which the princely states were included as a counterweight to the Congress.

This is all true enough, but it tends to divide Indian politics too neatly into two clear sides. The nationalist platform was not unanimous among itself, with the Congress divided between so-called naram (Moderate) and garam (Extreme) factions, and later between social radicals and conservatives. The prospect of more democratic institutions also nurtured a sense of distinctness among the Muslim population, many of whose leaders consistently stood away from the Congress model of nationalist self-government. Nor was there unanimity on the British side, where the problems of Indian government generated a spectrum of responses. Some kind of imperial decentralization was clearly necessary, as it was not possible for ministers in London to supervise the sprawling global portfolio that the empire had become. But precisely what powers should be delegated, and to whom, was very unclear in the case of India, where granting more local self-government was perceived as risking either revolt or secession.

There was also a change of political climate in Britain, with the appointment of a Liberal administration in 1905, confirmed by a landslide election victory in 1906. The reform packages of the next three decades were all the work of progressive cabinets, of Campbell-Bannerman's Liberals in 1909, the Lloyd George-led coalition in 1919, and the second Labour administration in 1929, which initiated the process that led on to the new constitution of 1935.

Over this period we can also see the final phase of the legitimacy strategy, with its distinctive polarity still intact. Before 1905 Curzon pursued a Tory version of legitimacy through uplift, forcefulness and competence; after his departure the emphasis switched to the liberal strategy of broadening political inclusion while retaining the reality of power.

In either case it remained an imperial priority not to hand over the running of India to the class most ambitious to take it on, and the battle between bourgeois liberal nationalists and old-school British imperialists remained the most intractable and distinct conflict throughout late Anglo-Indian history. Popular leaders finally emerged in India, at the head not of small provincial armies but of a national mass movement, rendering British claims to legitimate authority increasingly unconvincing. But at the same time, attempts to construct a national liberation movement based on a distinct 'Indian' identity were constantly disrupted by religious and provincial identities, overlaid on a left–right social and economic spectrum.

Almost anything the British did would now be either too much or too little, and some group somewhere could always cry foul.

The first example of this was Curzon's partition of Bengal. Though it was not inspired by religious motives, and merely took note of religious considerations, the reaction to it was unmistakeably religious in character. Bengali Muslims, who felt like winners in the process, remained quiescent, pleased with the enhanced importance of Dhaka, while Hindus expressed their outrage in mass protests. Civil liberties, never the Raj's strongest suit, were curtailed by a range of measures including restrictions on press freedom and public meetings between 1905 and 1910.

These post-1905 protests contained two new elements. The first was organized economic boycott. Refusing to buy British products, or replacing them with home-produced swadeshi goods, reduced imports from Britain by about a quarter. The second, after 1907, was terrorism, based on Irish Fenian and Russian anarchist models.

The numbers involved in terrorist activity were always very small, and the danger to the Raj was never mortal, but there were seventy-eight terrorist incidents in Bengal between 1906 and 1914. The district magistrate of Dhaka was killed in December 1907, a senior Indian official named Sir William Curzon Wyllie was shot dead in London in July 1909, and a bomb was thrown into the Viceroy's howdah as he rode into Delhi in 1912. Magistrates, policemen and informers were preferred targets, but several innocents were killed along the way. V.D. Savarkar, the father of Hindutva philosophy, was arrested in London for terrorist activities in March 1910 and deported to India, where he was sentenced to fifty years' imprisonment on the grim Andaman Islands.

This undercurrent of violence remained part of Indian politics until the mid-1930s, and revolutionary cells dedicated to the overthrow of the Raj proliferated before the First World War, especially among the Sikh community, both in the Punjab and abroad, principally in North America, where the Ghadar movement was formed in 1913. Of the 127 men hanged by the British for terrorist crimes, all but ten were Sikhs. The encouragement that these movements gained from hostile powers during the First World War was a source of constant concern to the Raj, and reflected an uneasiness in government that lingered till independence.

The first fruit of the new political energy in Bengal was the development of a specifically Muslim political viewpoint. Muslim leaders had maintained an almost apolitical stance for decades before 1905, and generally remained aloof from the Congress. It had been apparent to Sayyid Ahmad Khan that electoral politics were not a productive path for a community marooned in a permanent numerical minority, and that for Muslims self-government in the sense demanded by the Congress could only mean subjection to Hindu domination. There was, therefore, little to be gained by ousting the British, and Muslims were probably better off allying with the existing Raj than working to dismantle it. But the Hindu agitation following partition in Bengal, and the announcement by Secretary Morley in mid-1906 of an impending new scheme of reforms, changed the passive loyalism of senior Muslim figures. It became apparent to them that moves had to be made, first to pressure the British to recognize

Muslim concerns, then to create some kind of political vehicle for Muslim opinion. The result was the visit by a group of dignitaries to Simla in October 1906.

This august body, led by the Aga Khan, asked of Viceroy Minto (1905–10) that the Muslim community be granted due recognition within any scheme of reform. Crude numbers, they said, were not an adequate reflection of the 'importance' of the Muslim community. This was the kind of status-conscious Whiggism that had been losing ground in Britain over the previous century, but it made a good deal of sense to British ears in pre-democratic India. Minto, a traditional sort of aristocrat, was disturbed by Hindu militancy, and told the deputation that he was 'in accord' with their main points, of which he had been kept informed throughout their lengthy drafting. By the end of December a new political entity, the Muslim League, had been formed to contest the forthcoming elections.

Tensions resulting from Bengal's partition also found direct expression within Congress politics, which had hitherto been distinguished by gentlemanly restraint. The moderate, constitutional approach of Gokhale and Mehta had largely gone unchallenged, but now a more confrontational approach, developed by Tilak through the 1890s, gained credibility, and a 'New Party' formed around radical leaders who were disillusioned with gradualism and advocated direct, even violent action. This more vigorous, more specifically Hindu tendency was not numerically large, and its radicalism is easily overstated. Its chief spokesmen had regional rather than national followings, and the 'Lal, Bal and Pal' label traditionally attached to it makes it seem more of a united movement than it was. Lala Lajpat Rai in the Punjab was always measured in his language, and Bipin Chandra Pal in Bengal never became a substantial figure. It was Bal Gangadhar Tilak in the west that was the true nationalist bellwether, in both his ability to energize a wider audience and his willingness to step outside his Maharashtrian heartland to campaign in Bengal. Somewhat further out to the extreme wing was Aurobindo Ghosh, who had been involved in radical journalism in the 1890s and was now making plans for armed insurrection.

The Extremists caught the mood of exasperation which the partition of Bengal had focused, and they set out to win control of the Congress. By 1907, a split in the movement's senior leadership was looming, and the Moderates laid plans to thwart the militants. The annual session at Surat broke up in chaos, when Tilak was prevented from taking the platform, and the Moderates then rewrote the party's constitution to exclude hardliners. The movement remained split until 1916.

During these nine years the two factions fared very differently. The Extremists endured exclusion at the hands of their former colleagues and prosecution from British officialdom. The Moderates won short-term possession of the soul of the Congress, and they vindicated their strategy by practical results—the arrival of the reforms of 1907–9, drawn up by Viceroy Minto and Secretary Morley.

Many contemporaries were surprised that the bookish John Morley (1838–1923) ever entered politics, deeming him impractical and ill-suited to the rough and tumble of the trade. His slender personal means, coupled with a lack of patronage, made politics an unlikely, even an unwise, career. Nevertheless he rose to high office, and had a considerable effect on the political future of India.

He spent his early years scraping a living from tutoring and journalism, gradually building up a reputation as a literary and intellectual figure. Throughout the 1870s he published literary criticism, political articles, and several biographies of eminent men, including Voltaire, Rousseau and Burke. He also promoted, at every opportunity, the liberal ideas of John Stuart Mill, and he and Mill became personal friends. His most significant work was *On Compromise* (1874), an essay on the virtues of moderation, which was well known and admired in India. Jinnah claimed it had had a profound influence on his political development, and later recommended it to the attention of young people.

Morley was in his mid-forties when he finally found a way into Parliament in 1883 through a by-election in Newcastle, where the immigrant Irish population invited him to stand because of his well-known support for Irish Home Rule. This single cause gave him his greatest political presence in British politics, and he served two spells as Irish Secretary, from 1885 to 1886 and 1892 to 1895. On neither occasion did circumstances permit him to advance the Home Rule agenda.

His work in India was more enduring. In six years as Secretary for India (1905–11) he was co-author of the reforms of 1909, and it is in the contrast between his outlooks on Ireland and India that interest in his career chiefly lies.

His views on Ireland were shaped by meeting Irish expatriates in the United States on a visit in 1867. What he garnered from these encounters wedded easily with his liberal principles, turning him into a convinced advocate of Irish Home Rule. He drafted and sponsored Gladstone's unsuccessful Home Rule Bill of 1886.

His rather different attitude towards India stemmed from a reluctance, which he shared with many of his generation, to see India in remotely the same terms, despite the political congruity between the two situations. It is an irony that has not escaped historians that although the British were very wary about letting the Irish run Ireland, they were quite happy to let them run India. Through the 1890s, only Bombay was not at some point governed by an Irishman.

Morley was at heart a disciple of Gladstone, and Gladstone never took much interest in India, deterred by the 'difficulties' he claimed were involved. Morley stuck to the same general line. He never came to know Indians as he had come to know the Irish; he took little interest in Indian culture or history and never visited the country. Despite persistent demands for reform in India from 1905 onwards, he refused to move very far towards any kind of structural or ideological change in Britain's relationship with India. Although unconvinced about imperialism—he had been a staunch opponent of the Boer War—Morley tinkered with the Anglo-Indian relationship in the smallest possible degree.

His political ideas were fully formed by the mid-1870s and their peak relevance was during the 1880s. By 1905, in his late sixties, he proceeded to deal with India not so much as he had dealt with Ireland in the 1880s, but rather more like the British had treated the American colonies in the 1770s. Gokhale, who worked closely with him for four years over the reforms, summed up his attitudes very shrewdly, remarking that he was 'more for personal than national liberty'.[1]

The result was the 1909 Indian Councils Act—the Morley–Minto reforms—which increased Indian participation in provincial (Governor's) councils, while preserving an 'official' majority in the Viceroy's Central Executive and Legislative Councils.

The 1909 reforms were a slight advance on previous arrangements. All Legislative Councils, provincial and central, were expanded, and 'non-official' majorities were set up in the provinces, from a mixture of nominated and elected members. At the centre, the new Imperial Legislative Council consisted of sixty members, of whom just under half were to be elected, including nine from the provincial Legislative Councils. Non-official members could now introduce motions and ask a full range of questions concerning the budget. However, the resolutions of the Legislative Council were not binding, and the viceroy retained the power to force measures through.

The elective principle was extended, based on a limited franchise, heavily restricted by property qualifications and special interests, including religious communities. But the changes were scarcely more than cosmetic.

The power to override any inconvenient decision was retained and no real executive power, over either legislation or 'supply' (finance), was granted to any combination of Indian interests. The new assemblies were not very representative nor, despite their majority composition, did they possess the power to restrain the executive. In some ways this was a model of Tudor, not Edwardian, government.

Yet a new spirit of inclusion was apparent. Two Indian members were appointed to the Council of India in London in 1907, and the first Indian, Satyendra Sinha, was admitted to the Viceroy's Executive Council in 1909, as Law Member.

Overall, the status quo was largely maintained, because power was not devolved either to the viceroy from London, or from the centre to the provinces, or in any degree from British to Indians. The one great future pointer within the new arrangements was undoubtedly the establishment of the principle of separate electorates for religious communities, which was not dictated by their faith but by their political weight. This did not lay out some straight road to Pakistan, as is sometimes baldly stated. Two more reform packages, two world wars, and forty more years of political wrangling determined that journey. However, the reforms of 1909 set new ground rules that suited the Raj. Democracy in India came with a great many restrictive strings attached.

Morley disavowed any intention of introducing a parliamentary form of government to India. He maintained instead that he wished to introduce the 'representative principle' into Indian politics, not 'representative government'. He hoped to appease the Moderates, and to satisfy those who hoped for 'colonial autonomy' with 'being admitted to a fair and full cooperation'.[2] Gokhale considered the reforms disappointing, but by 1910 he and Jinnah were sitting as elected members in an expanded Central Legislative Council, a long-term Congress demand.

The Extremist leaders, meanwhile, had been much less fortunate. Lala Lajpat Rai was deported without a hearing to Burma in May 1907, while both Tilak and Aurobindo stood trial in 1908. Tilak was sentenced to six years in gaol, but Aurobindo was acquitted and fled to Pondicherry, where he remained for the rest of his life, pursuing his own spiritual growth. Bipin Chandra Pal fled to England, then spent an extended period as an impoverished itinerant writer, only returning to India after the First World War.

The British view of all these changes was telling. Morley was well aware that he had conceded the minimum necessary to support the Moderates against their more radical rivals. His original intentions had been to do rather more, and he had tried to introduce a degree of proportional representation, but he was outmanoeuvred by officials in both London and Calcutta, who drew up rules of qualification for candidates and electors that kept the new system as narrow as possible.

Restrained in part by the old conviction, running back to Mill and Macaulay, that a British-style representative political system was not suited to India, Morley was also hampered by the cautiousness of Viceroy Minto, who was persuaded by his senior officials to insist on the principle of separate electorates for religious minorities. Morley simply wished 'that it were otherwise'.[3]

Minto exerted a distinctly chilling influence on the whole process. An experienced, conservatively minded soldier-diplomat, who had been appointed by the outgoing Balfour government to replace Curzon, he owes his liberal reputation to his moderate use of repression, such as his pardoning of Lala Lajpat Rai after six months in the teeth of hard-line Anglo-Indian opinion. But his reluctance to countenance change was typical of the later Raj, as the future-blindness of true imperialism began to tell. The small extent of the progress merely underlined how difficult it was to achieve imperial reform through imperial institutions.

The reforms had less impact than Morley might have expected, but they did help the Indian cause indirectly. The calmer political atmosphere that followed them encouraged a gradual healing of the rifts in Congress ranks, and this process was aided by two exterior factors. The first was the announcement at the Durbar of 1911, held in Delhi to mark the coronation of King George V, that Bengal was to be reunited. Having alienated Hindus in 1905 with the original measure, the British now managed to alienate Muslims by reversing that decision. In another political faux pas, the British announced that Delhi, not Calcutta, was now to be the imperial capital. Residents of Calcutta, both Indian and European, were dismayed. Thus between 1905 and 1911 the Government of India managed to offend every interest group in Bengal at least once and sometimes twice.

The second factor which intensified the process of Indian political convergence was the position of Turkey in world affairs. The Turkish Sultan held the spiritual leadership of Sunni Muslims—the Khilafat (Caliphate)—and the repeated blows delivered by Western powers to the declining Ottoman Empire presented devout Muslims with a conflict of loyalties. Turkey's wars—with Italy in 1911–12, with other Balkan states from 1912–13, and eventually with Britain and her allies after 1914—convinced some that a Christian conspiracy to destroy Islam was afoot. More directly, these developments obliged all Muslims to weigh their spiritual and political loyalties between the British and the Ottoman Empires.

With Muslim opinion moving away from Raj loyalism, especially among younger leaders, and with a growing awareness in Congress circles of the benefits that a Hindu–Muslim alliance would bring to the nationalist cause, the two All-India parties drew closer. Jinnah's agreement to join the Muslim League in 1913 was a significant indicator of this rapprochement.

1914–19: War, Gandhi, Massacre

Economically and politically the First World War had complex repercussions on India. International trade was hit hard, and important markets in Europe were lost. But in terms of imports, the war had the helpful effect of cutting off foreign competition. Notable beneficiaries of this were the cotton, steel and coal industries. Wartime stimulated general demand; prices rose, and industry was more profitable. Employment went up too, as more labour was hired to meet increased demand. But inflation set in and the rupee depreciated. The net effect of all these various factors, especially the rise in agricultural prices, was to make the poor poorer.

Politically, war brought a wave of support for the Empire from moderate opinion all over India, and especially from the princes, who contributed men, money and personal service to the fight against German militarism and barbarism. Unfortunately Indians were to experience a good deal of militarism and barbarism at the hands of the British over the next five years, and a fair amount of incompetence too.

Indian troops fought in a number of theatres for the Empire, with a substantial contingent on the Western Front during the first two years of the war, holding the line while Kitchener turned a small volunteer British army into a mass conscript force. Indian troops were also deployed in the Middle East to fight the Turks, particularly in Mesopotamia, where the campaign was badly mishandled. But not all Indians were so loyal. Turkey's entry into the war on the German side in November 1914 forced some leading Muslims into open opposition to the Raj. Such hostility landed Maulana Abul Kalam Azad and the Ali brothers, Mohammed and Shaukat, in detention for the remainder of the war.

As the conflict dragged on, the consolidation of Indian nationalism continued with the return of the Extremist faction to the Congress fold in 1916. This became possible with Tilak's release from prison in 1914.

The path of reconciliation was also smoothed by the deaths of Gokhale in February 1915 and of Ferozeshah Mehta that December; the final details were ironed out by some skilful mediation from Annie Besant, the maverick English Indophile.

Reunited and reinvigorated, the Congress then negotiated a pact with the Muslim League at Lucknow in December 1916, which agreed a framework for Indian home rule within the Empire, including the retention of separate religious electorates. This pact represented the high tide of Hindu–Muslim political unity, and as 1917 opened, it seemed that the Indian political nation was at last pulling in the same direction.

Indian politicians were now in unprecedentedly close alliance. With the entry of the United States into the war that April on behalf of 'democracy', and after the release of the critical findings of the Mesopotamian Campaign inquiry in June, the need for a placatory gesture of some sort towards Indian desires for political inclusion became pressing. The London government worked out a formula, and here Lord Curzon had one last role to play in the story of British India. Recalled to the cabinet by Lloyd George in 1916, he drafted a statement which promised India some kind of self-government within the British Empire. Curzon had no wish to see India set free, and he managed to craft a form of words that avoided any clear commitment to do so, and left a great deal of room for interpretation and political manoeuvre.

Secretary of State Edwin Montagu then stood up in the Commons on 20 August 1917 and delivered the first-ever official statement on India's political future. He declared that the government's policy was to oversee the 'increasing association of Indians in every branch of the administration, and the gradual development of self-governing institutions with a view to the progressive realization of responsible government in India as an integral part of the British Empire'.[4] Fine-sounding words, but ultimately rather vague. Responsible to whom? Practical details were to be supplied after a fact-finding trip to India, which Montagu completed between November 1917 and April 1918. The report of Secretary Montagu and Viceroy Lord Chelmsford was then published in July 1918.

The new 'Mont-ford' reforms were discussed at a special Congress session that August, with a view to deciding whether to 'work' them or not. A general mood of disappointment among the majority prompted the moderate tendency to defect and form a new party, the National Liberal Federation. The leaders of this body, notably Sir Tej Bahadur Sapru and Srinavasa Shastri, continued to work with the government over the succeeding years. But they did not represent the way forward in Congress politics, which soon became permanently oppositional in outlook, in the hands not of liberal moderates in the Gokhale or Sapru mould, but of M.K. Gandhi, a populist radical.

Widespread economic distress and the call for swaraj (self-government) combined to produce a unique opportunity for a national popular movement, and Mohandas Karamchand Gandhi emerged as the person to lead it. He had spent twenty-one years in South Africa, from 1893 to 1914, fighting the colonial authorities for the rights of Indian migrants, and this background led to the introduction of one important extra factor in the Indian nationalist struggle—satyagraha. Developed by Gandhi in South Africa as a technique of non-violent mass protest, this was to have a unique significance in India's future.

Satyagraha (literally, 'holding on to truth') was far more than a means of protest, it was also a kind of disciplined spiritual self-development, designed to elevate not just its practitioners but its opponents too. It was a path designed to show a better way to people on both sides of any political conflict. Its themes of moral improvement, sacrifice, suffering, self-control and fearlessness made it unlike any previous political philosophy.

It was a fragile code, often imperfectly implemented, but it possessed an 'Indianness' that other contemporary political philosophies lacked, and it was extraordinarily self-sufficient, once fully appreciated. Satyagraha was an unlikely armament, and Gandhi an unlikely leader; he lacked conventional charisma, and had no great skill in oratory or any regional standing, and was thus unlike all the leaders of the previous generation. But his radical ideas were strong enough to sustain an attritional struggle that lasted much longer than the four years of trench warfare in Flanders.

This was also a struggle that the Empire was destined to lose, for Gandhi finally put together a combination of elements that struck the British hard in their two previously strongest areas: military might and moral assuredness. Gandhi's philosophy of ahimsa (non-violence) denied the relevance of British armed strength, while the spiritual dimensions of his message challenged the whole basis of imperial self-assurance, by completely reversing standard British notions of who was strong and who was civilized. Against the British claim, repeated endlessly across the previous century, that their purpose was to uplift the dilapidated Hindu, Gandhi averred that by meeting British violence with Indian non-violence, Indians were essentially civilizing their oppressors. This reversal of values infuriated the British, who could not deploy physical force against Gandhi's unarmed followers without proving his point.

Gandhi also forged a new type of political alliance within India, and this was at least as significant as the various forms of self-discipline and spiritual elevation that he promoted. He was the first person to operate above the limiting categories of class, region and faith, so that his nationalism, which was as broad and inclusive as he could make it, became a truly unifying force, untrammelled by economic interests or religious specifics. His language and his appearance had a distinctly Hindu flavour, but his enemy was always injustice, and his appeal was always to the dignity and self-worth of his listeners and their shared Indian identity.

He attempted to occupy a moral plane beyond the reach of his opponents, and he generally succeeded in thoroughly confusing the British, who never quite worked out what he was—fakir, politician or charlatan. Whatever he was (and the issue is still alive today) he managed to assemble a new type of mass movement that crossed many of the boundaries that had restricted previous political mobilizations. Thus the great movements he led drew their support not just in areas of established activism, like Bengal, Maharashtra and Punjab, but he also managed to revitalize the main theatre of the 1857 rising—the Gangetic heartlands.

In 1914 Gandhi was known in India principally as the author of *Hind Swaraj* (Indian Home Rule), a short book written on a voyage from London to South Africa in 1909. The nationalist ideas it contained were formed during a long pupillage under Gokhale, who had kept him abreast of Indian developments. Gandhi fully supported Gokhale's ideals of service, but remained unimpressed with the sporadic, dilatory and ineffective nature of Congress agitation compared to his own continuous, deeply personal and highly practical political methods.

Returning to India from South Africa via London in early 1915, he toured his homeland for a year, as he had promised Gokhale he would, to acquaint himself with the lives and conditions of ordinary Indians. During 1915–17 he then came to national attention through his activities on behalf of indigo workers in Champaran and mill hands in Ahmedabad, in the course of which he faced down not only Raj officials but also the Indian capitalist classes. During these years he made speeches that exhorted politicians to change their ways and to get to know the people they aspired to lead. He also began to use fasting as a moral weapon to shame his opponents. Leaving platform oratory to more conventional leaders, he developed what was to become his own unique political style, in which means and ends were perfectly reconciled, humility was all, and small things counted as much as large.

Gandhi began the war as a supporter of the Empire. He still believed that British rule conferred a greater degree of freedom on its subjects than the available alternatives. But he wanted swaraj, and expected that British fair play would deliver liberation to Indians if they supported the Empire in its hour of need. He continued to believe this till very late in the war, and remained essentially indulgent towards the failings of the Raj. He was not originally displeased with the Mont-ford proposals, but over the next two years he became not merely a critic of British rule but an implacable opponent, calling for its immediate removal. At the same time he converted what amounted to little more than his personal moral pre-eminence into effective political leadership of a national movement.

This transformation was not entirely his own work, but was the result of India's national reaction to a series of political developments: a law, a massacre, an inquiry, and a treaty.

By the end of the war in 1918, popular agitation and terrorist violence had thoroughly unnerved the Raj, while espionage and agitation in other countries during the war had done nothing to calm Raj pessimists. The Defence of India Act, passed in 1915, gave the government special powers of repression, but this was not applicable in peacetime. Therefore the Government of India commissioned an English judge, Sir Sidney Rowlatt, to make recommendations for measures to deal with sedition and terrorism after the war.

Rowlatt recommended granting the government drastic powers of search, arrest and internment without trial or appeal. When these measures were announced, the Indian political establishment erupted in furious protest. Someone coined the damning jingle: 'No vakil (lawyer), no daleel (proof), no appeal'.

Two bills became the Rowlatt Act, voted into law in early March 1919, despite the unanimous opposition of all non-official members of the Legislative Council. Jinnah resigned his seat and Gandhi called for a nationwide hartal, or day of mourning. Disorders in the Punjab led to the arrest and deportation of Gandhi from Lahore on 9 April, followed the next day by the forcible removal from Amritsar of two prominent local Congressmen, an affront that led to riots, resulting in both Indian and European fatalities. British officials panicked, and reinforcements were called in, under the command of General Reginald Dyer. Martial law was declared across the region, including a ban on public meetings.

What followed, as Dyer attempted to enforce that order, was the massacre in the Jallianwala Bagh on 13 April, in which an 'estimated'[5]

379 people were killed and over 1,500 injured, when Dyer ordered a small contingent to open fire on a peaceful crowd, assembled in a public park.

It was this incident, above all, that permanently changed the face of political India. The shootings were unforgivable in Indian eyes, yet enough of the establishment in England rallied to Dyer's cause to make it distressingly clear that double standards were in play. The official British inquiry into the affair, the Hunter Committee, largely exonerated Dyer, finding that he was justified in opening fire, because he was genuinely fearful of a riot that might have led to a general insurrection. However, the Report also stated that he should have issued a warning, and should have ceased firing sooner. He was also reprimanded for not taking care of the wounded. Dyer's feeble excuse was that the hospitals were open, and 'no application was made to him for help'.[6] The distance between Dyer's supporters and the average Indian was at least as wide in 1919 as the gap between British and Indians had been in 1857, but this time the loss of life was all on the Indian side.

Only weeks after the Amritsar Massacre, the Third Afghan War broke out, the first in which Afghans were the aggressors. The fighting, which lasted from 6 May to 3 June 1919, was largely the result of an opportunistic attempt by the new amir, Amanullah, to shore up his domestic position. He hoped that the unrest in the Punjab would be to his advantage, but his invading force failed to penetrate far into Indian territory. An interim settlement, known as the Treaty of Rawalpindi, was then signed in August. This returned to the amir the right to conduct foreign policy without reference to the British, and effectively made Afghanistan a fully sovereign nation, 'officially free and independent'.[7] Several details, however, remained problematic, and the Foreign Secretary, Lord Curzon, was reluctant to relinquish all control over Afghanistan's diplomatic dealings. A formal treaty was eventually signed in late 1921, which proved durable enough to outlast British India.

Anglo-Afghan tensions are sometimes cited as a mitigating factor in Dyer's conduct; they are supposed to have made him unusually nervous about the stability of the region. This is overgenerous; it was not the threat of invasion that led to the massacre, it was the uproar surrounding the massacre that led to the invasion.

The Jallianwala Bagh shooting opened a new oppositional phase in Indian politics. Prominent figures condemned it, with the nation's leading cultural icon, Nobel laureate Rabindranath Tagore, to the forefront.

Strangely, and in a way that would become characteristic, Gandhi did not blame the British so much as himself. He admitted to a 'Himalayan miscalculation' in having launched a non-violent campaign for freedom when the people were not yet ready for the discipline it required.

And it was not the massacre itself that disillusioned Gandhi; it was the official British reluctance, drawn out over many months, to condemn it. He took comfort from the Royal Proclamation of December 1919, which granted an amnesty to political prisoners, and he was still prepared to 'work' the new reforms. Even at this late stage he still believed that the British had honourable intentions towards India; it was over the next six months that he finally moved into irreversible opposition.

One factor that changed his mind was the harsh nature of the post-war terms that were to be imposed on Turkey by the Treaty of Sèvres, despite appeals made both to the viceroy in India and the government in London. The British government's refusal to soften its stance led to the formation of the Khilafat Committee, which rallied to the Sultan's cause as the Khalifa of Sunni Muslims.

Another was the publication of the Hunter Report in May 1920, with its lukewarm condemnation of Dyer. This was followed in July by a motion in the House of Lords supporting Dyer, and complaining of his unjust treatment. These things in combination seem to have persuaded Gandhi, now accorded the title of Mahatma by Rabindranath Tagore, that the Raj was not just incompetent or unworthily served, but actively 'satanic'.

India was now ready for radical leadership, and the necessary figurehead was at last to hand, for Gandhi was not only popular, he was also willing to take on board Muslim grievances in a way that Tilak, for instance, might have found difficult. Tilak did not like satyagraha as a tactic, but he died on 1 August 1920, the day that Gandhi launched what was to become known as the Non-Cooperation movement. This managed to collect under one banner the Khilafat Committee, the Muslim League and the populist wing of the Congress. The movement was very much Gandhi's affair, and he had to make considerable efforts to get the Congress to adopt Non-Cooperation. He managed to do this with two victories: at a special Congress session at Calcutta in September, then at a full session at Nagpur in December 1920.

How this came to pass makes a remarkable tale, involving popular pressure brought to bear at the right moments, the influx of Muslim members to open meetings, Gandhi's own quiet eloquence, and a kind of moral collapse among the senior Congress leadership, who felt unable to oppose an anti-government movement under the circumstances, despite their many reservations about the political wisdom, tactical soundness and intellectual coherence of what Gandhi was proposing. But Gandhi got his votes, and by the end of the Nagpur session Congress was committed to the Non-Cooperation–Khilafat movement, and had passed a resolution committing the movement to achieving swaraj within one year.

This was a moment of unprecedented unity, but it came at a cost. Gandhi only managed to obtain mass support by alienating moderates within the party who did not like close association of the Congress with a religious issue, and were concerned that boycotts and blanket non-cooperation with government would hit the poor especially hard. Chief among these defectors was Jinnah. However, despite the falling away of some moderates, Gandhi's campaign represented a new departure. The direction he set in 1920 fixed the Congress as the central fact of Indian politics for the next six decades.

It also saw the end of the active career of the remarkable Annie Besant. Annie Besant (née Wood) (1847–1933) played an unusual role as one of very few British figures who wholeheartedly espoused the cause of Indian nationalism. She did this as part of a personal spiritual journey from atheistic, socialist politics in Britain to transcendental religion in India. Always a complex mixture of serial rebel, social campaigner, inveterate attention seeker and credulous enthusiast, she divided opinion within British circles, yet was almost universally venerated by Indians.

Before arriving in India in 1893, Besant fought for a variety of progressive causes within English politics, a pattern she fell into after her first rebellion, against the intensely religious education she had received as a child. This rejection was triggered by the severe illness of her daughter, Mabel, in 1867, which brought on a crisis of personal belief in a benevolent God. She was married at the time to an Anglican clergyman, Frank Besant, but she left both him and her faith and moved to London, alone, in 1873.

Here she encountered two prominent figures of the British left. Under the tutelage of Charles Bradlaugh, the atheist republican, she became an effective public speaker and a prolific journalist, which led to her prosecution in 1877 under the Obscene Publications Act for disseminating information about birth control. Her next guru was Edward Aveling, whom she met in 1884. This drew her further to the left and led her to write *Why I Am a Socialist*, a pamphlet priced at one penny, published in 1886. Her new causes were Irish Home Rule and industrial conditions in England—she was an important figure in the agitation over the 'match girls' strike of 1888.

But this enthusiasm soon gave place to yet another, as she became interested in Theosophy, the occult teaching of Madame Helena Blavatsky. Besant rose rapidly within the movement and took over its leadership on Blavatsky's death in 1891. In 1893 she moved to Adyar, near Madras, to work with the movement's other founder, Colonel Henry Olcott, which pitched her into a whole new world of controversies.

She became entranced with Hindu philosophy and practice, while Olcott preferred the more cerebral charms of Buddhism. The two then fell out over the future direction of Theosophy. She was also drawn into the political and social issues of colonial rule in India, and gradually made herself a figurehead for nationalist causes, especially the 'regeneration' of Hindu learning; one of her early achievements was helping to set up the Central Hindu College in Benares (1898).

Olcott died in 1907, and shortly afterwards the confluence of Hinduism and Theosophy was completed when Besant declared that a young boy she had found near Madras, Jiddu Krishnamurti, was the incarnated 'World Teacher' that Theosophy had prophesied. This 'revelation' formed part of a set of larger scandals and struggles within the world of Theosophy, during which the movement lost ground intellectually, and many converts personally.

These problems were followed by the last phase of Besant's long career of advocacy when she espoused the cause of Indian swaraj. She joined the Indian National Congress in 1913, and took over a newspaper, *New India*, as a platform for her views. In September 1916 she formed her own Home Rule League, designed to run in parallel with another League formed earlier that year in the west of the country by Tilak. Besant's League was rather looked down upon by Congress leaders, and she was derided as a crank by Raj officials and the British press. But she picked up public support very quickly, and soon her activities and her outspoken press articles so goaded the British authorities that they imprisoned her in June 1917.

She was released in August, as a conciliatory gesture after Secretary Montagu's statement, and her popularity soared. The shock of seeing a white-haired old woman thrown into jail rallied public support, and she was elected president of the 1917 session of Congress. She was thus the fifth, and last, European to serve as Congress president: the others were George Yule (1888), William Wedderburn (1889 and 1910), Alfred Webb (1894), and Sir Henry Cotton (1904).

This proved to be the pinnacle of her career, for she fell back rapidly afterwards through a series of misjudgements and disputes. Most importantly, she disliked the methods and outlook of the rising star in Congress politics, M.K. Gandhi. Then, having been fiercely critical of British policy throughout the First World War, especially over the crushing of the Easter Rising of 1916 in Dublin, she became more of a loyalist as the war drew to a close. This was largely a tactical decision, because she believed that the time for confrontation had passed, and cooperation was a more likely way to produce concessions.

But while Gandhi was prepared to look for swaraj outside the Empire, Besant wanted to stay in. Where she believed in verbal politics, he believed in direct mass action. The whole thrust of Congress strategy was changed forever at the Nagpur session of 1920, and Besant effectively retired from national politics after it.

She lived on for another thirteen years, mostly in retreat at Adyar. In 1928 she was invited onto the committee that drafted the Nehru Report on the constitutional future of India, but this was her last contribution. Jiddu Krishnamurti's rejection of his mission in 1929 ended Theosophy as a coherent force, and she withdrew from public life.

She was always seeking ways to improve and elevate the human condition, and this was, perhaps, the unifying theme in her life. Her legacy, however, was slight.

Britain emerged victorious from the First World War, with greatly increased territorial holdings in the Middle East, but by 1920 the imperial relationship with India had suffered a series of severe blows. Along with Indian outrage at the Amritsar Massacre and the financial disruption caused by the war, Britain had ended up fighting side by side with the United States to uphold the principle of democratic self-determination—effectively against the idea of empire. Despite its attempts at reform, British India came out of the war politically, economically and ideologically worse than it went in.

10

1921–1939

NON-COOPERATION, DYARCHY, SWARAJ, PRINCES

1921–9: Non-Cooperation, Dyarchy

Non-Cooperation began in earnest in early 1921 and it proved to be a real trial of strength. Mass demonstrations demanding swaraj were accompanied by bonfires of imported goods. The government seemed paralysed, but an opportunity for progress presented itself with the arrival of a new viceroy in April. Lord Reading (1921–6) met Gandhi in May and took a liking to him, but he was in no position to make concessions as the disorder intensified. Mohammed and Shaukat Ali, whose inflammatory speeches seemed to be courting arrest, were interned (again) in July, and in August a large-scale rebellion broke out among the Muslim Mappilas of Malabar.

But the government began to feel that this was a storm it could ride out, and repressive measures were enacted relating to assembly and even clothing. When the Prince of Wales arrived in Bombay in November 1921, serious riots erupted. Reading was keen to ensure a warmer welcome for the prince in Calcutta, which he was due to visit in December, and he proposed to his seniors in London that formal negotiations might ease the situation. But the reply from London was unequivocal—no negotiations, no concessions.

A wave of imprisonments followed in January 1922, which put 20,000 behind bars, among them prominent Congress figures including Motilal Nehru, his son Jawaharlal, C.R. Das, Maulana Azad and Lala Lajpat Rai. The viceroy, who was more liberal in his views than either the cabinet in London or many of his own officials, put out feelers about talks, but Gandhi's list of preconditions ended the initiative. After that there was nowhere for either side to go, and the whole episode was ended by Gandhi himself, after twenty-two policemen were burned to death on 4 February 1922 at Chauri Chaura, a small town in the United Provinces. The Mahatma was distraught over the loss of life, and a combination of guilt and political instinct led him to call off the campaign, to the frustration of many younger, hotter heads, including Jawaharlal Nehru.

Gandhi had enjoyed a kind of invulnerability after launching the protests; the government remained hesitant to touch a man who seemed to be a dangerous mixture of Bolshevik and religious icon. The approach of elections, promised under the 1919 reforms, had also protected him, with officials eager to appear conciliatory in order to minimize opposition. But now, having already jailed so many, and with Gandhi in actively penitent mood, the authorities struck hard. In March 1922 Gandhi was arrested and tried for spreading 'disaffection' through magazine articles. He was sentenced to six years in prison, after his admission that he had fully intended to spread disaffection against the government, because the government thoroughly deserved it.

But the Raj survived, and both sides learned lessons. Henceforth the British tried to pick out individuals and co-opt them into the inner workings of government, leaving Gandhi and his followers to march in the streets. Gandhi, meanwhile, was forced to accept that India's masses were not yet ready for his kind of insurgency. After his release, he decided to retreat and build up the awareness of India's peasant millions through 'constructive' work in the countryside. Almost unnoticed, India's moment of maximum unity slipped away.

With Non-Cooperation tamed, the Mont-ford scheme could at last be given a chance. The new package represented a considerable advance on 1909. A new Central Legislative Assembly was created, consisting of 146 members, 106 of them elected. Above it, as a revising chamber, was a Council of State of 60 members, two-thirds of whom were elected. This structure carried an appearance of executive 'responsibility', but the viceroy remained unchallenged at its apex, and still held powers to overrule decisions made lower down. The main innovation was dyarchy (double government) in the provinces, where Indian ministers were to be chosen from elected assemblies by provincial governors, and given responsibility for a list of transferred powers, including agriculture, education and health care. Governors would retain a list of reserved powers, which were the traditional governmental functions of law and order, finance, and taxation.

The new electorates were small—membership of the central upper chamber was determined by around 17,000 voters—and special constituencies were retained. Overall about five million people, 3 per cent of the population, had a vote. The chief political aim of the system was to make it difficult for any one community to dominate any of the assemblies. Coalition governments would be necessary, and the active maintenance of coalitions was meant to be a safeguard against communal interests. In addition, the representative bodies at the centre were restricted in size and authority, so that day-to-day Indian politics would be a provincial, administrative affair.

There were several other important changes at this time. London gave the Government of India an expanded degree of diplomatic autonomy, with its own representation at the Versailles peace conference, admission to the League of Nations as a separate entity, and the appointment of an Indian High Commissioner in London. These things provided only marginal scope for independent action, but all three of these 'promotions' put India on the same footing as the Empire's Dominions.

A Chamber of Princes was created as a national forum for the variegated body of autocrats who still ruled about a quarter of India's population. By 1919 it seemed grossly anomalous not to have these 565 'independent' heads of state included in India's national life, especially as Montagu's Declaration of 1917 had referred only to India, making no distinction between princely and British India.

But the new Chamber, of 120 members, had several crippling political limitations. Firstly, because the states were sovereign entities with no formal position within British India, the Chamber had to remain purely consultative. Secondly, the largest twenty or so states, which already had separate diplomatic relations with the British Crown, had no incentive to use this shared forum, and might even prejudice their interests by doing so. Lastly, the smallest 300 states had to share delegates, which muted their input. This left only the middling states with much willingness or scope to use the place for political expression, but even among these there were historical and personal rivalries, and a wide diversity in terms of history, geography, wealth, size and religion.

Nevertheless the creation of the Chamber marked the re-entry of the princes to India's national political life, and with increased political importance came increased protection from London. The Indian States (Protection Against Disaffection) Act was passed by Parliament in 1922, specifically to protect the princely states from mass protests.

Finally, an official position on paramountcy had to be defined for the first time. The British had always preferred to be vague on the issue, but in 1926 Reading established a clear line, in a letter to the Nizam of Hyderabad over a dispute about Berar, which had been sequestered by Dalhousie in 1853 for arrears of subsidy, and which the nizam wanted back. Reading asserted the widest possible interpretation of Crown sovereignty over the princes, in all matters both internal and external, regardless of the detail of the treaties that actually regulated the Raj's dealings with them.

The last significant change at this time was the grant of 'fiscal independence' to the Government of India. This was deemed a necessary part of the new arrangements, because by 1919 a very large portion of the government's revenue came from customs, and to deny it full control over decisions that materially affected its liquidity would have been self-defeating. It was also a logical part of the transfer of responsibility for industry to provincial level. The clearest expression of this new freedom was the creation of a Tariff Board. But the Board was purely advisory and, like so much of the new constitution, proved to be of limited value to Indian aspirations.

Renewed optimism in government circles ran along with these new arrangements, and a burst of constructive self-criticism resulted. The Meston Committee (1920) on government finance, the Ackworth Committee (1920) on railways, the Muddiman Committee (1924) on the new constitution, and the Skeen Committee (1926) on the military, all made suggestions towards improvements, including accelerated Indianization. This looked constructive, even conciliatory, but it was more of a throwback to the mentality of Curzon—that India needed improved administration and was best spared real politics. And the Indianization was small and slow; the Skeen Committee envisaged a half-Indian army by 1952.

As the committees busied themselves trying to find ways to run the Raj more efficiently, the older school of paternalistic defeatism lived on. In 1925 Arthur Hirtzel, a senior denizen of the India Office, whose service went back to the Morley–Minto reforms, wrote to Harcourt Butler: 'If only we could go on doing nothing for a little longer.'[1]

With fresh elections scheduled for 1923 and Gandhi in prison, the Congress, which had boycotted the elections held in November 1920, was left without his guidance in deciding whether to cooperate with the new system. Staying out in 1920 had left the way clear for the liberals to monopolize provincial and central office, but this had been Gandhi's preferred course of action.

Now a substantial body of Congress opinion, led by Motilal Nehru and C.R. Das, favoured 'Council entry', if only to wreck the system from within. The Congress session of December 1922 at Gaya saw a showdown between the two factions, with Gandhi's line promoted by C. Rajagopalachari and Dr M.A. Ansari. The Gandhian 'No Changers' won the day, obliging their opponents to break away and form the Swaraj Party. The Swarajists then did well at the 1923 elections, and with over forty seats in the Central Legislature became the largest party. In alliance with other groupings they were regularly able to muster a majority against government measures. However, the viceroy's power to overrule votes in the assembly meant that the original objective of paralysing the government was hardly attainable.

Another significant development was the arrival in 1924 of the first Labour government in Britain. With the long history of socialist opposition to the idea of empire, this might have been expected to produce fresh thinking. But the new administration lacked a parliamentary majority, and lasted less than ten months. Furthermore, Labour voters were not always anti-imperial, because working-class interests were often closely bound up with the smooth running of empire. A multiplicity of well-paid jobs relied on imperial trade; empire delivered a good standard of living and cheap food for working people in Britain. There was little prospect that the incoming government could change any of this, or would even want to try. This led to a disappointing performance on the part of the new Indian Secretary, Lord Olivier, one-time leading light of the Fabian Society in the 1880s. Now, like Morley, he blue-shifted to the cautious end of the spectrum.

The Mont-ford reforms left much of Indian opinion unrepresented in formal or effective ways, and the years 1923–31 saw the revival or creation of religious and caste-based political movements, with an accompanying increase in communal violence. The Muslim League, in virtual abeyance since the creation of the Khilafat Committee in 1919, was reconvened in 1924, while its mirror image, the Hindu Mahasabha, became a revitalized national organization, led by conservative Congress leaders such as M.M. Malaviya and Lala Lajpat Rai. More militant Hindu opinion was catered for by a semi-militaristic 'cultural' movement, the Rashtriya Swayamsevak Sangh (RSS), formed in 1925 by K.B. Hedgewar, a close associate of another Mahasabha luminary, B.S. Moonje.

The Communist Party of India was formed in 1925, and there was a resurgence of revolutionary terrorism through the 1920s, although it remained a dispersed phenomenon, lacking central leadership. A Communist revolution or mass nationalist uprising may not have been in the offing, but there were a number of violent acts, with the killing of several officials, and even an attack on the central assembly itself by Bhagat Singh in 1928, for which he was later hanged. Viceroy Irwin narrowly escaped a bomb in December 1929. This climate of unease led to the arrest and prosecution of over thirty Communists in the notorious Meerut Conspiracy Case, which lasted from 1929 to 1933. All the defendants were eventually acquitted for lack of evidence.

The Congress remained the dominant force in Indian politics, but it began the long march to national government only slowly. Gandhi was granted early release from prison on grounds of ill health in March 1924, then concentrated his energies on home spinning, the promotion of Hindu–Muslim unity, and attacks on the institution of untouchability. He left the Swarajists to their work, giving them his blessing at the Congress session of 1924, which he chaired. All the while he deliberately kept clear of central wrangling.

Meanwhile, Jinnah was displaying his undoubted gifts as a central wrangler. He and Motilal Nehru dominated the Legislative Assembly until the Swarajists withdrew in March 1926, having accepted that their position was untenable and their objectives unattainable—incidentally proving that Gandhi had been right all along.

Jinnah became convinced of the necessity to refashion the Hindu–Muslim unity which he had done so much to promote at the time of the Lucknow Pact. To do this he decided that the Muslims had to drop their insistence on separate electorates—which he had never personally supported anyway, and in March 1927 he put together his 'Delhi Proposals', in which he offered to abandon separate electorates if the Congress was prepared to concede a fixed share of seats in the central legislature, along with some administrative changes that would give Muslims more majority provinces. The Congress eventually rejected this offer, a reflection of the confident view among the leadership that Jinnah was an irrelevant former party member whose opinions were unrepresentative, and with whom it was not necessary to do business.

But in all these schemes and strategies, Indian politicians began to suspect that they were engaged in no more than shadow-boxing with the Raj. Power was available to them only in the provinces, and a great deal of political activity all over the subcontinent reflected this. It was not national parties that were making progress, it was narrow interest groups that prospered when they managed to organize themselves into local alliances. These included landholders in the Punjab who formed the Unionist Party, and some caste-based groupings, such as the anti-Brahmin Justice Party in Madras. The one pointer to something different was the satyagraha against increased land tax, in the district of Bardoli in Gujarat, launched in 1926 by one of Gandhi's most prominent disciples, Vallabhbhai Patel. Eventual success in 1928 gave the Gandhians considerable encouragement, and hinted to the Raj that the weapon wielded crudely in 1920–2 might have more refined and effective uses.

The fractured national politics of the 1920s may have been what the British had intended to produce, with Indians busily training themselves for self-government through the experience of petty power in the provinces. But it was a British initiative that re-energized Indian politics on a national basis, and on a specifically nationalist agenda. This they accomplished with the appointment of the Simon Commission in November 1927.

The 1919 package had provided for a review of the reforms after ten years, but the Conservatives, returned to power in 1924, decided to bring forward the date in order to prevent a possible future Labour administration from appointing a pro-Indian panel. The task of selecting suitable men fell to F.E. Smith, Lord Birkenhead, a brilliant lawyer and possibly the most reactionary, least sympathetic Indian Secretary there ever was. He appointed a seven-man parliamentary commission, under the chairmanship of a Liberal, Sir John Simon, but with a solid Conservative majority.

News of the Commission's make-up caused immediate outrage in India, where it was not the political colour of its members that caused offence so much as the colour of their skin. The 'all white' Simon Commission, including future Labour prime minister Clement Attlee, arrived in India in February 1928 to massive protests. The political nation refused to cooperate with it, apart from a small faction within the Muslim League, and Dr B.R. Ambedkar, the leader of the Untouchables, who had no faith that the established parties would stand up for the 'depressed classes'. Birkenhead then rashly challenged Indians to come up with their own proposals, trusting in true imperial style that divisions would emerge. In this he was to be disappointed.

Indian ranks closed in defiance, and an All-Parties Conference was convened in Delhi in February 1928. A committee, chaired by Motilal Nehru, drew up a draft constitution for India known as the Nehru Report, published in August. Its main recommendations were a bicameral parliamentary system based on universal adult franchise, an end to special electorates, a declaration of rights and, most importantly, Dominion status for India along the lines enjoyed by Canada. This completely cut the ground from under the Simon Commission, which still had years of work to do before it submitted its own report. It also opened a possible divide within the Congress, many of whose younger members, including Motilal's son, were insistent on immediate and complete independence—purna swaraj.

The Congress, the Muslim League and the All-Parties Conference each met in Calcutta that December to discuss the Nehru Report. The upshot was that the Congress turned it into an ultimatum to the British, declaring that it would accept Dominion status if the Report was adopted within one year, i.e. by December 1929. Were it not to be adopted, satyagraha would follow. This bought off the radicals, led by Jawaharlal Nehru and Subhas Chandra Bose. The All-Parties Conference was less clear-cut, with Jinnah leading the objections. But he failed to carry the vote, leaving him isolated and despondent.

With the Congress buoyant, the political future of British India seemed to be dimming. Some if its oldest hands were coming to the end of their service, and were being replaced by fresher British minds and an increasing number of Indians. One of the grandest who slipped away at this time was Harcourt Butler.

Sir Harcourt Butler (1869–1938) was a brilliant and highly regarded civil servant, whose influence can be detected in areas of policy covering famine, education and relations with the princely states. His thirty-nine years of service, from 1890 to 1929, covered a period of constant administrative and political change in British India, which at the time included Burma. His general outlook, dominated by caution and pessimism, is broadly comparable to that of Alfred Lyall, whose service in India ended in 1887, three years before his own began. Like Lyall he was also unhappy in his marriage.

His clarity of mind was exceptional, and he is worth quoting on several central topics. In 1908 he accurately summarized the 'divide and rule' strategy by simply stating: 'We must reward loyalty and make it pay'.[2] He was also very clear-eyed about the reform process. Speaking of the Viceroy's Executive Council in 1915 he wrote: 'We are solving things in a truly British way. We admit Indians to our councils and then relegate the councils to insignificance.'[3]

Butler came from a middle-class family and had a top-drawer education at Harrow School and Oxford. He successfully sat the Indian Civil Service

(ICS) entrance exams in 1888 and made his way out to India after a 'probationary' period at Balliol College.

His first prominent position was as Secretary to the MacDonnell Commission (on famine), and its final report in 1901, with its emphasis on 'moral strategy', was largely his work. He served as Deputy Commissioner of Lucknow district from 1906 to 1908, then as secretary to the Foreign Department till 1910. At this point he was given responsibility for the newly created Department of Education, and with it a seat on the Viceroy's Executive Council. This was, effectively, as high as an ICS careerist could hope to rise. He then set out proposals for reform in a resolution of 1913, under which the monopoly of India's five major universities was ended and provisions were made for the development of a new independent sector.

In 1915 he was made Lieutenant-Governor of Burma, where his interest in education led him to press for the creation of an autonomous university in Rangoon, thus ending the subordination of Burmese colleges to Calcutta University. In 1918 he returned to the United Provinces (formerly the North West Provinces) as Lieutenant-Governor, where he developed Lucknow as a cultural and educational centre, and is credited with calming agrarian discontents in the region by persuading the local taluqdars to accept tenancy reform. After the 1919 Government of India Act his position changed in both name and nature. He became a Governor and was required, under dyarchy, to work with a locally elected assembly.

There were rumours that he was to succeed Lord Chelmsford as viceroy in 1921, and had this come about, he would have been the only ICS man ever to ascend to the post. But Lord Reading was given the position instead, and Butler had to make do with being sent back to Rangoon in 1923 to oversee the introduction of dyarchy into Burma, which was running two years behind the rest of India in the reform schedule.

The next step was the one that left his name in Indian history. In 1927 he became chairman of a commission of inquiry into the relations between the Government of India and the princely states. The Butler Commission reported in March 1929 and largely confirmed the existing position, as defined by Lord Reading in 1926. Butler found that 'paramountcy' was beyond judicial definition and did not depend on treaties. 'Paramountcy must remain paramountcy,' he declared, which also meant that it could not be transferred from the Crown to a future self-governing Indian dominion. This further made it necessary to recognize the existence of 'two Indias', which was the only piece of good news for the princes.[4]

The report was Butler's swansong. He retired in 1929 to accept the chairmanship of the newly established School of Oriental and African Studies in London.

Through the transit from autocracy to dyarchy, his attitudes hardly changed at all. In 1891 he wrote to his father that all that was required of the British in India was to dispense 'paternal government, stern, kind, just'.[5] He remained convinced of certain high imperial ideas, which he set out in a short book entitled *India Insistent*, written in 1931.

The book is worth quoting at some length, for its succinct phrase-making and its articulate exposition of what had become the 'official mind' of British India's senior servants. Most prominent were clear views about the role of government. 'India requires a steady progressive policy', he wrote, 'but, even more, a firm and efficient administration.'[6] It is noteworthy that he believed government in the twentieth century could be separated from policy. He believed this for a reason. 'The educated few are crying for self-government. The masses of the people want good government ... In our enthusiasm for goals we have almost forgotten to govern.'[7] This is the purest paternalism, and ran wilfully counter to the dictum of Liberal leader Henry Campbell-Bannerman, that 'good government is no substitute for self-government'.

Butler's unchanging view was that 'the people' wanted an unbiased, benign government that existed above their daily struggles. The British as rulers were not to take sides within Indian society. While governments elsewhere were very much taking sides—the US government was about to drag its people out of recession—government in India was supposed to shy away from too much 'policy'. Butler was clear: 'Of late the administration has unquestionably been subordinated to policy and the results have not been good.'[8] Indians, so he thought, did not want to be bothered with politics. 'The politically-minded portion of the population is so small,'[9] he wrote. For a 'rough perspective' on this, Butler pointed out that whereas about thirty-five million Indians had dealings with the courts every year, only about eight million could vote, and half of those didn't bother. This set the 'relative importance of administration and politics'[10] to the Indian people at a ratio of 35:4.

Overall, his experience had given 'a deep impression of the conservatism of India and the need for caution in political advance on western lines'.[11] And there were two background factors: 'The government is immeasurably strong if only it will show its strength',[12] and 'British peace has brought countless blessings to India and a prosperity which she had never before enjoyed'.[13] The argument was complete, but two main points had to be spelled out: '(1) the British cannot go and, (2) India, without the help of the British, cannot at present administer or protect the country'.[14]

Butler simply would not allow that change had occurred. The British had altered their policy—this he saw, and regretted—but Indians were still the same. All that was required was firmness of purpose, the preservation of order, and the prompt administration of justice, without fear or favour. At its heart, this attitude had a great deal in common with the views of Warren Hastings, Ellenborough or Frere. Apparently the myth of the 'unchanging East' had finally convinced the British of its reality, just as the Indians had determined that the East was, finally, about to change.

1929–39: Swaraj, Dominion Status, Princes

1929 offered new possibilities with the advent of another minority Labour government in Britain, led by Ramsay MacDonald, and as the year drew to a close, a rather vague offer came from London, through Viceroy Irwin (1926–31), to open talks about Dominion status. This was in line with the hope expressed by MacDonald the year before, while still leader of the Opposition, that soon 'a new dominion' would be added to the Commonwealth, by which he meant India.[15]

Irwin, who was a Tory appointed by the previous Conservative government, set up a series of meetings through November and December 1929 with a wide selection of Indian leaders in an attempt to broker a deal and head off another national resistance movement. But no agreement was forthcoming, and as the Congress met at Lahore in late December 1929 under the presidency of Jawaharlal Nehru, it was clear that rebellion was imminent. Jawaharlal himself raised the Congress flag in defiance on 31 December, declaring India to be, at last, independent. But the truth remained somewhat different.

Unruffled, the British waited for the report of the Simon Commission, which arrived in mid-June 1930. It avoided any mention of Dominion status, but recommended the granting of full provincial self-government, the creation of a federal structure including the princes, and the retention, for the time being, of separate electorates. These proposals were to be debated at a Round Table Conference in London, to which all interested parties were invited.

Congress meanwhile was waiting for Gandhi to launch the promised satyagraha. Finally, he decided to begin a new round of civil disobedience taking the salt tax, which had been increased under Lord Reading, as his main focus. Salt had long been a government monopoly in India, which the British thought was an important guarantee of the quality of a basic essential. The lack of contraband salt within the economy convinced officials that the tax was affordable. But that a substance so naturally abundant could be taxed struck Gandhi as unjust, so in March 1930 he set off from his ashram to walk to the sea, where he intended to break the law and make salt for himself. The journey soon became an international media circus as journalists and newsreel crews came from all over the world to watch how this new challenge to the Raj would be met.

The British held back for some time, reluctant to provoke widespread insurrection, but a month after Gandhi publicly boiled seawater on 6 April, he was arrested and imprisoned. Thousands more followed him into jail, and a large-scale protest at the government salt works at Dharasana ended in fatalities that were reported around the globe. Congress leaders refused to attend the Round Table Conference, which went ahead without them in late 1930.

It was soon completely apparent that no serious progress could be made without a Congress presence at the table, so Irwin sent intermediaries to Gandhi, and personal negotiations were opened in late January 1931. After three weeks of talks the Gandhi–Irwin Pact was agreed. Its main terms were a release of all political prisoners in return for an end to civil disobedience, and Congress attendance in London. Other provisions included the right for coastal dwellers to make salt for their own use, and for Congress supporters peacefully to picket shops selling British goods or liquor.

Some considered this a poor deal, believing that Irwin had got what he wanted—Congress compliance—and Gandhi had not made progress on any of the main Congress demands about swaraj, military cutbacks, taxation and so forth. Gandhi considered it a triumph that he had been treated as an equal; Winston Churchill found this idea 'nauseating'.

Having promised to go to London, Gandhi decided to travel as the sole Congress delegate. This gesture was intended to make a statement about Indian unity, but it also meant that he was overburdened with detail, which was never his strong point. This second session of the Conference lasted four months, from September to December 1931, and was no more productive than the first. Gandhi returned to India in January 1932, whereupon the civil disobedience campaign restarted. The new viceroy, Lord Willingdon (1931–6), clamped down hard on dissent, outlawing the

Congress and returning Gandhi to confinement, where he was joined by about 60,000 others.

Along with possible federal structures, one of the main issues at the Conference had been how to safeguard minority interests within the make-up of a national Indian assembly, and the deadlock was only resolved in August 1932 by executive order of Prime Minister MacDonald—known as the Communal Award, which laid down the exact proportions of minority representation. The Award's provision of separate electorates for the Untouchable community distressed Gandhi, who fervently believed that Untouchables had to be treated as Hindus and not as a separate community with its own interests. He wrote to MacDonald personally. The prime minister replied that he would only be able to change the Award in line with agreements reached voluntarily between Indian parties.

In view of this, Gandhi tried to open negotiations with Bhimrao Ambedkar, but was rebuffed. He therefore resorted to a fast, which ran in parallel with negotiations, undertaken within the Yerawada prison at Poona. A 'pact' was eventually agreed, which doubled representation of Untouchables and deferred a decision on the exact duration of separate electorates. Gandhi then broke his fast, which had brought him close to death.

Travel, work, imprisonment and fasting drained Gandhi's energy. There was also open criticism of his leadership and methods within the Congress from younger leftists, notably Subhas Chandra Bose. The formation of the Congress Socialist Party in 1934 was the result, although this was not so much a party as a lobbying group, intended to steer the Congress towards more socialist goals.

All this was too much for the Mahatma and he announced at the Bombay session of 1934 that he was giving up his membership of the party. He could not exactly resign because he held no official position, nor could he completely detach himself because his enormous moral authority meant that he was always a factor in Congress politics; meetings of the national leadership, the Congress Working Committee, continued to be held at his ashram near Wardha in central India.

Gandhi's political mantle passed unofficially to Jawaharlal Nehru, a quite different character with distinctly different political aims. Nehru was a believer in non-violence, but he wished to create a more explicitly socialist India, and his personal motivation was secular and materialistic as opposed to Gandhi's, which was essentially spiritual and idealistic. Congress under Nehru's guidance became a more conventional body, but it took another decade before Gandhi's influence was finally diminished to the point that his former lieutenants felt they could set aside his advice.

In 1935, after an eight-year period of consultation, the Government of India Act was passed in Westminster. The process had been started by the reactionary Birkenhead and was seen through by the almost equally neophobic Samuel Hoare. Unsurprisingly then, the Act that emerged was anything but radical.

The principal advance over the 1919 structure was the granting of provincial autonomy. Dyarchy and reserved powers were abandoned, and provincial ministries, under a premier appointed by the Governor, were made fully responsible to local assemblies, elected on an extended franchise, which now took in about ten per cent of the population. British India was divided into eleven Governor's provinces, and Burma and Aden were separated. The central assembly, of 375 seats, was now to contain representatives of the Native States; over one-third of the seats were allocated to the princes for them to fill either by nomination or election, as they saw fit. However, the system retained wide-ranging powers of veto for the viceroy and provincial governors. Rather in line with the previous two reforms, executive power remained revocable by senior officials, all of whom remained British, and none of whom were elected.

Dominion status was not granted, so the national bodies at the centre of Indian politics were not yet truly sovereign. Lines of accountability still led back to British ministers in Whitehall, not to Indian citizens or voters.

So what happened to Dominion status? It had little chance of surviving the London Conferences and the scrutiny of Parliament, for three main reasons.

Despite the retention of Ramsay MacDonald as premier, the National Government, installed in 1931, was dominated by Conservatives, meaning that sympathetic Labour politicians lost control of the negotiations. Next, the Conferences were attended by Raj officials opposed to radical change, who managed to convince the London politicians that their expert opinion should be respected.

Those politicians were all too ready to believe this, because Dominion status implied a series of political, constitutional and financial dangers. Britain was struggling with a global financial crisis at the time, and any kind of quasi-independence for India represented a potential credit risk, as India had no central reserve bank. One was duly set up in 1935, but this was a first step that London was not prepared to take simultaneously with the granting of greater autonomy. Lastly, there was a procedural issue.

British politicians wanted Indians to settle 'the communal question' among themselves before responsible government was conceded, and they failed to do so. This was a problem that was not about to go away.

The Act was thus a small step towards self-government rather than a leap into new territory. In a broadcast of 1 January 1935, Sir Samuel Hoare justified its temper, pulling out all the old arguments for 'prudent progress' and 'safeguards', explaining that provincial autonomy had to come before federation, that federation had to be an All-India federation including the princes, and that the whole edifice had to hang on 'responsibility with safeguards' at the centre, because the princes would 'not enter a federation controlled by Whitehall'.[16] This would have been a good argument, had 'responsibility' actually been granted in any real measure. But one element of the safeguards did appear, in the list of Scheduled Castes and Tribes attached to the Act, which later passed into the structure of independent India.

The reformed Indian state that emerged in 1935 was in some ways an even more egregious example of executive autocracy than before. The viceroy remained supreme, while below him a very thin layer of governors and senior civil servants ran the country. The nervousness that this represented slowly drove government into a smaller and smaller corner of Indian life, becoming more a matter of caretaking than leadership. The inability of the Raj to consult the people even-handedly proved a weakness at least as crippling as its related inability to tax the people equitably. The late Raj spent very little on public works, and what it did spend represented a fraction of what it spent on the military.

But a new level of Indian involvement had begun, and the first step towards this was the holding of elections in 1937.

Two principal parties contested the polls on a national basis, the Congress and the revived Muslim League, under the leadership of Jinnah, returned from semi-exile in London. The arrival of its master tactician did the League little good in the short term, and the Congress romped home in five provinces out of eleven, formed governments in seven, and eventually secured an eighth ministry in Assam. The Muslim League won no provinces outright, and it was only after several months that it was able to join a coalition government in Bengal.

As a foretaste of the new Indian politics, this was a little misleading, for the years 1937–9 saw a truly remarkable rise in support for the Muslim League. Jinnah completely reorganized the party, closely copying the Congress's constitution and regional organization. He also made a series of speeches warning that Islam was in danger, that 'Hindu raj' was coming, that Congress 'atrocities' were being committed against Muslims all over the country, and that Muslims could hope for nothing unless the League became the sole organ of Muslim opinion. Jinnah also made overtures to the viceroy, offering cooperation against the Congress ministries that represented a potential opposition bloc to the regime they were nominally serving.

Meanwhile demands for some kind of Muslim homeland gradually took on more definite shape and began to gather support. The first proposal had come in 1930 from the poet Mohammed Iqbal, but by the late 1930s a number of Muslim academics and political scientists were providing schemes for types of regional autonomy. By late 1939, Jinnah was working on his own scheme, an expression of an idea he was beginning to press hard—that India's Muslims were not a minority or a faith group or a community, but a 'nation', equal with other nations of the world, and entitled not to concessions as a minority, but to full statehood and a 'national home'.

Thus neither of the two main national bodies within Indian electoral politics was truly committed to its maintenance. The princes were hardly any keener. The new constitution of 1935 could only come fully into force when two-thirds of the princely states, by population, had signed up to the federal plan. The British tried hard to bring this about, but the princes, ever a disparate bunch, could not agree among themselves as to their best interests; after all, the possession of autocratic power is not a good entry point to common purposes. Among all the talented and honest men, drunkards, rogues and idlers, none of them felt they stood to gain much by joining a federal Indian state.

The dominant emotion among the princes was fear—fear that they would be bound into a sovereign India ruled by a Congress party sworn to the destruction of their rights and privileges. In the end, the princes never agreed to enter the 1935 system, and the new central assembly was therefore never inaugurated. Finally, with the outbreak of war in 1939, the attempt to integrate the Native States was indefinitely postponed.

Even the Congress had difficulty getting its lines straight. It decided in 1937, under Gandhi's direction, not to interfere with political agitation within Native States. But with an upsurge of popular unrest across princely India in 1938, Gandhi changed his mind and declared that Congress members should assist protestors in seeking democratic concessions. He explained his change of mind by maintaining that though it was unwise to rouse populations that had not stirred themselves, if people expressed a desire to be liberated then the Congress should help them. But by 1939 the whole topic was closed again when Gandhi, who had pressed the Raja of Rajkot into an agreement to set up representative government, decided to force him no further. Newly strengthened, the princes now felt able to ignore pressure to reform.

By this point the Congress leadership was in turmoil after the election of Subhas Chandra Bose as president in 1938. His victory was taken, principally by Bose himself, as proof that Gandhi's star was in decline, and that the Congress could now switch to his personal programme of revolutionary change. He set no store by non-violence and his ideals were pitched a good deal to the left of Gandhi's. His plans also included a large amount of leadership from himself.

This autocratic temperament alienated virtually the whole Congress high command, and when he forced himself into the presidency again the next year, the Working Committee revolted. Bose, bitter and broken in health, complained that the 'Rightists' had conspired to bring him down. This was true, but Bose, who seems to have had a talent for misreading situations, seriously overestimated the strength of his support—a significant miscalculation, for it led him to resign in order to create his own faction, the Forward Bloc, modelled on the kind of revolutionary national socialism fashionable across much of Europe at the time. His persistent and intemperate opposition to the British then led to his arrest in 1940, followed by his escape and subsequent flight overseas, to seek help against the British from the Axis powers.

Thus by 1939 there were at least four distinct species of Indian nationalism on offer, aside from Jinnah's own Muslim version. There was Gandhi's religious-conservative, socially radical version, Nehru's socialist democratic version, Bose's socialist authoritarianism, and the militant, culturally exclusive Hindu vision of Savarkar, Golwalkar and the RSS. Progress in constitutional terms had stalled, and it was not clear from where the energy or the consensus would come to resolve the status of India as a nation and a society.

Inevitably, it was the international dimension that dominated the course of Indian politics over the next six years, for war with Germany was clearly coming from 1938 onwards. In early September 1939 Viceroy Linlithgow (1936–43) summoned Gandhi and Jinnah to Simla for discussions, but only after he had already declared that India was at war. His omission of even a courtesy consultation before this announcement deeply wounded India's political classes. Linlithgow was not beyond his authority in doing what he did, but as with many events in the later Raj years, the insensitivity of the act served only to emphasize the subaltern nature of India within the Empire, a fact that at other times Raj officials took some pains to disguise.

Willy-nilly, India was at war before the viceroy asked the leaders what they intended to do. All gave some degree of support, even Gandhi, who was particularly torn. He had no love of fascism, but as a non-violent advocate of swaraj, he was reluctant to go to war to defend imperial rule in India.

The Congress faced a profound clash of political interests; it was running eight out of eleven provinces, yet its members could not in conscience support an alien regime which had shown precious little consideration for their wishes concerning the most important decision any country can make, namely, to go to war. Many in the party hated the whole 1935 scheme; Nehru had called it a 'charter of slavery' because it yielded so little real control of areas such as finance and foreign policy.

Congress now asked the viceroy for a clear statement of war aims before the party's support could be pledged. Assurances about swaraj were asked for, but not given, and the party decided to withdraw from government. Mass resignations followed in all eight provinces. Jinnah then declared 22 December 1939 to be a day of national jubilation, of 'deliverance' for all India's Muslims.

Though still half a world away, the war's immediate political effect was to split India three ways, into an imperial executive, a nationalist government in waiting, and a separatist opposition to it. The next eight years were to extend all these lines of policy to a point of irreconcilable conflict.

11

1939–1947

WORLD WAR, DETENTION, MEDIATION, PARTITION

1939–45: World War, Detention, Famine

The Second World War froze British India politically for nearly six years. While high levels of anxiety and uncertainty persisted, future arrangements could not sensibly be discussed. Nor were concessions going to be made to Indian nationalists with two die-hard imperialists in the War Cabinet: Winston Churchill as prime minister after May 1940, and Leo Amery as Secretary for India throughout. Churchill remained convinced right up to Independence that the Congress was unrepresentative, led by a small, self-interested clique. His contempt for the Hindu elite joined easily with his conviction that the majority of ordinary Indians were Empire loyalists, as demonstrated by the two million or so who came forward for military service, eventually constituting the largest volunteer force in history.

Jinnah took what advantage he could from the estrangement between government and the Congress. In March 1940, at Lahore, he demanded autonomous regional states for Muslims in the north-west and north-east of the country. Viceroy Linlithgow simply held his ground, making a formal statement in August 1940 that no alterations would be made to the government of India during the war, and that any changes made afterwards would not be implemented without the active consent of all parties. This was taken by Jinnah as recognition of an effective Muslim veto over future arrangements. From then on, his strategy was to wait for the end of the war while building up Muslim solidarity through regional organization.

Congress leaders remained undecided as to what degree of pressure to exert on the British. Gandhi was morally opposed to the exploitation of an opponent's distress, yet he had no wish to see the Axis powers triumphant. However, the situation demanded some sort of action because India was more than ever unfree, fighting a war she had not declared for herself and from which she stood to gain nothing. His solution was to launch a campaign of individual satyagraha in September 1940. It landed about 20,000 Congress supporters in prison, including Jawaharlal Nehru yet again.

The first major change in the situation was the entry of Japan into the war in December 1941, leading to the fall of Singapore in February 1942 and the rapid advance of the Japanese army into Burma. The Labour minority in the War Cabinet, led by Clement Attlee, persuaded Churchill that a gesture was necessary to shore up the Government of India. Stafford Cripps was sent out to make an 'offer', in the hope of assuring India's continued loyalty and galvanizing the war effort. Churchill felt there was no need to make concessions and Cripps was not mandated to negotiate, but the prime minister was willing to give the Labour group enough rope with which to hang itself. As Cripps flew east, Churchill, Amery and Linlithgow were all hoping he would fail.

Their wishes duly came true. On arrival Cripps made a formal statement that India would be granted self-government at the end of the war, but after that he seems either to have misunderstood his brief or to have overstepped it. Maulana Azad, the Congress president, came away from his first meeting with Cripps believing that the Congress was being offered an immediate share in government on a cabinet model, under the viceroy as a kind of constitutional monarch. This was not what Churchill had authorized. Confusion and much offence resulted.

At Amery's insistence, Cripps offered an 'opt-out' clause for any province(s) that did not wish to remain in a post-war Indian union. This was included as a sop to Muslim opinion, and it alarmed the Congress. Deadlock ensued. The British were not offering a full and immediate role in government, while the Congress would accept nothing less, and wanted an Indian minister of war. There was simply not enough on the table for them, and it was reported that Gandhi had likened the promise of self-government after the war to 'accepting a post-dated cheque from a failing bank'. Jinnah was initially attracted by the opt-out clause, which seemed to open the door to Pakistan, but it also opened up the possibility of multiple secessions and thus weakened his hand as a leader. In the end he too rejected the package. Cripps returned home empty-handed, and the Congress was left with no alternative but to withdraw cooperation from the war effort.

Gandhi now planned a new mass action—the Quit India campaign—and had only just carried a resolution supporting the idea in the Congress Working Committee when, in the early hours of 9 August 1942, the entire Congress leadership was interned, and the party was banned. Massive disorder broke out with strikes, riots and sabotage all over the country. Around 1,000 fatalities resulted, but the movement failed to dislodge the Raj.

The insurgency of that summer was compared by British officials to the events of 1857, and it was certainly the most widespread and violent challenge to British rule since that time. And it too failed, for roughly similar reasons.

Again the objective was clear enough—the expulsion of alien rulers—but the movement had several familiar weaknesses: lack of resources, and an absence of central leadership. This time there were no mutinous sepoys to do the heavy fighting, so the best form of attack would have been to use organized labour to paralyse industry. But wartime circumstances had split the Indian left, with the official Communists backing the war effort as part of the Soviet struggle against fascism, after the German invasion of Russia in 1941. Moreover, it was not entirely obvious that the best hope of a brighter, socialist tomorrow was to bring down the Raj only to let in the Japanese. And with most of the senior Congress leaders interned, the movement could only hope for a guerrilla-style disruption of government, not a head-on confrontation.

In the end the hard Linlithgow–Churchill line proved well judged. The Congress was faced down and India, still unfree, continued to fight Britain's war.

It might be appropriate here to explain Gandhi's views on swaraj and the continued presence of armed forces in the country. He was not listened to properly at the time, or much since, and it is not uncommon for conspiracy theorists looking for the roots of Pakistan to use Gandhi's alleged views on the subject as the prime reason for why the British felt the need to create a separate state as a proxy military base. Gandhi was in fact very cautious on this subject, and bent over backwards to be both clear and conciliatory.

He asked himself the relevant question in his magazine *Harijan* in June 1942. 'Q. Do you see a situation when after full independence is granted American and Allied troops can operate from India? A. I do.'[1] His point was always that this had to be by agreement—a not unreasonable condition for a sovereign power. Three weeks later the All India Congress

Committee passed a resolution stating: 'Nor does the Congress intend to jeopardize the defensive capacity of the Allied powers. The Congress is, therefore, agreeable to the stationing of the armed forces of the Allies in India, should they so desire, in order to ward off and resist Japanese or other aggression and to protect and help China.'[2] The only rider was that this had to be at the Allies' expense; again, hardly unreasonable. Finally, from prison the next year, Gandhi wrote to the viceroy to avoid all misunderstanding: 'The Allied troops would remain under terms agreed to between the Allied powers and the free India government.'[3] This position, like the previous two, was dismissed by the British not as unreasonable, but as irrelevant.

The year 1943 was a grim one for India. The Japanese continued to advance through Burma, while the Quit India campaign dragged on. In February Gandhi undertook a fast to protest against the accusation that he had sponsored or encouraged the violence. Linlithgow was prepared, with Churchill's approval, to let the old man die, but he survived his twenty-one-day ordeal. In July, an attempt was made on Jinnah's life by a Muslim extremist. Famine then came to Bengal, carrying off up to three million people. This was not the result of crop failure, but of a series of man-made circumstances. Requisitioning and hoarding drove up food prices, and incompetent and corrupt relief measures failed to ease the distress. Lord Wavell replaced Linlithgow as viceroy in October, and took vigorous measures to supply Bengal, rather to the annoyance of Churchill, who considered his actions as unhelpful to the war effort.

There was some improvement in 1944, and the tide of war turned against the Axis all over the world. Gandhi was released on medical grounds and had extensive talks with Jinnah in Bombay that September. The two cautiously explored each other's position, with Jinnah constantly one step ahead, forcing Gandhi to suggest more and more elaborate concessions to Muslim concerns. But Jinnah was not very serious; he was waiting for the end of the war, because he had no wish to settle directly and immediately with a Congress party that he was not convinced would deliver on its promises. He wanted to let the British enforce any agreement that he might make about Muslim regional autonomy. Gandhi could thus assure him of nothing he wanted to hear, and the two men parted, after seventeen days of talks, with no agreement.

Jinnah and Gandhi dominated Indian politics all through the war, which was not especially conducive to progress, because both were pursuing fairly limited 'one shot' strategies. Jinnah wanted Pakistan to be conceded in principle before any further details were discussed, and Gandhi adopted a similar approach in his demand for swaraj. The British had conceded independence in principle in 1929, and then again in 1942, but Gandhi had rejected both offers because the grant was neither immediate nor complete. The Cripps offer was not acceptable to Jinnah either, because its constitutional content was to be determined by a constituent assembly in which Muslims were guaranteed to be in a minority.

A more flexible British approach emerged after the war, mostly thanks to Wavell. Churchill disliked Wavell's liberal political views, and always thought of him as a stopgap viceroy for the duration of the war. With victory over Germany in sight, Churchill recalled Wavell for consultations in London that stretched across April and May 1945, though he did not greatly like what he heard; Wavell was determined to initiate a process of full consultation with Indian leaders.

But Churchill's hands were tied. With a war still to win in the East, this was no time to be replacing a viceroy. Nor was the domestic timing good. With the war in Europe over, the War Cabinet was due to stand down and fresh elections were imminent; such an important appointment should properly be left to the winning party. Victory was declared on 8 May 1945, the War Cabinet was dissolved on 23 May, with the polls set for 25 July. Wavell went back to India in early June, still in post.

On his return, he released the Congress leaders from prison as a prelude to assembling a conference at Simla, which began on 25 June. After three weeks of talking, no progress had been made because Jinnah insisted that the Congress could not nominate any Muslim to the projected Interim Government. The Congress, not unreasonably, responded that it was not up to Jinnah to dictate who could be in their party, which was open to all. Jinnah would not budge, because he absolutely had to have an exclusive right to speak for India's Muslims. If he did not, then he would be nothing more than the leader of a faction, not a 'nation'. The Congress, similarly, could not concede that it did not, within itself, represent the entire Indian nation.

This deadlock was a blow to Wavell, and there is a hint in V.P. Menon's *Transfer of Power* that Jinnah was encouraged in his obduracy by clandestine support from high up within the British establishment—from unnamed parties who wanted to play for time until a Conservative government could be elected with a full mandate. And Menon was right. Three members of the cabinet were opposed to the whole proceeding—Lord Simon (of the Commission), Sir P.J. Grigg and R.A. Butler—with Churchill in sympathy.[4]

But for all his unhappiness, Churchill never had the chance either to replace Wavell or to shape the demission process. In the general election that July, the first in Britain since 1935, the Labour Party, led by Clement Attlee, won a landslide majority. Churchill was dumped unceremoniously out of office in the hour of his triumph.

The long life of Winston Churchill (1874–1965) spanned the height of empire and its demise. As a young man he fought for the Queen-Empress in India, almost playing at war in a world of ripping yarns and unquestioned white superiority. He loved, and mourned, this world till the day he died, and during the Second World War he came to represent some of its best qualities, at least in its ideals of leadership, duty and patient endurance. But by 1945, when the voters of Britain turfed him out of office, he had become a romantic throwback to a faded imperial past.

He was born in the largest private house in England, Blenheim Palace near Oxford, ancestral home of the Dukes of Marlborough. His father, Lord Randolph Churchill, was third son of the seventh Duke of Marlborough and a prominent Conservative politician, who served as Secretary of State for India (1885–6), and narrowly missed becoming viceroy in 1888. His mother Jennie was American, a heritage that nurtured Winston's lifelong personal and political attachment to the United States.

Winston was, by popular legend, a dunce as a child, but he did well in subjects that interested him. This excluded mathematics, an unpromising beginning for a man who was later to serve as Chancellor of the Exchequer for five years. Winston himself often played up this alleged backwardness, telling a story that when he sat his entrance paper for Harrow School, he found himself unable to answer any questions, apart from filling in the space for his own name. He stared at the blank paper for a long time, then proceeded carefully to place a full stop after 'Churchill'. This would not seem to predestine any pupil for the Nobel Prize in Literature, which he won in 1953, but his backwardness was always a selective affair. He was bright and vigorous, but not intellectual; at the Royal Military College at Sandhurst he excelled in rifle shooting, fencing and horse riding.

Having secured a commission in the 4th Queen's Own Hussars in February 1895, he embarked for India and saw action on the North West Frontier over the next two years. His experiences were chronicled in a series of reports for the *Daily Telegraph*, and were eventually compiled as a book, *The Story of the Malakand Field Force* (1898). These early years showed his personal courage and hinted at his literary ability. They also saw his attitudes to India crystallize: he always thought of the British power as a protective and benign entity, and that Indians were happiest when under European leadership, which he viewed as their best protection from corruption and internecine strife. He also developed a lifelong prejudice against Indian landlords.

But he had no interest in a career either as a soldier or a journalist. It was politics that enthralled him, and after returning from service in the Boer War, he spent the rest of his years at the highest levels of British political life.

His career was a complicated affair, involving several changes of allegiance. In 1900 he was elected MP for Oldham in Lancashire as a Conservative, but in the 1906 election he stood for Manchester North West as a Liberal. He then held a clutch of senior positions—at the Colonial Office, the Board of Trade, the Home Office, and the Admiralty; during the First World War he moved on to become Minister of Munitions, then Secretary of State for War. He rejoined the Conservatives in 1924, and was made Chancellor of the Exchequer, a post he held till 1929, over four and a half years longer than his father had managed in 1888. Winston's time at the Exchequer is notable for the decision he made to put sterling back onto the gold standard, at the high valuation of $4.86. This, and his Gallipoli Campaign of 1915–16, are generally remembered as his two most serious mistakes in office.

Drifting between parties may seem to betray a man without principles, but in general he maintained what might be called a right-wing liberal stance, in favour of free trade and balanced budgets, imperialist but with a touch of social conscience.

After the installation of the second Labour government in 1929, he was bitterly critical of Ramsay MacDonald's Indian policy. He opposed the whole reform process set off by the London Conferences of 1930–2, and helped to form the Indian Defence League, an unashamedly imperialist body dedicated to protecting India—from Indians. He piled scorn on the Congress and Gandhi in particular. His famous description of him as a 'seditious Middle Temple lawyer' may have been prejudiced and uncharitable, but it was also wrong. It was the Inner Temple that Gandhi had attended, from 1888 to 1891.

At around this time Churchill was invited by former Viceroy Irwin to meet some Indian leaders who were in London, as an opportunity to update his views on Indian affairs. Hugh Dalton, a prominent Labour politician, records in his diary that Churchill replied: 'I am quite satisfied with my views on India. I don't want them disturbed by any bloody Indians.'[5]

He expressed those views very forcefully in the debates on the Government of India Bill. In late December 1934 he chided the Commons: 'A lot of this talk about liberty for India only means liberty for one set of Indians to exploit another.'[6] The possibility that Indians were already exploiting each other under British rule did not seem to occur to him. He also declared: 'There is no real, practical unity in India apart from British rule. Endeavour as you may to diminish British control and influence and Indianize the services of Government, to that very extent, step by step, you will see the unity of India decline.'[7] Even Sir Samuel Hoare was more optimistic than that, and the bill, the longest ever passed by Parliament, made it safely to the statute book.

The outbreak of war in 1939 brought Churchill back into the cabinet as First Lord of the Admiralty, and he became prime minister on 10 May 1940, as the political establishment sought stronger leadership than Neville Chamberlain could provide. While many around him were willing to make peace, Churchill was determined to fight on against Nazi Germany despite Britain's apparently hopeless position. But even with Churchill in charge, the situation deteriorated for a year or so before any light appeared on the horizon.

Meanwhile the country endured the retreat from Dunkirk, the sinking of capital ships *Hood* in the Atlantic and *Prince of Wales* and *Repulse* in the Far East, and, worst of all, the fall of Singapore. But Churchill held firm, and eventually, with both Russia and the United States in the war, Germany was invaded from both west and east, and forced to capitulate. The British electorate then dispensed with Churchill's services in July 1945.

He took this as a terrible blow, but it did spare him the pain of granting India her independence. Having personally defended British India as a young man, he was never able to free himself from a romantic attachment to the country. Even as late as 1944 he was still musing about 'peasant uplift' and rolling back the power of wicked landlords, if necessary by a Soviet-style collectivization of farms.

This demonstrates two typical aspects of Churchill's genius: the fertility of his imagination and his inability to tell the difference between his good ideas and his bad. To dream a way to victory among the disasters of 1940, to confront the daunting task of regrouping the British forces, to secure the vital recruitment of America into the war, to liaise with Stalin—all this took a determined and fecund mind. But throughout he was afflicted by moments of indiscipline or wilfulness, a consistent characteristic of his school days, frequently noted in his reports.

It was a piece of good fortune for India that in 1945 the electorate in Britain had its doubts about Churchill as a peacetime leader: the process of demission, difficult as it was, could only have been harder under the direction of a man who sincerely believed that the Anglo-Indian connection, as it then stood, was the bedrock of the welfare of both nations.

By the time Churchill was prime minister again, from 1951 to 1955, the Indian issue was long resolved.

1945–7: Mediation, Partition

Attlee's election victory marked a decisive turn in India's history, as the Labour Party came into office unambiguously committed to granting India her independence.

However, even the most progressive Labour politicians were unable to escape the reality that the British were rapidly losing their power to pressure the main Indian parties, which could not agree on central issues. Though earlier generations of British officials may have been all too willing to exaggerate divisions among Indians, disputes over the precise shape of an independent India were by now very real. All that any British politician could hope to do was broker an agreement.

It must be emphasized that Attlee, while determined to grant Indian independence, was not dogmatic about how this should be done. He was not convinced about the Congress Party's claims to represent the entirety of the nation, and like so many other British leaders he proved much more cautious in executive authority than might have been expected.

The first step was to ascertain India's national post-war mood, and elections were scheduled for the winter of 1945. These turned out, for the first time, to be a straight fight between the Congress and the Muslim League as national parties. Each side won its 'natural' constituency, with the League winning all the reserved Muslim seats, and the Congress winning all but a few of the general seats they contested. Such clarity was not, however, especially helpful to the general process of demission, because Jinnah had treated the election as a plebiscite on Pakistan, and it was hard for the Congress now to dismiss him as an ephemeral figure peddling an unpopular dream.

Two distinct visions of a free India now needed to be reconciled. Congress leaders aspired to create a secular, inclusive Indian state, with a strong central government, capable of modernizing Indian society and industry, and able to make a strong impression internationally. The Muslim

League had no vision of an 'Indian' state at all. They wanted a decentralized structure, predicated on Muslim distinctiveness, with a high degree of regional autonomy, and constitutional safeguards against potential oppression by the Hindu majority.

The British had a preferred outcome of their own—a unitary but probably federal India. This would be much the best solution from the point of view of British strategic and diplomatic interests. The voluntary creation of a united independent India was also the Congress ideal, but this was incompatible with the Pakistan demand. Jinnah had therefore to overcome opposition from both the British and the Congress. He had the most radical demand, yet the least leverage, and was therefore forced to compensate for his weakness by tactical acumen. He persistently refused to compromise, and demanded more concessions whenever he felt cornered. As justification, he relied simply on the credo that the Muslims were a 'nation' and could not be expected to live within another 'nation'. There were many layers of inconsistency and contradiction within this idea, but the emotional appeal of it was very strong, and it became both a call for political liberation and a rallying point for religious fervour.

One central point needs to be made here about British intentions. The preferred British option was the maintenance of a unitary India, inside the Commonwealth. All political manoeuvrings and manipulations were to this end, and there is a mound of official documentation to support this assessment. Any other scenario was worse. A unitary India outside the Commonwealth was obviously undesirable, and any division into two states carried multiple risks. Not even the creation of two states that remained within the Commonwealth would avert the danger of war between them, while having one in and one out carried the risk of having to back one against the other. Finally, two states outside the Commonwealth was the worst of all—even worse than a unitary state outside, for it carried the possibility of war but with no leverage available to stop it.

The creation of a sovereign Pakistan was not the best option for British interests, or even a good one, despite attempts by revisionists to show that it was, by using selective quotation from the confidential opinions of senior military figures. A divided India was seen as a surer way to let the Russians in than to keep them out. This reluctance to divide the country was not secret and was not merely strategic. In a book written in late 1945, Lt Col. C.B. Birdwood commented: 'Partition is against every creative instinct which has stimulated our constructive work in India.'[8]

With no agreement emerging on the subcontinent, in March 1946 Attlee sent a three-man Cabinet Mission, to mediate and make recommendations. Its nominal head was Lord Pethick Lawrence, Secretary for India, but its real leader was Sir Stafford Cripps, back in India for the first time since his abortive 1942 trip. After an extended period of consultation, during which Jinnah was forced for the first time to specify in detail what he actually wanted, the Mission unveiled its proposal on 16 May. Jinnah was not offered a fully sovereign Muslim state, nor did the Congress get a centralized, united India. The plan was for a complex, 'three-tier' structure. At the top would be a central authority responsible for foreign affairs, defence and communications. Below would come federated groups of provinces, and within the groups would be individual provinces, based on existing boundaries.

This plan was rather more politically comprehensible than it was administratively workable. It was designed to grant the League a sort of 'soft' Pakistan, at the same time as giving the Congress a vaguely unitary state. But as in all federated systems, the devil was in the detail. Jinnah had serious reservations about the way the new constitution was to be agreed—by a national Constituent Assembly in which Muslims, as ever, could be outvoted. The Congress disliked the whole idea of 'groups' and the way these related to the centre; whether the plan made 'grouping' compulsory or not was a major concern for the Congress. Another objection was that Assam, a Hindu majority province, was to be grouped with Bengal, a narrowly Muslim majority province. Yet despite their various reservations, both the Muslim League and the Congress agreed to proceed on the basis of the 16 May proposal.

Like the 1942 offer, the Mission's plan had two strands. One dealt with constitutional structures, the other concerned the formation of an Interim Government, to be appointed by the viceroy from leaders who had signed up to the three-tier plan. Both main parties had done so but, in late June 1946, the Congress changed tack, and declined Wavell's invitation to enter the Interim Government, because of Jinnah's insistence that the Congress could not nominate Muslims for office. Wavell was left with the prospect of forming a cabinet involving only the minority parties, and he baulked.

Jinnah was furious and accused everyone else of bad faith. Nehru then made a public declaration on 6 July that he considered the grouping proposals unacceptable, and that Congress members would enter the new Constituent Assembly bound by no prior commitments about the shape of a future India. This was too much for Jinnah. In a speech of 28 July he renounced constitutional methods and called for 'direct action' on 16 August in support of the Pakistan demand. On the chosen day Calcutta exploded into violence, and the bloodshed surrounding independence began, with around 5,000 deaths. Over succeeding months, retaliatory violence was to spread across much of eastern Bengal and Bihar.

All parties were sobered by these developments, and in early September Wavell put together a Congress-led government, which Muslim League members joined in October. But this expanded cabinet rapidly descended into squabbling, as its members tried to frustrate and undermine their opponents' proposals. The Muslim League then decided to boycott the Constituent Assembly, elected in July and due to meet later in the year. By December, therefore, India had a deadlocked central government, a lop-sided Constituent Assembly and a background of communal violence. Prime Minister Attlee called the leading representatives to London for talks, but nothing came of them.

In this impasse, Attlee took the decision to replace Wavell, although he did not tell him so at the time. Attlee approached Lord Louis Mountbatten to take over as viceroy, and after some negotiation about the details of his remit, Mountbatten accepted.

Attlee unveiled the appointment of Mountbatten in the House of Commons on 20 February 1947. He also named an end date to British rule in India, which would come no later than June 1948. This declaration was designed to concentrate minds, but otherwise Attlee was only announcing a change of personnel, not of policy. Mountbatten was still to implement the Cabinet Mission's plan of May 1946. Only if this were not possible was he allowed to explore other options.

The arrival of Mountbatten in late March 1947 transformed the political situation. He was a younger, brusquer man than Wavell, and keen to make a fresh start. He immediately set about talking to everyone that mattered, noting their positions and confronting them with the problems he foresaw. By mid-April he had come to the conclusion that partition was the only feasible outcome, and the politicians, who had been going over much the same ground for rather longer, did not seek to disagree with him.

Jinnah had consistently demanded partition; it was only the terms that concerned him. The main change at this point was that Congress leaders finally accepted the principle of regional self-determination, to which they had been paying occasional lip service since 1940. J.B. Kripalani, the Congress president, told Mountbatten this in private on 17 April,[9] and in a meeting with the viceroy on the 25 April, Sardar Patel accepted partition if the Muslim League refused to implement the Cabinet Mission plan, as he believed they would.[10] Nehru and Rajendra Prasad both announced much the same in public by the end of the month, Nehru in the United Provinces,[11] Prasad in the Constituent Assembly.[12] Partition was then the only way forward.

This left Mountbatten to devise a means of making the separation, and his first attempt was curiously mishandled. In late April he sent a draft plan to London for approval. It was based on a mixture of the Cabinet Mission's second tier and the old 'opt-out' clause, with provinces allowed to join either India or Pakistan, or neither. When this plan returned from London with cabinet approval in early May, Mountbatten showed it to Nehru, who angrily rejected it in its entirety. Nehru immediately saw that no matter how equitable the plan, in its grant of extensive rights of self-determination to provinces, it was not at all acceptable to the Congress, because it threatened to destroy all central authority—to 'balkanize' the new India. Mountbatten was initially taken aback, but a revised plan was soon drafted by his Reforms Commissioner, V.P. Menon, who had close links to Sardar Patel.

Menon had in fact presented something very like this new proposal to Wavell the previous January, and had discussed its outlines with Patel. The Menon plan provided for two Constituent Assemblies—one for each successor state—and required all provinces to opt for either India or Pakistan, thus removing the principal objections of both Jinnah and Nehru to previous plans. It also recognized the two Constituent Assemblies as sovereign bodies, to which power could be transferred under the existing 1935 legislation. This meant that independence would be granted immediately, leaving complex constitutional questions to be resolved at leisure. Privately, both party leaders also accepted that the two new sovereign states would take up Commonwealth membership, which ended the potential for embarrassment, and assured both of economic and military help from Britain.

Mountbatten flew back to London with the new plan on 18 May, obtained cabinet approval, and was back in India on 31 May. Indian leaders saw the final text on 2 June, and Mountbatten asked them to give their approval the next day. He pitched his words carefully, requiring only 'acceptance' of the plan, not 'agreement' with it. No one was satisfied with the final settlement, but all parties acknowledged that there was no better deal to be had. The Viceroy, Nehru, Jinnah, and Baldev Singh for the Sikhs all made separate broadcasts to the nation that evening.

Mountbatten announced to the world the next day that the transfer of power would take place on 15 August. His reasons for naming such a close date have never been satisfactorily explained, by himself or anyone else, but in general he considered that waiting longer would produce more problems than there already were. An early date also ensured that no matter what problems still remained, they would not be a British responsibility.

All that remained was the formality of passing the necessary legislation in the imperial Parliament. Some Tories, including Churchill, did not like the title that Attlee gave the measure, the Indian Independence Bill; it seemed humiliating. On 10 July, in the debate on the bill, Sir Stanley Reed, former editor of *The Times of India* and now Conservative member for Aylesbury, approved of the measure but wanted to call it 'the Fulfilment of India Bill', because he believed that it was the fulfilment 'of all our work in India'.[13] The idea died very hard.

In the settlement Jinnah got most of what he had asked for, but not all. His original demand had been that Sind, the North West Frontier Province (NWFP), Punjab, Bengal and Baluchistan should become his new Pakistan. Three of these units had clear Muslim majorities—Sind, the NWFP and Baluchistan, and in the Punjab and Bengal there were small Muslim majorities of around 55 per cent and 52 per cent respectively. He also staked a claim to Assam, where there was no overall Muslim majority, just a substantial minority, largely concentrated in the area of Sylhet. In the end, only Sind, the NWFP and Baluchistan went to Pakistan in their entirety; Punjab and Bengal were divided, and Sylhet was added to the eastern half of Bengal.

Mountbatten did to Punjab and Bengal what Jinnah had proposed should be done to India; he partitioned them in order to protect the interests of a minority population. Jinnah continued to resist this logic until very late in the process, but was eventually forced to concede the point in order to secure the larger object of a separate Muslim nation-state. This left around thirty million Muslims under Hindu raj, and the new Muslim homeland was unstructured and poor, especially its eastern wing, which contained the least developed parts of Bengal.

Pakistan was obliged to finance its armed forces and administration based on only 17 per cent of the assets of imperial India. The British were convinced that this was not enough for a viable state, and Jinnah was repeatedly told this during the negotiations, but he refused to be deterred. Many senior Raj officials and Congress politicians considered that Pakistan would be back inside a federal Indian union within about a decade.

Jinnah remained obdurate, but the Pakistan he was given was no better than offers he had rejected several times before, notably in the Bombay talks with Gandhi in 1944. Ultimately he was asking for too much, and once the Congress had accepted partition, he lost the ability to extract concessions by delaying, which was always his best tactic. The Congress essentially called his bluff as soon as it became clear that there would be no better offers from him, and no intervention by the British.

Mountbatten fulfilled his brief; he ended the Raj by agreement, at a minimal cost in blood, treasure and prestige to the British.

Louis Francis Albert Victor Nicholas, Earl Mountbatten of Burma (1900–79) was the last British figure to have a direct influence on India's history. But where others had extended or reformed British India, Mountbatten gave it back to the Indians, as he had been told to.

He still divides opinion very sharply. At the time, most of the British establishment said, at least in public, that he did a wonderful job, as well as it could have been done, and better than anyone else available at the time could have done it. But to many Indians, and to most Pakistanis, he is remembered as a bringer of mayhem and mass murder. This disparity springs from a characteristic he shared with men like Clive and Curzon, that he carried within him both virtues and vices on a grand scale. His story cannot be related without constant reference to his charm, energy and broad-mindedness, but it is also impossible to overlook his vanity, ambition and flexible allegiance to truth.

Born into the minor German princely house of Battenberg, young Louis—who as an adult was always known as Dickie—was the great-grandson of Queen Victoria, which gave him confidence, prestige and access to almost anyone in British society. The other great influence on his career was the tradition of naval service that was particularly strong in the British royal family, which his father had also followed.

The first great setback in his life arrived with the outbreak of the First World War, when an upsurge of anti-German feeling forced Mountbatten's father, also called Louis, to resign his position as First Sea Lord—the senior serving officer in the Royal Navy. This humiliation, which shattered Louis senior, remained with Dickie for the rest of his life, and his lasting ambitiousness within the navy is commonly attributed to a desire to expunge this blot on his family's honour. The other immediate effect of the war was that the house of Battenberg changed its name to the more English-sounding Mountbatten, at the same time as the royal family also anglicized its name from Saxe-Coburg-Gotha to Windsor.

Mountbatten then served continuously in the Royal Navy until he accepted the viceroyalty of India from the post-war Labour government in late 1946. He bargained hard for wide powers of negotiation and the right to appoint this own personal staff, but most importantly he insisted on a deadline for his term of office. The date eventually chosen was June 1948, which brought a new factor into the Indian independence process. So Mountbatten flew out to India with an entirely different brief and broader powers than any previous viceroy.

It must be emphasized that Mountbatten did not set out to partition India, a charge so commonly made by Indian writers that it would seem beyond argument. In reality, Mountbatten was under specific instructions to hand over power in three possible ways, ranked in order of desirability. He was instructed first to seek agreement to some version of the Cabinet Mission plan of May 1946; if this did not appear by October 1947, he was to implement any settlement that could be reached by agreement; then, if even this were not possible, the British would withdraw in June 1948, having handed power to whoever seemed most able to exercise it in the regions concerned.

This was not a plan for partition, though it did provide for that possibility if agreement could not be reached. Nor was it hidden. It was stated as public policy by Attlee in the House of Commons. The only secret was that Mountbatten also had private instructions from the king, his cousin, to try to ensure that India, or any successor states, should be persuaded to remain in the British Commonwealth.

Mountbatten landed in Delhi with no predetermined ideas, but his first fortnight in India appears to have made up his mind that the Cabinet Mission plan was a dead letter, that agreement was not achievable, and that some sort of partition was the only way forward. He floated this idea with his staff, and again in a meeting with his provincial governors in mid-April. All the while he was becoming increasingly alarmed, as were politicians and officials, at the severe deterioration in public order.

Violence in the Punjab and the NWFP convinced him of the need for urgent action, and he managed to get his final plan into the hands of Indian politicians on 2 June. His combination of speed, charm and high-handedness trumped all objections and the leaders formally agreed the plan the next day, though Jinnah tried to defer a decision by claiming that he could not agree to the plan without the approval of the League's Working Committee. Mountbatten simply rode roughshod over this delaying tactic, telling Jinnah that he would take responsibility himself if the Committee's approval were not forthcoming. Jinnah later secured the formal agreement he needed without objection.

The next six weeks were a blur of activity on political, administrative and military fronts. Votes were taken in the provinces affected by possible partition; a separate department to deal with the princely states was created; a Partition Council was set up to divide the assets of British India between the two new states; military arrangements were put in place to separate the Indian army into two new forces with separate command structures; and a Boundary Commission under an English judge, Sir Cyril Radcliffe, was appointed to determine the border between the two new states through the intricately mixed communities in Punjab and Bengal. Amid all this governmental activity, communal violence continued to escalate, especially in the Punjab.

The formal transfers of power were ceremonially played out on the afternoon of 14 August in Karachi and the same evening in Delhi. Widespread rejoicing followed, but with the announcement of the Boundary Award on 17 August, massive migrations began in both directions across the Punjab as individual Hindus, Muslims and Sikhs discovered which of the new countries they found themselves in.

For all this, Mountbatten has endured trenchant criticism. He is accused of speeding up the process of partition unduly, of making too little provision to suppress communal violence, and of interfering in the decisions of Sir Cyril Radcliffe. He certainly hastened the process of partition, and in doing so he is generally reckoned to have served Congress purposes rather than those of the Muslim League. Nehru and Patel were keen to be rid of the British and were anxious to wield power themselves after such a long wait, much of it spent in prison. Jinnah on the other hand was keen to slow the process down, well aware that he had to set up an entire new government from scratch.

But Mountbatten, by accelerating in the way he did, was mostly serving British purposes—to make Indians and Pakistanis responsible for their own destinies as soon as possible, and to minimize British exposure to risk, both military and political. Could he have gone slower? Yes, of course, and this might have saved lives. But it might also have led to the effective decentralization of both the new successor states, as local concerns became paramount to everyone involved. The chaotic state of China served as a lurid, contemporary example of what could happen if central authority were to crumble.

It is not easy to make out a cast-iron case that a slower process would have rendered the practicalities on the ground any easier. What might have made a difference was a cooling of sectarian feelings, but all parties agreed at the time that speed was more likely to do this than delay.

In trying to suppress the violence, Mountbatten had no easy task. It would have been hard for him to take strong action before the transfer of power, because the use of military force was highly distasteful to Indian politicians, and also difficult for the British, who were trying to scale down their involvement. Control of the civilian population was also not feasible by deploying the army. As large numbers of people began to move across the Punjab from the middle of the summer, the Indian army was neutralized as an effective force by the process of separation and reintegration it was undergoing, in order to be reallocated to the two new states. Mustering a non-partisan peacekeeping force was not possible while operative fighting units were being dismantled and thousands of soldiers were in transit all over the subcontinent. The great fear was that they might begin to fight among themselves, and the protection of civilians from each other ranked as a lower priority.

It was also impossible for Mountbatten personally to take measures to suppress the violence after 15 August, because from then on he was only Governor-General of the new Indian state, and as such was the servant of India's politicians, not their master. By then it was for the politicians to impose order. They did indeed take on this task, but the failure to control so many hundreds of thousands of desperate people is hardly surprising. The excessive concentration of central power in Delhi was matched by a fatal absence of authority on the ground.

Lastly, the decision to publish the Boundary Awards after the formal declaration of independence was definitely Mountbatten's responsibility, and he did it specifically to ensure that the celebrations were not marred by unpleasantness. Like Radcliffe, Mountbatten guessed that not everyone would be satisfied with the eventual awards, and he was right. In consequence, the smooth running of the festivities in Karachi and Delhi was paid for in blood by thousands of people whose dissatisfaction might have disfigured Mountbatten's moment of triumph.

Whether he directly interfered with Radcliffe's decisions is less certain, but it seems extremely likely that he made representations over the area of Ferozepur. Originally destined for Pakistan, it went to India for a number of strategic reasons, including the provision of water to the state of Patiala (which had opted to join India) and the presence of a large military arsenal in the district. In this, as in several other elements of his viceroyalty, Mountbatten seems to have exhibited a distinct bias in favour of India.

Conspiracy theories still surround Mountbatten's dealings with British and Indian politicians; all are over-imaginative and easily discredited. There is, however, one persistent strand in these theories which has a basis in fact and therefore deserves some consideration. This is the relationship between Mountbatten's wife, Edwina, and Jawaharlal Nehru. Some sort of intimate friendship certainly existed, although if or when it became more than friendship is open to dispute. The main protagonists and nearly all the eyewitnesses are now dead, and no one ever wrote a definitive account of their dealings.

But even though the bond between them may have been real, there is no evidence at all that it actually affected political realities during the partition process. Therefore, any attempt to discuss this subject involves entering the realm of boudoir politics, where everything becomes a matter of nods and winks. No documents, no proof, just endless supposition. We speculate about whether Edwina had purposes of her own, or whether she was simply a willing conduit for Nehru's ideas, or whether she had any real influence over her husband in political matters. Who, indeed, was influencing whom? And *why*? Edwina did not have any personal political interest in the demission process, and there are perfectly plain and well-understood strategic reasons why Mountbatten took the decisions he did.

For lovers of tittle-tattle this story will run and run, but as a historical quest for truth it is a dead end. The later phases of the relationship/affair between Edwina and Jawaharlal are genuinely touching, and there is no reason to believe that their connection was ever primarily about politics or power. It certainly survived any conceivable utility it might have had for either of them.

Mountbatten was generally congratulated in Britain for his work. Privately, though, some senior soldiers, principally Auchinleck and Montgomery, thought he had made a mess of it. Churchill congratulated Prime Minister Attlee and the Viceroy in the House of Commons. Like most other parties to the settlement, he considered it was, by then, the best deal available, though he regretted the abandonment of minorities to Hindu majority rule, and felt that the princes, who had been unswervingly loyal, were badly treated.

Other diehards agreed, and for some years Mountbatten was known disparagingly as 'the man who gave India away'. Suffice it to say that India was never his to keep, and that he had explicitly been told to give her back. At the time of his final departure, in June 1948, Mountbatten was massively popular with the Indian public, which was prepared, in quite unforced displays of affection, to cheer him and his wife to the echo as they left. It was a later generation of Indian writers that thought fit to assail his decisions and his integrity.

Mountbatten went on to occupy many senior naval posts, emulating his father by becoming First Sea Lord in 1954. He rose even higher when he was appointed as the second-ever Chief of Defence Staff in 1959. After retirement he devoted himself to numerous charitable causes, but never wrote a memoir, choosing instead to let history deliver its verdict in due time.

In the end it was not enraged Indians or Pakistanis that caught up with him. He was killed by Irish nationalists, who exploded a bomb on his yacht off the west coast of Ireland in 1979.

It is remarkable that in all the writing surrounding Partition, Clement Attlee (1883–1967) is given so little space. Conspiracy theorists and partisan polemicists have produced whole books of speculation about secret deals, Mountbatten's untruthfulness, Jinnah's villainy and Lady Mountbatten's flirtations with Nehru, but all of this misses one central point, which is that it was always Attlee who had the final say in proceedings.

He was the man who granted India her independence, ending the 182-year involvement of Britain in the government of India. That alone would assure him a place in history, but this quiet, unassuming character also took a leading role in the shaping of the modern British state, as head of a government that nationalized mines and railways and set up the National Health Service. All this he did as a man who rose to the top of the Labour Party without working-class credentials or close connections with the trades union movement. By any standards this was a remarkable career that belies Churchill's quip about him, that he was a modest man with much about which to be modest.

Attlee took a central role in the negotiation of India's independence, a greater part than a prime minister would usually play in what was essentially a matter of foreign policy. In this one area the Foreign Secretary, Ernest Bevin, stood aside and gave the prime minister a free hand. This was very much Attlee's wish, as he had developed a keen interest in Indian affairs while a member of the much-reviled Simon Commission of 1927–30. In the long discussions that preceded the Government of India Act of 1935, he had submitted an alternative report, usually known as the Attlee Draft, which would have largely granted Indian demands as detailed in the Nehru Report of 1928. Then and afterwards, he showed a willingness to meet Indian aspirations, though he always harboured reservations about Congress's claims to represent all of India's people.

Attlee was not anti-Congress in disposition, unlike Churchill, who had a visceral dislike of the seditious Gandhi and the socialist Nehru, but he felt caution was in order. He wished to bequeath India a new constitution that would give all Indians safeguards, security and freedom, and he doubted that simply handing Congress leaders the seals of office would guarantee this sufficiently.

He was keen to give India her independence for several reasons. Ideologically he was happy to unpick the seams of empire, but his willingness was enhanced by the extremely serious economic crisis that gripped Britain after the Second World War. This became a principal consideration in determining the speed of the departure from India, which in turn was closely linked to the degree of military spending that was likely to be required in any other scenario.

His first decisive act was to send the three-man Cabinet Mission in March 1946, and its failure was a blow to him. Having accepted that agreement about the shape of an independent India was unlikely to appear spontaneously, he made further changes by withdrawing Viceroy Wavell and sending Mountbatten to replace him.

The Chancellor of the Exchequer, Hugh Dalton, threatened to resign in January 1947 if foreign commitments were not reduced, so Attlee's only options after that were cheap ones. The cheapest was waiting for Indians to agree among themselves, and this is what he instructed Mountbatten to do, with a further cheap option to follow on—withdrawal without agreement in place.

Mountbatten therefore flew out with a strict time frame in which to work, carrying detailed instructions rehearsed by Attlee in the Commons a month before.

The cabinet closely supervised all of Mountbatten's dealings between March and June 1947, and were sufficiently alarmed at his antics to call him back for consultations in mid-May. During Mountbatten's visit to London between 18 and 29 May, all the details of the final partition agreement were finalized with Attlee's approval, while the political ground was cleared by obtaining Churchill's agreement, as Opposition leader, to the substance of the Indian Independence Act. Churchill had to be conciliated, partly as a matter of propriety on an issue of such magnitude, but also to ensure a rapid passage of the bill, because by that stage it was not only Mountbatten that was deeply convinced of the need for rapid action.

Despite his central involvement in the whole process, Attlee recorded in his autobiography, *As It Happened* (1954), that in his view 'it was by the decision of the Indians themselves that a partition was made'.[14] This might serve as a reminder that political memoirs can be both selective and exculpatory. Attlee was one of the few people who could have issued instructions that avoided partition, but he did not. He cited the deterioration of public order as his main reason. Another was that the education of Indians in self-government had reached a natural conclusion; he, for one, considered that the 'work' was over.

Writing in 1954, he was not prepared to take full responsibility himself, which would have been the constitutional position, or to blame any other individual, which would have been only human. 'India' does not even appear in the index of the book. Perhaps Partition did not lie too heavily on his conscience.

The other forgotten man of Partition is General Wavell, who had possibly the most difficult job of all, and received precious little recognition for what he managed to achieve.

A successful and well-regarded soldier in his own time, Archibald Percival Wavell (1883–1950) grew up in India, son of a military family. Personally he had an air of reticence, but was always well liked by his men and respected by his fellow officers, who considered him something of a theoretician. Even Field Marshal Rommel, a soldier's soldier if ever there was one, is reported to have carried one of Wavell's books with him on campaign.

He fought in the Boer War, lost an eye on the Western Front in the First World War, and commanded the Middle East theatre in the early years of the Second World War. Appointed Commander-in-Chief, India, in 1941, he was replaced in the Middle Eastern command by General Claude Auchinleck, who subsequently followed him to India as Commander-in-Chief, when Wavell became viceroy in 1943. At that time the Japanese army was advancing through Burma, severe famine had gripped Bengal, and the leadership of the Congress Party was in prison. Things, therefore, were hardly running as normal. Unfortunately, Wavell's task never became appreciably easier.

The job of a viceroy in war was primarily to get the most out of India for the war effort, and Wavell did this well enough. But his responsibilities became much more complicated with the end of hostilities in 1945, when self-government, long promised, was to be granted.

The extended negotiations and abortive plans that followed mark out what was viewed at the time as the dimming of Wavell's star. He was accused of naivety, of political inexperience and of ineptitude. This assessment has since been revised, partly because of the publication of his highly articulate and detailed journals, and partly because the reputation of his successor, Lord Mountbatten, has suffered in the opposite direction. Wavell's attempts to find agreement are now widely seen as generally well judged, but ultimately doomed by the intractability of the issues.

It is certainly unfair to compare his efforts too directly with those of Mountbatten, for Wavell laboured under several disadvantages that his successor was spared. Firstly, he was denied a clean political start; he had been in India too long by 1945 to try new tricks. Secondly, Mountbatten was given a different brief—to reach agreement at all costs—whereas Wavell was required to reach a consensus by persuasion. Thirdly, Mountbatten had a definite end date to his posting, whereas Wavell did not, and so was never able to push any situation as hard as Mountbatten could.

As a matter of political skill, Mountbatten had the edge in obvious charm, and as a younger man he conveyed more energy—and less subtlety. But the ending of the war converted Wavell from a military autocrat to a political referee, and this change sat uncomfortably with the idea of coaxing agreement out of India's argumentative politicians.

Famously, Wavell despaired of prolonging the Raj, and he completed a detailed plan of evacuation in September 1946. This was titled Operation Breakdown and provided for an orderly withdrawal of British forces and civilians while there was still time and manpower to secure their safety. Unfortunately the plan did not reassure senior British officials, but only convinced them that Wavell had lost his nerve and was planning an ignominious 'scuttle'.

Attlee then decided to replace Wavell with Mountbatten in December 1946. He had no great faith in Wavell and wanted a change of face, of pace and of attitude. Wavell's presentation in February of another plan of retreat, named Ebb Tide, did nothing to contradict the impression that Attlee had sacked him for defeatism. It was Wavell's peculiarly bad luck to be considered too much of a liberal by Churchill, and too much of a soldier by Attlee.

Indian politicians generally thought well of him, perhaps because he never pushed them too hard. He was also a transparently humane man; he released Gandhi on compassionate grounds from the Aga Khan's Palace in 1944 after his pneumonia, and later wrote him a note offering condolences on the death of his wife. It was also Wavell that fought the corner of famine-hit Bengalis in 1943 against the cabinet in London, which had no wish to divert ships and food from elsewhere to help relieve the distress. It has been suggested that perhaps Wavell remembered his Indian childhood and retained some understanding of and affection for the Indian people. Nevertheless, in the dark days of autumn 1946 the Congress leadership eventually tipped Attlee the wink that they would prefer a new man, and his fate was sealed.

As a lover of poetry, a great deal of which he knew by heart, he was hardly a conventional soldier. It was generally his ill fortune in life to be given especially difficult jobs at times when it was most difficult to do them. Such men rarely shine, but they should be remembered with a certain admiration.

12

1947–1950

AFTERMATH

Pakistan was created at great speed, and in many important areas of public policy the new entity's aims and aspirations were never properly defined. Both before and after independence, Jinnah's speeches seemed to indicate that he had an all-inclusive, secular vision of the new Muslim state. He repeatedly declared that all would be free to worship and behave as they wished in his Pakistan, and that no one should have any fear of living there. He may have been clear in his own mind about the constitutional details of his creation, but he did not live long enough to flesh them out. This incomplete legacy and its meaning are still contentious today.

The splitting of the armed forces was what had most concerned British strategists at the time but, in the event, it was this aspect of demission that ran most smoothly. With the two successor states both joining the Commonwealth, their armies were able to retain their senior British officers. Not a shot was fired between them during the Partition process.

The official Congress line was that Partition was necessary—to be rid of Jinnah's endless cavilling, to permit the growth of democracy without special reserved electorates, and to give India a strong centre that would promote social and economic progress. Nehru and the senior leadership were tired of waiting, of prison and of Jinnah. They also felt, as did many on the British side, that Pakistan would not last long and that a reunification might not be far off—five or ten years perhaps.

No one expected the bloodbath. Yasmin Khan, in her meticulous and comprehensive account, writes: 'Partition set in motion a train of events unforeseen by every single person who had advocated and argued for the division.'[1] Gandhi talked in terms of bloodletting at times, but he thought that a British presence would make it worse. He had no illusions that the birth of the new nation would be easy; he had already seen carnage in rural Bengal and Bihar, but he wanted the British to leave as a matter of urgency. If the new nation had to 'pass through the fire', he was quite clear that Indians should be left to sort out the details. And if they had to learn self-control through experience of their own violence, then so be it. The long-term results, in his view, would be worth it.

Constitutionally and politically, V.P. Menon's plan was a triumph, at least in the short term. The problems of Partition came from two other directions. The first was the civil disruption and violence. The killings and mass migrations across the Punjab did not begin in earnest till after independence, because the decisions of the Boundary Commission were not revealed until after the formal transfer of power. They therefore dropped into a vacuum of government in the rural Punjab. Problems of some sort would certainly have occurred, because the population of the region was so intermixed, but had there been a little more lead time while civil authorities were still in place, the migrations could perhaps have been slowed and the scale of the bloodshed minimized.

On the other hand, politicians on both sides had been at pains to underplay the likely effects of Partition, and had even hailed the existence of 'hostage' populations within the two new states as a guarantee of safety for all. The necessity for an 'exchange of populations' had been repeatedly dismissed as unnecessary. Everyone assumed that to show too much pessimism before the event would undercut the politicians, and might lead to panic on an even wider scale.

The other calamity was the conflict in Kashmir. This grew out of the wider problem of the princely states, all 565 of which were notionally sovereign powers, linked by treaty to the British Crown. The Menon plan, therefore, made no provision for their future, because they were third parties, and Menon was only concerned with the dealings of His Majesty's Government (HMG) and the two successor states.

The Cabinet Mission statement of May 1946 declared that British paramountcy was to lapse at independence, because it was part of bilateral treaty relations between HMG and the individual sovereign princes. It therefore could not be transferred to any successor state(s). Mountbatten realized that political measures had to be taken to fill this gap, and once the main business of Partition was agreed, he threw himself into persuading the princely states to accede to either India or Pakistan. He immediately made it clear to all the princes that none of them would be recognized as independent states by HMG, and would therefore not be eligible for Commonwealth membership.

Sardar Patel and V.P. Menon were given charge of a new States Department in July, and standard terms for accession were drawn up. Most states had a straightforward decision to make, based on geography, and few of them could seriously contemplate sustaining an independent existence. Thirteen eventually went to Pakistan, the rest to India.

Three princes looked seriously into their options. One was the Nawab of Junagadh, the rather eccentric Muslim ruler of a small state on the coast of Gujarat, bounded by the sea and India. He opted for Pakistan, in defiance of topography and the wishes of his majority Hindu population. The Indian army walked in, and the nawab fled.

This was a minor matter, easily resolved. But the two largest states by area, Hyderabad and Kashmir, presented more serious difficulties. Hyderabad had a Muslim ruler and an overwhelmingly Hindu population. Independence was hardly a viable option for a landlocked enclave within India, but the nizam prevaricated for months, despite ever-increasing pressure to accede to India and a rising tide of violence in the state. Eventually, after Mountbatten had gone home, Patel authorized a 'police action' named Operation Polo. Indian troops marched into Hyderabad in September 1948, and it was annexed.

Things were more complicated in Kashmir. It was the inverse of Hyderabad in that it had a Hindu ruler and a largely Muslim population, but Kashmir's options were different, because it bordered both India and Pakistan. Its ruler, Maharaja Hari Singh, refused to commit to either. Nehru encouraged him to join India, and in August 1947 Mountbatten sent Gandhi to try to persuade him. But the internal politics of Kashmir were convoluted, and the distribution of its religious communities complex. The maharaja had even imprisoned the chief pro-Indian politician in his state, Sheikh Abdullah, who was a Congress supporter and partisan of India, despite his Muslim faith.

The deadline of 15 August went by without a decision from the maharaja. This was unfortunate, because up to this point all parties would have been compelled to accept a freely made decision by him, either way. Two more months of silence passed, until an incursion by irregular forces from Pakistan—who were responding to reports of violence against Muslims—prompted the maharaja to appeal to India for help. Mountbatten, standing on formality, insisted that the Indian army could not be used to defend Kashmir unless the maharaja signed an Instrument of Accession to India.

He did so on 26 October 1947, whereupon reinforcements were immediately flown to Srinagar. Again, this was unfortunate, because accession meant that India was subsequently unable to withdraw from what was now claimed as Indian territory. Thus Pakistan became involved in Kashmir too informally, and India too formally. Armed conflict was then highly likely to escalate.

The roots of the Kashmir problem are deep, and virtually all of the details in the story, large and small, are disputed. Whether Mountbatten could have forestalled the problem is not clear; constitutionally he could not have pressured the maharaja to accede to India while he was still viceroy. Critics have considered his punctiliousness about the Instrument of Accession to have been unnecessary, but in one important way it was vestiges of such formality that prevented full-scale war, because the Commanders-in-Chief of the two national armies were still British. Between the two of them and Mountbatten they agreed that the conflict should remain local.

A great deal of the blame must also fall on Maharaja Hari Singh, who seemed incapable of making a decision no matter how much time he was given or how much advice he was offered. Here was a man who was still capable, in 1947, of wreaking havoc on a personal whim, which must count as the sourest legacy of the British decision to prop up autocratic princes. The Kashmir impasse can thus be accounted the most enduring result of 1857.

Had the British knocked over all the hereditary princes of India at the height of their power—which they were well capable of doing—they would doubtless have been accused of imperial arrogance. But they spared their feudal friends, and were then obliged to abide by their decisions. The new leaders of India and Pakistan were thus forced to cope with the unfinished business of not one but two outdated political systems.

Kashmir rapidly became a sump into which all the bitterest personal rivalry between Jinnah and Nehru was poured. The two men did not like each other and had not needed to form a respectful relationship in order to achieve the independence settlement. When it came to the first serious problem between them, both men suspected the other of the worst possible motives. By failing to talk to each other or keep each other informed, mistrust was allowed to grow into full-blown paranoia. Unfortunately neither leader was able to take a proper grip on the situation: Nehru could not control the maharaja, Jinnah could not control the razakars (militias).

Both leaders also drifted into difficult issues of consistency. Nehru had already overturned a ruler's decision in Junagadh, so would be awkwardly positioned if Jinnah decided to do the same in Kashmir. Jinnah, meanwhile, was reluctant to challenge the decision of the maharaja, because in late 1947 he still hoped to get Hyderabad through its autocratic ruler's personal decision. Neither man found a good way forward. Jinnah resorted to armed intrusion, while Nehru propped up his position by allowing for a plebiscite—which was never held because of the military instability in the region. The deadlock has yet to be broken.

India should have conceded Kashmir to Pakistan on the same logic as she took Hyderabad. But she took both, by force.

The last tragedy of Partition was Gandhi's own. In the final phases of the negotiations he was virtually excluded. Although Mountbatten liked Gandhi, he thought him unrealistic, as did most of the Congress leadership by that stage. The Mahatma was then eased out of the process by harder-headed men. He was shot dead on 30 January 1948 by a Hindu extremist, convinced that Gandhi's concern for Muslims was somehow to blame for India's misfortune.

The long road to freedom and independence did not end in August 1947. The Menon plan left India as a Dominion with a Governor-General—Mountbatten—but without a settled constitution. After the great haste of that summer, the situation gradually resolved itself over the next three years. The Constituent Assembly finished its work in December 1949, producing a very long and detailed constitution for the new Indian Republic that was declared on 26 January 1950. By then India had a President—Rajendra Prasad—though not yet a freely elected prime minister. This lack was duly supplied in 1952, when Jawaharlal Nehru led the Congress Party to a sweeping victory in the country's first general election.

By then Nehru had managed to renegotiate the basis of the organization formerly known as the British Commonwealth. As an independent republic, no longer acknowledging allegiance to the British monarch, India was only prepared to continue her membership if King George became merely a symbol of shared, free association, described as the 'Head' of the Commonwealth, which was no longer to be 'British'.

This was agreed in London on 28 April 1949. Thus modern India, once home to personal rule and despotic forms, finally brought to an end the largest monarchical structure the world has ever seen.

PART THREE

RETROSPECT

13

REVIEWING THE STORY

The British liked to think that they had won the Second World War, but in truth they were only on the winning side. Emerging indebted and exhausted, within two years Britain had lost a possession that was an empire in itself.

As some had foreseen and many had feared, the end of British India did indeed portend the end of the British Empire, of which it had always been by far the largest piece. Within a decade, pretensions to imperial dignity proved impossible to sustain, with defeat over Suez, independence for Ghana, and insurrection in Malaya, Kenya and Cyprus. All the gloomiest predictions came true; without the Indian keystone to the arch of empire, Britain slipped back from the ranks of Great Powers.

For more than a century the Indian connection had occupied a central place in the British psyche, providing a sense of moral mission and cultural confidence, linked with justifications for a range of cherished ideals, including social hierarchy, religious superiority and racial destiny. The 'work' in India had always brought more uplift to British hearts than to Indian peasants, and the severing of the relationship left an enormous hole in the cultural firmament of the British military and administrative classes. 'Glorious' became something that only the weather could be. The collapse of scale involved was devastating, and took probably two generations to absorb.

The long-term effects on Britain of the Anglo-Indian relationship have never been fully or rigorously explored. During the Raj, it was not considered good form to speculate on how India might be changing the imperial homeland, for fear of admitting that a gradient of power and influence did not exist, or that the mother country had anything to learn from those it sought to civilize. The assumption was that the effects were all travelling one way, and were all for the better. Surplus trade balances and a supply of soldiers for imperial operations were the acknowledged substance of the link, along with well-paid albeit demanding employment for a small cadre of educated officials and an even smaller band of high-born Governors.

In the modern era it is now possible, though not easy, to search for subtler, unacknowledged influences. These might include the extended survival of the British hereditary ruling classes, who preserved themselves as 'natural' rulers, not of Britain, but of India. The Indian Empire was a source of marvellously flattering stories of aristocrats in action, ruling in ways they were no longer allowed to at home. Photographs of white men with large dead animals, surrounded by small brown servants, depicted the natural imperial order, a sepia Raj of unchanging hierarchy. In the hands of the likes of Sir James Fitzjames Stephen, this served as a model for the governance of Britain. Indeed, many of the ideals that developed through the later Raj to justify British rule in India had a definite appeal to those wishing to justify aristocratic privilege at home: important decisions should be the preserve of a far-sighted, educated elite, who were best excused the inconvenience and indignity of consulting a mass of ignorant, atavistic underlings. But such attitudes only emerged late in the drama and remained the preserve of a minority.

The main domestic effect of government in India was that the British political classes were compelled to broaden their thinking beyond oligarchical, aristocratic Whiggism and hierarchical, monarchical Toryism. Neither was adequate to the new demands of overseas empire, and British thinkers began to perceive problems of government as universal. Here lay the British discovery of liberalism, whose central belief was that political rights exist independent of economic and social status.

Some of the early British thinkers about India deserve credit for the way they faced up to liberal tenets, despite their obvious implications for the ultimate fate of British rule. Many British politicians deserve censure for the way they did not follow through the implications of those ideas with anything like sufficient energy or dispatch.

And what of the effects on India? Politically, the impact is clear. The Indian leaders who promoted the cause of self-government after 1857, and those who ultimately took it on, were shaped by their experience of British rule and by British principles of government. And the elements of British rule that they most resented when in alien hands—the strong executive, the bureaucratic system, centralized control of economics, protection of minorities—were carefully preserved by Congress leaders after independence. But though much of the social reform agenda was implemented after independence—the abolition of Untouchability, equal rights for women, adult suffrage—other major elements, such as land reform and the standardization of family law, were resisted by conservative forces. The Congress thus ended up with both the Raj's ruling system and its familiar inability to bring about real change. Nowhere was this clearer than in the issue of language, where the modernizers wanted to impose Hindi, but regional objections forced the retention of English.

The course steered by the Congress in government was essentially the path of least resistance, which meant dragging a large measure of British influence into independent India. This included much of the 1935 reforms, such as the provincial-federal structure and the schedules of castes and tribes. The judicial-legal system was largely retained, and the state's machinery of self-protection was modelled on colonial repression, including the very broad law of sedition. Importantly, two distinctly British political traditions were also preserved—state neutrality in religion and the non-political role of the armed forces.

Meanwhile India's railways still went where the British had wanted them to, and all of the largest cities, with the exception of Ahmedabad, carried a heavy imprint of British strategic and economic interests. For the moment, provincial boundaries stayed where the British, often quite randomly, had seen fit to draw them, while India's international frontiers retained a similarly pragmatic outline. Nepal and Bhutan were never incorporated into British India for largely prudential reasons, and Burma was separated in 1937 as a matter of administrative efficiency.

The British legacy was thus pervasive, and many of the choices made by the Congress were more apparent than real.

The ironic point here is that the British increasingly abandoned constructive use of their influence in the later Raj, and it was progressive Indians, after Ranade and Naoroji, who picked up the momentum. Nevertheless, the creation of the modern Indian nation was undoubtedly a joint alien–native project. The British initially injected enough violence to break down interest groups, and the Indians then slowly developed a new and distinctive identity around which to coalesce. The skeleton of the new India had a British shape; the flesh and blood were Indian.

The British took an absolutely central role in unifying modern India, though not always in the ways they sometimes thought. A string of leaders, from Ellenborough to Churchill through Lytton and Curzon, believed that

British rule was something Indians could unite behind. Nationalists, from the 1880s on, saw it as something Indians could unite against. With an alien all-India structure in place, the challenge for nationalists was to confront it on equal terms, and this enormously helped the drive for unity. The ultimate inability to turn British India into one independent entity was not a failure of ambition, but a combination of over-ambition in philosophy, coupled with a refusal to copy British methods. Non-violence was enough to see off the declining colonial power, but not enough to face down all the Congress's domestic competitors.

But beyond acknowledging their joint role in nation-building, the British in India still stand indicted as rulers. They never discharged their own conception of their obligations well enough, and never managed to develop a proper plan to give the governance of the country back. India's future was effectively confiscated between 1765 and 1917, and remained hidden beyond a distant horizon that never seemed to move appreciably closer. After 1917 the theft was acknowledged, but would only be remedied on condition of good behaviour.

The idea that sovereignty lay with the people had been fought for and established in England by 1689, and the central iniquity of the colonial enterprise in India was that this principle was seen by very few as a compelling truth that had, for the sake of consistency and natural justice, to be extended to parts of the world that were not England. This never occurred to the early conquerors, because they were primarily Whigs, and Whigs were concerned with defending the rights of Englishmen, not the universal rights of mankind. But later generations were made uneasy by this discrepancy, and attempts to justify imperial rule, from J.S. Mill onwards, were intended to cover this weakness. India was represented as either somehow different, or not ready, or better off ruled by a neutral, umpiring class.

Another serious indictment of colonial rule should be that the British took so much power while bringing so little prosperity to Indians. Continuing poverty in India was not the result of deliberate destruction, but it was certainly a matter of under-stimulation, and calculated reorientation and manipulation of the Indian economy. This was massively to the disadvantage of independent India; in terms of development she was set back by decades, though not centuries.

The way that the British handled the Indian economy was more complicated than a straightforward act of national plunder. Wealth was certainly brought to Britain from India, but this was not originally organized by the British state. Between 1600 and 1757, wealth came back through the EIC, whose profits, in the good times, were conventional and legitimate. The plunder of Bengal after 1757 was different, but was largely a private matter, as was involvement with the debts of the Nawab of Arcot. The plunder of Bengal happened not because the Company was strong but because it was weak.

And none of this 'financed the Industrial Revolution'; the sums involved were too small and went to the wrong hands. The wealth transferred to Britain in the three decades after 1757 was spent on country houses and playing politics, not funding power looms. After 1800 the profits in trade with India earned by the EIC were modest, and its surplus came from its dealings in China. Positive balances on trade only grew substantially in the 1830s. Until then, British trade with the West Indies was larger than with India.

Anyone who wishes to maintain that India somehow funded the Industrial Revolution in Britain will have to do three things: to show in what years the EIC made a profit or how much named nabobs brought home, how these sums relate to patterns of investment in machinery, and how the money could plausibly have got from EIC stockholders, or the nabobs, to factory owners in the north. Otherwise it is simply a pleasing fantasy, harped upon by demagogues chasing easy popularity.

The most apparent and direct drain of wealth from India was by means of the Home Charges, but they were always much smaller than implied by nationalist economists; one modern account has estimated that they barely exceeded 0.5 per cent of GDP.[1] Dadabhai Naoroji was wrong about some of the detail, but right that India's wealth was used within the imperial system for purposes that did not benefit India, such as military expenditure, and that the use of preferential tariffs and the manipulation of foreign trade balances within the global economy diverted substantial sums that might have been used for other, more constructive purposes in India.

The British altered India's manufacturing sector in various ways that included swinging the textile industry away from weaving cloth to spinning yarn, while India's agricultural base remained largely unchanged, with a shift towards indigo and, later, jute, cotton, tea and wheat. Indians eventually became consumers of European goods, which they had not been in the days before industrial mass production and cheap ocean transport. Inadequate tariff protection was certainly an issue for manufacturing within India, but it was not fundamentally a lack of protection that hobbled India—it was lack of investment.

How can we judge the disadvantages that India suffered? Socially, the impact of alien rule was neutral to beneficial, with the British able to do many things that progressive Indians wanted to do and might have found hard to accomplish without centralized state power. Culturally it was a unifying force, but it also generated a debilitating inferiority complex. Politically it was advantageous, but only in the long run. Economically it was very damaging.

Seen in the longer perspective, there is one important point on which to peg economic comparisons. At around 1870 the proportion of national wealth spent by governments was roughly the same in India and Britain. From then on it began to rise all over the West, but stayed low in India, where the population could not dictate the government's priorities. Indians were left under a lighter burden of taxation by a government that remained afraid to impose itself, and which took on proportionately less responsibility for the public sphere than its Western counterparts. India was left behind, saddled with a government too timid and cash-starved to evolve into a modern state. This appeasement of the upper classes has persisted. One long-term legacy of colonial rule has been the inability (or unwillingness) of the modern Indian state to tax its wealthiest citizens.

The overall result is often summed up in the shameful statistics on literacy and life expectancy in 1947, usually quoted as 12 per cent and 31 years respectively. In some ways, therefore, the claim made by the Congress in 1930 that Britain 'ruined' India has some force. A subtler charge would be that whatever progress an unrestrained India might have made in the modern world was denied her; the decisions that determined her evolution were not made by her own people, and were not directed for her benefit.

However, one frequently used statistic needs to be challenged. Angus Maddison's work is commonly used to assert that in 1700 India generated about 23 per cent of the world's wealth, but by 1947 it was only 3 per cent. This certainly looks damning, especially if the assumption is made that all the missing wealth was carted off to Britain. But these figures cannot be taken as evidence of a simple plundering of India's economic capacity, and they absolutely do not mean that India's economy shrank by a factor of more than eight; actually it trebled in size over the same period.

When India was generating about 23 per cent of global wealth, she contained around 23 per cent of the world's population. By 1947 she had 20 per cent of the global population and 3 per cent of its wealth. So the ratio of global population to wealth had fallen from 23:23 to 20:3. What happened in the interim was that technological and financial breakthroughs in Europe massively increased the productivity of Western populations, whereas industrialization hardly benefited India's economy at all. The resulting disparity related to expansion, not the transfer of existing wealth. It was simply that the conditions for growth—infrastructure, education and the availability of capital—were never competitively developed in India.

In 1700 the world's economy was based primarily on agriculture, and the size of India's population guaranteed that she enjoyed a similar proportion of global wealth—i.e. second behind China. The luxury sector of the Indian economy was glittering enough to attract and impress visitors, but it was tiny compared to the agricultural sector. Now, in the twenty-first century, India still has the second-largest agricultural output in the world, and China is still number one. The advantages of land area and population have not changed over three centuries. They were not destroyed by colonialism; they were simply outstripped by industrialization. The idea that a super-rich India was reduced to super-penury by colonialism is an attractive myth, but it relies on far too many unsubstantiated assumptions and a manipulation of statistics that borders on fraudulent.

The world economy grew enormously from 1757 to 1947, but India did not share proportionately in that growth, and imperial policy must shoulder a large part of the blame. We can attribute this imperial failing to malice, as some still insist, or perhaps to ignorance, confusion, incompetence or indifference. Britain had no direct interest in the impoverishment of India. Indeed India needed to run a trade surplus with the rest of the world in order to pay for her deficit with Britain.

The British wanted India to be stable and content or, if not content, then at least quiet. What the British never did was to prioritize Indian interests over British. This was the effect and procedure of colonialism in a nutshell.

Could any of this have been different?

The 'what if?' questions of Anglo-Indian history tend to run back to the events of 1857, and it is worth addressing the biggest of them. What if the rebels had won? What kind of India would then have emerged? Would a newly resurrected Mughal dynasty have been any more successful at uniting the country? And what if there had been no new Akbars, but only Aurangzebs? Or, worse, simply more Zafars? Would south India have taken any more kindly to Zafar's successors than to Aurangzeb, just because they weren't John Company?

And what of the presidency towns? The modernizing classes in Indian society found much to gain from British rule in its early phases, and they supported the British in 1857—at least to the point of not joining the rebels. The fact that the eventual reward for this support was meagre and grudging does not mean that the best and brightest of the new urban India would have submitted to a restored Padshah.

What was there, indeed, to admire in late Mughal Delhi? The idea that the twilight Mughal durbar represented a pinnacle of enlightenment or possessed a culture of lost greatness is misplaced. In reality, Zafar's court could boast only the thinnest record of achievement, apart from a great deal of ingenious debauchery. One poet doth not a culture make, and the Mughals can take little credit for the great Ghalib, except for paying him; court intrigues actually kept him from the highest honours.

The most likely outcome of a rebel victory in 1857 would have been extensive decentralization and the appearance of a chequerboard of petty local domains; in other words, fragmentation and warlordism, perhaps akin to the years 1707–65. Had they succeeded, the rebels of 1857 would not have overthrown any of the world's great powers, while they would have significantly diminished India's ability to defend herself against them. This could have led to either of two longer-term outcomes: that India entered the twentieth century like China—nibbled at the edges while chaos reigned in the centre—or like Africa—divided up in a 'Scramble for India' that might have started as early as the 1870s, and would probably have included Japan. Anyone who rejoices that India has had a unitary political existence and has emerged as a democratic state should not mourn the failure of 1857.

There is one other counterfactual question that is rarely asked, but should be. What if the revolt of 1857 had never happened? This last scenario represents the only likely way there ever was that the British might have readmitted Indians to self-government earlier than they did. Without the British reaction to the Uprising, the feudal class in India would not have taken hold of the country so securely, and profitability within the Indian economy might have risen sooner and faster than it did, driven by a search for profits away from agriculture. The most constructive partnership possible within India—between British technocrats and progressive Indian entrepreneurs—might have had a chance to flourish, nurtured by a government more dedicated to local growth. But this did not happen, and the legacies of 1857—the alliances it encouraged and the memories it bequeathed—remained the greatest obstacle to any handover of power.

Seen like this, modern Indians have little to celebrate about 1857. The revolt had far greater effects on India than Britain—all of them negative. In India, its failure led to a kind of throwback, and eventually to stasis. In Britain, it led to self-congratulation and a vastly expanded sense of moral superiority. It was thus a central factor in the creation of high imperialism, justifying the mission to civilize, while the memory of it acted as a constant brake on any intentions of giving Indians a place within colonial institutions.

The best scenario, therefore, for the creation of a modern India made with the least British interference is one in which the revolt of 1857 never happened at all.

Were there other turnings that were missed, that might have led on to other endings? It is possible to propose at least four.

There was a good opportunity in the 1820s, when the overall situation was relatively uncomplicated. The early wars of security were over, and India's princes were adapting to the British as they had adapted to Mughal rule. There was a chance to create a progressive, low-cost government that could have included Indians increasingly closely. Senior Company men on the ground were thinking in this way, notably Sir Thomas Munro, and a generation of enlightened and talented Indians were available for recruitment. But the moment was lost because of continuing British obsessions with security of all kinds—military, fiscal and political—and the unhelpful intervention of liberal economic theory in the matter of 'rent', which justified high revenue demands.[2] Political tensions, the exclusion of Indians and a depressed rural economy were the results.

Again in the 1850s a period of peace presented an opening for greater Indian inclusion, and Lord Dalhousie seemed prepared to go at least a small way in this direction. But first the caution of Charles Wood, then the bloodbath of 1857, closed off that possibility.

A third window opened after 1900, when an economic upturn and a brief moment of imperial optimism coincided with sufficient maturity in Indian political self-awareness to allow constructive dialogue, especially with the older generation of Congress leaders. But any chance of accommodation was thrown away by Curzon, who took better times and the conciliatory tone of Indian politicians as reasons to continue doing the 'work' he deemed necessary, unaided by Indians.

Then the First World War widened all the cracks in the imperial edifice, and led the British into a series of disastrous decisions that virtually destroyed all remaining hopes for a full Anglo-Indian partnership in government. Economically, ideologically and politically the years 1914–19 produced multiple ruptures in the skein of Anglo-Indian connections, and led to the crisis of 1919–22. Yet even in all the confusion and heightened emotion, one small chance remained.

In 1921 Gandhi led the largest coalition of indigenous political forces ever assembled, and faced a Liberal Secretary, Montagu, and a Liberal viceroy, Reading, who were adopting as mild a tone as they could, to try to get the new Mont-ford constitution off the ground. But at the head of this powerful force, Gandhi, the great conciliator, was not prepared to meet his opponents in the middle, while Lloyd George's government in London was being encouraged to take a hard line by senior officials in India. A bespoke version of Dominion status might have been worked out, along with the many other changes that followed the Great War. But the chance was always slim, and it too was lost.

Over the next decade the Indian political scene fragmented; the Congress split, the Hindu Mahasabha became politicized, Lala Lajpat Rai floated schemes of religiously based partition, senior Muslim League leaders referred publicly to the 'United States of India', the Communist Party was launched, and the worst inter-communal violence ever seen peaked in 1926.

Nor did the British end of the relationship ever recover a truly positive mindset. Had the Labour Party in Britain been stronger or bolder, or had it won a substantial majority in the 1929 election, things might have played out differently. Had the Conservative party been less in the grip of anti-Communist panics and worries about imperial decline, then perhaps the reforming agenda through the 1927–35 period might have produced greater agreement.

Overall, the British never made sufficient concessions to the Congress Moderates, because they were never convinced that they needed to. This crippled the one class that had the best chance of taking a united India into independence. The Moderates in their turn made insufficient attempts to accommodate the leaders of India's Muslims, and thus undermined their own chances of building a unitary state.

For the British, armed strength was always the great panacea for political problems; successful warfare ends arguments, and military power remained the real guarantor of British rule. But between campaigns there was a pattern of gambits and responses, which made up the legitimization project, the long-running search for non-military ways to continue to rule India.

To provide active political support for this project, the British also repeatedly attempted to make alliances within Indian society, with existing classes, emerging classes and classes they tried to manufacture. From 1793 they tried to create a new zamindar class in the north-east; overtures were made to peasant cultivators from about 1800 to 1857 in the south and west; and in the towns the emerging middle classes were seen as natural collaborators from around 1820. Then, through the declining years of the Raj, elite Muslims and hereditary princes were courted but, in a disastrous misjudgement, the one social group that really would have helped—the class of educated, urban babus—became viewed as an untrustworthy, self-serving opposition faction.

All these social alliances were tactical and provisional, and none would have been sufficient to support British rule on its own. But Indian social conditions usually meant that classes could not easily ally among themselves, and the lack of united opposition took the place of active support in prolonging British control.

Here we can review the Indian quest for unity, and we must ask: if the Raj lacked active support, and also faced endemic local insurrection and large-scale rebellion, why did it last so long?

The answer favoured by post-colonial writers is that the British were so powerful. It was British policy to talk up their strength in public, but this does not mean that they were ever as strong as they claimed, and we should examine imperial boasts closely. British India was strongest, militarily, from 1842 to 1857, but soon afterwards the army began a long decline into inefficiency and obsolescence. From 1859 to 1885 the Raj was at its political zenith, but economically its best years were 1900–14, when the government was financially solid, the rupee was stable, the famines of the previous twenty-five years ended, and there was a boom in jute. The fact that these various peaks were not synchronized hints at the contingencies that lay beneath the assured exterior of British rule. The colonial archive is full of worried assessments of the Raj's weaknesses. Why should we believe that such damaging admissions, made in secret, were not true?

A better, though much less acceptable, answer to explain the Raj's longevity, and one that has been proffered by very few commentators, is that the crucial factor throughout was the diffuse and weak nature of Indian resistance, particularly its inability to unite around a sufficiently clear alternative that transcended regional loyalties and class interests. No one has ever had any political incentive to put forward this thesis, and many have had strong disincentives to dare suggesting it.

But time and again, Indian resistance lacked central direction or clearly agreed objectives, from the south Indian wars of the late 1700s, through 1857, right down to the Quit India movement. Indian divisions also played a determining role around the moment of demission in 1947, when there was still no agreed way forward out of colonial status. To attribute this disunity to a covert British policy of divide and rule is only a partial explanation—and one that always risks infantilizing Indians in the way the imperial British were prone to do. It is also a flawed argument because it assumes its premise in its conclusion—that the British were so powerful that they could persistently divide and rule an Indian population which otherwise would have known its own mind. The British were powerful, it says, ergo they could do with Indians as they wished, according to a coherent plan. Indians never had any say in the matter. We know this because the plan worked. QED.

The deeper truth is that both sides, colonizers and colonized, were weak. Indian conditions tended to undermine or hamper all national political movements, not just in the British period but all across history. This was because of a range of well-understood factors, such as diversity of population, problems of scale, and difficulties of communication. Indian history from 1757 to 1947 shows all sides struggling to overcome their own structural weaknesses. The history of these years was not a parade of strength. On the contrary, it was a carnival of bluff.

To a great degree, the success of the Raj relied on demonstrating military superiority and getting Indians to pay for it, while proclaiming moral superiority and getting Indians to accept it. Until Gandhi. Using non-cooperation to strike at taxation and administration, using non-violence to render armed force irrelevant, and with unshakeable confidence in Indian moral superiority, the Mahatma found the needles to burst the Raj's prettiest balloons.

But this was still not enough. The formation of the Indian National Congress was a valiant attempt to kick down the fences that kept Indians apart, but although it had a truly national philosophy, the Congress always struggled to represent the whole nation in its ranks. Many would not join because, variously, the Congress was too modern, not modern enough, too Hindu, not Hindu enough, too radical, too conservative, too keen on industrialists' interests, not keen enough on princes' rights—and so forth.

There were thus two national forces by the 1920s, both claiming to represent the 'voiceless millions'—the Raj, defending the ryot against the moneylenders and landlords, and the Congress, defending all Indians against the Raj. The Congress claimed to embody the nation; Raj die-hards denied there was any nation to represent. Meanwhile Jinnah aspired to represent all Muslims, but faced resistance and even derision. All through the story, none of the sides was strong enough to make good its own claims.

Instead, as demission approached, a divided insurgent force faced a demoralized military regime; the former too diffuse to push hard, the latter too undermanned to resist firmly. In the darkest days of 1857, the British had managed to find new reserves of strength, both military and moral. But in 1947, instead of confidence and resolve, there was self-doubt and exhaustion. Imposing a settlement at this stage was not only impossible in practical terms, it was also unthinkable in moral terms, and a disastrous incoherence was the result. By then, the British only had preferred outcomes.

The Partition settlement was the result of a contest between three weak players. Though apparently the weakest, the Muslim League had the clearest objective and the most focused leadership. Had this not been so, perhaps there would have been no Partition at all.

This book has tried to understand Anglo-Indian history in a wider context than usual, by assessing how developments in England determined what kind of colonial government—and governors—India received, and what sort of India would emerge from colonial rule.

The later sections of this narrative revolve around the failed dialogue between British and Indian politicians, a dialogue that the British regarded first as unnecessary, then as inadvisable until Indians could agree among themselves. Meanwhile they preferred simply to carry on working for India's good.

Ex-Viceroy Irwin, by then the Earl of Halifax, conveniently set out the British attitude to their labours for an American audience in April 1942. As the Cripps Mission was falling apart, he said: 'Since the latter half of the eighteenth century we have been trying, firstly, to give unity to India where there was, and still to a great extent persists, disunity. Secondly, we have been trying to give security to India. Thirdly, we have tried to raise the general level of social and economic standards. Lastly ... we have tried to develop India's political life. In other words, we have been trying within the British Empire to foster the creation of a United India, sufficiently at one within herself ... to permit us to devolve upon her people the control of their own affairs.

'And if the outcome of our efforts was to endure, it has been plain that this outcome must evoke not only the respect but the loyalty of the whole of India, content, as I would hope, to realize its full destiny through Imperial partnership. We have always thought that, if and when that unity could be achieved, our work in India would be finished.'[3]

A good deal of history was being recast in these words, but Halifax was a politician not a historian and, in a sense, he spoke truly; he was giving an accurate summary of what he, and those like him, thought they were doing.

Five years later, and still undone, the 'work' was cut short. India was handed back, and an important part of the story concerns by whom it was received. The British, latterly, had always engaged most closely with the least radical parts of Indian society, and this affected how the story ended. Gandhi's non-violent philosophy may not have been the only factor in ending colonial rule, but that approach, in tandem with Nehru's genuine commitment to plural democracy, ensured that India had the least internal animosity and the best political platform upon which to build a future.

There are a few final summary points to be made.

- The British Raj was not planned, but neither was it an accident. Each stage in its construction had its own logic, and sometimes even a detailed strategy, behind it. The beginning of the story was all circumstance and opportunism; the drive to complete the task, however, was conscious. Once the military machine was in place, and the benefits of control were properly channelled within domestic British society, the last segment of the conquest, under Ellenborough and Dalhousie, was attractively attainable.
- The British were able to go further than Ashoka or the Mughals, because of the extent of the resources they committed, the flexibility they showed in making alliances, and the fact that once territory passed into British hands it never came out. The British imported a 'conquest culture' that avoided succession disputes, regencies of minors, or breakaways by provincial rulers who had become confident in their own strength or who feared for their lives at court.
- In doing all this the British had one great advantage—timing. India became governable as a single entity as soon as the distances of the country had been shrunk by the use of steamships, railways and the telegraph.
- The Raj, once established, was sustained by a genuine conviction that Indians could not govern themselves, and should not be allowed to try, for fear of a return to feudal exploitation and civil disorder. Despite its

obviously self-serving elements, this conviction was entirely real, and it overshadowed the second half of the British presence in India. Whenever there was violence or disorder, that conviction was reinforced. Whenever the servants smiled or local dignitaries were pleasant, this was taken as proof of Indian approval.

– Once British rule in India was a fact, it was a daunting task to volunteer to disentangle all the strands within it. Commercially, administratively and politically, it became extraordinarily difficult for senior British policy-makers to see a good way out.

The longer the British presence lasted, the more difficult it became to leave a peaceful India behind. What the British should have done is what they did in Canada—grant devolved self-government—and for decades this is exactly what the senior Congress leadership asked them to do. It would have taken political courage, but it would not have been impossible to work out such a system, especially after the Imperial Conference of 1926. But unrest in India constantly retriggered the British instinct to suppress disorder.

The last decades of British rule were not especially beneficial to the British commercially—the balance of trade reversed in the 1930s—but India stood at the front of a long queue for self-government that included all the African colonies, which still had real value to Britain. The 'white' Dominions, long given home rule, could be expected to stay onside in global political terms. Not so India, or the squadron of non-white territories behind her.

Deliberate or accidental, intentional or involuntary, well informed or ignorant, the 'work' undertaken by the British certainly affected India, especially in the spheres of economic development, political institutions and legal structures. That work did therefore endure, as Curzon believed it would, though not in the happy manner he seems to have envisaged. The end was too slow and too bitter.

There was never a good enough reason, or at least no pressing, practical reason, for the British to grant India self-government, until the 1940s. The forces of conservatism that the British had nurtured in Indian affairs weighed down all progress. By the time there *were* good reasons, including mass protests, the best window for resolution had gone. Playing for time was an enormous mistake on the British behalf, and it gradually worsened local conditions at the same time as making the leap to swaraj more and more daunting. If ever there was an example of the dangers of elite isolation or political procrastination, it must surely be the ultimate fate of British India.

Lastly, the essentially conservative nature of India's nationalist revolution has often been remarked upon, and a great deal of energy has been expended in trying to explain why this was, especially by the Subaltern Studies project. But the answer does not lie with sweeping statements about the character of bourgeois revolutions, the universalizing mission of capital, the nature of colonial discourse as a discourse of power, or any other post-Marxist sociological construct.

So why was it? There are three main factors to consider.

1. The proletariat in India was very small, because of underdevelopment in the industrial sector. Instead there was an agrarian society that the British had frozen.
2. There was a climate of moral denigration of Indians that only Gandhi seemed capable of overcoming, and he stood some distance away from modern leftist positions.
3. After the British had decided they had work to do in modernizing India, they excluded the educated middle classes, which they themselves had helped create, from sharing in the work.

This left no class or leader or grouping capable of developing an effective campaign for radical social change. The only central organ of Indian politics, the Indian National Congress, had a strong interest in its own acquisition of power, but none in real revolution. India remained administratively centralized, but not socially organized in a way propitious for revolution.

The India that emerged had a sense of nationhood—a shared experience of struggle against a common enemy—but not a sufficiently agreed local view of modernity to make social reform easy. The equality agenda, so central to modernity in the West, passed to progressive minds like Nehru's, but it was not directly in the interests of India's existing elites to carry it through.

Modern Indians might yet admire the courage of the insurgents of 1857, and forgive their mistakes, but they should give thanks for their failure too, because it made room for later generations of patriotic Indian to make better decisions. It is very hard to trace a credible line of development between where the sepoys were heading and the secular, democratic India of today.

In an epic twist of irony, the British, once restored to full power, ended up actively supporting the religious privilege and feudal rulers that the defeated sepoys had fought to restore. The anti-colonial revolution in India was conservative because the British made it so; the revolt of 1857 undoubtedly helped them to do it.

Would a free, united India have been a liberal democracy without the legacy of British rule? There is no way of knowing. But India, like Britain before her, was spared violent social upheaval, and stayed out of the Communist fold after 1947. This has had an enormous effect on world history. Those with a natural aversion to liberal democracy may lament it, but India, with much more colonial intervention than China, saw no peasant revolution. India's British connection and liberal inheritance were undoubtedly major factors in determining the course of the Cold War.

The Anglo-Indian connection is the axis that defined and nurtured liberal parliamentary democracy, that developed modern governmental skills, and defined new ways of mounting and sustaining political opposition. The post-war world carries an Anglo-Indian stamp.

We must all accept that the Raj failed repeatedly in detail, and it had a pronounced bias towards British interests. But there was humanity and concern too, in among the various self-serving devices used to catch the eye at home and to recruit support in India. Yes, the British supported injustices in India, but it was with the support of, and for the benefit of, classes of wealthy and powerful Indians. Claiming that injustices in modern India are the fault of the British is to offer the old schoolyard excuse—a big boy did it then ran away.

All colonial governments may have had their compradors, but in India there was an entire ruling class willing to compromise with the intruders, because those intruders were smart enough to leave them alone. 'Oblige and rule' was subtle, effective and highly sustainable.

Indians were not kept in subjection by daily experience of extreme violence, or even a more distant threat of severe violence. Indians were kept in subjection largely by an existing social hierarchy which the British did very little to dismantle.

The British defended the areas of industrialization and, to some degree, of modernity for themselves, and left the rest to their social allies. The result was the rural poverty and undercapitalized industry that India possessed at independence. The British never solved the problems of rural production, despite repeated efforts at stimulation. It took the 'green revolution' of the late 1960s to provide a solution.

Finally, it is worth stressing the issue of internal disarmament, which is the one thing Britain gave to India that Indians would have found very difficult to give themselves. Demilitarization was a violent process, founded in self-interest, but it had massively beneficial consequences. The brightest and best that India had to offer learned to trust each other in the space it created. They also adopted peace as a method, a method that allowed the least violence in demission and the fewest scores to settle afterwards.

The British made the peace and the Indians made modern India.

NOTES

1. RESHAPING THE STORY

1. See J. Keay, *The Honourable Company*, London, HarperCollins, 1993, p. 178.
2. N. Robins, *The Corporation That Changed the World: How the East India Company Shaped the Modern Multinational*, London, Pluto, 2012.
3. Ibid., p. xii.
4. Hoh-cheung and Loma H. Mui, *The Management of Monopoly*, Vancouver, University of British Columbia Press, 1984, p. 56.
5. C.H. Philips, *The East India Company 1784–1834*, Manchester, Manchester University Press, 1961, p. 303, n. 2.
6. www.youtube.com/watch?v=VcWc7WqcS5M.
7. Titled *Inglorious Empire* in the UK and *An Era of Darkness* in India.
8. F.H. Sykes, *From Many Angles: An Autobiography*, London, Harrap, 1942, p. 523.
9. S.N. Sen, *History of Modern India*, New Delhi, New Age, 2006, p. 142.
10. Essay on Warren Hastings: http://www.columbia.edu/itc/mealac/pritchett/00generallinks/macaulay/hastings/txt_complete.html.
11. M. Edwardes, *British India 1772–1947*, New Delhi, Rupa Publications, 2011, p. 232.
12. B. Ghose, *Selections from English Periodicals of 19th Century Bengal*, Calcutta, Papyrus, 1978, vol. 4, p. 278.
13. R.K. Mookerji, *The Fundamental Unity of India*, Calcutta, Longmans, Green and Co., 1914, p. 24.
14. V. Joshi, *India's Long Road: The Search for Prosperity*, Oxford, OUP, 2016.
15. R.C. Majumdar, *The History and Culture of the Indian People*, Bombay, Bharatya Vidya Bhavan, 1977, vol. XI, p. 140.
16. R.P. Dutt, *A Guide to the Problem of India*, Gollancz, London, 1942, pp. 87–9.
17. B. Chandra, *Communalism in Modern India*, New Delhi, Vikas, 1987, p. 244.
18. S. Gopal, *British Policy in India 1858–1905*, Cambridge, CUP, 1965, p. 194.
19. R.N. Sharma and R.K. Sharma, *History of Education in India*, New Delhi, Atlantic, 2000, p. 29.
20. H.B. Sarda, *Hindu Superiority: An Attempt to Determine the Position of the Hindu Race in the Scale of Nations*, Ajmer, Rajputana Printing Works, 1906.
21. Quoted in J. Roach, 'Liberalism and the Victorian Intelligentsia', *Cambridge Historical Journal*, vol. 13, no. 1 (1957), p. 64.

22. See P. Gopal, *Insurgent Empire: Anticolonial Resistance and British Dissent*, London, Verso, 2019.
23. S. Sarkar, *Modern India 1885–1947*, New Delhi, Macmillan, 1983, p. 21.
24. W. Dockter, *Churchill and the Islamic World: Orientalism, Empire and Diplomacy in the Middle East*, London, I.B. Tauris, 2015, p. 88.
25. Quoted in T.H. Beaglehole, *Thomas Munro*, Cambridge, CUP, 1966, p. 123.
26. G. Prashad, 'Whiggism in India', *Political Science Quarterly*, vol. 81, no. 3 (September, 1966), pp. 412–31.
27. C.A. Bayly, *Empire and Information: Intelligence Gathering and Social Communication in India, 1780–1870*, Cambridge, CUP, 1996, p. 214.
28. L. Fraser, *India under Curzon and After*, London, Heinemann, 1911, p. 488.
29. Hansard, vol. 145, cols. 994–1068.
30. J.A. Hobson, *Imperialism, A Study*, London, George Allen and Unwin, 1902, p. 288.
31. Ibid., p. 287.
32. Z. Baber, *The Science of Empire: Scientific Knowledge, Civilization, and Colonial Rule in India*, New York, State University of New York Press, 1996, p. 206.
33. Fraser, *India under Curzon*, p. 2.
34. A.B. Keith (ed.), *Speeches and Documents on Indian Policy*, Oxford, OUP, 1922, vol. 2, p. 73
35. Ibid., p. 75.
36. Fraser, *India under Curzon*, p. 488.
37. J.R. MacDonald, *The Awakening of India*, London, Hodder and Stoughton, 1910, p. 184.
38. Sarkar, *Modern India*, p. 86.
39. S.A. Kochanek, *The Congress Party of India*, Princeton, Princeton University Press, 1968, p. 336.

2. 1600–1740: SPICES, RIVALS, CHAOS, PEACE

1. Keay, *The Honourable Company*, p. 178.
2. Ibid., p. 145.

3. 1744–1784: WAR, GOVERNMENT, PLUNDER, REGULATION

1. Letter to Chairman Rous, April 1765, in G.W. Forrest, *The Life of Lord Clive*, London, Cassell, vol. II, pp. 256–8.
2. Keay, *The Honourable Company*, p. 375.
3. P. Griffiths, *The British Impact on India*, London, Cass, 1965, pp. 78–9.
4. F. Thackeray, *A History of the Rt. Hon. William Pitt, Earl of Chatham*, London, Rivington, 1827, vol. II, p. 131.
5. Forrest, *The Life of Lord Clive*, vol. II, p. 396.
6. Keith, *Speeches and Documents on Indian Policy*, vol. I, pp. 13–18.
7. R. Holmes, *Sahib*, London, HarperCollins, 2005, p. 184.

8. Hastings to Laurence Sulivan, 10 Feb. 1772, BL, Add. MS 29126, fol. 125.
9. G.R. Gleig, *Memoirs of the Rt. Hon. Warren Hastings*, London, Bentley, 1841, vol. 1, p. 404.

4. 1784–1813: LAND, LAW, EXPANSION, VICTORY

1. Keith, *Speeches and Documents on Indian Policy*, vol. 1, p. 163.
2. Quoted in E. Malins, 'Indian Influences on English Houses and Gardens at the Beginning of the Nineteenth Century', *Garden History*, vol. 8, no. 1 (Spring, 1980), p. 50.
3. B.W. Hill, *Edmund Burke on Government, Politics and Society*, Glasgow, Fontana, 1975, p. 264.
4. Ibid., pp. 274–5.
5. Quoted in R. Travers, *Ideology and Empire in Eighteenth-Century India*, Cambridge, CUP, 2007, p. 220.
6. A. Cobban, *Edmund Burke and the Revolt against the Eighteenth Century*, London, George Allen and Unwin, 1929.
7. Letter to Arthur Lee, 1 October 1786. Quoted in J. Majeed, *Ungoverned Imaginings*, Oxford, OUP, 1992, p. 30.
8. J. Keay, *History of India*, London, HarperCollins, 2000, p. 20.
9. P.J. Marshall, *Problems of Empire: Britain and India 1757–1813*, London, Allen and Unwin, 1968, p. 94.
10. Keith, *Speeches and Documents on Indian Policy*, vol. 1, p. 197.

5. 1813–1839: ROMANTICS, LIBERALS, EDUCATION, REFORM

1. J.W. Kaye, *Lives of Indian Officers*, London, Strahan and Co., 1867, vol 1, p. 375.
2. Ibid., p. 144 n.
3. A.J. Arbuthnot, *Sir Thomas Munro*, London, Kegan Paul, 1881, vol. 1, p. 94.
4. Ibid., p. 100.
5. P. Woodruff, *The Men Who Ruled India*, London, Jonathan Cape, 1954, p. 196.
6. Arbuthnot, *Sir Thomas Munro*, vol. 1, p. 149.
7. Ibid., p. 149.
8. G.R. Gleig, *Life of Sir Thomas Munro*, London, Colburn and Bentley, 1830, vol. 2, p. 310.
9. M. McLaren, *British India and British Scotland, 1780–1830*, Akron, Ohio, University of Akron Press, 2001, p. 220.
10. Ibid., p. 182.
11. Kaye, *Lives of Indian Officers*, vol. 1, p. 131.
12. Ibid., vol. 1, p. 289.
13. Ibid., p. 443.
14. Ibid., p. 444.
15. Ibid., vol. 1, p. 194.

16. J. Malcolm, *Malcolm: Soldier, Diplomat, Ideologue of British India*, Edinburgh, John Donald, 2014, p. 543.
17. J.S. Cotton, *Mountstuart Elphinstone*, Oxford, Clarendon Press, 1892, p. 128.
18. Kaye, *Lives of Indian Officers*, vol. 1, p. 456.
19. Ibid., p. 399.
20. J. Malcolm, *Sketch of the Political History of India*, London, Murray, 1826, vol. 1, p. 9.
21. Quoted in S. Sastri, *Ramtanu Lahiri*, ed. R. Lethbridge, n.p., 1907, p. 69, http://rupkatha.com/V7/n3/26_intoxication-in-19th-century-colonial-bengal.pdf.
22. M. Jain, *Sati: Evangelicals, Baptist Missionaries, and the Changing Colonial Discourse*, New Delhi, Aryan Books, 2016.
23. J. Rosselli, *Lord William Bentinck*, London, Chatto and Windus, 1974, p. 84.
24. W. Dalrymple, *The Last Mughal*, London, Bloomsbury, 2006, p. 62.
25. Quoted in P. Carson, *The East India Company and Religion, 1698–1858*, Woodbridge (UK), Boydell Press, 2012, p. 208.
26. Lady Holland, *A Memoir of the Rev. Sydney Smith*, London, Macmillan, 1869, p. 234.
27. G.O. Trevelyan, *Life and Letters of Lord Macaulay*, London, Harper and Bros, 1876, p. 21.
28. J.W. Barley (ed.), *Life and Letters of Lord Macaulay*, London, Macmillan, 1914, p. 7.
29. L.C. Sanders (ed.), *Lord Melbourne's Papers*, London, Longmans, 1889, p. xii.
30. http://www.columbia.edu/itc/mealac/pritchett/00generallinks/macaulay/txt_minute_education_1835.html.
31. Ibid.
32. http://www.columbia.edu/itc/mealac/pritchett/00generallinks/macaulay/hastings/txt_complete.html.

6. 1839–1858: DISASTER, SUPREMACY, MODERNITY, MUTINY

1. J.W. Kaye, *History of the War in Afghanistan*, quoted in K. Meyer and S. Brysac, *Tournament of Shadows*, London, Little, Brown, 1999, p. 61.
2. W.F.P. Napier, *The Life and Opinions of General Sir Charles Napier*, London, John Murray, 1857, vol. 1, p. 435.
3. H.T. Lambrick, *Sir Charles Napier and Sind*, Oxford, OUP, 1952, p. 33.
4. Napier, *The Life and Opinions of General Sir Charles Napier*, vol. 2, p. 218.
5. E. Thompson and G.T. Garratt, *Rise and Fulfilment of British Rule in India*, London, Macmillan, 1934, p. 361.
6. M. Yapp, *Strategies of British India*, Oxford, OUP, 1980, pp. 426–8.
7. C. Greville, *The Greville Memoirs, 1814–1860*, London, Macmillan, 1938, vol. 2, p. 235.
8. E. Stokes, *The English Utilitarians and India*, Oxford, OUP, 1959, p. 248.
9. Carson, *The East India Company and Religion*, p. 223.
10. F. Warre Cornish, *The English Church in the Nineteenth Century*, London, Macmillan, 1910, pp. 375–6.

11. Letter of 28 August 1858, 'The Sahib and the Nigger', quoted in R. Gandhi, *A Tale of Two Revolts*, London, Haus, 2011, p. 176.
12. Carson, *The East India Company and Religion*, p. 207.
13. Decennial Missionary Tables, quoted in J.F. Riddick, *The History of British India*, Connecticut, Praeger, 2006, p. 151.
14. Gandhi, *A Tale of Two Revolts*, pp. 115–19.

7. 1859–1885: RECOVERY, INVESTMENT, DEBT, DEVOLUTION

1. R.G. Sanyal, *The Life of the Hon. Rai Kristo Das Pal*, Calcutta, Bengalee Press, 1886, p. 190.
2. Wood to Canning 3 January 1860, quoted in Gopal, *British Policy in India*, p. 13.
3. R.J. Moore, *Sir Charles Wood's Indian Policy, 1853–66*, Manchester, Manchester University Press, 1966, p. 199.
4. Wood to Elgin, 3 March 1862, quoted in Gopal, *British Policy in India*, p. 35.
5. Quoted in J.W. Burrow, *Whigs and Liberals*, Oxford, OUP, 1988, p. 105.
6. R. Temple, *Lord Lawrence*, London, Macmillan, 1893, p. 139.
7. Stokes, *The English Utilitarians and India*, p. 244.
8. Arbuthnot, *Sir Thomas Munro*, p. vii.
9. Stokes, *The English Utilitarians and India*, p. 268.
10. R.B. Smith, *Life of Lord Lawrence*, London, Smith, Elder and Co., 1885, vol. 2, p. 30.
11. B.R. Nanda, *Gokhale: The Indian Moderates and the British Raj*, Princeton, Princeton University Press, 1977, pp. 21–2.
12. Sir J.W. Kaye and Colonel G.B. Malleson, *History of the Indian Mutiny of 1857–8*, London, W. H. Allen, 1889–93, http://www.ibiblio.org/britishraj/KayeMalleson1/authorpreface.html.
13. G.B. Malleson, *Indian Mutiny of 1857*, New Delhi, Rupa, 2005, p. 276.
14. Holmes, *Sahib*, p. 181.
15. Stokes, *The English Utilitarians and India*, p. 286.
16. Quoted in Lady G. Cecil, *Life of Robert, Marquis of Salisbury*, London, Hodder and Stoughton, 1921–32, vol. 2, ch.4.
17. Quoted in Nanda, *Gokhale*, p. 23.

8. 1884–1905: CURRENCY, CONGRESS, COMMISSIONS, CURZON

1. Salisbury to Lytton, 30 August 1876, quoted in Gopal, *British Policy in India*, p. 115.
2. B.R. Nanda, 'Moderates and All That', *Economic and Political Weekly*, vol. 14, no. 40 (6 Oct. 1979), p. 1672.
3. *The Indian National Congress ...*, Madras, G.A. Natesan and Co., [1908?], pp. 92, 256, 460, http://www.archive.org/stream/indiannationalco00madrrich/indiannationalco00madrrich_djvu.txt.
4. Edwardes, *British India 1772–1947*, p. 287.
5. J. Masselos, *Indian Nationalism: A History*, New Delhi, Sterling, 2002, p. 79.

6. Gopal, *British Policy in India*, p. 189.
7. A.C. Lyall, *Asiatic Studies Religious and Social*, London, Murray, 1882, p. 304.
8. Ibid., p. 305.
9. Ibid., p. 306.
10. Ibid., p. 2.
11. D. Gilmour, *Curzon*, London, John Murray, 1994, p. 144.

9. 1905–1920: COUNCILS, WORLD WAR, GANDHI, MASSACRE

1. Quoted in Nanda, *Gokhale*, p. 486.
2. Keith, *Speeches and Documents on Indian History*, p. 83.
3. Ibid., p. 93.
4. B.R. Nanda, *The Making of a Nation*, New Delhi, HarperCollins, 1999, p. 109.
5. Report of the Hunter Committee.
6. Ibid.
7. L.W. Adamec, *Afghanistan, 1900–1923: A Diplomatic History*, Berkeley, University of California Press, 1967, pp. 182–3.

10. 1921–1939: NON-COOPERATION, DYARCHY, SWARAJ, PRINCES

1. Quoted in W. Golant, *The Long Afternoon*, London, Hamish Hamilton, 1975, p. 93.
2. Nanda, *Gokhale*, p. 488.
3. Ibid., p. 489.
4. R.J. Moore, *The Crisis of India Unity 1917–4*, Oxford, OUP, 1974, pp. 127–9.
5. D. Gilmour, *The Ruling Caste: Imperial Lives in the Victorian Raj*, London, Pimlico, 2007, p. 253.
6. H. Butler, H., *India Insistent*, London, Heinemann, 1931, p. viii.
7. Ibid., p. 103.
8. Ibid., p. viii.
9. Ibid., p. 103.
10. Ibid., p. 105.
11. Ibid., p. vii.
12. Ibid., p. 108.
13. Ibid., p. 109.
14. Ibid., p. 116.
15. G. Lansbury, *Labour's Way with the Commonwealth*, London, Methuen, 1935, p. 64.
16. *The Times*, 2 January 1935, p. 6.

11. 1939–1947: WORLD WAR, DETENTION, MEDIATION, PARTITION

1. *Harijan*, 21 June 1942, in *Collected Works of Mahatma Gandhi*, vol. 83, p. 11.
2. Ibid., p. 446.
3. Ibid., p. 361.

4. A.I. Singh, *The Origins of the Partition of India 1936–1947*, Oxford, OUP, 1987, p. 122.
5. Quoted in Golant, *The Long Afternoon*, p. 108, n. 1.
6. Hansard, vol. 296, col. 456.
7. Ibid., col. 459.
8. C.B. Birdwood, *A Continent Experiments*, London, Skeffington, 1945, p. 169.
9. H.V. Hodson, *The Great Divide*, Karachi, OUP, 1985, p. 236.
10. Ibid., p. 244.
11. L. Fischer, *The Life of Mahatma Gandhi*, London, Granada, 1982, p. 581.
12. M.N. Das, *Fateful Events of 1947*, New Delhi, Standard, 2004, p. 154.
13. Hansard, vol. 439, col. 2482.
14. C.R. Attlee, *As It Happened*, London, Heinemann, 1954, p. 215.

12. 1947–1950: AFTERMATH

1. Y. Khan, *The Great Partition*, New Delhi, Penguin, 2007, p. 10.

13. REVIEWING THE STORY

1. A.K. Dasgupta, *A History of Indian Economic Thought*, London, Routledge, 1993, p. 83.
2. See R. Matthews, *Flaws in the Jewel*, New Delhi, HarperCollins, 2010, ch. 9.
3. http://www.ibiblio.org/pha/policy/1942/1942-04-07a.html

INDEX